SOCIO-ECONOMIC CONDITIONS OF HANDLOOM WEAVERS

SOCIO-ECONOMIC CONDITIONS OF HANDLOOM WEAVERS

By

DR. K. VENKATA SUBBAIAH

M.A., Ph.D.

Reader in Economics

Dr. S.R.J. Degree College

Atmakur-524322

(A.P.)

DISCOVERY PUBLISHING HOUSE PVT. LTD.

NEW DELHI-110 002

Published by:
Tilak Wasan
DISCOVERY PUBLISHING HOUSE PVT. LTD.
4383/4A, Ansari Road, Darya Ganj
New Delhi-110 002 (India)
Phone : +91-11-23279245, 43596064-65
Fax : +91-11-23253475
E-mail : parul.wasan@gmail.com
discoverypublishinghouse@gmail.com
web : www.discoverypublishinggroup.com

***First Edition:* 2012**

ISBN: 978-93-5056-017-4

Socio-economic Conditions of Handloom Weavers

Printed at:
Shree Balaji Art Press
Delhi

Dedicated

to

My Parents

Sri K. Venkata Subbaiah & Smt. Govindamma

Preface

Since time immemorial the handloom industry has been playing a vital role not only in the Indian Economy but also in the Andhra Pradesh Economy. It is by far the largest and most important cottage industry, next only to agriculture. The industry attained a high degree of excellence, centuries before the machines were invented to produce cloth. It continues to be so even now. Andhra Pradesh occupies the second position in India with 5.29 lakh looms which is 17.50 per cent of the national total of 30.22 lakh looms.

The present study is basically a socio-economic study of handloom weavers in Cuddapah district of Andhra Pradesh. The unique feature of handloom industry in the district is that the industry in eastern zone of Cuddapah district is providing gainful employment to the handloom weavers, whereas the industry in western zone is producing traditional varieties and not able to improve the socio-economic status of the handloom weavers. The present research work is a modest attempt in the direction of analyzing the reasons for disparities in the socio-economic status of the handloom weavers in these two sectors viz., eastern and western zones of Cuddapah district. Data pertaining to the evolution of handloom industry for over a period of 20 years (1970-90) had been collected and analyzed. The study tries to identify the important factors responsible for the existing inter regional disparities of the handloom weavers in the eastern and western sectors of Cuddapah district.

The thesis comprises of seven chapters. The *first* chapter presents the introduction to the handloom industry and outlines the objectives of the study. The policy of the Government, before and after independence, has been analyzed in the *second* chapter. The general nature and characteristics of the handloom Industry are dealt with in chapter *three*. Detailed comparisons of the socio-economic conditions of handloom weavers in eastern and western zones of Cuddapah are presented in chapter *four*. The *fifth* chapter deals with the cost structure, price and capacity utilization of handlooms in different regions of Cuddapah district. The *sixth* chapter is devoted to the study of evolution or the process of change the industry has undergone over a period of time. The *seventh* and last chapter is exclusively devoted to present the main issues, findings and conclusions.

In the difficult and arduous task of completing the present study, many people helped me in many ways. It is difficult to say where the list should end. But I know where to begin it. Towering above them all, is my Research Supervisor Prof. M.L.Kantha Rao, Former Principal and Head of the Dept., of Economics, S.K.University College, Anantapur, who led me through the completion of the study. His valuable suggestions and constructive criticisms ultimately helped me to tide over the difficulties usually encountered in such a work. His informal dealings, apart from the benefit derived from his scholarship and experience, will remain ever fresh in my mind. To him I owe an incalculable debt. I take the opportunity of thanking Smt M.L.Kantha Rao for her motherly affection and encouragement.

I am deeply indebted to Dr G.Satyanarayana, Sr.Research Officer, C.P.D.S and Dr M.D.Bavaiah, Lecturer, Department of Economics, S.K.University, Anantapur for their valuable help in processing the data.

I am thankful to the authorities of Sri Krishnadevaraya University, Anantapur for enabling me to register for Ph.D degree and for providing necessary facilities to pursue my research.

I am thankful to the ICSSR, New Delhi for granting me 'study grant' for two months which enabled me to stay at New Delhi, for the collection of necessary data.

In the course of investigation I had the opportunity of meeting some of eminent personalities, well-versed with the problems of my study. Important among them are Prof D.U.Sastry, Institutue of Economic Growth, New Delhi, Late Prof N.G.Ranga, former M.P, Late Sri Pragada Kotaiah, former M.P., Dr Akurathi Venkateswara Rao, editor, 'Chenetha' telugu journal. I offer, my respectful thanks for all of them for their inspiring guidance which helped me in the successful completion of my work.

The Offices of the Asst. Director of Handlooms and Textiles, Cuddapah, Director of Handlooms and textiles, Hyderabad, Commissioner for Handlooms and Textiles, New Delhi, are the major sources of secondary data. I acknowledge my deep sense of gratitude to all of them for their help and co-operation in getting required data.

At all times I received constant encouragement and inspiration from Prof T.K.Meti, Karnataka University, Dr Bathaiah, Professor, Dept., of Econometrics, S.V.University, Tirupati, Dr Sarangapani, Reader in

Economics, P.G. Centre, Machilipatnam. I offer my sincere thanks to all of them.

My cousin late Sri Kasala Sivaramaiah, a treasure of information on handloom industry and the leader of handloom movement had immensely helped me with lot of literature on my research problem. I cannot but acknowledge the help he rendered to me.

I acknowledge the co-operation extended to me by the respondents during the course of primary data collection and those who helped me in many ways during the field survey.

I would not have taken up the present research work, had I not been inspired by my beloved teacher Late Sri P.Prabhakar Rao, Lecturer in economics, Govt., Degree College, Venkatagiri town. My brothers Sri K. Narayana and Sri K.V.Chalapathy and my borther-in-law Sri Malluru Subbarayudu have been great help and inspiration to pursue my research work. I express my deep sense of gratitude to all of them.

I cannot forget the libraries I had visited and their librarians. I wish, especially to thank the librarians and the staff of Delhi School of Economics, Indian Institute of Public Administration, ICSSR, Nassdoc, New Delhi, Osmania University, Centre for Economic and Social Studies, National Institute of Rural Development, Hyderabad and S.K.University, Anantapur, for their co-operation.

I acknowledge with thanks the help and encouragement I received from Sri Jonnadula Yanadaiah, Correspondent, Dr S.R.J. Degree College, Atmakur, Nellore dist, Sri T. Madhusudana Das, Principal and all the staff members of Govt., Junior College, Kanchikacherla, my friends Dr Divanji, Lecturer, Dept., of Statistics, S.K. University, Anantapur, Sri Manduru Venkata Subbaiah, Dr A.Mahankalaiah, Dr B. Harihara Nath, Sri Sadhu Subbarayudu, Dr M.Veera Raghavulu, Sri Sunkulaiah and Sri Gopal.

Finally I am grateful to Sri K.K. Azam Khan, Research Scholar, Department of Instrumentation, S.K.U, Anantapur and Sri Gurunatham, B.Tech for their help in computerizing and processing the data.

Last but not least, I thank my wife and my children Chi K.V. Ramakrishna and Chi Sai Sudha for their co-operation.

K. Venkata Subbaiah

Contents

1 Introduction

In India, handloom industry is the oldest industry[1]. Since times immemorial handloom industry has been an integral part of India's economy. This industry, by far the largest in the unorganised sector, ranks next only to agriculture in terms of income and employment it generates. There are over three million handlooms in the country employing over 10 million persons.

The Industry has displayed an innate resilience, despite competition from powerlooms and mill sectors by producing exquisite fabrics to meet the challenges, demands and fashion trends of modern times. It has shown remarkable capacity for survival against tremendous odds.[2] It is not only very ancient but also unique in the sense that in no other country hand-weaving is being carried out on a nation-wide basis.

The handloom industry is highly labour-intensive. The 10 million people that are in the handloom industry are mostly from rural areas on over 3 million handlooms[3]. About 27 per cent of the total textile production in the country emanates from the handloom sector. Thus the handloom industry occupies a place of pride in the decentralised sector in terms of employment and production. Hence in any scheme of restructuring the textile policy, the handloom sector will have to be adequately taken care of.[4]

Further, handlooms have been successful in preserving technical designs and skills which have world-wide repute, one of the good things about handloom industry is that it has kept to the traditional patterns.[5] These artisans are artists and the fabrics are products of the art. They have the inherited skill, and an acquired but expert knowledge of colour chemistry. They possess sensitive artistic mind that envisaged new designs which reflected the culture of the land, suited to change in seasons, changing tastes and fashions. No other country in the world can boast of a similar skilled artisan like the Indian handloom weaver. The nation owes a debt of gratitude to the Indian handloom weaver who deserves to be congratulated for preserving his art form throughout the centuries across.[6] Excellent workmanship and ingenuity are the hallmark of the Indian craftsman.

Handloom industry constitutes the larcest labour intensive household industry in the country and has a long tradition of expertise. The handloom industry is hereditary in nature and inspite of the passage of time, it has not very much changed its hereditary character.[7] It is coming down from father to son and on to generations beyond.[8] The entire work from preparatory stage to the weaving stage is shared by all members of the weavers family including women and children.

The handloom industry is dispersed in different parts of the country, particularly in rural areas. The systematic sound of the looms can be heard in almost all the villages, for well over 2000 years, India enjoyed a prominence as a producer of textiles.[9]

Handloom Industry in Retrospect

The history of the handloom Industry in India could be traced back to the hoary past. It dates back to the epic times and is reported to have been in a highly developed stage even then.[10] In the Vedas and Puranas there are innumerable references to the exquisite qualities and wide range of fabrics worn by the Goda, kings and the people at large. Goda were said to have been very much fascinated by the exotic designs and textures of fabrics worn by women of the earth, and there are stories of such Goda falling in love with mortal ladies by their dress.[11]

Weaving is one of the oldest of man's industrial arts and with its allied industrial art of spinning, it led off the industrial revolution. There was solid evidence that man was practicing the art of weaving in the mid 5th millennium B.C., and the evidence indicates that at that time weaver had been practising it long enough to have grown fairly sophisticated in his technique. In the 18th century he took the first major step towards turning the weaving art into an industry in the modern sense of the term. There is evidence of the existence of loom as early as 4400 B.C., a loom pictured on a potter dish found in a woman's tomb at Albari[12].

Early History

India's hand-weaving industry has vast inherent potentialities and it had a glorious past. No other country in the world has preserved and upheld this very ancient hoary craft in such pure form or with such traditions left behind as India does now. Weaving has become an integral part of the lives of large sections of our people and an important part of our economy through the centuries.[13]

The cotton handloom industry is as old as the Indus valley civilization. From first century B.C to the 18th century A.D Indian cotton textiles were regarded as a wonder of the world and were eagerly covered by nobles and kings in Europe, Africa and other far off lands.[14] The weaver with variegated designs and colour combinations was able to meet not only the simple demand of the village woman but was in a position at the same time to satisfy the fastidious requirements of the princess in the palace. The prince as well as the peasant had to look upon the weaver for his clothing requirements.[15]

The marvelously woven tissues and sumptuously interwrought apparel,[16] of ancient India were not only famous in this country but also found their way into many countries. A little more than 2000 years ago, cotton was practically unknown to the civilised nations of the west.[17] Thus Europe was in primitive darkness, when India was in comparative light. The Indian handloom products were the craze of fashionable woman all over the world.

Important Varieties Produced in the Ancient Handloom Industry of India

Since the dawn of civilization, India has been the home of peerless art and craft tradition that has survived sweeping changes.[18] Right from ancient times, across the centuries the high quality *Muslins** of Chanderi, Gozzamer Silk *Brocades** of Benaras, the *Tie & Die** products of Orissa, the *Chintas** of Machilipatnam, the *Hiroos** of Hyderabad, the *Khes** of Punjab, *the Prints** of Ferukhabad, the *Phenek* and *Tongar* and *Bottle designs** of Assam and Manipur, *the lungis** of Madras, *the Maheswari sarees** of Madhya Pradesh, the Patola* of Baroda etc., have been quite famous.

Even in the good old days cloth of highly superior variety was produced. It has been said that muslins* of Dacca using yarn upto 500 counts measuring several yards was reported to have been drawn through a finger ring and parcelled in a match box.[19] As recorded in the history emperor Aurangzeb was startled by his daughters appearing almost naked before him in court, where upon the young princes remonstrated that she had as many as seven muslin suits on her person.[20]

---

* Regional names of clothes.

The writings of the great historians, politicians and kings and poets speak much of the handloom industry and its past glory. In the annals of history the travel accounts of Huantsang, Uarthima, Bernier, Carrird, Travirnier, General Orni, Marcopolo spell out the glory of the handloom industry of the bygone days.[21]

George Phillips in the Instructive article on Menuan's account of the Kingdom of Bengal shows the progress of the handloom industry in the 15th century. From what Manuan, the Chinese traveller, wrote in his account, five or six kinds of fine cotton fabrics were manufactured in India.

Marcopolo the first Christian traveller refers to the (1290 AD) production and manufacture of cotton in Gujarat and other places. Referring to Machilipatnam, he said that they produced the finest and most beautiful cottons to be found in any part of the world.[22] The waves of comquest which commenced from the eleventh century, no doubt greatly hampered Indian Industrialists and Industries for some time. But the establishment of the Mughal empire and the safety and security of the reign of Akbhar seem to have fully revived Indian Industries and handicrafts.[23]

In Nawab Alliwardy Khan's time a weaver was chastised and turned out of the city of Dacca for neglect in not preventing his cow from eating up a piece of Abroon (a type of cloth rolled around head) which he spread and carefully left on the grass.[24]

Foreigners were very much attracted by the beautiful fabrics produced on the handloom industry. The merchants of Europe were lured by the trade and prosperity of India. The establishment of English factories in India was due to the discovery of the English merchants that the products of India, especially Calicoes, Silk and Salt petre, were very profitable articles of merchandise and to their strong desire to carry them to Europe.[25]

Travernier in admiration of the fine cloth manufactured in India tells us of a Persian ambassador who took for his sovereign, on returning home a coconut of the size of an ostrich's egg, enriched with precious stones and when it was opened, a turban was drawn from it 60 cubits (30 Yards) in length, and of a Muslin so fine that would scarcely know that you had it in your hands.[26]

There is another poet who had described that when the princess walked into the swayamwara pandal clad in gorgeous dress, a feeling went through that a rainbow has come down on the earth.[27]

Handloom Industry Before Independence

Inspite of its glorious past, if one looks at the Handloom Industry in retrospect, one will find that its history is dotted with a series of injustices inflicted on it by the Mills[28] In the early period (Before Independence) heavy import duties were levied on yarn intended for handlooms. There were duties on every registered loom and woven thread. The village officer had to register and visit every loom at work and stamp the cloth in preparation before it was sold. If the cloth was bleached or coloured, the dhobi had to pay another duty from the wages he received.[29]

Handloom Industry Under East India Company

Before independence the weavers were weaving for the East India Company. The weavers continued to weave only because of the advances given to them by the Company through the *Copdars** who acted as middlemen between them. The copdara never gave these advances in full, leaving the weavers to be flogged by the company's servants if they could not deliver the goods on time.

The Copdars never allowed the weavers to be directly engaged nor did they give them any share in their enormous profits. The Company was only interested in getting as much cloth as possible. Their sympathetic representations did not receive any favourable attention from the Board of Trade. The weavers themselves protested in vain against these dishonest and cruel Copdars, who were getting the lion's share of the advances given by the Company agents. The weavers were made to work at very poor rates in spite of the rise in the prices of thread and food stuffs.

As the Company never trusted the weavers the copdars continued to have uncontrolled sway over the weaving settlements. They used to go with peons to harass the weavers, not as men of business, but of ostentation and authority, for sorting and rejecting the woven cloth, rather than for assisting and supporting the weavers. The Company agents and the Board of Trade knew the villainous methods of the copdars but they never interfered to check these malpractices for fear of incurring their displeasure which might adversely affect their investments.

Every loom was subject to the imposition of heavy moturpha (a Tax), unless it was engaged by the Company for export to Europe when it was exempted from it, as it was an inducement to attract the reluctant weavers, unwilling to work for the Company.

---

*Middlemen named as 'Copdars'.

Handloom Industry During the World Wars

The greatest havoc was wrought to Handloom Industry during the two world wars. At the time of war, the demand for cloth was high, the mills increased their production, beyond all proportions, by usurping the yarn normally meant for handlooms. This situation had continued till the middle of 1949. When all the foreign countries were busy, with the preparation for warfare, the import of mill cloth to India was reduced considerably. This situation was well exploited by the Indian Textile Mills, by way of producing more and more of cloth and deprived the handlooms of their share of yarn. The major problem, the Handloom industry had faced was with regard to the unsteadiness of the supply of yarn in abnormal times.[30]

During the war period, all the Mills whether spinning, Composite or Weaving were made to work to their full capacity in the name of war efforts. The interests of the handloom weavers and of the consumers were thus, for the time being, ignored and the yarn which was previously available for the handloom weavers and the cloth which was available for the consumers were considerably curtailed and both of them were diverted to war requirements. The Mllla were given not only full work and abnormal profits but also all facilities and protection demanded by them. Even the labour strikes were declared illegal.[31]

Effect of the First World War on the Handloon Industry (1914-18)

The progress of the Handloom Industry was very much hampered due to unsteadiness of the supply of yarn during the world war. For, nearly the whole of its yarn supply, the handlooms under the new dispensation came to depend on mills, both home and foreign. This resulted in the handlooms sharing in the ups and downs of the mill industry to a considerable extent. The dangers of this dependence was felt for the first time during the War of 1914-18. Imports of cloth having diminished and the internal demand for cloth having increased, Indian mills used up much more of their yarn themselves and left much less for the handlooms. Of the total yarn available in the quinquennim 1911-12 to 1915-16, mills took only 1,295 million lbs (51 per cent), * while 1,248 million lbs., (49 per cent) went to Handlooms, but in the next quinquennim, 1916-17 to 1920-21, of the total yarn available, mills took as much as 1,644 million lbs., (60 per cent) while only 1,097 million lbs.,(40 per cent) went to the Handlooms. The result of this can be seen from the Table 1.1.

Table 1.1 : Production of Cloth by Mills and Handlooms

Year	Consumption of yarn (in million Lbs.) by Mills	Estimated production of cloth (in million yards) by Mills	Estimated consumption of yarn by Handlooms (in million Lbs)	Estimated production of cloth (in million Yards) by Handlooms
1910-11	219	1047	227	908
1911-12	238	1133	261	1044
1912-13	254	1214	260	1040
1913-14	244	1166	267	1068
1914-15	246	1176	272	1088
1915-16	313	1496	236	945
1916-17	336	1606	149	598
1917-18	338	1616	185	741
1918-19	310	1482	224	894
1919-20	341	1630	127	506

Sources:

1. From 1910-14: M.P. Gandhi—The Indian Cotton Textile Industry—Its Past, Present and Future—p.82, G.N. Mitra, The Book Company Ltd., Calcutta, 1930.
2. Data from 1914-20: The Fact Finding Committee p.8, Government of India, 1942.

Thus, the estimated production of handloow cloth increased from 908 million yards in 1910-11 to 1088 million yards in 1914-15. But the production of handloom cloth fell from 1088 million yards in 1914-15, to 506 million yards in 1919-20. Till 1910-11, the annual handloom production had been more than the mill production and in some years nearly double. But from that date mill production began to increase steadily and rapidly, and in the years 1911-12 to 1914-15 both the lines of production became nearly equal. Then came the war, and taking advantage of the cessation of imports, mills made a serious effort to increase production and capture the home market. Handlooms were finally beaten and not only beaten but probably severely crippled for the time being.[32]

Although the total output of handloom cloth suffered a set back in the period, the condition of the industry was in other ways not so discouraging. The decline of imports during the war and the preoccupation of the Indian hills with war supplies with little possibility of adding to mills machinery enabled the handloom industry not only to maintain but to expand its production especially in the field of women's garments.[33] However, this revival of production and prosperity was not shared by many centres. When the prices of fabrics rose, wages also rose, although not correspondingly, owing to the inevitable time-lag, but the scarcity and high prices of yarn was a great handicap to the weavers who had managed to keep their independence, and led large numbers of them to take up contract work under *mahajans** or to work as labourers in the *karkanas*.** The scarcity and consequent high cost of dyes also affected the handloom industry during the war of 1914-18. The net imports of dyes fell from a pre-war quinquennial average of over 15 million lbs to 0.7 million lbs.

In the years following the War of 1914-18, the handloom sector was able to obtain more yarn and there was a partial revival in the industry, judging from the increased quantities of yarn that went to it year after year.

Handloom Industry During the Second World War (1939-45)

The Second World War gave the mills a rare opportunity of capturing the Indian market. During the first world war, the mill industry was in a state of underdevelopment and could meet only 30 per cent of the home demand. But by 1939, it supplied more than 85 per cent of the home demand, and from 1940 onwards the stimulus came from huge Government orders and from increasing exports and dwindling imports.

During the war, the prices of textiles were very high. So, in order to control the prices of cloth, the 'Standard Cloth Scheme' was introduced by the Government of India, in the year 1943, to make the cheap and standard cloth available to the poor sections of the community.[34]

During this war, the handloom weavers had to pay 12 1/2 to 20 per cent more than the ex-mill prices of yarn besides taxes. Yarn was not available in sufficient quantity and in required counts and the weaver was compelled to purchase yarn in the black market. There were times when the handloom weavers could not get enough yarn to employ themselves even for four days in a month.[35] As a result the production fell down during the war period as shown in Table 1.2.

Exploitation by middlemen was quite conspicuous during the War. Before the war, the price of 40 counts yarn, was ₹ 6.25 for 10 pounds. But during the war the price of the yarn increased to ₹ 45. The price of cloth was Re. 0.50 (Half Rupee) per yard before the war, and it increased to

---

* Rich Master weavers who supply raw materials to weavers.

** Weaving Sheds.

₹1.75 during the war period. The increase in the price of cloth and the benefit that accrued was enjoyed only by the middlemen.[36]

Table 1.2 : Production of Cotton Cloth in Mills and Handloom Sectors in India

(In Million Metres)

Year	Mill cloth production	Handloom cloth production	Total cloth production
1937-38	4029	1477	5506
1938-39	4297	1946	6243
1939-40	3790	1820	5610
1941-42	3720	1600	5320
1942-43	3290	1500	4790
1943-44	4410	1600	6010
1944-45	4300	1500	5800
1947-48	4310	1259	5578

Source: Prasad, K. 'Technological Choice under Developmental Planning (1963), Popular Prakashan, Bombay, p.26.

Handloom Industry After Independence

Independence and simultaneous partition of the country made the position of handloom industry much worse.[37] Soon after attaining independence, the National Government in the name of making more cloth available for internal consumption, banned the exports of handloom cloth, with the result, the long established foreign markets for handloom cloth in Middle and Far Eastern Countries like Aden, Burma, Ceylon, Malaya and Indonesia etc., for varieties like lungis, Sarees etc., were lost.

During the year 1952, the industry faced a serious crisis owing to the unprecedented slump which prevailed immediately after the Korean war. In order to overcome this catastrophe, the Government of India, created the 'Cess Fund' with the levy of cess at the rate of quarter anna for every square yard of mill fabric manufactured.

Having traced the growth of handloom industry in India, till the beginning of the planning era (India got independence on 15th August 1947 and launched its First Five year plan w.e.f 1.4.1951), let us now defer the description of the developments in the handloom industry to the succeeding pages. But meanwhile an attempt is being made to have a brief survey of the literature on the handloom industry. This survey not only indicates the need for the present study by the author but also indicates the developments that took place in the handloom industry in India, particularly in the later half of the 20th century.

Survey of Literature on Handlooms

There ia not much of printed literature on the subject, as the handloom industry was a rural-based one and did not attract adequate attention of the authorities concerned, although the history of the handloom industry dates back to some thousands of years. Statistics are not available about the handlooms as in the case of many other sectors of the Indian Economy.[38] However, a brief review of the literature on the subject is presented in this section.

Prof. N.G.Ranga[39] in his survey conducted during 1925-26 entitled 'The Economics of Handlooms' explained the Mungani system* and apprenticeship system, which showed that monthly earnings of the weavers ranged from ₹ 8 to ₹ 25 depending on their hardwork and that in a majority of the cases the income was not sufficient to make the both ends meet and that they were heavily indebted. The position remains the same even now. Starvation deaths also are reported.[40] The author was of the opinion that the inventive skills of the weavers were not of a high order and that they were slow in adopting themselves to changes in the methods of production.

The unique contribution of the study was that it gave a fairly good account of the important handloom centers of production, pattern of production, structure of the markets, earnings and expenditure of the weavers and the like in those centres. The study was the first authentic account of the structure of the handloom industry in Andhra Pradesh. The author also estimated the poverty line for the handloom weavers.

According to the author, most of the workers were being badly exploited by heartless and inefficient employers and a proper system of Trade Boards was urgently needed to safeguard their interests. The author advocated the setting up of better *Sizing*** machines and common workshop facilities to make it possible for the woman members of weaving households to take part in this work.

A master piece of R.G. Kakade, the 'Socio-economic Survey of Weaving Communities in Sholapur' is worth mentioning in this context. This work is based on his Ph.D thesis submitted to Bombay University and published by the Gokhale Institute of Politics and Economics, Poona in 1946.

The work was undertaken with a view to studying the handloom industry of Sholapur—one of the prominent places of Handloom industry

* The system whereby Master Weaver supplies the required inputs in their proper proportion at the doorstep of the weaver worker and gets fabrics after due payment of wages, fixed.

** Sizing is the preparation of length-wise yarn known as warp.

in India—in a comprehensive and detailed way and to study the sociological aspects of the communities engaged in the industry. Kakade had to start his study with a thorough census of the weaving communities of Sholapur in the absence of reliable information. He had followed 'Systematic Sampling' method and the data were collected by personally canvassing the questionnaire. Out of a total of 1376 karkanas, 107 units which were representative both in character and size were selected for intensive study. The size of the sample was 12 per cent of the size of population. The socio-economic conditions of 541 families were studied out of 7,870 Padmasali families. Apart from this, another 60 families were selected on a random basis from communities other than Padmasale. Thus information was collected from 601 families, and it was used for intensive study.

In the chapter—Reform and Reconstruction of Handloom Industry and proposals for the future, he indicated how the handloom industry was facing the competition from the Powerloom and Mill industries. He gave very valuable suggestions to protect the handloom industry from the Mills and Powerlooms.

According to Kakade, there are four possible ways of protecting the handloom industry, from the competition of Mills and Powerlooms. They are: (1) Completely prohibiting mills from producing those goods that are produced on handlooms and in which competition exists; (2) Without restricting mill production, regulating mills through the market by dividing it between the mills industry and the handloom industry, under a statutory enactment, accompanied by a duty, if necessary to prevent encroachment of the handloom market by the mill sector; (3) Without restricting the production of mills to impose a duty on mill-made cloth which enters into competition with the handloom weavers; (4) Without restricting the output of the Mill cloth to pay a subsidy or subvention to the handloom weavers on the basis of their production.

An important suggestion of Kakade was that the industry needed technological improvement. The inefficiency of the handloom weavers is proverbial.[41] When we speak of increasing the efficiency of weavers it must be remembered that efficiency is one of the functions of the technical equipment available in the industry.[42]

In a chapter devoted to the study of 'Social and Economic Conditions of Padmasalis', data were collected on such aspects as: the number of persons of the family, type of family, economic status, housing, food, addictions, savings, debts etc. Another interesting aspect of the study was the attempt to determine the cut off level of income for poverty determination. According to the study 89 per cent of the weaving families were below the poverty line. About 53 per cent of families were steeped in dire poverty and the remaining 36 per cent were on a slightly higher level[43], but certainly below the poverty line. The poverty of Padmasali workers had been mostly attributed by many observers to the vices they had. The author argued that their poverty was largely due to the injudicious expenditure of their incomes.[44]

Kakade had discussed the 'Ethnology, Mythology and Religion of Padmasalies' also. He described the historical origin of weaving castes. According to him weaving began with the manufacture of coarse blankets from the wool of the sheep tended by shepherds, and was originally a shepherd's occupation.[45]

A survey conducted by the National Council of Applied Economic Research[46] of India regarding the economics of handloom industry (in the year 1958) in the five districts of the then Karnataka State is note-worthy. The study included in it, among other things an estimate of the degree of under-employment and assessment of cost structure, production potential of the industry, organisational and financial problems of the industry.

The study used the 'Stratified Sampling' method, for the collection of data. The handloom centres in Karnataka were stratified into two strata viz., rural and urban. Then the centres were classified according to the number of establishments. Each sub stratum was further classified into three size classes on the basis of specified number of looms in each establishment viz., with 1 to 3 looms, 4 to 8 looms and 9 looms and above. Out of the sample of 714 households, 215 belonged to 38 selected rural centres and the remaining 499 to the 9 selected urban centres.

The study clearly explained the low levels of earnings and low standards of living of handloom weavers. According to this study the earnings in the urban centres were considerably higher than those in the rural centres.

According to this study, the subsidies, rebates and other sorts of protection extended to the handloom industry were short-term solutions only. The permanent solution to the problem lies in strengthening the co-operative system.

One of the limitations of this study however was that it did not explain the reasons why the earnings in urban centres were higher than the rural areas.

Another work worth mentioning is that of Nagen C.Das viz., 'Development of Handloom Industry—Organisation—Production—Marketing'. It is based on his Ph.D thesis, submitted to Gauhati University and published by Deep and Deep publications, New Delhi in 1986. Das, in his work, explained in detail the historical background of the origin and development of handloom industry, its relevance to the State economy, organisation of handloom industry in co-operatives and non-co-operative sectors, production inputs and outputs, marketing, finance and modernisation of handloom industry etc. Some concrete suggestions were also made by the author for the further development of handloom industry. The study is based on both primary and secondary data.

According to the author, in the initial stage of planning process and particularly under handloom development schemes, the progress of the primary and central weavers' societies seemed to be encouraging, yet, the societies could not show any marked improvement during the later years. It is evident from his analysis that the very low membership of the societies and the presence of some vested interests with in the societies managing committees indirectly hampered the initiative of persons to become weaver-members. Another reason given by the author for the poor state of co-operative system in Assam was the reluctance of the weavers to become members of weavers' co-operatives because of the inability of the societies to deliver the goods and services required by the members.

The author suggested that processing facilities should be improved through the Governmental assistance and intervention. The State Government should come forward in this sphere.[47] He also suggested that primitive looms should be replaced by modern looms.

The author had recognised the importance of working capital for the healthy growth of the handloom industry. The working capital that the weavers availed themselves from the commercial Banks was not recovered due to important reasons. The blame for poor recovery of Bank loans cannot entirely be attributed to the weavers alone. According to Das, the major obstacle in the non-payment of Bank loans by the Loanees, was the absence of proper marketing outlet where the weavers might readily dispose of their products.

The credit accommodation made available to Master weavers by both private and public sources was found to be satisfactory. This is because the Master weavers have their own marketing outlets which helped in making timely repayment. This is one of the findings of Das.

Das had tried to focus light on the marketing problems of the handloom cloth. The individual weavers were mostly in a disadvantageous position for marketing their produce. At times they are forced to dispose of their products through distress sale. The researcher had the opportunity to acquaint himself with the nature of marketing problems faced by the individual weavers. It was stated that some weavers because of their indebtedness, to village traders or financiers and mahajans, were required to sell their products at throw away prices. Some merchants and traders also directly dealt with individual weavers by supplying yarn and buying back the cloth.

Finally the author suggested that a comprehensive plan was highly desirable for the industry, and that it should embrace all the aspects of handloom production, promotion and development.

Mahapatro's work on the "Handloom Industry of Orissa' (Year 1986) is also worth mentioning. According to the author, it is the first of its kind in the State of Orissa. It was therefore exploratory in nature. The study examined the relevance of the industry to the economy of the State. It scrutinised the general characteristics of the Industry. Capital and organisational structures of the industry were given due coverage in the study. Output and employment aspects of the industry were also studied. In addition, the incomes of the weaving households and their economic conditions were analysed. The major problems faced by the industry were also been pinpointed. The study envisaged a planned programme for a gradual technological change (as against phased and selective development) so that the resultant transformation will be as painless as possible.

The master piece of Abdul Zahir entitled 'Handloom Industry in Varanasi', an unpublished thesis submitted to Banaras Hindu University, in the year 1966 deserves to be mentioned. The author had the added advantage in selecting this industry for field investigation, because he belonged to the same community which owns and runs this industry. As such, he is familiar with a large number of local terms used in the various processes and practices of the industry aa well as with the working conditions, process o£ production, types of products, costs and marketing practices etc. At first it was decided to collect information from more than 100 establiahments., but later on the number was reduced to 65-70 establishments.

The work of Abdul Zahir has been divided into twelve chapters, each dealing with only one aspect of the industry. In this work, the historical development of the industry in Varanasi during the last so many centuries was explained in detail. It also throws light on organisation, structure and size of the industry, Capital structure, raw materials, process of production, employment, wages, output, marketing and sales etc.

The study of Zahir emphasises the need for giving encouragement to the handloom industry of Varanasi not only on the ground that it absorbs a significant section of the community that would otherwise remain unemployed, but also because it produces a specilised and distinct type of handloom products, having wide internal and foreign markets. It was also advocated that unless the small weavers are improved no structural improvement in the industry can be thought of.

The author emphasised the need to improve the co-operative base of the handloom industry. He advocates that the societies must be run on the lines of a business organisation with trained and experienced person at the helm of affairs.

The author concludes by saying that any phased programme of development technological, structural or otherwise—as envisaged above, is directly linked with the general uplift of the weaver community.

An unpublished Ph.D thesis of Angadi,(1976) entitled 'Handloom Industry in Karnataka' is a study of Handloom and Powerloom industries of Bijapur district in Karnataka State. The study analysed in detail the economic, techno-economic and non-economic aspects of the industry, regarding organisation, size, equipment, capital, output, labour, income, pricing, market, finance, debt etc., along with family budgets and other general characteristic features of people engaged in the handloom industry.

The final part of the study gives an integrated comparative and comprehensive picture of the case studies of 8 handloom weaving centres. It also discussed the problem of reservation of certain products to the handloom industry.

The author showed that more than 90 per cent of the handloom establishments in the district were found to be un-economic, particularly in rural centres, almost all establishments are un-economic in size. According to him, certain improvements are to be brought in the processes of production viz., warping and weaving. In order to increase the earning capacity of the weaver, automatic frame looms should be widely popularised, and to improve the quality of production on jacquards and improved *dobbies** are to be introduced. The study further points out that the indebtedness of weavers demoralise the weaving communities. Consequently a common weaver miserably lacks good human qualities like honesty, contentment, sincerity, discipline and hardwork. According to this study the monthly income of the household was less than ₹ 100 in 1976 and almost all workers suffered from malnutrition.

A.V.Ramana Rao[48] in his book entitled 'Economic Development of Andhra Pradesh (1776-1957)' narrated how the handloom industry had

* Jacquards and dobbies are the instruments used for designings in the fabric.

suffered under British Rule and gave a detailed account of various handloom centres and products produced in the State of Andhra pradesh.

'The loom of Interdependence'[49] by Yvone J.Arterburn is a case study of what makes co-operatives succeed rather than fail the everyday life of silk handloom weavers in neighbourhoods and homes of Kanchipuram in India is painted as a backdrop to their successful fight for greater control of their co-operatives. It analyses how weavers have an indigenous ethic of brotherhood and equality and use skill and craftmanship as a source of pride in work and evaluation of status, the book shows.

The work of S. Hariharan viz.,[50] 'Handloom Industry in Tiruchy District (Tamil Nadu)', a project sponsored by the ICSSR, New Delhi, and completed in 1989., explains the important contributions of the handloom industry, in terms of employment and earnings of foreign exchange to the country. He has rightly pointed out that instead of aiming at helping and sustaining a stagnating industry, the need is for making it a really self-sufficient industry, more dynamic, more competitive with faster rate of growth. He further states that though the industry has been growing, the rate is not fast enough and it has to be improved. He admits that the possibilities are great for the production of new varieties of sarees and shirtings in the industry and the encouragement on these lines, must be given priority along with promoting the skills of artists, making new designs for the sarees etc.

Another point that he make is the industry cannot survive in urban areas, because of lack of space and consequent overcrowding. The author suggests that the encouragement should be given for weavers' settlements in new housing areas specially demarcated for this purpose.

The author also fears that the weavers are moving out of the industry and this would ultimately lead to demand for higher wages.

He is also of the opinion that the shortage of working capital can be met through the pursuit of a more liberal policy by the Commercial Banks. According to him handloom industry should be notified as a priority sector and instructions be given to the Nationalised Banks to treat this industry with greater consideration particularly in the provision of working capital.

With regard to the marketing of handloom products the author suggests that it may not be possible to have handloom marketing centres in every town, but it should be possible to have one in every district headquarters—a centre where handloom products produced by the Master weavers and Independent weavers find a place. Similar to marketing centres, export centres must also be established in every district. He wants that the Government should take initiative to start workshops and to utilise the expert designers who can give their debt for the development of new designs for the growth of the industry. Publicity, Salesmanship and advertisement on modern lines are a must for this industry not only in India but abroad too.

The work of Subramanyam and Rama Mohan Rao on 'Socio-economic Conditions of Weavers in East Godavari District'(1982), a Mimeo, is worth mentioning here. It throws light on social and economic conditions of the weavers in East Godavari district.

Relevant information has been collected from five villages viz., Bandarlanka, Kothapeta, Mori, Vellore and Uppada in East Godavari district, based on purposive stratified random sampling. The handloom industry is mostly concentrated in these villages. The survey covered 5 per cent (325 households) of the total establishments in the selected villages.

The study explains that the Master Weaver sector is dominating the industry. A little more than half of the weavers work for the Master Weaver, and 30 per cent work the co-operatives and only 7 per cent were independent producers. The rest worked for more than one organisation.

Excepting for a negligible few, handloom weaving is the full-time occupation for the majority of the weaving population. According to this study, the average monthly income of all the weavers was around ₹ 300 and it ranged between ₹ 70 and ₹ 600 in 1982. A significant percentage of weavers say, 76 per cent got a monthly income of ₹ 300 or below. According to this study, institutional financing was quite negligible and nearly 75 per cent of the credit requirements of the respondents was met by both moneylenders and master weavers together. The average debt per establishment was around ₹ 850 and the average value of fixed assets was ₹ 2010 per establishment. Ramamohan's work entitled 'Development of Handloom Industry—A Case Study of Socio-economic, Production and Marketing Characteristics of Handloom Sector in Karimnagar District' an unpublished thesis submitted to Andhra University, Waltair, throws light on many aspects of the handloom industry in Karimnagar district.

On the basis of the number of looms in each taluk, five taluks which account for nearly 70 per cent of total loomage in the district were selected. Three important villages from each taluk having large scale concentration of looms are selected. Thus, 375 household (25 from each village) units of 15 villages were selected. Out of 1218 primaries existing the five taluks, 45 co-operatives were selected for appraising, their performance. Random sampling technique was used for selecting both the household units and co-operatives.

According to the study, all the respondents in the district belong to padmasale community. Independent organisation is more predominant in this area. About 13 per cent of the respondents worked for the Master weavers, 27 per cent for the co-operatives and the remaining are the Independent weavers. The annual income of the weaver varied between ₹ 1000 to ₹ 10,000.

An unpublished Ph.D thesis of S.T.Surendra submitted to Osmania University, Hyderabad in 1984, entitled 'Co-operatives in Andhra Pradesh' deserves to be mentioned. The study covers such aspects as growth, organisational structure and effectiveness of Weaver Co-operative Societies, vertical disintegration vis-a-vis factors of production, marketing and finance, functioning of the Apex Weavers' Co-operative Society, apart from the socio-economic survey of the weavers of Mahaboobnagar district.

The author finds that the socio-economic conditions of the weavers are far from satisfactory and the weavers live in poverty, indebtedness and illiteracy. The living conditions are unsanitary and unhealthy. He is unable to make both ends meet, even after decades of efforts must be made to bring more and more weavers into co-operative fold and all necessary facilities must be extended to improve the socio-economic conditions. The survival of the industry itself depends on the weaver and his well-being, who is the backbone of the industry.

An unpublished report entitled 'Employment Factor in Handlooms[51] by Dr. B. Sudhakar Rao and others(1986), prepared on behalf of NIRD, Hyderabad, studied in detail employment generation capacity of the handlooms. It also attempted to estimate the under-employment and unemployment prevailing among handloom weavers. The study throws light on existing institutional support such as supply of raw-material, credit, marketing of fabrics etc, needed for the over all development of handloom industry. The study also suggested various measures both policy and programme related, necessary to safeguard and strengthen employment factor in the Industry.

An unpublished Ph.D thesis of B. Sarangapani entitled 'Organisational Pattern and Levels of Living of Handloom Weavers—A study in coastal Andhra Pradesh (1987), submitted to Andhra University, Waltair throws light on some important aspects of the weavers. It also explains the organisational pattern in the industry and levels of living of handloom weavers. It also made an attempt to examine the relationship between production pattern and levels of living of handloom weavers and migrational aspects etc. The study is restricted to Pedana and Mangalagiri towns of Krishna and Guntur districts respectively.

According to the author, Pedana and Mangalagiri had the largest number of looms in Krishna and Guntur districts. There were 4,392 looms in Pedana constituting about 57 per cent of total looms in the district and the rest are in different parts of Krishna district. In Mangalagiri Taluk alone, there were 6,000 looms constituting 77.42 per cent, and the rest were in different parts of the district. Both the centres are well developed and have access to markets.

The weaving households have been classified into four categories viz. 1) Independent Weavers; (2) Weavers working for Co-operatives; (3) Weavers working for Master Weavers; and (4) Cooli Weavers. A minimum of five per cent of the households in each of the 4 categories of the households, was covered. In the case of Coolie weaving households, the size of the sample was limited to 100. Accordingly the overall size of the sample came to 5.29 per cent of the total weaving households.

The evolution of the industry was explained in detail. Almost all the looms in the area surveyed are pit-fly shuttle looms (99.42%). The production in the area surveyed is heterogeneous in nature and hence wages are paid according to the counts, quality and intensity of weaving.

According to the study, the incidence of poverty is more among the coolie weaving households (60%), followed by households working for Master Weavers (54.39%), households working for co-operatives 47.06 per cent and for Independent weaving households it is 25 per cent. It is advocated that the incidence of poverty is more among the sample households in Pedana when compared to that of the sample households in Mangalagiri.

The average size of the sample weaving household was 4.54 and the average number of participants in weaving per household was 1.60. To cross the poverty line, net earnings per loom per month must be ₹ 266. From the- study of Sarangapani, it is found out that the proportion of households earning more than ₹ 266, was more in Mangalagiri than in Pedana. However there are inequalities in the distribution of net earnings per loom per month and per household in both the centres of production. Next to the independent weaving category, Co-operative weaving was having better prospects for the weavers in the study area, as far as their earnings were concerned.

Pragada Ketaiah[52] in his article on 'Don't Kill the Handlooms' described the difficulties, the industry had to face during 1965-66, with the rise in export duties and customs on chemicals, dyes and yarn. The author in another article on 'Neglect of Handloora weavers'[53] rightly pointed out that while handloom industry was starving for want of finance and raw materials, it was unjust to provide finance to the power-loom industry.

In another article[54] the author describes the handloom Industry as a "Motherless child'. He feels that the competition between handloom and powerloom Industries is acute. In the words of the author. The competition that the powerloom presents to the handloom is of a more serious character than that of a composite or a weaving Mill. He suggests that certain items of cloth production should exclusively be reserved for the handloom industry.

Chowdary Ram Sewak[55] in his article on the 'Role of Handloom Board in the Development of Handloom Co-operatives' feels that the Co-operative societies must be provided adequate amount of working capital to provide full employment to the weavers depending on the societies. It was also observed that the societies make no efforts to change the pattern of production to suit the tastes of their consumers. So the production in weavers co-operative society hould be oriented by the changing pattern of sales, to suit the tastes of the consumers.

Ansari[56] in his article on the 'Pattern of Government Assistance to Handloom Industry' felt that the co-operative societies have failed to provide continuous employment to the weavers working for them. The uncertainty of continuous work is a powerful factor for the weavers to cling to the master weavers. The author suggests in this article that the Government should see that the units outside the co-operative fold are not neglected and that while framing the credit policy of the major nationalised banks, this industry should also be provided with adequate credits.

C.S. Rao[57] in his article on 'Employment in Handloom Industry' explains in detail the employment potential of the handloom industry, which according to him is highly labour intensive. According to the author, the present utilisation of the existing capacity of the industry is 55 per cent only, mainly due to inadequate supply of yarn, working capital and marketing problems. He advocated that a major thrust is reuired to be made in formulation and implementation of the handloom development programme by the Centre, and State Governments, keeping in view the need to provide cheap credit and raw materials. It is also necessary to improve the production techniques by training the weavers and supply the improved tools and equipment and market the goods.

In an article on 'Utilise Capacity of Handlooms in Full' Somappa.M[58] opines that the potentials of the handloom industry are not exploited full due to shortage of supply of raw material yarn and competiton from Mill industry. The author suggests that Mill should concentrate on export market and the vaccum thus created in the internal market by auch increased exports will be met easily by the Handloom sector.

A study brought out by the Commerce Research Bureau[59] opined that factors like very low output, very meager returns, the high cost and erratic supply of inputs like yarn, dyes and chemicals, the absence of adequate marketing facilities and know-how, the chronic iIndebtedness of the weavers and their exploitation at the hands of middlemen and moneylenders, the poor organisation of the industry and the failure, by and large, of the co-operatives in the field have all been responsible for the present plight of this sector.

In an article on 'Handloom Industry' H.V.R. Athre[60] feels that to improve the industry further Mills should be made to stamp on each hank[61] the minimum strength of yarn and weavers should be trained for weaving special varieties. Improved equipment like jacquard[62], long warping sheds should be supplied at subsidised rates and young weavers should be trained in power-looms and all the existing handlooms must be converted to powerlooms ultimately. Finally he concludes that the Co-operative Societies must be strengthened to function as a clearing house for stocks and liberal credit facilities should be given to society.

G.S. Kamat[63] in an article on 'The Yarn Requirements of Handlooms and the Role of Co-operative Spinning Mills' opined that there was need for a face-lift for the industry.

He covered various aspects such as gaps in yarn requirements, potentials for handlooms, Reservation policy of the industry, Regional imbalances etc. The major thrust was on yarn requirements of the industry keeping in view the wide fluctuations in the yarn prices and supply position he suggests that it is extremely necessary that buffer stock arrangements are to be made and channels of distribution are be progressively co-operativised and strengthened to avoid instabilities.

In an article on 'Progress and Problems of Handloom Weavers' Co-operatives in Karnataka State, K.N.Venkatappaiah[64] opined that the prime factor in the production of handloom fabrics is getting and supplying of raw materials to the weavers at controlled rates without which it is difficult for the weaver to earn his livelihood. Because of non-availability of raw materials at reasonable rates, the looms are in lame position. He emphasized the importance of producing quality fabrics and bottlenecks have to be got rid off for the smooth working of the handloom industry.

J.D. Bathra[65] in his article on 'Petrofils to the Aid of Handloom Co-operatives' feels that the industry should switch over to produce superior variety of cloth by using polyester filament yarn. According to the author it would fetch the higher wage to the weavers. In another article on "Programme for Weavers Prosperity'[66] the author opines that the industry suffered from organisational strength, un-economic working conditions, want of regular supply of raw materials at stable prices, shortage of credit and lack of proper marketing facilities not to speak of competition from the more powerful mill and powerloom sectors. The viability of handloom units depend largely on the regular and adequate supply of inputs at reasonable prices. The basic elements consist of yarn and credit.

T.S. Srinivasan[67] in his article on 'Handloom Industry—Looking for a New Deal' states that the Government should frame rules for the concrete and definite relationship between composite mills, powerlooms, handlooms and the man-made fibre textiles.

R.G. Kulkarni[68] in his article on 'Improved Handlooms' described how the Industry evolved from the time immemorial. The author feels that the handloom weavers will have to be provided with improved tools which will bring in more return at least double the present level. He rightly emphasised the defects of pit looming. According to the author, the *Sevagram loom** is the best substitute for the existing pit loom.

K.P. Radha Krishna in his article on 'Poverty and Unemployment—The Case of Handloom Sector'[69] feels that for the poor economic conditions of the Indian economy the solution lies in popularising the handloom sector., which needs significantly less amount of capital. He concluded that the development of the handloom sector offers the right answer to the problem of providing better economic well-being to this under privileged section of the society within the framework of the policy objective of the Government. He feels that capital should flow into rural areas rather than labour flow out into urban areas. Moreover this attempt at providing year round employment to the handloom weavers combined with the creation of additional jobs at the farm will narrow the gap between rural and urban real incomes.

In an article entitled 'Organisation of Handlooms' Kantikumar R. Podar explained in detail, the problems that the industry has been facing and made several suggestions. The study observed that relevant and reliable statistics must be made available regarding number of looms, types of products produced on the Industry, marketing aspects etc.

---

* Technically improved loom by Institute of National Handloom Technology, Varanasi.

The study further observed that any industry can prosper in the long run not through giving continuous protection, but by enabling it to stand on its own feet through a sound commercial and organisational set up.

J.D. Batra[70] in his article on 'Protection for the Handloom Industry' reiterated the need for strict implementation of reservation policy by the Government. According to the author the Government should not permit any expansion in the weaving capacity of the organised mill and powerloom sectors. The Government should enforce the existing reservation and further extend it to other items.

T. Yagaiah[71] in his article on "Handloom Industry in India' strongly emphasised the importance of strong co-operative system. One of his observations was that the condition of weavers working for the co-operatives was better than of other weavers. The problems of weavers, who are either working for other agencies or on their own account, should get special attention for their wages are less than they should be. So, he strongly pleaded that all the weavers should be brought under the co-operative fold.

S. Arasaratham[72] in his article on 'Weavers, Merchants and Company: The Handloom Industry in Southern India 1752-1790' narrated the historical facts pertaining to the industry, such as, relation between weaver and trader, caste system prevailing in the industry, products produced, financial assistance provided for the industry, involvement of family members in general and children in particular, marketing aspects, looms tax, socio-economic background of the weaver during 1750-1790, etc.

K.G. Srivastav[73] in his article on 'Handlooms in Madhya Pradesh' explained the progress of the handloom Industry under centrally sponsored schemes. The author opined that there was need for a new approach and strategy. In the new strategy initially priority will have to be given for making the handloom cloth more and more popular and the availability of it to the consumers at reasonable rate if not cheaper than the mill made cloth.

L.C. Jain[74] in his article on 'Handlooms Face Liquidation—Powerlooms Mock at Yojana Bhavan' expressed the view that the powerloom industry was eating away the market reserved for the handloom sector. A substantial portion of powerloom cloth, (as is well known) was shown as handloom production. He felt that this was not an innocent error; it is smoke-screen for concealing the cannibalisation of handlooms by powerlooms. The resultant loss of employment in weavers' households is unimaginable; and one-half of those who lose their jobs are women since women are engaged in pre-weaving processes and in certain areas, in weaving as well.

S.L. Kukraja[75] in his article on 'Co-operativisation Programme in Handloom Sector' felt that Co-operative sector should be strengthened. In order to achieve the overall target of 60% coverage, then set for the Sixth Five Year Flan, as per the recommendations of Sivaraman Committee, the author suggested that the then existing programmes of assisting Primaries and Apexes should be continued and that they should be suitably augmented by new schemes like managerial subsidy for appointment of paid Secretaries, modernisation, renovation, purchase of new looms in the Co-operative sector and assistance for setting up industrial type handloom weaver co-operative societies.

In an article on 'Handloom Industry in Coastal Andhra—Survey[76] B. RamaKrishna Rao and G. Subramanyam explained in detail the socio-economic conditions of the weavers in Coastal Andhra. They emphasised the need for strict enforcement of minimum wage for handloom weavers, introduction of Provident Fund scheme in both private and co-operative sectors. They also felt that the Government should come with a heavy hand and should snub the malpractices adopted by the Master weavers.

In monographs entitled 'Wither Handlooms'[77]. The voice of Handlooms'[78]. 'Handlooms in the Fourth Plan'[79]. 'Handlooms Crave Justice'[80]. 'Fair Deal to Handlooms'[81] M. Somappa gave a detailed account of various types of crisis the industry had undergone at different times. In all these monographs he described that powerlooms are a greater threat to handlooms than even the organised mill weaving industry. He had opposed the idea of converting the handlooms into powerlooms. He further adds that it is the duty and responsibility of every citizen of India and of the Government, (Central and State) to see that the handloom weavers are relieved from their present ugly predicament by strictly enforcing the reservations in regard to production of cloth. Public also should patronise the use of handloom cloth. In all his works the author emphasised the importance of handlooms for the Indian economy. In order to keep the industry on sound economic footing, the author recommended certain short term measures such as Rebate on the sale of handloom cloth, purchase of handloom cloth by State Trading Corporation, provision of working capital, loan through the Cess Fund, and long term measures viz., restricting the mill cloth production, strict enforcement of cloth reservation, grant of higher rebate for export of handloom cloth, and elimination of powerlooms.

A monograph entitled 'Self-employment Solves Unemployment' of Sri Pragada Kotaiah[82], a well known leader of Handloom weavers and a champion of cottage industries, is a valuable contribution. Kotaiah had highlighted in this paper the constructive contribution that the handloom industry made. It can help the rapid growth of National Income and facilitate the solution for unemployment problem, at less cost to the Government and in a shorter time, without bringing in the complications and conflicts associated with employer-employee relations in factor and service sectors.

Kotaiah in another monograph entitled 'Wither Handlooms'[83] explained in detail the problems that the industry was facing and suggested remedial meaauree alao. He advised the Government, to introduce certain welfare schemes viz., Medical aid, Housing facilities, Thrift Fund Scheme etc. to the handloom weavers.

Now that we have completed the survey of literature regarding the history and problems of Handloom Industry in India, we should now concentrate on a statistical picture of the Handloom sector in India.

In the period prior to installation of looms driven by motive power, handloom industry enjoyed pristine glory. Inspite of the decline, handlooms have managed to survive and have been playing an important role in the national economy. In our country there are over three million handlooms. About 10 million people are engaged in weaving alone. In associated activities auch as pre-weaving, post-weaving etc., quite a large number of people are employed. The State wise break-up of the handlooms in the country is presented in the (*See on next page*) Table 1.3.

Production of Handloom Cloth

Though information on production is readily available regarding Mill sector, same ia not the case with regard to unorganised industry like hand-weaving, pursued in small units scattered all over the Country.[84] Under these circumstances we have to fall back upon some method of estimating production in other ways, utilising such data as are available. Thus, all the figures available the production of handloom cloth are only estimates and not actual figures. The estimates of production by the handloom sector are based on the free yarn supplies to the decentralised sector as a whole, of which a certain percentage is assumed as the consumption by handlooms.[85]

Handlooms consume yearn in hank form. In arriving at production estimates, it is assumed that all marketed hank yarn goes in to the production of handloom cloth. The cone yarn yields 20 metres of powerlooms cloth and like wise 1kg of hank yarn yields 10 meters of handlooms cloth.[86] The total production of cloth in the decentralised sector, therefore, cannot exceed the total availability of hank yarn and cone combined.

The estimated production of Handloom, Powerloom and Mill cloth in India is presented in the Table 1.4 (*See on p. 28*). According to the information available in the table, the share of mill production in total cloth production came down from 79 per cent to 21.4 per cent; during 1950-51 and 88-89. The share of Handloom Cloth production in the total production has also came down from 29.10 per cent in 1950-51 to 26.12 per cent in 1988-89. It is evident from the table 1.4 that power-looms, whose share in the total cloth production was significant in 1950-51; i.e 17.90 per cent; increased to 52.47 per cent by 88-89. Thus power-looms

Table 1.3 : Number of Handlooms in the Country

Sl.No.	State\Union Territory	Total No. of Handlooms	4 as a per centage of total looms
1.	Andhra Pradesh	5,29,000	17.50
2.	Assam	2,00,000	6.62
3.	Bihar	1,00,000	3.31
4.	Gujarat	20,000	0.66
5.	Haryana	41,000	1.36
6.	Jammu & Kashmir	37,000	1.22
7.	Karnataka	1,03,000	3.41
8.	Kerala	95,000	3.14
9.	Madhya Pradesh	33,000	1.09
10.	Maharashtra	80,000	2.65
11.	Manipur	1,00,000	3.31
12.	Orissa	1,05,000	3.48
13.	Punjab	21,000	0.70
14.	Rajastan	1,44,000	4.77
15.	Tamilnadu	5,56,000	18.49
16.	Tripura	1,00,000	3.31
17.	Uttara Pradesh	5,09,000	16.84
18.	West Bengal	2,21,000	7.01
19.	Other States\Union Terruitirues	37,000	1.13
	Total	**30,22,000**	**100.00**

Source: The Annual Report of the Co-op. Spinning Mills Ltd., Bombay, 1984-85, p. 144.

Map 1.1

have occupied a significant place in the production of cloth by encroaching on the markets of handloom industry and mill industry.

The powerlooms, which have several advantages in production compared to handlooms and they are free from all problems of taxation. In addition to this advantage, powerlooms are encroaching upon the handlooms by producing items reserved for handlooms. The origin of the textile crisis can be traced largely to the unauthorised and unprecedented powerlooms growth. As rightly pointed out by M. Somappa, a leader of handloom movement, it is the powerlooms that are delivering a deadly blow to the handlooms.[87]

Exports of Handloom Goods

The Textile Industry in India is the largest single industry in terms of its contribution to foreign exchange its share being arround 25 per cent in the total ort from India[88]. Further 1/10th of the output of the Handloom sector is exported.[89]

Table 1.4 : Production of Cloth

(In million Meters)

Year	Handloom cloth production	Powerloom cloth production	Mill cloth production	Total cloth production
1950-51	1013 (21.00)		3727 (79.00)	4740 (100)
1970-71	2283 (29.10)	1409 (17.90)	4157 (53.00)	7849 (100)
1980-81	2540 (30.40)	2298 (27.60)	3502 (42.00)	8340 (100)
1981-82	2626 (23.91)	4547 (41.41)	3132 (34.68)	10981 (100)
1982-83	2788 (26.27)	4694 (44.22)	3132 (29.51)	10614 (100)
1983-84	2956 (25.14)	5315 (45.20)	3487 (29.66)	11758 (100)
1984-85	3137 (26.11)	5445 (45.32)	3432 (28.57)	12014 (100)
1985-86	3236 (25.89)	5886 (47.10)	3376 (27.01)	12498 (100)
1986-87	3449 (26.56)	6222 (47.90)	3317 (25.54)	12988 (100)
1987-88	3508 (27.00)	6457 (49.70)	3027 (23.30)	12992 (100)
1988-89 Estd. (Apr-Dec)	2597 (26.12)	5217 (52.47)	2129 (21.41)	9943 (100)

Source: Annual Report 1988-89, Ministry of Textiles, Govt, of India, p.74.

Export of handloom fabrics ia not a new development of the recent past. Handwoven fabrics of India established their reputation in the international markets long before the Industrial revolution in the West. The Handloom Industry in India was not only producing enough cloth to meet internal demand but they were also exporting numerous special and artistic varieties, in the shape of cloth and garments, to the highly industrialised affluent and advanced countries of the world to cater to

Graph 1.1 : Cloth Production in India

(In Billion Metres)

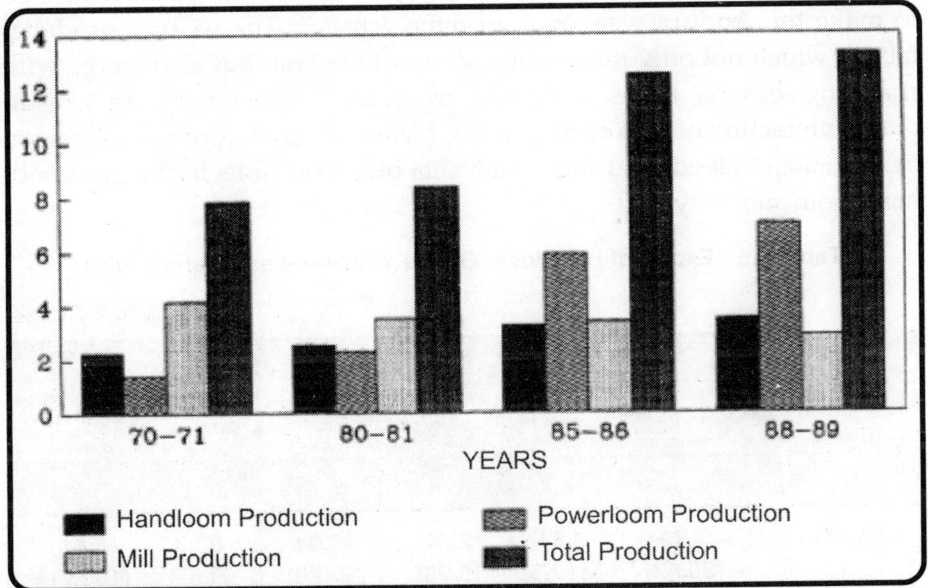

the fast changing tastes of the sophisticated consumers in those countries. Handloom cloth even now is competing with the cloth produced on the modernised machines and thus the weavers are earning the valuable foreign exchange to our country.[90]

Handloom industry in India had been catering mainly to the traditional markets in the Far East like Malaysia, Singapore, Burma, Srilanka, Middle East and East African Countries. The items exported consist mainly of traditional items like lungis, Sarees etc. In fact, the industry has captured market of almost all the countries in the world. As indicated in table No. 1.5 exports of handloom sector increased by 22 times during 1970-89 i.e. from ₹ 25.61 crores in 1970-71 to ₹ 5691.51 crores in 1988-89.

Handloom Industry in Andhra Pradesh

Proud of her past, India houses the largest number of handlooms of the world. In the same way South of vindyas, handloom industry in Andhra Pradesh occupies a place of pre-eminence in the economy next to agriculture.[91] From times immemorial A.P.Textiles, bright brilliant and bewitching, found their way to the west as well as the East and won the hearts of the peoples, the world over. The creative urge of the Andhra weaver found full expression in myriad forms of loveliness. Inherited but unrivaled skills, an acquired but expert knowledge of colour chemistry, a sensitive but quick changing artiste mind have all combined to make the Andhra weaver a supreme artists.[92] The weaver produces fabrics which not only reflect the culture of the land but also merge with changing seasons, tastes, and fashions almost every where. As a result of the interaction of historical, geographical and Social forces, each region in the State evolved over the decades its own traditions in the growth of handloom industry.

Table 1.5 : Export of Handloom Goods Year-wise and Variety-wise

(Value in ₹ Crores)

Year	Cotton			Slik items	Other non cotton Items	Total
	Fabrics	Made-ups	Garments			
1	2	3	4	5	6	7
1970-71	7.79 (30.42)	5.54 (21.63)	2.07 (8.08)	10.04 (39.20)	0.17 (0.67)	25.61 (100.0)
1971-72	10.01 (33.29)	6.71 (27.32)	5.94 (19.75)	7.15 (23.78)	0.26 (0.86)	30.07 (100.0)
1972-73	16.63 (34.32)	7.02 (14.49)	16.01 (33.04)	8.30 (17.13)	0.50 (1.03)	48.46 (100.0)
1973-74	32.06 (35.79)	9.53 (10.64)	35.00 (39.07)	12.37 (13.81)	0.62 (0.69)	89.58 (100.0)
1974-75	29.14 (24.09)	13.25 (10.96)	65.00 (53.74)	12.29 (10.16)	1.27 (1.05)	120.95 (100.0)
1975-76	39.35 (20.17)	13.20 (6.77)	123.56 (63.39)	16.47 (8.44)	2.40 (1.23)	195.00 (100.0)
1976-77	53.18 (19.69)	22.22 (8.23)	173.64 (64.28)	20.50 (7.59)	0.61 (0.21)	270.15 (100.0)
1977-78	81.59 (31.57)	34.54 (13.37)	109.42 (42.37)	31.61 (12.23)	1.27 (0.49)	258.43 (100.0)
1978-79	62.80 (20.73)	28.91 (9.54)	168.94 (55.77)	42.27 (13.95)	—	302.92 (100.0)
1979-80	72.29 (24.89)	38.19 (13.15)	130.76 (45.03)	49.17 (16.93)	—	290.41 (100.0)
1980-81	75.23 (23.05)	60.90 (18.66)	135.45 (41.51)	52.38 (16.05)	2.37 (0.73)	326.33 (100.0)

(contd...)

1	2	3	4	5	6	7
1981-82	119.57 (32.43)	50.02 (13.57)	127.35 (34.54)	71.81 (19.46)	—	368.75 (100.0)
1982-83	83.08 (25.11)	39.50 (11.94)	130.00 (39.29)	78.31 (23.66)	—	330.89 (100.0)
1983-84	73.69 (28.09)	46.56 (17.75)	44.00 (16.77)	94.48 (36.02)	3.59 (1.37)	262.32 (100.0)
1984-85	104.93 (30.08)	63.84 (18.30)	45.01 (12.90)	122.88 (35.22)	12.20 (3.50)	348.86 (100.0)
1985-86	87.97 (24.33)	73.36 (20.29)	31.38 (8.68)	156.17 (43.19)	12.71 (3.51)	361.59 (100.0)
1986-87	83.51 (21.31)	82.16 (20.97)	18.74 (4.78)	194.94 (49.75)	12.40 (3.19)	391.81 (100.0)
1987-88	100.57 (19.48)	137.07 (26.55)	81.71 (3.62)	244.83 (47.43)	15.03 (2.92)	516.21 (100.0)
1988-89 April 88 to Feb 89)	104.16 (18.29)	151.95 (26.68)	17.20 (3.02)	289.26 (50.79)	6.94 (1.22)	569.51 (100.0)

Source : Office of the Commissioner for Handlooms and Textiles Govt, of India, New Delhi.
Note : Figures in brackets are per centages to their respective totals.

Graph 1.2 : Export of Handloom Goods

(In crores of Rupees)

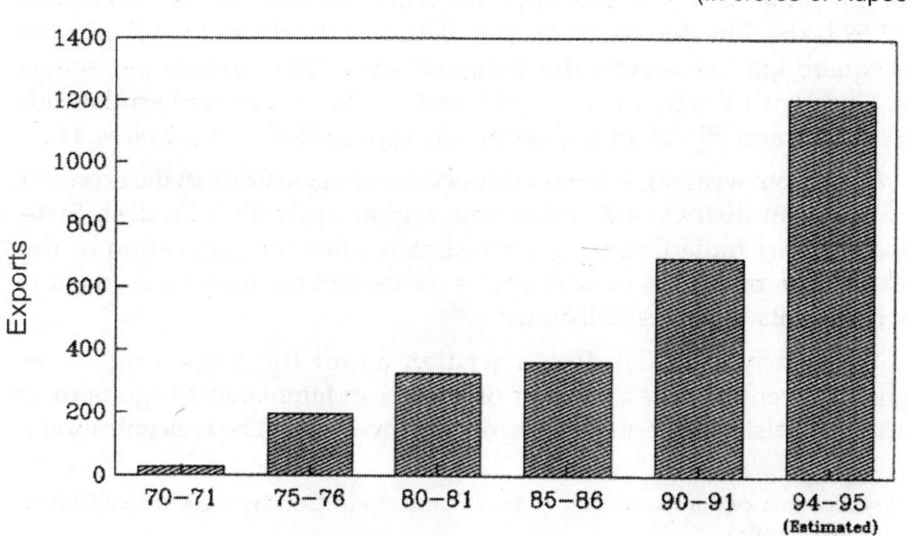

Till the end of the 19th Century, the handloom fabrics of Andhra Pradesh were in great demand in England, France, China, Persia, the Mauritius, Bourbone, Egypt, Ceylone, the shores of Pacific and the Mediterranean and the Red Sea in spite of severe competition from the cheap Mill-made textiles of England.[93] But by the end of the 19th century, handloom industry as such began to lose ground all over the World with the progress of Industrial revolution. The weavers were put to lot of difficulties due to low wages. In Andhra Pradesh wages were very low compared to the high prices of the food stuffs and hence the powerloom products proved cheaper.

As shown in the Table 1.6 (*See on page 33*) there are about 6.00 lakhs of handlooms in Andhra Pradesh of which 5.28 lakhs are registered. The State has the highest number of handlooms in the country next to Tamilnadu. Andhra Pradesh is the fifth largest state in India both from the point of view of geographical area and population. Perusal of the table reveals that the Handloom industry is concentrated in the districts of Cuddapah, Karimnagar, Prakasam, Warangal, Nalgonda, Nellore, Guntur, Medak and Mahaboobnagar districts. The average number of handlooms per district works out to 22,413. The handloom industry provides employment to more than 10.0 lakhs people in Andhra Pradesh State mainly in rural and semi-urban areas.[94]

Handloom Industry in Cuddapah District

Cuddapah district is one of the 23 districts of Andhra Pradesh State and one of the four districts of Rayalaseema region*, which is a chronically drought-prone area. The total population of the district as per 1991 census is 22.59 lakhs. The density of the population of the district is 147 persons per square km., as against the state average of 241 persons per square km. Cuddapah lies between 13° -43' and 15°-14' of the northern latitude and 77°-55' and 79°-29' of the eastern longitude (*See Map 1.2 on p. 34*).

Handloom weaving is next in importance to agriculture in the economy of Cuddapah district of Rayalaseema region in Andhra Pradesh State. Even the East India Company immediately after the acquisition of this area in 1800, made this district one of its sources for the procurement of textiles for its Army establishments.[95]

The Kaifiyat of Gandikota written about the beginning of the eighteenth century lists a number of villages in Jammalamadugu taluk of Cuddapah district as centres of handloom weaving. The concentration is

---

* Rayalaseema region consisting of four districts viz..Cuddapah, Kurnool,Chittor, and Anantapur.

Table 1.6 : District-wise Loohage in Andhra Pradesh

Sl. No.	Name of the District	Looms			Total No. of looms	Per cen tage
		Cotton	Wool	Silk		
1.	Srikakulam	13215	—	—	13215	2.50
2.	Vizayanacaram	8015	—	—	8015	1.52
3.	Visakhapatnam	4484	—	—	4484	0.83
4.	East Godavari	44003	—	143	44146	8.35
5.	West Godavari	14585	29	—	14614	2.76
6.	Krishna	23263	—	—	23263	4.40
7.	Guntur	38419	41	—	38460	7.27
8.	Nellore	23752	—	—	23752	4.49
9.	Prakasam	47936	—	—	47936	9.07
10.	Chittor	20441	50	—	20491	3.88
11.	Cuddapah	35671	—	—	35671	6.75
12.	Anantapur	1683	644	7458	9785	1.85
13.	Kurnool	19805	466	—	20271	3.83
14.	Hyderabad	2664	—	—	2664	0.50
15.	Rangareddy	2358	1898	—	4256	0.81
16.	Mahabubnagar	16736	12162	3464	32362	6.12
17.	Warangal	28312	1945	120	30377	5.75
18.	Karimnagar	71745	4333	—	76078	14.39
19.	Nizamabad	10867	478	100	11445	2.16
20.	Nalgonda	32565	3973	1242	37700	7.15
21.	Khammam	4850	—	—	4850	0.92
22.	Adilabad	3203	2644	—	5847	1.12
23.	Medak	17169	1739	—	18908	3.58
	Total	**485741**	**30402**	**12527**	**528670**	**100.00**

Source: Director of Handlooms and Textiles, Govt. of Andhra Pradesh, Hyderabad.

immediate vicinity as those of Veparala, Dommaranandyala and Moragudi. These weavers are drawn not only from the traditional weaving castes of Padmasali, Thogata, Devanga and Malas but also from

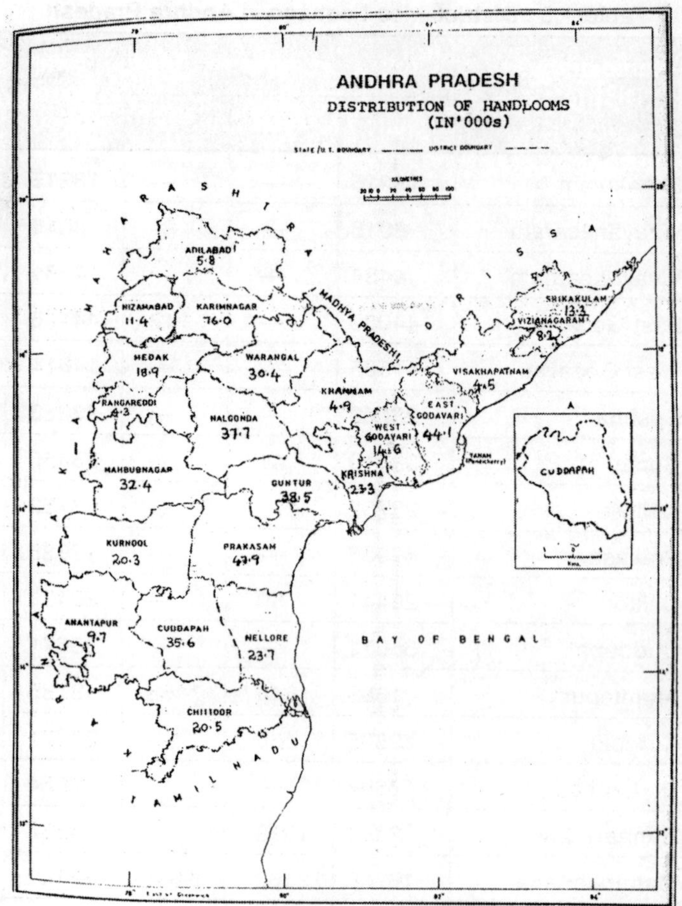

Map 1.2

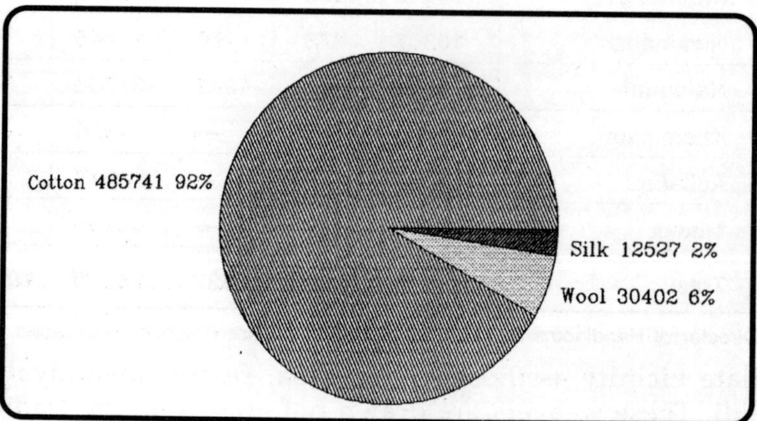

Graph 1.3

among Dudekula and even Mangalas and Matharachas, besides Christian and Muslims.[96]

From the point of view of the number of weavers, Proddatur town is next in Importance to Jammalamadugu. But there is hardly any concentration of the artisans in this or any other area of the district remotely comparable to that in Jammalamadugu.

The speciality of Kamalapuram is its art Silk sarees and Shirtings, though coarse cotton sarees are also woven in some places. The weavers in this area are mostly Thogatas. The industry is spread over quite a few villages including Uppalur, payasampalle, Kalamalla, Uruturu, Koduru, Veldurthi nd Palagiri, Uppalur is the best known of these villages and it is claimed that it is next only to Iladhavaram and Pullampet in its importance as a weaving centre in the district.

Though Rayachoti has a large number of weavers, the only striking feature about the Industry in the taluk is the manufacture of *pattemarpu** sarees. The yarn used ranges from 40 to 60 Counts, even finer ones being used in certain cases. The Pattemarpus with their squares of red, black, green etc., are dispatched to Madras. It is reported that they are exported overseas for Countries such as Malaya and Egypt. Some art Silk ia also woven at Veerannagatlupalle.

The Mandal of Vontimitta has the largest number of weavers in the district next to Jammalamadugu. They are heavily concentrated in a compact area spread over the revenue villages of Madhavaram, Kondamachupalle and Boyanapalle. The important places in this tract include, besides Madhavaram, the hamlets of Upparapalle, Beripalle, Boyanapalle, Chinnapureddypalle, and Kondamachupalle. Pure zari sarees are produced in this area. All the weavers in the district belong to Padmasale Caste.

Although weavers are not so numerous in Rajampet area, as in Jammalamadugu and Proddatur, the surrounding villages such as those of Puttanavaripalle, Kommanavaripalle, Appayyarajupet, Kothapet, Peddoratnpadu are well known for the industry. The weavers in this area belong mainly to Padmasale. *Pure zari*** border sarees are produced in this area.

Silk weaving was also practiced in the district particularly in places like lladhavaram, Sidhout, Muddanur and Uppature in the 19th century. A descriptive catalogue of the Madras exhibition of 1857, records the

* Name of a particular type of saree.

** Golden thread which is used in the process of weaving sarees particularly for designs and border.

display of the some silk pieces from this district as well. Similarly one of lladhavaram weavers who exhibited samples of excellent workmanship at the Industrial and Arts exhibition conducted at Madras in 1903 and in Mysore in 1911, seemed to have secured a silver and a bronze medal and two silver medals respectively[97]. At present the silk weaving is not so significant in the district.

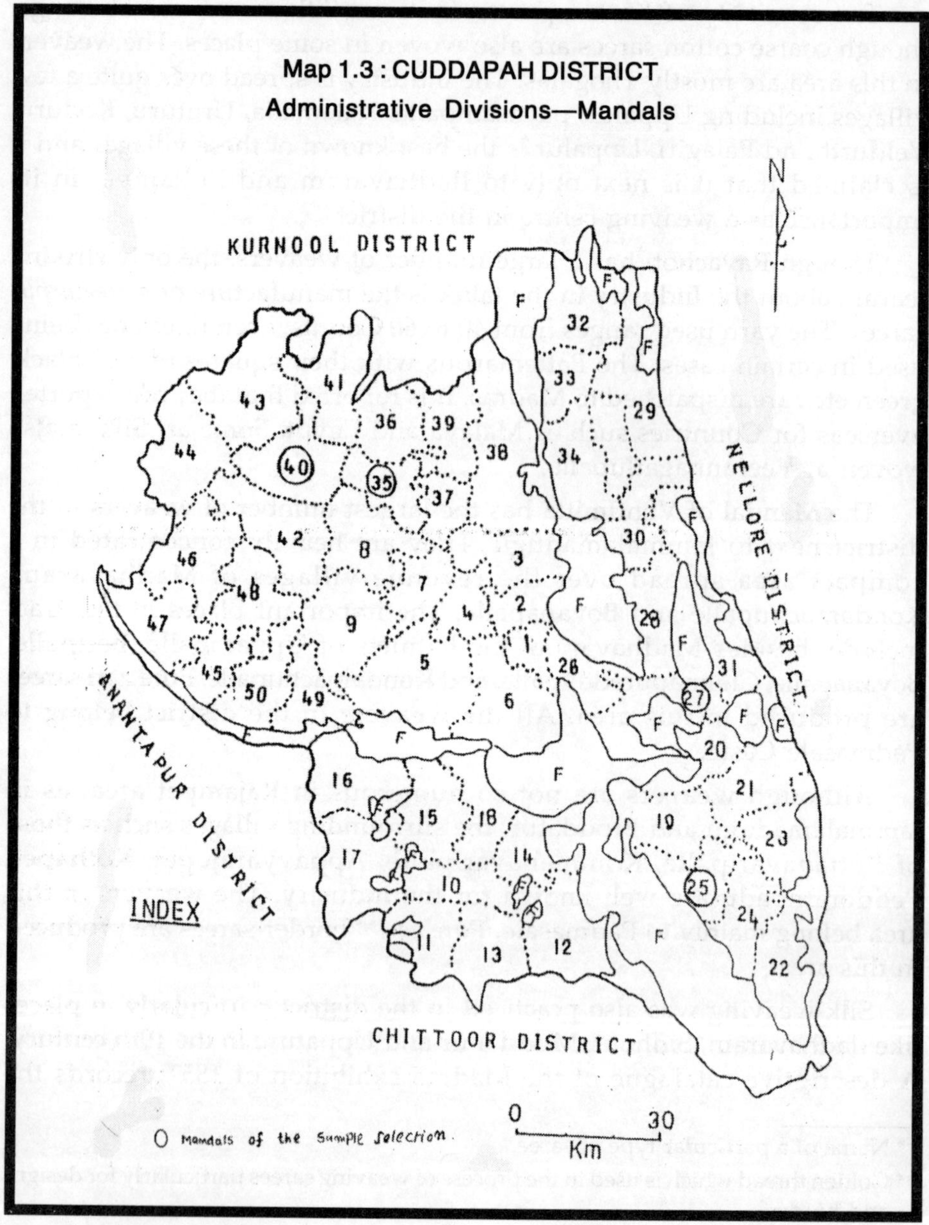

Map 1.3 : CUDDAPAH DISTRICT

Administrative Divisions—Mandals

O Mamdals of the Sumple selection.

List of Mandals in Cuddapah District

1.	Cuddapah	26.	Sidlhout
2.	Chonnur	27.	Ontimitta
3.	Khajipeta	28.	Atiooru
4.	Valluru	29.	Porumamilla
5.	Pendlimarri	30.	Badvel
6.	Chlnthakommadinne	31.	Gopavaram
7.	Kamalapuram	32.	Narasapuram
8.	Yerraguntla	33.	B. Koduru
9.	Veerapunayunipalli	34.	B. Mattam
10.	Raynchoty	35.	Proddatur
11.	Chinnamandam	36.	Rajupalem
12.	T. Sundupalli	37.	Chapadu
13.	Sambepalli	38.	Mydukuru
14.	Veeraballi	39.	Duvvur
15.	L.R. Palli	40.	Jammalamadugu
16.	Chakrayapeta	41.	Peddamudium
17.	Galiveedu	42.	Muddanur
18.	Ramapuram	43.	Mylavaram
19.	Rajampet	44.	Kondapuram
20.	Nandalur	45.	Pulivendula
21.	Penagalur	46.	Simhadripuram
22.	Kodur	47.	Lingala
23.	Chitvel	48.	Thondur
24.	Obulavaripalli	49.	Vempalli
25.	Pullampeta	50.	Vemula

Details of the Industry

Cuddapah district which is chosen for an intensive study of handloom industry is the eighth largest district in the state in order of concentration of looms in Andhra Pradesh. Among the four districts of Rayalaseema* region, Cuddapah district stands first in respect of handlooms. Out of 77,600 looms in Rayalaseema, 45.97 per cent are in Cuddapah district alone.

Active Looms and Idle Looms in Cuddapah District

Table 1.7 shows that, out of 26,521 looms in the district 98.61 per cent looms are active looms, and the remaining 1.39 per cent are idle looms.

* Rayalaseema region consisting of Cuddapah, Kurnool, Chittor, and Anantapur districts.

Each household on an average has 1.56 looms in the district. The percentage of idle looms concentration is more in urban areas than in Rural areas.

Caste-wise Classification of Weavers

The weavers in the district belong to Padmasale Community, Thogata, Dudekula and other castes viz.,Scheduled Castes and Scheduled tribes. Out of 17,407 weaving households in the district, 177 households are of Scheduled Castes and 31 households are of Scheduled Tribes.

Table 1.7 : Number of Weaving Households and Looms in the District

Area	No. of Households	No.of Working Looms	No.of Idle Looms	Total No. of Looms	Average Looms Per Household
Urban	11001 (63.20)	15074 (57.64)	341 (92.66)	15415 (58.12)	1.40
Rural	6406 (36.80)	11079 (42.36)	27 (7.34)	11106 (41.88)	1.73
Total	**17407**	**26153**	**368**	**26521**	**1.52**

Source: Asst. Director of Handlooms and Textiles, Cuddapah (1990)
Note: Figures in brackets are the per centages to their respective totals.

Different Types of Yarn Used

Cotton yarn is the chief raw material used in the district for making fabrics. Of all the looms in the district, 87.92 per cent of the looms are using cotton as the raw material. Other important raw materials used in the order of Importance are Silk (8.17%), polyester blend (1.60%), wool (1.41%) and Viscose including Art Silk (0.89%).

Table 1.8 : Number Engaged in Weaving and Preparatory Activities

Category of of weaving population	Weaving		preparatory Activities		Total	
	Full time	Part time	Full time	Part time	Full time	Part time
Men	19306	666	1545	87	20851	753
Women	7134	1861	13598	733	20732	2594
Children	33	60	2160	409	2193	469
Total	**26473**	**2587**	**17303**	**1299**	**43776**	**3886**
Average	1.01	0.10	0.66	0.05	1.67	0.15

Source: Asst. Director of Handlooms and Textiles, Cuddapah.

Organisational Distribution of Handlooms in Cuddapah

From Table 1.9 it ia clear that the Master Weaver is dominating the scene of handloom industry in Cuddapah district. Co-operative Organisation, Independent weavers are next in order of importance after the Master Weaver organisation.

Table 1.9 : Status of Handloom Weavers in Cuddapah District

Organisation		Rural	Urban	Total	percentage of total weavers
(a)	Independent	2124	529	2653	10.00
(b)	Under M/W	7883	8311	16194	61.22
(c)	Under Co-op	4680	1735	6415	24.20
(d)	Under HDCs	63	79	142	0.54
(e)	Under KVIL	—	10	10	0.04
(f)	Under Private Owners	616	443	1059	4.00
	Total	**15366**	**11107**	**26453**	**100.00**

Source : Asst. Director of Handlooms and Textlles, Cuddapah(1990)
HDC : Handloom Development Corporation
KVIL : Khadi & Village Industries Limited.
MW : Master Weaver.

Need for the Present Study

The survey of literature presented in this chapter clearly brings out the fact that no integrated survey on the living conditions of Handloom weavers in Cuddapah district has been undertaken so far, though this district ranks first among the four districts of Rayalaseema region of Andhra Pradesh State, in the concentration of Handlooms.

It is also stated that in the Western zone of Cuddapah handloom industry is worse off, while it is prospering in the Eastern zone of Cuddapah. Therefore, an attempt is made to study the factors responsible for the superior socio-economic status of the weavers in the Eastern zone than in the Western zone of Cuddapah.

The present study is a modest attempt in that direction and has taken care to cover some of the gaps in the earlier studies.

Objectives of the Study

The main purpose of the study is to examine the socio-economic conditions of the handloom weavers in Cuddapah district. The following are the specific objectives of the study.

1. To study the evolution of the Handloom industry in Cuddapah district.
2. To study the general characteristics of the Handloom industry in Cuddapah district.
3. To study the socio-economic conditions of the handloom weavers in Cuddapah district and to ascertain whether there has been an improvement in their socio-economic status.
4. To observe the changes that took place in the income, employment and indebtedness of the persons engaged in the industry during the last 20 years (i.e 1970-90).
5. To ascertain whether handloom industry in Cuddapah district has undergone any structural changes during the last 20 years including improvement in the skills of the workers.
6. To study the problems and prospects of handloom industry in India.

Choice of the Study

Cuddapah district is selected for the intensive study for the following reasons:

1. The concentration of handlooms in Cuddapah is more than in the other three districts of Rayalaseema.
2. Even with in the district, the handloom industry in the Eastern parts of the district is flourishing better than the Western zone.
3. The handloom industry is equally spread in both Eastern and Western zones of Cuddapah district.
4. The handlooms are concentrated in both urban and rural areas in both the regions of the district.

Apart from the above, considerations of proximity and familiarity of the researcher with this region also weighed in favour of the selection of this district.

Methodological Aspects of the Study

Collection of Data: The present study is based mainly on primary data. Some information is collected from the secondary sources also. Data from secondary sources were collected mainly from the records available with the Asst. Director of Handlooma and Textiles., Cuddapah, Director of Handlooms and Textiles, Hyderabad, Commissioner for Handlooms and

Textiles, Ministry of Industries, New Delhi. The sources of the Secondary data are indicated in the study as and when required.

The Survey Design

The researcher used multi-stage sampling method for the collection of primary data. In the first stage, the district has been divided into Eastern and Western zones. In the second stage each zone has been divided into urban and rural centres based on the concentration of handloom industry. then, the researcher selected two centres each from urban and rural centres drawn both in Eastern and Western zones. Thus, in total, the researcher selected 8 centres as specified in Table 1.10.

Selection of Sample

About 3.5 per cent of the total units from each cluster have been selected from the villages identified at random. Due weightage is given, in the process, to units belonging to different organisational categories. The number selected from each of the categories of weaver households was in proportion to its ascertained relative strength in the village. Table No.1.10 shows the number of sample observations drawn from the selected clusters.

Table 1.10 : Details of Sample Selection

Cluster No.	Name of the cluster	Number of Handloom Households	Number of households selected	4 as % of 2
1.	Madhavaram (WU)	1003	35	3.49
2.	Pullampet (WU)	571	20	3.50
3.	Upparapalle (WR)	569	20	3.52
4.	Kothapet (WR)	429	15	3.49
5.	Proddatur (EU)	1286	45	3.49
6.	Jammalamadugu (EU)	857	30	3.50
7.	Kannelur (ER)	571	20	3.50
8.	Chowtapalle (ER)	857	30	3.50
	Total	**6143**	**215**	**3.49**

Source : Asst. Director of Handlooms and Textiles, Cuddapah,(1990) for columns 2 & 3.
WU : West Urban WR = West Rural ER = East Rural
EU : East Urban.
Note : Classification of areas viz., Rural and Urban, is made by the office of the Asst.Director of Handlooms and Textiles, Cuddapah.

However, the field survey had to be restricted to a manageable number of important handloom centres on account of time and resources constraint. The unorganised nature of the industry and its wide dispersion in location has given rise to difficulties of coverage. The weavers' reluctance to give information and the absence of the account keeping habit among them are the other difficulties.

The Interview Schedule

A well structured schedule (vide Appendix—I) has been used as an instrument for the collection of data during the field survey. The schedule is well integrated and carefully prepared. Questions were both of close ended and open-ended nature. The schedule was framed with the objective of collecting quantitative data as well as securing information of a qualitative nature. It was designed keeping in mind the nature of the persons to be interviewed, the mode of administration, the nature of information sought and the kind of analysis intended. The Schedule was pre-tested before the start of field survey. After pre-testing, the Schedule was finalised with the necessary modifications. During the field survey the heads of the sample household units were interviewed and their responses were recorded in the Schedule.

Informal Observation and Interviews

Informal observation and conversation methods were also used, in addition to the interview Schedule, to collect the data from the primary sources.

The field survey provided an opportunity to come into close contact with the cotton handloom weavers in the areas visited. Thus their socio-economic status, customs, traditions and working conditions which greatly influence their weaving activity directly or indirectly could be observed from close quarters. Proximity of the investigator to them made the task some what less difficult when conversing with them. Apart from the weavers, important persons in the industry in the area concerned, and Government officials were also contacted, and problems and prospects relating to the industry were discussed. Information obtained through such informal interviews has been tabulated properly in the study.

Limitations of The Study

The present study is limited to one district, based on which certain generalisations are made. Other limitations may be those incidental to the design, conduct and coverage of the survey, given nature of the industry and the persons to be contacted.

A majority of the respondents are illiterate and answers given by them to some of the questions as such can only by approximate figures. The possibility of understatement or overstatement by the interviewed, under the circumstances, might not be ruled out in spite of precautions taken.

The non-availability of the required and reliable information from both published and unpublished records is the another major limitation.

The problems faced by the weavers form a complex web of economic, social, political and many other causes. Hence, their problems cannot be fully analysed through economic tools alone.

The study therefore is to be interpreted and understood within these limitations. However every possible care has been taken to present the information in an unbiased and clear manner, keeping in mind the need for objectivity, accuracy and clarity.

Chapter Scheme

The study ia divided into 7 chapters. *First* chapter deals with the introductory part of the handloom industry. *Second* chapter is earmarked to explain the policy of the Government and its assistance to the handloom industry. The *third* chapter deals with the general characteristics of the handloom industry. *Fourth* chapter is devoted for an indepth study of socio-economic conditions of the handloom weavers in the district. *Fifth* chapter deals with the cost of production of and capacity utilisation of the handloom units, price spread etc. The *sixth* chapter is devoted for the study of evolution or the process of change, the industry has undergone over a period of time. A brief summary of each chapter is not only presented at the end of each chapter but *seventh* and last chapter is exclusively devoted to present the main issues, findings and conclusions.

REFERENCES

1. Powerloom Enquiry Committee Report, p.155, Government of India, New Delhi-1963.
2. Speech of Late Prime Minister Mrs. Indira Gandhi, ICMF Journal p.691, February 1976.
3. Annual Report (88-89), Ministry of Textiles, p.17, Government of India 1989.
4. Report of the Expert Committee on the Textile Industry, Government of India, p. 7, Ministry of Supplies and Textiles, April I985.

5&6. ICMF Journal, *ibid*-p.691, February 1976.

7. Report of the Handloom Committee, Industries and Commerce Department, p.15-Hyderabad, Government of Andhra Pradesh, also known as B.R.K. Sastry Report 1975.

8. Somappa, H. Handlooms in Fourth Plan's Brochure, February 1969.
9. Sreenivasan, R. 'Commerce', journal, p. 1, Vol. 139. 3565 13th October 1979.
10. All India Handloom Board 'Handlooms of India, year of publication is not mentioned, p.1.
11. S. Padmanabhan, 'Souvenier'—All India Handloom Convention, Madras, 24th July 1974, pp. 18-19.
12. Encyclopaedia of Britannica, Vol. 23, pp. 342-353-USA-1968
13. Speech of Smt.Indira Gandhi, Late Prime Minister of India, ICHF Journal, p. 691. February 1976.
14. Commerce Research Bureau, 'Commerce'—Journal, p. 315, No. 3353, August 1975.
15. All India Handloom Board 'Handlooms of India', p.I.
16. Report of Fact Finding Committee, Government of India, p. 5, 1942.
17. M.P. Gandhi—The Indian Cotton Textile Industry, Its Past, Present and Future—G.N. Mitra Esquir of the Book Company, Bombay-1930, pp. 6-7.
18. Akurathi Venkateswara Rao, APCO—A Broachure, p. 3, year of publication not mentioned.
19. Akurathi Venkateswara Rao—'APCO'—A Brochure, p. 3.
20. APCO Year Book (1978-79)
21. B.R.K. Sastry Report, *op. cit.*, p. 1.
22. M.P. Gandhi, *op. cit.*, p.4.
23. M.P. Gandhi, *op. cit.*, p.4.
24. P.T. Thomas 'Modern Review'—Journal, p. 4, January 1924.
25. *Ibid.*, p. 23.
26. *Ibid.*, p.11.
27. S. Padmanabhan—A Souvenier—All India Handloom Convention—24th July 1974, p. 18.
28. M. Somappa—'The Voice of Handlooms'—A Brochure—2nd April 1958, p. 2.
29. Ramana Rao, A.V. 'Economic Development of Andhra Pradesh'—p-107-Popular Book Depot, Bombay, 1958.
30. Fact Finding Committee Report, p. 9, Government of India,1942.
31. Andhra Pradesh Handloom Weavers' Congress—'Handlooms and Their Future, p.63, year not mentioned.
32. The Fact Finding Committee Report, *op. cit.*, p. 8.
33. *Ibid.*, pp. 9-10.
34. Andhra Patrika, Daily, pp. 4-13, March 1943.
35. The Madras Provincial Handloom Congress: Memorandom and Answers to the Questionnaire Issued by the Textile Enquiry Committee, Nidibrolu–1953.
36. Kotaiah, Pragada: 'Andhra Patrika', p. 5, 13th June 1943.
37. Kotaiah, P. 'Handlooms and Their Future'—Handlom Weavers Congress, Nidubrolu, 2nd November 1964, p. 64.
38. Sreenivasan.T.S '*Kurukshetra*', p.12, May 16th 1977.
39. Ranga, N.G. 'The Economics of Handloom Industry in Madras, Taraporewale Sons & Co, Bombay, 1930.

40. Ramachandran,V.K.; *The Hindu*—Supplement, p. 8, 26th April, 1992.
41. Kakade, R.G., *op. cit.,* pp.108-109.
42. Kakade, R.G., *op. cit.,* pp.108-109.
43. Kakade, R.G., *Ibid.,* p.155.
44. *Ibid.,* p.156.
45. *Ibid.,* p. 167.
46. National Council of Applied Economic Research, Survey of Handloom Industry in Karnataka and Sholapur, Ashia Publishing House, Bombay-1959.
47. Nagen C.Das., 'Development of Handloom Industry', p. 217, An unpublished Ph.D thesis, 1986.
48. Popular Book Depot, Bombay, pp. 106-13, 1958.
49. Hindustan Publishing Corporation (India), Delhi.
50. Department of Post-graduate Studies and Research in Commerce, National College, Tiruchirapalli, 1982.
51. National Institute of Rural Development, Hyderabad, 1986.
52. *Swarajya*—A Weekly from Madras, Editorial, 3rd April 1965.
53. *Swarajya*—Editorial-3rd December 1967.
54. *Swarajya*—p. 9-11th July 1964.
55. Indian Co-operative Review, pp. 499-512-July 1969.
56. Indian Co-operative Review—A journal, pp.259-64-January 1970.
57. *Kurukahetra*—Monthly, pp. 20-22, 1st October, 1973.
58. All India Convention—A Souvenir, pp.1-2, Madras, 24th July 1974.
59. Commerce-Journal, No. 3353, pp. 315-21, 23rd August 1975.
60. Mysore Economic Review-Monthly, pp. 9-13, December 1975.
61. Hank Yarn is specially made for the use in handlooms.
62. Jacquard is an instrument used for designing in the texture.
63. Indian Co-operative Review, Monthly, pp. 337-43, July 1976.
64. Indian Co-operative Review, pp. 129-40-January 1977.
65. *Kurukshetra*, pp. 24-25, 16th June, 1979.
66. *Khadi Gramodyog*, Monthly, pp. 286-87, March 1977.
67. *Kurukshetra*—journal, pp.12-13, 16th May, 1977.
68. *Khadi Gramodyog*, Monthly, pp. 507-11, July 1978.
69. *Khadi Gramodyog*, pp.125-27, Nov. 1978.
70. Commerce-Journal-weekly, pp.27-29; 23rd December 1978.
71. *Yojana*, Fortnightly, pp. 9-12, 16th December, 1979.
72. The Indian Economic and Social History Review, pp. 257-81 Vol. XVII, No. 3, July-September, 1980.
73. *Yojana*- 1st September, 1980, pp. 28-29.
74. *Economic and Political Weekly*; 27th August 1983, pp. 1517-26.
75. *Co-operator*, Vol. No.15, February 1984, pp. 32-35.
76. Kurukshetra, March 1977, pp. 14-18 and 34.
77. All India Handloom Fabric Marketing Co-op, society, Bombay, 15th December 1954 pp.1-24, Jupiter Press Pvt. Ltd., Madras, 18.
78. Weavers Co-op.Society Ltd., Yemmiganur, 25th April 1958.

79. All Indian Handloom Fabrics Marketing Co-op. Society Ltd. Bombay, pp. 1-19, 1st February 1969.
80. -do-, 3rd January, 1968.
81. Weavers Co-op. Society, Yemmiganur; 8th October 1956.
82. All India Handloom Weavers Congress, NIdubrolu—24th April 1971, pp. 1-12.
83. All India Handlooms and Handicrafts Board, Nidubrolu, Guntur District. (A.P)- pp. 1-19.
84. Fact Finding Committee Report, p. 43, Govt. of India, 1942.
85. Powerloom Enquiry Committee Report, 1963, Govt. of India, p. 126.
86. Govt. of India, Ministry of Commerce : Report of the Study Group on Employment in Handloom Industry, 1980.
87. M. Somappa, Handloom in Fourth Plan. All India Handlooms Fabrics Marketing Co-operative Society Ltd., Bombay, 1st February, 1969, p. 10.
88. Annual Report 1988-89, Ministry of Textiles, Govt. of India, p. 1.
89. Annual Report 1985-86, Ministry of Textiles, Govt. of India, p. 41.
90. Report of Handloom Committee, Govt.of A.P. 1980, p. 15.
91. Director of Handlooms and Textiles, A.P. 1979, p. 5.
92. A brochure issued by the Dept. of Information and Public Relations, Govt. of Andhra Pradesh 'Twenty years of Andhra Pradesh Handloom Industry'. 1976, p. 1.
93. Ramana Rao, A.V. Economic Development of Andhra Pradesh (1766-1957), 1958, Popular Book Depot, Bombay, p. 106.
94. Govt.of Andhra Pradesh, Survey of Economic Trends and State Plan-1992-93, p.65, Govt. Central Press, Hyderabad, March 1992.
95& District Gazetter of Cuddapah, pp. 362-1967.
96.
97. *Ibid.,* p. 367.

2

Assistance to Handloom Industry *Government Policy*

A brief survey of the Governmental assistance and Government policy towards the handloom industry will provide the right perspective for understanding the problems of the Handloom industry. As auch the present chapter makes an attempt to examine the policy of the Government towards the handloom industry, in general and some of the important forms of assistance given to it in particular.

Government Policy and Assistance in Retrospect—from Negligence to Protection

Government policy towards the handloom industry in India prior to independence, amounted to purposeful negligence and incidental protection.[1] The import duty on piece goods during the British rule, was intended primarily to protect the mills, and this intention was adequately fulfilled.[2]

From 1896, the import duty on cotton piece goods was 3.5 per cent and valorem, but as there was a countervailing excise duty to offset this advantage, the duty had no protective effect to the handloom industry. In 1917, as a war measure, the import duty on cotton piece goods was raised to 7.5 per cent and coupled with the transport difficulties, this had a powerful protective effect. The position was further improved by the enhancement of the duty to 11 per cent in 1921 and 15 per cent in 1930, and by the removal of the excise duty in 1926.

Between 1930 and 1931, the duty on British plain greys' was increased to 4.5 annas* per lb. At the same time, the duty on foreign plain greys

* 16 annas = one Rupee.

was raised from 3.5 annas to 6.75 annas in 1933. By 1934, there was further classification and the duties on cotton piece goods imported from the United Kingdom stood at 4.5 annas, and on those imported from foreign countries, at 5.25 annas. Thus within a short time, the Government of India raised a rather high tariff wall to protect the Indian Cotton Textile Industry, though it has been slightly lowered there after. Even then the Tariff still ranged from 12.25 per cent to 15 per cent on British piece goods, and 50 per cent on foreign.

At the same time, an import duty on yarn was also imposed. In 1922, a duty of 5 per cent ad valorem was levied and in 1927 a duty of 1.5 annas per lb., was imposed as an alternative. The import duty was increased in 1931 to 6.25 per cent per lb. In 1934, the duty on British yarn of 50 Counts and below was lowered to 5 per cent or 1.25 annas per lb., on yarn of counts above 50s; while British yarn paid 5 per cent, other foreign yarn 6.25 per cent. These duties were in operation till 31st March 1942.

It has been claimed by the Mill Owners' Association, Bombay in the memorandum submitted to the Fact Finding Committee, that the protective measures adopted by the Central Government benefited the handweaving industry equally along with the mill industry.[3] The findings of the Fact Finding Committee did not support this conclusion. Judged by the test of protection, the effect of the Tariff Policy on the handloom industry had not been perceptible.

We may now examine the different aspects of the Tariff Policy and see how each of them affected the hand-weaving industry. The removal of the 3.5 per cent excise duty in 1926 created an immediate handicap to the hand-weavers. Not that the hand-weaving industry had any over whelming claim to the continuance of the excise duty, for it was not conceived as a measure of protection to the handloom and whatever benefit the handloom received was incidental. Nevertheless, it has to be admitted that while the mills got an immediate relief by the removal of this duty, the handlooms received a set back.

The import duties on cotton piece goods were primarily intended to protect the mills. But it does not appear that those benefits accrued to the handlooms. On the other hand wills with the assistance provided, had grater ability to fight the handloom industry.

Nevertheless, the Handloom Industry also secured the benefit through the Tariff Policy of the Government. If the mill had been strengthened for attack, the hand weaver had been strengthened at least for defence.[5] Subsequent experience however has shown that the handloom industry has not been very much strengthened even for defense. Taking advantage of protection, the Indian mills have taken to fine weaving and dumped the markets with similar class of fine goods which were earlier produced by the handloom weavers alone.[6] The duties thus strengthened the mills not only against the foreign mills but also against the indigenous handloom industry.

If the import duties on piece goods were of doubtful value, the duty on yarn placed a definite burden on handlooms, as they consumed the great bulk of the imported yarn. It was true that owing to exchange depreciation and other causes, yarn prices subsequently fell. The point to be noted is that the hand weaver had to buy his raw material at a higher price than he would otherwise have had to.[7]

However as the imposition of this import duty came soon after the removal of the cotton excise duty, the hand weaving industry got an immediate set-back. The Indian mill section of the industry was in a better position to compete against the handloom industry which was definitely handicapped by the Tariff on yarn particularly that required for the production of cloth with finer yarn, (especially of higher counts as a result of this protective policy). This helped.the mills to compete with the handlooms more effectively, for it was with such yarn Indian mills could put into the market superior sarees which displaced the handloom products. However, it must be admitted that the protective duty on yarn strengthened the Indian Textile industry by decreasing its dependence on foreign yarn imports. As a result of the protective policy, Indian mills had increased their production of yarn, especially of higher counts.[8]

Measures Adopted by the Provincial/State Governments

The non-availability of yarn of finer counts to the handloom industry and the consequent serious condition of the weavers aroused the interest of the Government of India. Earlier, the handloom industry could not attract the attention of the Government of India to any great extent. Only the provincial Governments had been trying to help the industry as much as they could. The first concern of these Governments was the introduction of improved appliances, especially fly-shuttle sleys.[9] The intention of the Government was to spread the new technique by imparting training in industrial schools. It was soon realised that the demonstration of improved appliances to the weavers' children in a few industrial schools, had salutary effect and therefore demonstration parties were organised for serving the different areas one after another. Such efforts gained momentum after the reforms of 1919.

The then Government of Madras province maintained a Textile Institute in Madras and gave grants-in-aid to several weaving schools maintained by private bodies. In Bombay, nine weaving schools moved from one place to another imparting training and rectifying mistakes. In addition, eleven demonstration parties were also at work. In the United Provinces (U.P), at first, there were peripatetic weaving schools, but these were abolished and model schools were started in certain centres, with the charge of demonstration work also. Punjab had no regular touring parties, but improved methods were demonstrated at fairs and exhibitions. In Bihar and Orissa, a school and ten peripatetic parties were maintained. The Bengal Government, established 8 fixed weaving schools and 26 peripatetic schools.

Besides giving training in improved methods, some of the leading textile institutes also carried on research work in the various preparatory processes, weaving, dyeing and printing. Owing to such efforts, the use of fly-shuttle sleys, dobbies, jacquards and other improved appliances had increased. Demonstration was not confined to improved looms and preparatory processes only; special dyeing demonstration parties also were organised in Madras and Bombay.

The Government of India's Grant-in-aid

The foregoing measures taken up by the Government did not help the hand-weavers very much in counteracting the forces working against them after 1930. Hitherto, the handloom industry had not attracted the attention of the Central Government to any considerable extent.[10] It was only the provincial Governments which were trying to help the industry, but found they could not do anything effective by themselves. The problem had to be tackled on an all India basis. It would not be possible to prevent further deterioration in the condition of millions of handloom weavers without the co-operation of all provincial Governments and the Centre. The provincial Governments which earlier zealously guarded themselves against interference from the Centre, gradually realised the urgency of combined action.[11] The Government of India also recognised that the handloom industry was hit by the import duty on yarn.[12] Realising the problems, the Government made available a grant to the handloom industry equivalent to the proceeds of an Import duty of 1.25 anna per pound on imported yarns upto 50 counts., since 1934-35. The grant which eventually amounted to ₹ 5 lakhs annually, was distributed in the year 1934-35, and was utilised by the provinces for approved schemes. There was however no uniformity between the provinces in regard to the mode of utilisation of funds and financing methods.[13]

In Madras, the grant was administered through the provincial handloom weavers' society at Madras. The management of the society vested in a Board of Directors with fifteen members, of whom the Registrar of Co-operative Societies, the Director of Industries and Commerce and the Principal of the Government Textile Institute were ex-officio members. It was first contemplated to make the Director of Industries and Commerce the administrative officer for the grant, but later the control was transferred to the Registrar of Co-operative Societies. Members of the Staff of the Industries Department were always available for technical advice.

The Provincial Society for the Development of Handlooms was established in 1935 with an authorised capital of ₹ 5 lakhs. The provincial Society had to arrange for the supply of yarn to the primary societies from mills at wholesale prices on its own guarantee. Cash loans were also granted to the societies for the purchase of yarn directly from the bazaar when such purchases were found more profitable. The provincial societies also helped the primary societies by sending its expert designers, by maintaining several marketing officers and inspectors and by giving them marketing facilities at its sales emporia.

The estimates of the benefit derived from the in different provinces also varied widely. Considering the meagreness of the funds spent in Madras, the work must be regarded as a great success. The comparative success of Madras was due partly to the vitality of the co-operative credit movement in that province and the spade-work done by the weavers. Primary societies in existence before the scheme was put into operation.[14] Goods worth ₹ 40 lakhs had been marketed during the six years ending with 1940-41. The Provincial Society of Madras complained about the competition that the new scheme had to face from 'Sowcar weavers' and 'Mahajans[15&*].

However, it was soon realised that financial aid, however generous, was not sufficient to remove the handicaps that were hampering the industry's progress. Therefore, a Fact-Finding Committee was appointed in 1941 to investigate the problems of the handloom industry, the types of production, the difficulties in getting yarn, marketing of finished products, the state of handloom technique, the lines on which the industry could be reorganised and the possibility of demarcating a special field for the handlooms etc.[16]

The Fact-finding Committee was of the opinion that both the mills and the handlooms have their place in the Indian economy and stressed the need for reconciling the interests of both.[17] Further the Committee

* Sowcar weaver means master weaver who supplies necessary raw material to the weavers. Mahajans are the traders of the handloom goods.

recommended the establishment of an Indian Handloom Industry Board as a Semi-public Corporation for Co-ordinating all the efforts made for the development of the handloom industry.[18] The All India Handloom Board was set up in 1945 by the Government of India in response to the recommendation of the Committee.

Government Policy and Assistance after Independence

Government Policy During the Plan Periods

Steps were initiated immediately after the grant of Independence to India in 1947 to ameliorate the miserable condition of the handloom weavers.

First Five-Year Plan (1951-56)

The First Five-Year Plan fully recognised the employment potential of the Village and Small Scale Industries. For the first time an effort was made to understand the difficulties and problems in the development of these industries—from an all India angle and in an integrated manner.[19] The First Five Year Plan was thus the starting point of economic resurgence of Village and Small Industries.

Although the handloom industry was the largest industry next only to agriculture, strangely enough the planners had not provided adequate funds for the handloom industry in the first year of the First Five-Year Plan. For the first time the Government of India realised the size and magnitude of the handloom industry and its important role in the National economy, during the great crisis of 1952. When there was migration of weavers' families in search of employment due to the unprecedented glut in textiles. Relief centres had to be opened by the State Governments. It also provided funds of the order of ₹ 4 crores every year under the Cess Fund Scheme to be administered by the Government of India under the advice of the All India Handloom Board. Under the Cess Fund Scheme Programmes were accepted and implemented by the Government of India, such as, organisation of weavers into co-operative societies, financing of weavers' cooperative societies by way of share capital and working capital loans, rebate on the sale of handloom cloth, introduction of improved handlooms and appliances, marketing (both internal and external), encouraging the starting of co-operative spinning mills etc.

Government assistance was canalised through the State Governments and a ceiling for assistance was fixed for each year in respect of each State. The ceiling was fixed on the basis of the state of the industry in each state. The amount sanctioned as well as the expenditure incurred during the years 1953-54 to 1955-56 were ₹ 1,190 lakhs ₹ 1071-81 lakhs and 969.52 lakhs respectively.[20] Production of handloom cloth in the Country increased from about 810 million yards in 1950-51 about 1,449 million yards in 1955-56 against the set target of 1700 million yards.[21]

With the introduction of the First Five Year Plan in 1950-51, the attention of the States came to be focussed on cooperation as a suitable organisation for undertaking programme of economic development in several fields. The setting up of All India Handloom Board is an example. The Handloom Board concentrated on developing the handloom industry on co-operative lines. The objective of developing the industry on co-operative basis has been renewed from plan to plan and may be considered the main plank in the development of the handloom industry.[22]

The First Five Year Plan was more or less concerned with taking the preparatory measures to rehabilitate and stabilise the industry at first and then to achieve its development. The policy in the First Five Year Plan was based on the promise that there should be a common production programme for the cotton textile industry as a whole. The essential points of this common programme were-that the supply of the basic raw materials should be assured, a sphere of production earmarked and Cess enforced on mill industry.[23] The common production programme would necessarily imply a measure of control by the Government, especially over the organised large-scale industry.[24]

In a nut shell, the Government Policy during the First Five Year plan was aimed at exercising control over the productive capacity of the mills with a view to minimising the area of competition from the large scale industry to the handloom industry and to give a wider scope to the later. Accordingly, granting of licence for installation of additional looms in the composite mills was stopped.[25]

Second Five Year Plan

The Industrial policy during the Second Five Year Plan was mainly based on the Industrial Policy Resolution of 1956 of the Government of India. Under this policy Small Scale and Village Industries were to be strongly patronised and given a crucial role in the basic strategy of the Second Five Year Plan, because, a comparatively small amount of capital in these industries could generate a great volume of employment and could alao aupply additional consumer goods for sale[26].

The programme for Village and Small Scale Industries envisaged during the Second Five-Year Plan and the problems connected with their implementation, had been reviewed by a committee. The Village and Small Scale Industries Committee', which was appointed by the Planning

Commission in June 1955. The Committee envisaged that even in the traditional village industries like handloom industry, to the extent immediately possible, technical improvements should be adopted, and for the future there should be a regular programme of gradual transition to better techniques. It also admitted that the concept of decentralised economy was not necessarily related to any given level of technique or mode of operation.[27] What it implies is that technical improvements should be adopted, in such a manner and to such an extent so as to permit comparatively small units which are widely scattered throughout the Country. Obviously, the approach conforms to the recommendation of the Kanungo Committee for gradual conversion, in phases, of handlooms into semi-automatic powerlooms.

Thus during the Second Five Year Plan the Government of India decided to have 35,000 powerlooms installed under the scheme of conversion of handlooms into powerlooms. Against this set target, only 3,500-4,000 powerlooms could be installed during the Second Five Year Plan.[28] To improve the technological efficiency of the handloom industry and to provide necessary supervisory and skilled personnel required for the developmental schemes of the industry, all over Country, the Government of India in 1956 established weavers' Service Centers in the principal handloom centres. These Service Centers were intended to extend technical advice and assistance in the pre-loom, loom, and post-loom production processes. The Government of India in 1956 took over the Government Central Weaving Institute in Varanasi and the Textile Institute In Madras, (Later on shifted to Salem)[29] and began to run them as two All India Institutes of Handloom Technology—one to cater to the needs of Northern States and the other to the Southern States.

One of the objectives in the plan was that the industry should be enabled to stand on its own feet. Government help should be for a short time, until the base of the industry is strengthened. It envisaged that the cost of the scheme of protection afforded to village and small industries should be readily measurable and schemes of protection should be so planned that they could be withdrawn within a reasonable time.[30] It was intended that the role of subsidies, rebates on sales and sheltered markets should be progressively reduced and efforts should be directed more and more for improving the productivity of the worker through more positive forms of assistance.

The approach during the Second Five Year Plan period was that the handloom industry was to be organised and more on co-operative lines so as to enable the handloom weavers to secure the advantages of buying raw materials and selling the products on a large scale, and getting access to institutional credit and of utilising improved techniques of production.[31] Keeping this in view, the weavers Apex Co-operative Societies were set up in the States. The Reserve Bank of India scheme for financing the Weavers' Co-operative Societies was also launched during the Second Five Year Plan.

The handloom industry had to undergo a critical phrase during 1957 and 1958, when it had to encounter the grave slump created as a result of over-production due to avariciousness of the owners.[32]

The Second Five-Year Plan outlay for the Handloom Industry was 55 crores out of total outlay of ₹ 59.5 crores for the weaving industry.[33] At the end of the Plan, handloom cloth production increased to about 1900 million yards per year against the target of about 2,100 million yards[34].

Thus the policy of the Government during the Second Five Year Plan was more on protective measures and organising production and marketing on co-operative lines, and gradual transformation of handlooms into powerlooms.

Third Five Year Plan

The Third Five Year Plan had kept the following objectives in view while formulating programme for Village and Small Scale Industries.

1. To improve the productivity of the worker and reduce production costs by placing relatively greater emphasis on positive forms of assistance such as improvement of skill, supply of technical advice, better equipment and credit etc.;
2. To reduce progressively the role of subsidies, sale rebates and shelter markets;
3. To promote the growth of the industries in rural and small towns.
4. To promote the development of Small Scale Industries as ancillarles to large industries; and
5. To organise artisans and craftsmen on Co-operative lines.[35]

There was no change in the basic policy towards the handloom industry during the Third-Five year Plan period. However the principal aim of the handloom programme during the Third Plan period was to bring about further expansion of handloom production through fuller employment of the handloom weavers and the introduction of improved techniques[36]. Emphasis was laid on revitalising the weak Co-operative Societies. As a part of the conversion of the handlooms into powerlooms on a Co-operative basis, it was decided install 90000-95000 powerlooms for which sanction had already been made during the Second Plan[37]. The progress in this direction was very slow. It was claimed effective steps had been taken to check the installation of powerlooms except by the handloom weavers' co-operatives[38]. In this plan, a higher priority was accorded to the supply of improved appliances, provision of facilities for processing and training, introduction of improved designs and purchase of yarn requirements increasingly from Co-operative Spinning Mills.

The expenditure incurred for the development of the handloom industry during the Third Plan period was ₹ 25.37 crores.[39] The production in the decentralised sector was 3,197 million meters in 1967[40]. The progress of the handloom industry was encouraging during the first two years of the Third Plan, then slowed down for various reasons including the shortage of raw materials, following the hostilities of 1962 and 1965[41].

Annual Plans (1966-69)

The policy and pattern of assistance towards the handloom industry followed so far was continued during the Three Annual Plans also. During the three annual plans from 1966-1969, expenditure incurred on handloom industry amounted to ₹ 13.0 crores[42].

Fourth Five Year Plan (1969-74)

The policy of positive assistance to the handloom sector and phased conversion of handlooms into powerlooms continued during the Fourth Five Year Plan. The objectives of the Small and Village Industries programme were:

1. To improve progressively the production technique of small industries so as to enable them to produce quality goods and to bring them to a viable level;
2. To promote decentralisation and dispersal of industries;
3. To promote agro-based industries.[43]

The Fourth Plan envisaged an outlay of ₹ 27.1 crores for the States and Union Territories. The actual expenditure incurred was ₹ 29.0 crores.[44] Under this plan efforts were made to obtain credit from the State Co-operative Banks for the handloom Co-operatives. Steps were taken to arrange regular supply of yarn and other essential raw materials at reasonable rates. Training in improved appliances and enforcing effectively the restrictions on production of special varieties of cloth were reserved exclusively for the handloom sector. The value of handloom exports was estimated to increase from about ₹ 8.2 crores in 1968 to about ₹ 15 crores by 1973-74. Most of the objectives of this plan could not be fully achieved due largely to the rapid growth of unorganised powerlooms, shortage of yarn, inadequancey of credit facilities, high per centage of dormancy among handloom weavers societies and marketing difficulties.[45]

Production of cloth in the decentralised sector was expected to increase to 4,250 million meters in 1973-74 from about 32,350 million meters at the beginning of the Fourth Plan[46]. Against this target the actual production in 1972-73 was 3,830 million metres. In 1973-74 production of cloth in handloom sector was 2,132 million meters.[47]

At the end of the Fourth Five Year Plan the Ministry of Commerce on 29th Dec, 1973, constituted a High-power Study Team, under the Chairmanship of B. Sivaraman, to make an in-depth study of the problems of the handloom industry in order to suggest a programme for its development in the Fifth Five Year Plan. The report was submitted to the Government in July 1974. The Important recommendations of the Committee were as under.

Report of the High Powered Study Team on the Problems of the Handloom Industry

The study team had started the work with the following objectives:

1. To suggest procrammee for development of the handloom industry in the Fifth Plan;
2. To suggest measures for the maximum utilisation of the export potential of the Handloom industry;
3. To suggest measures for building infrastructure and providing adequate inputs, particularly finance to the handloom sector; and
4. To review the position regarding reservation and to suggest changes in policy.if necessary.[48]

The high power study team made an intensive study of the Handloom Industry and made the following recommendations for their implementation in the Fifth Five Year Plan:

1. The All India Handloom Board Should be activised and converted into a Statutory Board.
2. A separate directorate for handlooms should be created in the Ministry exclusively to look after the problems of this Society.
3. A separate body should be created in the form of an All India' Handloom Research and Design Association' for drawing up and implementing effectively a programme of research and development in the handloom industry.

4. A programme should be drawn up for the training of weavers, especially for imparting to them technical and managerial expertise.
5. At least 60 per cent of handloom weavers should be brought into the co-operative fold by the end of the Fifth Plan period.
6. For the effective development of handlooms outside the Co-operative fold, an intensive development scheme should be drawn up. Units of 5000 to 10,000 handlooms each in compact geographical area should be taken under this scheme. Not more than 25 such units should be taken up during the Fifth Plan period.
7. The management of the Technological Institutions and the weavers' Service Centres should be entrusted to a seperate body designated as the All India Handloom Research and Design Development Association.
8. The production and adequate supply of yarn to the handlom sector is a basic requirement. The Fifth Plan programmes should be directed towards substantially augmenting the production of yarn, especially hank yarn.
9. The establishment of Co-operative Spinning Mills should receive particular emphasis with a view to meeting the yarn requirements of the handloom sector especially the co-operative sector, adequately. The yarn availability of mills managed by government should be linked reasonably with the requirements of handlooms outside tre co-operative sector.
10. Financial arrangements should be made with Industrial Finance Corporation and other agencies to ensure funds required for investment in these mills.
11. Arrangements for adequate and timely supply of other input such as dyes and chemicals should be made.
12. Schemes for modernising handlooms in the States should be taken up as centrally sponsored scheme.
13. Processing facilities should be developed in the centrally sponsored schemes and should be linked up with the marketing organisations being developed either through Apex Co-operatives or Corporations set up by the States so that there is an effective link production, processing and marketing.
14. In cases where the Central Bank is weak and unable to obtain finance, direct financing from the Apex Bank should be arranged.
15. The norms set by the Reserve Bank of India are not exclusively strict. The Co-operative Societies should observe the financial

discipline laid down by the Reserve Bank and improve their own operating efficiency within the framework of the RBI schemes.

16. The limits laid under the RBI scheme may be revised upward in view of the rising cost of production.
17. Nationalised Banks should be persuaded to finance handloom weavers.
18. The Reserve Bank of India should follow the policy of making the credit to the handloom Co-operativea effective and for this purpose, should bring in various methods which have been inducted in the field of agricultural credit.
19. The supply of yarn and arranging for the marketing of produce in the area covered under the intensive programme should be the main lines of activity of the handloom financing and Trading Corporations. They should obtain ways and means of credit from Scheduled Banks, outside plan frame, for their trading operations.
20. The Apex Societies must take responsibility for the supply of yarn for a reasonable per centage of weavers'requirement and arrange to market at least 50 per cent of the production of the Primary Weavers' Societies.
21. The State owned corporations/Emporia should deal with the marketing of the produce of the individual weavers.
22. Apex Societies and State Corporations should be given a subsidy for putting up their show rooms. A managerial subsidy should also be given for a period of three years on a tapering basis. The expenditure should be shared by the Centre and the States.
23. The Rebate subsidy may be phased out over a period of three years by tapering it off annually.
24. A common facility Service Centre equipped with improved machinery, may be provided for an area covering 500 to 600 looms engaged in export orders.
25. Research should be undertaken and facilities should be developed for post-loom processes, like pre-shrinking finishing etc.
26. The problem of getting a large number of experienced cutters, designers and production managers should be examined and a suitable training scheme formulated for their training in the latest techniques.
27. It is necessary to develop, under an export-oriented project scheme, 50 production units in important handloom centres in the country which are now contributing to the export market which have highly

qualified handloom weavers. Supplies of yarn, Credit and Marketing or production should be arranged by each centre. Funds for modernising equipment pre-loom processing and post-weaving, finishing facilities and for training of weavers should also be arranged by the Centre.

28. The handloom industry needs special protection, as the handloom programme is one of the most important Programmes for raising minimum consumption level of the lowest three deciles of the population, besides being the extremely important means of rural employment, providing a living wage.
29. Powerlooms which have taken advantage of their favoured position in the excise-structure, should be brought on par with the organised mill industry and excise duties on powerloom cloth should be suitably revised and a Tax structure evolved which will act equitably and in favour of the handloom sector.
30. Additional revenue realised from additional duties on powerlooms should be utilised for the development of the handloom sector.
31. The system of 'Tex mark' for powerloom cloth should be re-introduced.

Almost all the recommendations of the Sivaraman Committee Report, were accepted by the Government and implemented with immediate effect. For example the Office of the Development Commissioner for Handlooms was created. This office under the Ministry of Commerce, serves as the focal point for handloom development in the country. In accordance with the recommendations of Sivaraman Committee, by 1980-81 a network of 18 State Handloom Development Corporations had come up. Steps had been taken to bring more looms under co-operative fold.

Fifth Five Year Plan

The recommendations of the 'High power Study Team' on the problems of Handlooms were accepted by the Government and were incorporated in the development programme for handlooms in the Fifth Five Year Plan. The plan emphasised the need for positive and promotional assistance to the handloom sector. Stress was laid on improving the technique of production and intensive development of handlooms. A number of schemes have been formulated for the development of the handloom sector.

The plan envisaged to strengthen the co-operatives in order to reduce dependence of the weavers on Master Weavers and moneylenders. It was proposed to establish new Institutions of Technology and Service Centres, designs research and extension services and the promotion of exports and domestic sales. It was also proposed to resume quantities of yarn of the categories and varieties required by handloom weavers and for arranging their supply at reasonable prices.[49]

By March 1980 about 25 Intensive Handloom Development Projects (IHDPS) with a coverage of little more than 1 lakh handlooms and 21 Export-oriented Production Projects (EPPs) with a coverage of about 10000 looms had been set up. But performance of these projects had not been uniformly satisfactory because of poor coverage of loom, low productivity of weavers, static product mix and inadequate institutional finance and marketing support.[50] Another important scheme in the handloom sector introduced during the Fifth Plan period was the production and distribution of Janata Cloth, a counterpart of controlled cloth of the Mill Sector. The scheme was started in October, 1976 and the production of such fabrics went up from a level of about 8 million square metres in 1976-77 to about 287 million square meters in 1980-81.[51] The scheme involved payment of subsidy at the rate of ₹ 1.50 per square metre.

It was hoped that by implementing the scheme a substantial could be made on the under employment of weavers, apart from the opening up of new employment opportunities.[52]

The Janata Cloth Scheme was, no doubt, beneficial to the consumers, especially those belonging to the weaker sections of society, as they got cloth at cheap prices. But it was not advantageous to the skilled weavers, as weaving of Janata Cloth required less amount of skill. The real purpose behind the introduction of the scheme was to save the mills from the losses. The mills were obligated since 1948 to produce and pack the stipulated minimum quantity of controlled cloth required for mass consumption, and any contravention was punishable under the Essential Commodities Act. The mill sector was considering this as a burden and as a major factor contributing to its sickness. The mills were given the option in 1968 to pay compensation in respect of deficiency in production of controlled cloth. Most of the mills preferred paying the compensation rather than producing controlled cloth. Consequently the production of controlled cloth declined substantially. Ultimately under the scheme of Janata cloth production, the burden of producing coarse cloth was shifted from the mills to the handlooms in the name of creating employment in the handloom sector[53].

Low priced cloth of coarse varieties was produced under the scheme. From the long term point of view, nothing could be more disastrous to the handloom industry than wasting the skill of the weavers on producing fabrics that require low level of skill. During the field survey it was noticed that many weavers were weaving Janata Cloth for Co-operatives, only as an obligation. Many weavers preferred to weave other varieties of cloth for the Sowcar weavers*, as the piece-rate wages for weaving Janata cloth with yarn of lower counts were lower than those of for weaving fabrics with higher counts of yarn, especially with intricate designs. Only less skilled weavers benefited under this scheme. They take up weaving of Janata cloth, other wise they may remain unemployed or underemployed.

The Fifth Five Year Plan expenditure in the public shector of the handloom industry was 99.92 crores.[54] The share of the handloom industry in cloth production was kept at 3,000 million meters out of the total target of 10,000 million meters of cotton cloth.[55] Against this target, the actual production in handloom sector in 1978-79 was about 2, 720 million meters.[56]

Sixth Five Year Plan (1980-85)

There has been no major change in the approach towards the handloom industry in the Sixth Five Year Plan from that of earlier ones. The major strategy adopted during the VI plan period for the development of the handloom sector was to promote the organisation of Weavers' Co-operatives. In order to provide a non-exploltatlve organisational infrastructure to handloom weavers for production and marketing activities, a number of programmes and schemes were devised to promote co-operativisation.[57]

The Sixth Five Year Plan emphasised the importance of promotional and protective assistance to the handloom industry to bring about a faster rate of growth in the villages. Promotion of village and Small Scale Industries continued to be an important element in the National development strategy particularly because of their favourable capital output ratio and high labour intensity.[58] It was envisaged that during the Sixth Five Year Plan period the major thrust of the programme was on augmenting the supply of hank yarn to weavers through the setting up of additional spinning capacity, setting up of a National Development Corporation to facilitate, inter alia, the supply of hank yarn and other inputs at reasonable prices. It was also proposed to bring 60 per cent of the handlooms under effective Co-operative coverage and to increase productivity through modernisation and renovation of looms. Another

* Sowcar weavers are those who deal in the trade of handloom cloth.

important emphasis of the plan was to strengthen the technical extension systems for improving the quality and design of handloom products and reservation of looms In the North-East.[59] Accordingly, the National Handloom Development Corporation was set up in 1982. The plan also aimed at integration of the promotional programmes in the VSI (Village and Small Scale Industries) sector with the other area development programmes and adoption of a cluster approach for the traditional industries.[60]

The 'National Bank for Agriculture and Rural Development' (NABARD) was set up in July 1982 to achieve effective implementation of the concept of integrated Rural Development as envisaged in the Sixth-Five Year Plan. Further, a new institute of Handloom Technology was set up in 1982 in Gauhati to help produce diversified and commercial production of handloom cloth.

In keeping with the emphasis on development of handloom during the Sixth Plan, its production was expected to increase from 2, 900 million meters in 1979-80 to 4,100 million meters (including 500 million meters of Janata cloth) in 1984-85 with a growth rate of 7.2 per cent per annum as against 5.2 per cent during 1974-80[61]. The Sixth plan outlay in the Public Sector for the handloom industry was ₹ 310.93 crores.[62]

Seventh Five Year Plan (1985-90)

The strategy for the Seventh Five Year Plan for the development of the handloom sector drew its strength from the 'New Textile policy' announced in June, 1985. The Seventh Five year plan document admitted that the targets set for the Sixth Five Year Plan in terms of production, employment and exports could not be achieved. The estimated production in the handloom sector went up from 2900 million metres in 1979-80 to 3,600 million metres in 1984-85. During the same period, employment in the handloom sector increased from 61.50 lakh persons to 74.66 lakh persons the per capita production of handloom cloth also increased from 471.5 tttrs to 481.9 Mtrs during this period. The exports of handloom products in value terms went up from ₹ 290.41 crores in 1979-80 to ₹ 348.86 crores in 1984-85[63].

The target for production of handloom cloth was placed at 4,600 million metres and additional employment to be generated was estimated at 23.47 lakh persons for the seventh Five Year Plan. Exports of handloom products to increase from ₹ 348.86 crores to 485 crores.[64] The seventh Five Year Plan outlay in the public sector for the handloom industry was Rs. 512.26 crores.[65]

Handlooms and Textile Policy (1985)

The major thrust of the new Textile policy announced on 6.6.85 was to focus mainly on sickness of the mill industry. All other things are residual.[66] The following are the highlights of the Textile Policy of 1985.

"I. The Textile Industry shall be viewed in terms of the stages of its manufacturing process, namely spinning, weaving and processing.

II. The industry shall be provided with fuller flexibility in the use of various fibres.

III. The industry shall be subject to more pragmatic policies regarding creation or contraction of capacities by units in order to increase competition and promote healthy growth in the industry."[67]

In order to preserve the unique role of handlooms and enable them to realise their full potential as also to ensure higher earnings for the handloom weavers, the following steps were in corporated in the Textile Policy 1985.

1. Development of handlooms through co-operatives and Co-rporations were intensified.
2. Greater emphasis was placed on the modernisation looms and provision of technological and other inputs for improving productivity of handlooms and the quality and finish of handloom products.
3. Special efforts are to be made to ensure adequate availability of yarn and other raw materials to the handloom sector.
4. The production of mixed and blended fabrics on handlooms are to be encouraged with a view to improve the wages and earning of the weavers.
5. Protection to handlooms is to be provided by reserving articles for their exclusive production in the handloom sector under the 'Handloom Reservation of Articles for Production Act 1985.' The provisions of this Act shall strictly enforced and the machinery for doing so shall suitably strengthened.
6. To improve the competitiveness of handlooms steps should be taken to remove, as far as possible, the cost handicap of the handlooms vis-a-vis the powerlooms by suitable financial measures.
7. To improve the marketing of handloom products, infrastructure of marketing complexes, training of marketing personnel and intensive publicity should be organised. Steps should be taken to

upgrade the technical, managerial and administrative skills of personnel employed in the handloom sector.

8. To strengthen the data base for the handloom sector for better planning and execution of handlooms development programmes, a census of handlooms should be strengthened.
9. The responsibility for the entire production of controlled cloth should be transferred to the handloom sector by the end of the Seventh Plan.

The Textile Policy 1985 was in a way the logical culmination of the processes initiated during the laat decade.[68] Protection for handlooms against unequal competition from mills and powerlooms has hither to been the corner stone of the Textile policy. The survival of handlooms depends on Reservation Policy.[69]

The Textile Policy 1985 seems to have knocked out any possibility of saving the handloom industry with all its significance for rural employment.[70] The New Textile Policy expected the handloom industry to depend on its own muscle power to chase away the killers-powerlooms and Mill industries.

With the introduction of the Textile Policy 1985 all capacity restrictions were withdrawn on Mills and powerlooms but all conceivable financial, fiscal and other assistance has been offered to enable them to occupy the market rapidly leaving little space for the handlooms except for some controlled crumbs.

The Textile Policy of 1985 aimed at an increasing the production of cloth to make it available at cheaper rate for the masses. The main objective of 'New Textile Policy' is to increase the production of cloth of acceptable quality at reasonable prices to meet the clothing requirements of a growing population.[71] Controlled cloth scheme was in operation for more than two decades earlier. It was mainly intended to meet clothing needs of the poor. Until June 1985 National Textile Corporation Mills and handlooms shared the responsibility of the production of controlled cloth. In 1979 the statutory obligation of mills to produce controlled cloth was discontinued. Under the Textile Policy 1985, the entire responsibility of the production of controlled cloth was to be eventually transferred to the handloom sector by the end of the Seventh Five Year Plan. The object of producing cheap cloth for the masses is undoubtedly laudable, but the manner in which the scheme was operating did not help in achieving the objective. The policy of eventually shifting the entire production of controlled cloth on the handloom sector is patently a wrong policy to follow, whatever the argument of providing assured market for handlooms. It is not clear why handlooms should at all undertake the production of such low value controlled cloth on no profit no loss basis.

The objective of the Textile Policy of 1985 treating powerlooms and mills on par had worked against the interests of handlooms. What was wrong with the 1985 Textile policy was not the policy but its deliberate violation by private-profit seekers and Government's own political and administrative elite and enforcement machinery. Instead of removing the thorn the 1985 textile has done away with the body itself.[72]

With the Textile Policy of 1985, the entire responsibility of producing Janata Cloth thus was shifted to the handlooms. The scope for even accidental survival of handlooms has been diminished by the wholesale sickness transferred on their shoulders in the form of 'responsibility for production of controlled cloth'—an activity which it is claimed made the healthy mills sickened sick mills sicker.[73] The handloom weavers were forced to work below capacity; as they are asked to produce cheap variety of cloth. The production of cheaper cloth does not help the weavers since wages are lower for coarser varieties.[74] Given the pattern of demand for textiles and product mix in the hill and powerloom sectors, handlooms, if they were to produce controlled cloth, have to depend entirely upon the patronage and subsidy of the Government, without any hope of improving their competitive strength. The handloom weavers have to work in a declining branch of the oldest manufacturing industry at subsistence wages. It was feared that the 1985 Textile Policy would make a large number of weavers unemployed or under employed. At least a million persons—men and women—in the handloom industry would be thrown out of employment in less than five years.[75] Most of the displaced would be in remote rural areas which have no power and no alternative employment opportunities. Under this New Policy, employment in even the mill sector will shrink significantly, as hi-tech automatic machines will be utilised to step up cloth output in the machine sectors with 'soft loans' to be liberally supplied by the Government.

Thus the experts on the Handloom Industry made a big hue and cry to restructure the 1985 Textile Policy for the benefit of the handloom industry.

Objectives and Strategies in the VIII Five Year Plan

As a part of the working group on Textile Industry, constituted in the context of the preparation of the VIII Plan, it was decided to set up a Sub-group to formulate an approach for the development of the Handloom sector during the VIII plan. The sub-group was accordingly set up on 21-12-1988, under the chairmanship of Shri V.K.Agnihotri, Development Commissioner for Handlooms, New Delhi.

As envisaged by the sub-group the broad objectives of Planning for the handloom sector during VIII Plan are:

1. To sustain and create avenues of employment in the handloom sector;
2. To improve the socio-economic status of handloom weaver;
3. To improve productivity, quality and cost competitiveness of handloom products; and
4. To preserve the unique role of the handlooms in the country's development efforts.

While the broad objectives of planning for the handloom sector remained the same for the VIII plan, the sub group in the light of the National Handloom Census data and its analysis by IRMA[76] recommended changes in the strategies for achieving these objectives.

The Sub-group is of the view that in the operationaliaation of the strategy for development of handloom sector during the VIII Plan, the following should be the guiding principles:

"1. There should be a flexibility of approach in providing assistance to handlooms both in terms of schemes and in terms of interventionist organisation.

2. Identification of low earners, medium earners and high earners should be made with reference to fabric types and their constructions.

3. Reservation of products for exclusive production on Handlooms must continue. At the same time, reservation must be supplemented by stimulating the development, production and marketing of designs and constructions vhich have a comparative advantage for handloom vis-a-vis powerlooms.

4. Fiscal concessions for the handloom sector must continue to bridge the cost handicap.

5. Given the strategy of beneficiary weaver being the centre piece for State assistance, the management information system should have built-in provisions for monitoring production details (fabric and construction types) and the earning of the beneficiary weaver. Concurrent beneficiary evaluation and periodic sample surveys are to be conducted for constant analysis and course corrections.

6. Products of high earners should be marketed at high levels of efficiency and surpluses of high value products should be used to cross-subsidise products of low-earning weavers.
7. As the marketing infrastructure of the State organisations in the rural areas is weak, there is need for the State agencies to tie up distribution, particularly of low value items, with the private sector, while intensifying their marketing effort for the medium and high value items in domestic urban and International Markets.
8. There is need for induction of a new breach of professional managers in interventionist organisations who would be effective in business entrepreneurship as well."[77]

The Sub-group was convinced that the strategies as discussed earlier would stimulate production in the handloom sector ao as to reach the targeted level of approximately 30 per cent of total textile production in the Country during the VIII plan period. Employment generation in this sector is also expected to increase. On the basis of census data, employment generation in the handloom sector during 1987-88 was of the order of 627 million man-days. It is estimated that employment generation will reach a level of 869 million man-days by the terminal year of the VIII Plan period. The production, employment and export targets are as given under.

Target of Production of Handloom Cloth During VIII Plan

Assuming a 5 per cent annual growth rate for handloom cloth production during VIII Plan, the Sub-group recommended the following target (Table—2.1) for the production of handloom cloth during the VIII Plan period.

Table 2.1 : Targeted Production of Handloom Cloth

(In Million Metres)

Year	Cotton	Blends	100* Non Cotton	Silk	Wool	Total
1990-91	3875	50	500	150	125	4700
1991-92	4075	60	520	165	130	4950
1992-93	4250	75	550	185	140	5200
1993-94	4435	90	575	205	145	5450
1994-95	4665	100	600	230	155	5750

Source: VIII Plan Report of the Sub-group on Handlooms Development Commissioner for Handlooms, Ministry of Textiles-p.39.

Yarn Requirements

The requirement of yarn based on the production targets are shown in Table 2.2.

Anticipated Exports During VIII Plan

Indian Handloom industry produces a wide range of exquisite products. India's handloom products have been among the best known commodities exported to Asian and other countries since ancient times.

Table 2.2 : Reuirement of Yarn Supplies during Viii Five Year Plan

(In million Kgs)

Year	Cotton	Viscose Spun/ filament	Polyester Spun/ filament	Silk	Wool	Other man made fiber yarn	Total
1990-91	338	21.6	12.1	8.8	20.8	18.7	420.00
1991-92	408	22.8	12.7	9.8	21.7	19.7	494.70
1992-93	425	24.4	13.7	10.8	23.3	21.3	518.50
1993-94	444	26.1	14.6	12.0	24.2	22.6	543.50
1994-95	467	27.4	15.4	13.5	25.8	23.8	572.90

Source: VIII Plan Report of the Sub-group on Handlooms, *op. cit*, p.41.

Exports of handloom products have shown a remarkable growth during the past few years. These have increased from ₹ 256 mllion($ 32 million) in 1970-71 to about ₹ 3646 million ($371 million) in 1981-82. The estimates for 87-88 was ₹ 5162 million[78]. In order to substantially improve the level of handloom exports, the production and the processing plan of Handloom cloth need a major thrust[79]. The target for export of Handloom cloth for the VIII Plan are given in Table 2.3.

Table 2.3. For Exports during VIII Plan

Year	Exports (In million ₹)
1990-91	6940
1991-92	7950
1992-93	9130
1993-94	10540
1994-95	12050

Source: VII Plan Report of the sub-group on Handlooms-p.171.

Important Specific Measures for the Development of Handloom Industry

1. The All India Handloom Board

The Thomas Committee, also known as 'The Fact Finding Committee, appointed by the Government of India in 1941 was historically the first Committee to study the state of affairs of weavers extensively and it made very valuable recommendations for the development of handloom sector. Based on the recommendations of the Committee the first All India Handloom Board' was constituted in 1945. The functions of the Board were confined largely to the action of supplying raw materials to handloom weavers, the mathod of marketing handloom fabrics and the administration of grants-in-aid. However, nothing could be done beyond the stage of recommending various steps for the improvement of the industry.[80]

Nonetheless, it should be admitted that a real practice oriented and concrete programme of action for setting the handloom industry on sound economic footing was made with the reconstitution of the Second 'All India Handloom Board' in October, 1952, since then several schemes have been implemented for the growth of the handloom sector in the country though confined mostly to weavers working in co-operatives. The Board was entrusted with the functions of the handloom industry, to examine the schemes for the improvement and development of the industry and to make their recommendations for assistance from the Handloom Fund.[81]

The All India Handloom Board till 1958 was directly responsible for formulating the State Plan Schemes for the development of the handloom Industry, after discussion with the concerned State Governments, for scrutinising and sanctioning individual schemes and for watching and reviewing their implementation by the States. The position however, underwent a radical change since 1958 with the new procedure for the release of Central assistance for State plan Schemes.

It was proposed in the revised procedure formulated by the Planning Commission that the schemes for handloom development which were continuous in nature, should be sanctioned by the State Governments under their normal procedure and that no financial sanctions as such would be iaaued from the Centre. The State Governments had to obtain the technical approval of the All India Handloom Board in respect of the new schemes.

Keeping in view the important role played by the All India Handloom

Board, the High Power Study Team recommended that the Board should be constituted as a statutory body with adequate financial resources and powers to formulate and implement the schemes for the development of Handloom industry. The Sivaraman Committee recommended that the handloom Board should once again be brought back to its premier position as the eyes and ears of the Government of India in the matter of Handloom development.[82] The Central sector financing should be with the advice of the body. The Board should be provided with adequate financial resources and powers to formulate and implement the schemes for the development of Handloom industry. The All India Board was reconstituted in 1978, in response to the recommendation, as the highest advisory body to the Government of India in Handloom matters.[83]

Reservation of Fields of Production

Consistent with the objective of providing adequate protection to the handloom sector, the growth of the powerloom sector has been regulated and monitored within the framework of a Reservation Policy.[84] The Handloom Committee (1949) of the All India Cottage Industries Board recommended that a suitable field of production should be exclusively reserved for the handloom industry. The committee while recommending this, recognised that such reservation should not affect mill production for export nor should it operate to the disadvantage of the poor classes.

It is well known that the handloom Industry would never be able to market its cloth at a competitive price as compared to that of mill-made cloth. This criticism can be justified from the fact that the handloom industry is still craving for protection even after three decades of planning.[85] It was feared at the same time that the consumer would have to pay a higher price if he is forced to take his requirements of certain varieties of cloth solely coming out of the handloom industry.[86] Inspite of it, the Government of India decided to reserve certain verieties of cloth production to the handloom sector and prohibited Mills and Powerloom factories from producing those varieties after First July 1950. Powerloom establishments with four looms or less working on cottage industry basis and not coming with in the scope of Factories Act, 1948; are exempted from the operation of these restrictions.

Effective steps to reserve certain products for the Handloom Industry were taken even in 1985. The Government of India have enacted the Handloom (Reservation of Articles for Production) Act, 1985 to protect the interests of the handloom industry. The said Act came into force with effect from 31st March 1986. The main objective of the Act is to reserve certain fabrics for exclusive production on handlooms and leave the rest to powerlooms and mills. It also intends to ensure that the areas of production actually reserved for handlooms are not encroached upon by powerlooms. Under this Act 22 types of fabrics have been reserved exclusively for production by the Handloom Sector and the Government of India issued an order on 11th March 1986. If this Act is implemented effectively and all the 22 items are produced only on handlooms, it would go a long way in increasing the production and improving the welfare of the handloom weavers. Most of the powerloom owners who have formed their own Association, filed writ petitions challenging the Development Commissioner's Notifications and got Court orders staying the implementation of the Reservation Act.The Government of India moved the Supreme Court of India to get all the cases in various High Courts transferred to Supreme Court so that these could be argued and a verdict is obtained at the earliest at one single point. The Supreme Court of India has admitted the Government of India's 'Transfer Petition'. The office of the Development Commissioner for Handlooms is making efforts to get it decided at the earliest.

In the meantime, the Government of India with a view to protecting the handloom industry and to enforce the provisions of the Handloom Reservation Order, have set up an Enforcement Machinery with Head-quarters at New Delhi and three Regional Offices at Delhi, Pune and Coimbattore from 31st March 1986.

As per the Textile (Control) Order 1986, the State Governments have been authorised to issue Registration certificates to all kinds of authorised and unauthorised powerlooms. Owing to this liberalisation and relaxation of rules and procedures relating to registration of powerlooms there was no control over the growth of powerlooms. Hence, keeping the problem in mind, the Government of India decided to enforce the provisions of the Reservation Act effectively which would require periodic inspection of the powerlooms scattered all over the States, by implementing the scheme for establishment of enforcement machinery at the State level.

The Reservation Scheme was fully funded by the Government of India during the VII Five Year Plan. From the First Year of the VIII Five Year Plan it is proposed by the Sub-group of VIII Plan that the Central assistance to the States should be reduced on a tapering basis, i.e., the State Government will bear 20 per cent of the expenditure of the Enforcement Machinery during the First Year of VIII Five Year Plan, 40 per cent during the Second Year of VIII Five Year Plan period and so on, so that by the terminal year of VIII Five Year Plan, the entire expenditure for the purpose will be met out of the funds of the States. On the other hand the expenditure could also be met from out of the powerloom registration fees collected at ₹ 250 per powerloom and credit it to Government account. The Central assistance is available to meet recurring and non-recurring expenditure for the purpose. Quite recently, the Abid Hussain Committee on the Review of Textile Policy, has recommended that handloom Reservation should be changed from fabric to fibre. It suggested that all natural fibre like cotton, silk and wool should be reserved for handloom and all man-fibers should be reserved for others.

Conflicting views have been expressed about the efits accruing to the handloom industry from the reservation of the fields of production. Nevertheless, the Reservation policy helped the industry in its survival. In addition to the demerits of the scheme, its proper implementation has not been possible. Items reserved for handlooms should be produced on Handlooms only. Any breach of this order, should be punishable under the Essential Commodities Act. In actual practice, however the orders are honoured more in breach than in compliance and there is very little of prosecution under the Essential Commodities Act[87]. A household unit possessing 4 powerlooms is exempted from following Reservations and they have taken good advantage to prosper. It is another lacuna in the Reservation Policy. As the decentralised sector is littered with small powerloom units, along with the unauthorised powerlooms, they have taken advantage of the reservation schemes at the expense of the handloom sector.[88]

Rebate

With a view to improving the marketability of handloom cloth by reducing the price gap between the mill-made and handloom cloth, an attractive rebate on sales of handlootn cloth at 20 per cent, on certain occasions usually synchronising with festivals, was introduced. The difference between Handloom cloth and Mill cloth was estimated by the Power-loom Enquiry Committee, in the year 1964 to be not less than 27 per cent as the mills were adding the extra cost incurred for reeling yarn into hanks for bundling and baling, transport etc., not to mention the profits of the mills and other middle men.[89] When the scheme of 'Rebate' was first introduced in 1954 it was hoped that it would not only create preference for handloom cloth among the consumers, but reduce the price gap between mill cloth and handloom cloth. One of the measures to boost the sales of handloom cloth is the grant of rebate to consumers[90].

In the beginning Rebate was being allowed at 2 annas in a rupee or 12.5 per cent normally and at about 20 per cent on special occasions. Not only Weavers' Co-operative Societies but private merchants selling handloom cloth exclusively, were also permitted to allow rebate. Though all the claims for reimbursing the rebate allowed to consumers was subject to checking and certification by Government officers; it was soon found that this 'Rebate' was being misused by the private merchants. Therefore 'Rebate' was denied to private merchants within a year after it was started. The Government of India, at present, is providing a special Rebate of 20 per cent for 30 days in a year as a matching grant. The Central Government gives 10 per cent and the State Governments also give an equal amount of Rebate for a period of 30 days in a year spread over several spells coinciding with the festivals and occasions.[91]

Though the idea behind the Rebate scheme is good for the industry, it did not yield the expected returns. The Rebate scheme which was intended to be a boon has become a bane to the handloom industry.[92] It was only after the starting of 'Rebate' scheme, that many Weavers' Co-operative Societies in Andhra Pradesh worked at heavy losses and gradually became dormant.[93]

The Rebate Scheme introduced by the Government to encourage sale of handlooms is boomeranging, because of the delay in reimbursement of the amount.[94] This amounts to a flow of credit in the reverse direction i.e from the handloom weavers to the Government.[95] It may be mentioned in this context that apart from the loss of interest to Societies on the heavy amount of 'Rebate' which remained without reimbursement for long periods, this 'Rebate' disturbed the Co-operative Societies. The primaries were selling the cloth produced by their members, to outside merchants at a cheaper price than to the Apex Society because no rebate was allowed on the sale of cloth to Apex Society by the Primaries. For instance, a Society sells cloth produced by it at a cost of ₹ 100 by adding 10 per cent as its margin. Out of the selling price of ₹ 110 so fixed, a rebate of 10 per cent or ₹ 11 is deducted and it is sold to a merchant at a net price of ₹ 99. But when the same cloth, is sold to Apex Society, the later is expected to pay some margin to the Primary Society over the cost price of ₹ 100. Even if 5 per cent margin is allowed, the Apex Society must pay ₹ 105. On this purchase price the Apex Society adds about 20 per cent before selling the cloth through its sales units allowing a Rebate of 10 per cent on the retail selling price of ₹ 126. Thus the consumer pays ₹ 126-12.60 i.e ₹ 113-40.But the private merchant who purchases it only for ₹ 99 from the Primary Society, can sell it for ₹ 110 and yet make a Profit of ₹ 11. The Apex Society sells the same cloth for ₹ 126 when no Rebate is allowed.

When Primaries thus sell their cloth to private merchants at lower prices, the Apex Societies could not get supplies of required varieties of cloth for sale through their sales units because merchants purchase away all salable stocks as long as there was a heavy demand in the market. When the market slackened, the primaries were locking to the, Apex Societies for purchasing their unsold stocks. If the Apex Societies wanted to give yarn in exchange to cloth, the Primaries were often pointing out that yarn was being sold in the market at lesser prices.[96]

Considering all these complications and conflicts which arose out of 'Rebate' neither the primaries nor the Apex Societies need feel sorry for the stoppage of Rebate in future. Instead, we must welcome other alternative forms of assistance which can strengthen their financial base and which can also lead to better co-operation between the individual weaver members and primaries and between Primaries and the Apex Societies. Ue quite realise that a change over from the system of subsidy to a system of no subsidy may not be immediately accepted. It is true that the Subsidy system, along with other protective measures, affords time and opportunity to the handloom industry to gain the necessary strength to develop on its own. Obviously the Rebate system should be considered as a temporary measure. In view of the mounting expenditure on the payment of Rebate by the Government, the Government is not able to give any substantial funds to other necessary sectors for development of Handlooms.[97] Hence the High Power Study Team felt that this system should gradually wiped out during the next three years by tapering the Subsidy.[98]

Technical Development

Technology is the base for the survival and development of any industry. The growth of Small Scale Industries in India has not been satisfactory despite the various provisions for its technological development in the industrial policy of the country. One of the major handicaps of the small-scale sector has been the absence of the latest technology which alone can ensure quality and a high rate of productivity. The small industrialist, therefore, should keep himself abreast of developments in technology.[99]

'Low productivity' is one of the basic problems with which the industry has been confronting, and hence the income of the handloom weaver is very low. In order to increase the productivity, and income of the handloom weaver, technological upgradation is the sine qua none in the handloom industry. To raise the volume and value of the product it is essential to impart know-how to the weavers in the latest production techniques and designs.[100] The Handloom weavers will have to be provided with improved tools which will bring in more returns at least double the present level.

The old and outdated looms are still in use in the industry. One of the reasons for low earnings and the poverty of handloom weavers is that most of the handloom weavers are still working on old and outdated handlooms and technology. Using obsolete techniques of production and design by handlooms, the quantum of production is very low and it is not suited to market demand.[101] All the plans and schemes intended to bring technological development in the industry did not meet with success. Being a cottage industry a majority of the looms are concentrated in rural areas throughout the country. The weavers are mostly residing in small huts without adequate space even for dwelling. The impact of technological developments such as introduction of new designs, new weaving and colour combination is not felt at all.[102] The resistance to change emanates out of their unwillingness to take risks, despite their awareness that production of the same traditional varieties would lead to stagnation and accumulation of stocks. Similarly there has also been resistance to introduction of new technology as weavers feel that sophistication would mean more work.[103]

The low productivity in the industry raises the cost of production of cloth to level which the market cannot absorb. Consequently, the handloom industry couldn't compete with the mill and powerloom industries. In fact much has been done for the technological development in the handloom industry. For example a number of innovations such as take-up and let-off motions, improved looms with multiple shuttles and pedal looms were made by the Institute of Handloom Technology and a large number of Weavers Service Centers have been established in different parts of the country to speedily transfer these improved technology.[104] All this technology did not help to bring any substantial increase in the earnings of the weavers. These technology improvements have not been transferred to the Industry in a big way.[105] Therefore, there is need to ensure swift and smooth transfer of technology from the Research Institutes to the handloom weavers.[106]

The survival of handloom industry, like any other traditional cottage industry, depends very much upon its ability to adopt itself to the changing conditions by constantly improving its techniques of production[107]. Unfortunately its absence is conspicuous in handloom industry[108]. Most of the weavers are in the Indian rural sector. They are unaware of modern designs and by the time they use them, they become outdated in the market. Hence, there is great need to educate and train the weaver in such a way that he can observe and produce the cloth in accordance with the changing fashions of the consumers. It is imperative on the part of the Government to promote a number of weavers' Service

Centres in various handloom concentrated areas in the State to ameliorate the living conditions of handloom artisans.

Training is another essential input in the handloom development programme as this will enable handloom personnel to acquire necessary skills and will equip them in the modern management techniques. The scheme of technical training is one of the important schemes for technical improvement of the handloom industry.[109] Low pace of technological development in the handloom industry is a hindrance for the healthy growth of the industry. Weavers in the industry, therefore, should keep abreast of developments in technology and changing tastes and preferences of the consumers. As weavers are not exposed to advanced technological innovations, they are unable to orient their production to the ever changing tastes and preferences of the overseas market.[110]

Conversion of Handlooms into Powerlooms

For the first time in India, the problem with regard to the uncontrolled growth of the powerlooms, was recognised in 1942 by the Fact Finding Committee. The Committee had stated that a new rival has come into the field, namely single, unit powerloom worked in cottages and small powerloom factories'[111]. Where ever these little powerloom units have grown they have seriously affected the handloom industry. In this respect handlooms have been the worst hit.[112] Thus powerlooms are the greatest menace to the handloom industry.[113]

The Textile Enquiry Committee, (1952) for the time, flashed the idea of converting the handlooms into powerlooms. The smaller powerlooms unit, however, is almost invariably a step in the evolution of the industry from a predominance of the handloom to one of the powerloom.[114] The Committee felt that it would increase the productivity and earnings of the handloom weavers. It finds little difference between powerloom and handloom industry. The cottage powerloom unit is a little different from the handloom unit, except that in the case of the former, the weaver produces per unit of time about four times as much cloth as the handloom weaver and, therefore, earns a better total wage than the handloom weaver.[115] Having in view the similarity between the small powerloom unit (Having less than 5 looms) and a comparable handloom unit, the Government of India decided to allow to the small powerloom industry the same benefits of reservation of certain varieties for production which were conferred on the handloom industry in 1950. Since 1951, the installation and working of powerlooms on cotton yarn has been very stringently controlled under the Cotton Textiles Order 1948, with a view to ensuring the maximum possible share to the handloom industry from out of the meager available supplies of yarn[116].

The 'Powerloom Enquiry Committee' 1963, strongly recommended a phased conversion programme of handlooms into powerlooms with a view to improving the economic position of the weaver. The Government of India accepted the recommendatlons of the Committee and implemented the scheme during the Second Five Year Plan. The main conditions of the policy governing the Installation of the powerloom in the handloom sector were[117]:

(a) The allotment of looms would be on a co-operative basis as in the existing handloom industry.

(b) The existing co-operative societies would be assisted to change over to powerlooms.

(c) Power-looms should normally be housed in weavers' cottages themselves.

(d) The co-operative unit of powerlooms to be formed should normally be small in size say of 10 looms.

(e) Powerloom units should be located only in rural areas. For this purpose a town with a population of 30,000 or less will be considered as a rural area.

(f) Only one. powerloom to each weaver normally should be allotted.

(g) It is not necessary to insist that where a powerloom is put into commission, the handloom should go out of commission.

(h) Powerlooms under this scheme are meant exclusively for production of cotton cloth only.

In accordance with the recommendations of the committee the Government of India decided to allow the installation of 35,000 powerlooms in the handloom sector during the Second Five Year Plan and allocated a specific production target of 200 million yards of Cotton cloth to be manufactured by these powerlooms.[118] Under this scheme, 13,469 powerlooms were sanctioned to the various handloom Co-operatives.[119] The response from the State Governments was not equally encouraging. The Government of Andhra Pradesh kept aloof while the Government of Madras got 15 looms sanctioned on an experimental basis.[120] The Government of India reviewed the scheme and in 1961 it was discontinued, except allowing installation of powerlooms in the cases where irrevocable commitments had been entered into.[121]

While the State Governments were proceeding with the installation of powerlooms on a phased programme, backed by considerable amount of financial assistance by way of looms and grants, it came to light even in 1959 that a very large number of powerlooms had come into existence without any Governmental help and in contravention of the restrictions placed over the acquisition or installation of powerlooms in the Country.[122] It was also maintained that in some cases, the benefits from setting up of powerlooms accrued to the Mill ownera than to the ownera of the poverlooms[123]. It was also held that the amount spent on the installation of powerlooms could be more usefully utilised for the improvement of the general standard of production of handlooms and for promoting their exports with a view to augmenting Foreign exchange.[124]

The Powerloom Enquiry Committee had accepted that the scheme of converting handlooms into powerlooma did not meet with full success—because the weavers did not take to the scheme with enthusiasm, but mainly because of the following factors[125].

1. Insufficient financial assistance provided for working capital.
2. Absence of simultaneous arrangements for providing pre-weaving facilities, Winding, Warping, Sizing etc., for supply of yarn in sized beams as also post-weaving finishing arrangements.
3. Absence of arrangements to ensure that in the allocation of looms, in the co-operatives, the net befits arising there from did really get distributed among all the members of the co-operatives.

The committee further observed that there was considerable time lag between the formulation of the scheme and its actual implementation.

The need for introduction of superior technology in the handloom industry is irrefutable. But opinions differ on the degree of technological change over. In the running controversy over how much labour intensity is to be intalned and how much mechanisation is to be allowed, the weaver is being forced to continue the traditional labour-intensive approach which involve drudgery some times of the entire family, with a small return in value added for the time employed. The primary approach in the strategy should be the evolution of an intermediate technology, a suitable mix of mechanical process for the industry so that those parts of the operation which involve heavy drudgery and expenditure of time, without adequate value added for time spent, are suitably mechanised.[126] If the preliminary process is mechanised, the weaver and his family can employ their time in a better way in actual weaving, where their skill comes into operation and where value added for time spent ia reasonable.

Summary

The policy of maximising employment in the process of making cloth has been the corner stone of our textile policy. Accordingly handloom sector was given priority in successive Five Year Plans. Since Independence a number of measures have been taken up for the protection and development of the handloom industry. On the organisational side, emphasis is being given on expansion and strengthening of the co-operative sector. Attempts have been made to bring more number of handlooms into Co-operative fold, by extending finance and marketing facilities. Efforts have been made to make available institutional finance. The policy to expand the capacity of the Spinning mills and to set up new ones in the co-operative sector in order to ease the yarn problem, is a step in the right direction. Adequate measures have been taken to protect the handlooms against competition from the mills. A special field in the textile market has been demarcated for the handloom sector through the scheme of reservation. Rebate facility is provided to encourage the demand for handloom cloth. Excise duty is imposed on powerlooms and mill industry for the benefit of the handloom industry.

Government efforts in the direction of increasing the productivity of handlooms did not meet with success. Technology intended for the development of the handloom industry did not reach the weaver. Government efforts to convert the existing handlooms into powerlooms also is a failure because of weavers reluctance. Hence technological development in the handloom industry is a major problem to be solved.

After an analysis of all the Government Plans, any one would be forced to come to the conclusion that serious efforts are not directed towards making the industry economically viable. The industry is made to live on doles and on reservations for years. Consequently, the industry will continue to drain the resources of the public exchequer, and the consumers will continue to pay a high price for cloth. So, the Government Policy must help the industry to stand on its own legs, by means of producing superior varieties of cloth, which the powerlooms and mills can not produce, and the weavers producing plain varieties of cloth must either be trained to produce artistic varieties of cloth, or they must be engaged in the powerloom industry.

When all is aaid and done, the Textile Policy of the Government of India also is not without deficiencies. Following are the important deficiencies;

1. The policy doesn't have a long term and clear perspective for the development of the handloom industry.
2. The policy doesn't help improving the technological base of the handloom industry, and hence there is no perceptible progress in increasing the productivity of the handloom weaver. Consequently

the competitive ability of the handloom sector has drastically decreased compared to earlier periods.

3. The policy of treating handlooms on par with power-looms, has been detrimental to the healthy development of the handloom industry. The advantages that the powerlooms have over the handlooms with their better technology and almost the same level of excise vis-a-vis the handloom sector has to be set right so that the powerlooms are no longer in a position to underbid the handlooms in their legitimate markets.[127]
4. The policy has seriously neglected the private sector whose role is vital in the industry, which constitute about 80 per cent of the total looms in the country. There are large concentrations of looms outside the effective Co-operative fold and the Master Weaver fold for which an effective rehabilitation programme will have to be drawn up.[128]
5. The policy of fixing targets quite below the capacity of handlooms in the country is quite unjustifiable. Even to realise the targets set, arrangements were not made through the supply of raw materials and credit. The Weavers are put to hardships due to inadequate and irregular supplies of raw materials and fluctuating prices of yarn.zari, dyes and chemicals.
6. The removal of capacity restrictions, with the implementation of Textile Policy of 1985, worked against the interest of the handlooms. Steps should be taken to impose restrictions on the strict implementations of reservation policy to protect the handloom industry.

From the foregoing analysis, we can conclude that the Government should prepare a long term perspective plan for the development of the handloom industry. The technological developments in the handloom industry should be passed on to the weavers, and they should be convinced of the utility of the technology. The Government should take care of the private sector, while formulating Handloom Development Plan. The fiscal concessions so far extended to powerlooms on par with handlooms should come to an end., and the powerlooms should be treated on par with mills. Free and adequate supply of raw material should continue to help the Handloom Industry., and the production targets of the Handloom Sector should take into consideration the optimal productive capacity of the industry. Steps must be taken to restructure the Textile Policy of 1985, and the compartmentalisation system should be reintroduced in view of protection required by the handloom industry.

REFERENCE

1. The Fact Finding Committee Report, Govt.of India, p. 13, 1942.
2. Mahapatro, P.C..Economics of Cotton Handloom Industry in India, p. 205, Ashia Publishing House, New Delhi, 1986.
3. The Fact Finding Committee Report, *op. cit.*, p. 13.
4. The Fact Finding Committee, *op. cit.*, p. 13.
5. The Fact Finding Committee, *op. cit.*, p.13.
6. *Ibid.*, p.14
7. *Ibid.*
8. The Fact Finding Committee, *ibid.*, p. 22.
9. The Report of the Fact Finding Committee, *op. cit.*, p. 22.
10. The Fact Finding Committee Report, *op. cit.*, p. 22.
11. *Ibid.*, p. 23.
12. *Ibid.*, p. 24.
13. The Fact Finding Committee, *op. cit.*, p. 184.
14. Fact Finding Committee Report, *op. cit.*, p. 189.
15. *Ibid.*, p. 188.
16. *Ibid.*, p. 25.
17. *Ibid.*, p. 243.
18. *Ibid.*
19. Govt.of India-Planning Commission-Report of the Village and Small Scale Industries Committee, p. 5-1956.
20. Report of the Committee of the House to Enquire into the Activities of Handloom Co-operative Organisations Relating to the Misuse of Rebate—Govt. of Andhra Pradesh–1976, p. 13.
21. First Five Year Plan–Govt.of India, p. 76.
22. Indian Co-operative Review-Editorial, p. 502, July 1969.
23. The First Five Year Plan-*Ibid.*, p. 331.
24. *Ibid.*, p. 318.
25. Report of the Textile Enquiry Committee—Government of India—1954, p. 7.
26. Mahalanobis, P.C (1955) 'The Approach of Operational Research to Planning in India'—Sankhya, pp. 3-130-16th Dec. 1955.
27. Second Five Year Plan-1956-Govt.of India, New Delhi, p. 432.
28. Third Five Year Plan—Planning Commission, Govt.of India, 1961, p. 430.
29. All India Handloom Board—Fourth Report(1956-59)-Rajkot, Ministry of Commerce and Industry, Govt. of India,1959, p. 32.
30. Second Five Year Plan-1956, *op.cit.*, p. 435.

31. Second Five Year Plan, *Ibid.,* pp. 31-32.
32. Somappa, M-Brochure-Weavers' Co-operative Society Ltd., Yemmiganur, 20th Aug 1960, p. 10.
33. Second Five Year Plan, *op.cit.,* p. 441.
34. Third Five Year Plan, *op.cit.,* p. 43.
35. Govt.of India., Planning Commission (1961)—The Third Five Year Plan, Summary, pp. 113-14.
36. *Ibid.*, p. 430.
37. The Third Five Year Plan, Summary, *op.cit.,* p. 439.
38. *Ibid.*
39. Fourth Five Year Plan 1969-74-Draft, p. 227.
40. *Ibid.*, p. 219.
41. *Ibid.*, p. 218.
42. Editorial-Commerce-19th May, 1979, p. 2.
43. Govt. of India., Planning Commission(1971)-Fifth Five Year Plan, p. 218.
44. Editorial., Commerce—19th May, 1979, p. 2.
45. Report—Committee of the House—To Enquire into the Activities of Handloom Co-operative Organisations Relating to the Misuse of Rebate in A.P–1976, p. 14.
46. Fourth Five Year Plan, Draft-1969-74, p. 226.
47. Draft of the Fifth Five year Plan-1974-79, p. 162.
48. Report of the High Powered Study Team on the Problems of Industry, 1973, Govt. of India, p. 3.
49. Fifth Five Year Plan (1975), Govt.of India, Planning Commission, pp. 67-68.
50. Sixth Five Year Plan (1978), Govt.of India, Planning Commission; p. 197.
51. Basic Statistics on Handlooms (1982), Commissioner for Handlooms and Textiles, p. 25.
52. Eastern Economist., Editorial—A Big Hand for Handlooms-71(2) 14th July 1978, p. 66.
53. L.C.Jain—Handlooms Face Liquidation—Powerlooms Mock at Yojana Bhavan—*Economic and Political Weekly*, 18(35)–27th aug. 1983, pp. 1525-26.
54. Seventh Five Year Plan (1981)-Planning Commission-Govt. of India, p. 190.
55. Draft Fifth Five Year Plan-1974-79, Vol. II, p. 167.
56. Basic Statistics of Handlooms, *op.cit.,* p. 5
57. VIII Plan report of the Sub-Group of Handlooms-Development Commissioner for Handlooms, Ministry of Textiles, Govt. of India, Feb, 1989, p. 30.
58. Sixth Five Year Plan (1979)—Govt.of India, Planning Commission, New Delhi, p. 197.
59. Sixth Five Year plan, *Ibid.,* p.191.

60. *Ibid.*, p.197.
61. 8th Plan Report of the Sub-Group, *op.cit.,* p. 197, Feb 1989.
62. *Ibid.*, p. 190.
63. Seventh Five Year Plan-85-90 Vol. II, 1985, p. 106.
64. *Ibid.*, p. 107.
65. *Ibid.*, p. 104.
66. Sastry, D.U.-An Alternative to the New Textile Policy—Presidential Address to the Fifth Annual Conference—Andhra Pradesh Economic Association—SKU, Anantapur-17/1/87.
67. *Financial Express*—7th June 1985, p. 8.
68. Eapen.M.(1985) The New Textile Policy'—*Economic and Political Weekly*, Vol. XX, Nos 25 & 26, p. 1072.
69. Sastry, D.U., The Cotton Mill Industry in India, 1984, Oxford University Press, p. 17.
70. L.C.Jain., 'End of Handloom Industry'. *Mainstream*, July, 20th, 1985, p. 1.
71. *Financial Express*-Editorial, 8th June 1985.
72. Jaln, L.C., End of Handloom Industry, *Mainstream*, 20th July 1985, p. 3.
73. L-C. Jain, End of Handlooms, *Ibid.*, p. 3.
74. Goswami, Omkar (1985); Indian Textile Industry C1970-84), An Analysis of Demand and Supply, *Economic and Political Weekly*, Vol. XX, No. 38, p. 1613.
75. Jain, L.C., End of Handloom Industry—*Mainstream*, 20th July 1985.
76. IRMA—Institute of Rural Management, Anannd.
77. VIII Plan Report of the Sub-group on Handlooms, *op.cit.,* pp. 34-35.
78. VIII Plan Report of the Sub-group on Handlooms, p. 85.
79. *Ibid.*, p. 87.
80. M.P. Gandhi,The Handloom Weaving Industry: 1950-51, Annual Vol. II, Oct 1951, Bombay; Gandhi & Co., p. 36.
81. All India Handloom Board, First Annual Report, Bombay, Ministry of Commerce and Industry, Govt. of India, 1954, p. 2.
82. Report of the High Powered Study on Handlooms, *op.cit.,* p. 11
83. Report on Village & Cottage Industries., National Committee on the Development of Backward Areas, Planning Commission, Govt.of India, p. 13-1981.
84. Report of the Sub-group on Handlooms for VIII Plan-Commissioner for Handlooms, Govt. of India, New Delhi-1989, p. 60.
85. Mahapatro, P.C., Economics of Cotton Handloom Industry in India-Ashish Publishing House, New Delhi, p. 228.
86. Gandhi, M.P, *op.cit.*, pp. 15-16.
87. High Power Study Team, Govt.of India-1974, p. 81.
88. Powerloom Enquiry Committee Report, Govt. of India-1964, pp. 133-34.

89. Report of the Handloom Committee—B.R.K. Sastry—Govt. of Andhra Pradesh-1980, p. 50
90. Editorial-Commerce-19th June 1982, p.1059.
91. Surendra, S. T. Co-operatives in Andhra Pradesh—An unpublished Thesis-1984, p. 268
92. *The Hindu*—1st Nov, 1985, p. 19.
93. B.R.K. Sastry Report, *op. cit.,* p. 50
94. *The Hindu*—1st Nov 1985, p. 19.
95. Jain, L.C., Handlooms Face Liquidation—Powerlooms Mock at Yojana Bhavan, *Economic and Political Weekly* 18)35), 27th Aug 1983, p. 1522.
96. R.K.Sastry Report, *op.cit.,* p. 50.
97. Report of the High Powered Study Team-1973,*op.cit.,* p. 68.
98. Idem.
99. Vasanta Desai., Problems and 'Prospects of Small-scale industries in India, Himalaya Publishing House, p. 9.
100. Kantikumar R. Podar-Commerce-Dec 23, 1978-Organisation of Handlooms-p. 22.
101. Editorial-Commerce-19th May 1979, p. 848.
102. Sankara Subaiayan-Commerce,13th Oct, 1979, p. 36.
103. Rajula Devi, A.K., Plight of Handlooms—A Study—*Kurukshetra*, Jan,1983, p. 21.
104. National Institute of Rural Devlopment, Hyderabad, Employment Factor in Handlooms-1986, p. 73.
105. *Ibid.*, p. 99.
106. Report of the Expert Committee on Handloom Technology—April, 1986 Govt. oi India, p. 22 para, No. 2.66
107. Planning Commission., Govt.of India, Programme Evolution Organisation-1967, p. 56.
108. Ramakrishna Rao, B-Handloom Industry in Coastal Andhra, *Kurukshetra*-Mar,1987, p.14.
109. Planning Commission, *op.cit.,* p. 64-1967.
110. Export Promotion of Handloom Goods—Indian Journal of Marketing, July-Aug 1983, p.10.
111. Fact Finding Committee Report, *op.cit.,* p. 19.
112. *Ibid.*, p. 20.
113. Somappa-Faire Deal tc Handlooms-Oct. 1956-The Jupiter Press Pvt. Ltd, Madras, p. 7.
114. The Textile Enquiry Report—Govt. of Indla-1952, *op. cit.,* p. 7.
115. *Ibid.*, p. 8.
116. *Ibid.*, p. 9.

117. Powerloom Enquiry Committee Report, *op.cit.,* p. 59.
118. Powerloom Enquiry Committee Report, *op.cit.,* p. 29.
119. Idem
120. *Ibid.,* p. 60.
121. *Ibid.,* p. 29.
122. *Ibid.,* p. 60.
123. Powerloom Enquiry Committee Report, *op.cit.,* p. 60.
124. *Ibid.,* p. 61.
125. *Ibid.,* p. 65.
126. Report on Village and Cottage Industries, National Committee on the Development of Backward Areas, Planning Commission, Government of India, 1980-p. 17.
127. High Powered Study Team, *Op. cit.,* para No. 82, p. XXIV.
128. *Ibid.,* para No. 8, No. IV.

3 General Characteristics of the Handloom Industry in Cuddapah District

An examination of the 'General Characteristics of Handloom Industry' is useful to understand overall picture of this industry. As such, the characteristics of this industry in Cuddapah, generally pertaining to such aspects—as the nature and size of the industry, year wise establishment of looms, number of years spent by the individual weavers in the industry, distribution of looms on the basis of production, organisational distribution of looms, distribution of looms among different organisations and the various products of the industry, number of handlooms producing zari cloth and non-zari cloth, active looms and idle looms, details of ownership of looms, involvement of family members in the process of production, details of yarn used, and holidays observed by the weavers etc.,- are explained in detail in the following pages.

Nature of the Industry

The Cotton Handloom Industry in Cuddapah district, as in the rest of the country, is basically a household industry. The manufacturing work viz., pre-looming, looming or weaving, post-looming processes are carried on by the members in their own houses. Handloom Kharkanas or Sheds are completely absent in this district.

Establishment of Handlooms in Cuddapah District

The history of the development of handloom industry in Cuddapah district shows that, 88 per cent of the existing looms were established prior to 1980 and the remaining after 1980 (Table 3.1).Weavers within the age group of 18 to 70 years are found engaged in the Handloom Industry.[1]

Table 3.1 : Establishment of Looms—Period-wise Analysis

Areas	Prior to 1930	1931-50	1951-70	1971-80	After 80	Total
West Rural	—	8	32	21	11	72
	—	(11.11)	(44.44)	(29.17)	(15.28)	(100.0)
Uest Urban	—	14	36	29	20	99
	—	(14.14)	(36.36)	(29.29)	(18.13)	(100.0)
Total West	—	22	68	50	31	171
		(12.86)	(39.77)	(29.24)	(18. 13)	(100.0)
East Rural	2	7	17	15	3	44
	(4.54)	(15.91)	(38.64)	(34.09)	(6.82)	(100.0)
Eaat Urban	—	14	39	18	—	71
	—	(19.73)	(54.95)	(25.33)	—	(100.0)
Total East	2	21	56	33	3	115
	(1.74)	(18.26)	(48.69)	(28.69)	(2.62)	(100.0)
Grand Total	**2**	**43**	**124**	**83**	**34**	**286**
	(0.70)	**(15.03)**	**(43.36)**	**(29.02)**	**(11.89)**	**(100.0)**

Source: Field Survey Data.
Figures in brackets are the precentages to their respective totals,

Out of 286 looms surveyed only 2 looms established prior to 1930 were in active operation. The distribution of handlooms in the district has been as shown in Table 3.2. In the Western part of the district 82 per cent of the total looms in that area were established between 1930-80 and the remaining 18 per cent looms were established after 1980. But in Eastern Zone 97 per cent of the looms were established prior to 1980 and the remaining looms after 1980.

From Tables 3.1 and 3.2 it is clear that the percentage of weavers that entered the handloom industry in the last ten years (i.e after 1980) is relatively more in Western Cuddapah (18 per cent) than in Eastern Cuddapah (3 per cent). This was largely due to non-availability of alternative job opportunities for the weavers in Western Cuddapah. However, in Eastern Cuddapah (as the author could observe during the survey) the younger generation could get diverted to other field and take up jobs in education, business, services etc., to improve their living conditions.

Table 3.2 : Spatial Distribution of Weavers and Years of Experience/Work

Areas	Total Years of Experience									
	Below 10 years	11-20	21-30	31-40	41-50	51-60	Above 60	Total	Average	S.D.
West Rural	14 (20)	28 (40)	10 (14)	17 (22)	2 (2)	1 (2)	—	30 (100)	21.00	4.42
West Urban	26 (25)	40 (40)	12 (13)	14 (15)	7 (7)	— —	— —	99 (100)	18.78	3.37
Total West	40 (23)	68 (40)	22 (14)	31 (18)	9 (5)	1 (1)	— —	171 (100)	19.32	4.27
East Rural	4 (9)	15 (34)	7 (17)	11 (26)	2 (13)	5 (11)	— —	44 (100)	27.34	2.63
East Urban	— —	23 (33)	29 (40)	9 (13)	7 (11)	3 (3)	— —	71 (100)	27.27	2.67
Total East	4 (3)	38 (33)	36 (31)	20 (18)	9 (8)	8 (7)	— —	115 (100)	27.30	2.67
Grand Total	**44 (15)**	**106 (37)**	**58 (21)**	**51 (18)**	**18 (6)**	**9 (3)**	— —	**286 (100)**	**23.11**	**4.97**

Source: Field Survey Data.

Figures in the brackets are percentages to their respective totals.

On the basis of the survey it has been observed that the maximum period upto which a weaver could be engaged in weaving activity is 60 years.

The nature of the industry in Western Cuddapah is such that it makes the weaver retire early. This may be due to the fact that weaving of coarse varieties in Western Cuddapah, is rather hard and needs great vigour and strength; consequently weavers get early retirement in Western Cuddapah, unlike weavers in Eastern Cuddapah, who have been engaged in the production of yarn of higher counts which is relatively easy to weave and weaver does not get exerted too much during the process of production.

Size of the Handloom Industry

The cotton handloom industry in Cuddapah is essentially a household one. The manufacturing processes are carried out by the household members in their own houses. This industry consists mostly of small household units having one or two looms each. Out of 215 households surveyed only one household in the district has 3 looms. Two households in Eastern Cuddapah and Western Cuddapah have four looms each.

The distribution of looms among the 215 households is shown in Table 3.3. It shows that 71 per cent of the sample units had one loom each and 27 per cent had two looms each. These two groups taken together constituted 98 per cent of the total number of sample units. Only 2 per cent of the respondents had four looms each, and only one household than 0.4), had three looms. The position is almost in all the regions of the district. This clearly shows the preponderance of small units with only one or two looms.

In terms of the average looms per household, West-Rural Zone occupied the first position with 1.44 looms per household, and East Rural Zone had the lowest with 1.26 looms per household. The average number of looms per household is relatively more in Western Cuddapah (1.37) while it is less in Eastern Cuddapah (1.28). In other words 5 households on an average had a total of 7 looms and 6 looms each in Western and Eastern zones respectively. This may be due to the following reason. The physical structure of the loom in Eastern Cuddapah is entirely different from that of Western Cuddapah. Looms in Eastern Cuddapah require more space. For example, looms in Eastern Cuddapah require 6×12 feet, while it is only 6×6 feet in Western Cuddapah. Hence two looms of Western Cuddapah can be accommodated in the space of one loom of Eastern Cuddapah. Therefore, the average loomage per household is more in Western than in Eastern Cuddapah.

Table 3.3 : Size of Handloom Units

Areas	Number of Handlooms						Average looms per Household
	One	Two	Three	Four	Total Looms	No. of Households	
West Rural	30 (60)	19 (38)	—	1 (2)	72 (100)	50	1.44
West Urban	54 (72)	19 (25.33)	1 (1.34)	1 (1.33)	99 (100.0)	75	1.32
Total West	84 (67.2)	38 (30.4)	1 (0.8)	2 (1.6)	171 (100.0)	125	1.37
East Rural	26 (74. 28)	9 (25. 72)	—	—	44 (100)	35	1.26
East Urban	43 (78.18)	10 (18.18)	— —	2 (3.69)	71 (100.00)	55	1.29
Total East	69 (76.67)	19 (21.11)	— —	2 (2.22)	115 (100.0)	90	1.28
Grand Total	**153 (71.16)**	**57 (26.52)**	**1 (0.46)**	**4 (1.86)**	**286 (100.0)**	**215**	**1.33**

Source : Field Survey Data.

Figures in brackets are the percentages to their respective totals.

Type of Handlooms in the House

Neither the total number of looms in a household nor the number of working looms in the zone can explain fully the true nature and size of the handloom industry. The of the looms in use has its own impact. Almost all looms are pit looms with fly shuttles.[2] Throw shuttle pit looms were in existence long ago. The oldest looms in India worked with the Throw Shuttle Sleys[3]. Prior to 1922 the number of fly shuttle looms were far less. The rapid increase in their number was due to active endeavours of the Government to popularise them.[4] The respondents opined that Throw-shuttle looms were in use upto 1965 in Western Cuddapah and 1970 in Eastern Cuddapah. The introduction of Fly-shuttle pit loom in 1950 completely replaced the Throw Shuttle Pit Looms. The Fly-shuttle Pit looms helped the weavers in increasing their productivity and reducing the difficulty in weaving.

Pit-fly Shuttle Looms

The Fly Shuttle Pit Looms were first introduced in England in 1733 by John Kay. By this device, the shuttle is propelled by hammers placed at the ends of the lathe which is lengthened for the purpose and thus weaving can be done more rapidly. The Fly Shuttle Sleys were introduced in India long ago.[5]

In this Fly Shuttle Loom, there will be a small pit of about two feet deep and 1.5 foot width and 2 feet length. The weavers seat will be just under the cloth roller, a few inches below the ground level and the weaver works keeping his legs in the pit conveniently to operate the treadles.

The Pit Loom as it existed, had both merits and defects. It costs less and therefore, within the reach of all weavers. Its construction being simple, it could be repaired even by a village carpenter. It was not heavy for working. The pit below maintained proper hygroscopic condition. When the open part of the warp rests on a pit the dry surrounding air has very little action on the warp and it can be kept in proper condition for weaving without breakages.[6] Thus the pit provided the simplest and cheapest form of humidifier.

The greatest defect of the pit loom was that the different weaving operations such as Shedding, Picking, Beating, Taking up etc., were required to be done by the weaver with his hands and feet. Thus the loom greatly taxed both the brain and the body of the weaver. While weaving, he had to sit upright in a steady position, minding all the operations, which unnecessarily strained his spinal column and tired him out after one or two hours of uninterrupted work.

Fig. 3.1 : Weaving (Eastern Cuddapah) A Dobby used for border designing

Fig. 3.2 : Weaving (Western Cuddapah)

The other defect was that there was no arrangement for a warp beam. It is the pit that harbours and invites many ailments in weavers' households, pit looms should not be allowed in the interest of the weavers health. All sorts of filth gather in the pit. Mosquitoes make it their abode and the poor weaver becomes a victim of malaria, filariasis and other diseases.[7]

Working Looms and Idle Looms[8]

The total number of looms in the industry cannot give a correct picture of the size of the industry. Working of looms in a cottage is not like that of looms in a hill. If weaving in a mill ceases to be profitable, looms are discarded. But a domestic loom is like any other family operated. Looms will not be discarded for any rate for some years and they will fetch little if they are sold.[9] Therefore the total number of looms actually working may be considered more appropriately as an indicator of the size of the industry than the total number of looms. The number of looms turned idle increased, with the passage of time.[10] Keeping this in view, the data pertaining to idle looms were collected through the field survey.

As presented in Table 3.4 (*See on next page*) out of 215 sample units covering 340 looms, 16 per cent of the total number of sample looms were reported idle. The percentage of idle looms in different regions of Cuddapah district ranged between 13 per cent to 21 per cent. The percentage of idle looms to total looms is almost the same both in Western and Eastern Cuddapah.

Some of the important reasons for the looms remaining idle are as under—In the first place, artisans with good educational background give up weaving activity, if conditions permitted them to do so. Secondly under moderniaation schemes also weavers have replaced the Throw Shuttle and primitive looms for Fly-shuttle and modern loons. Thirdly the weaver leaves the loom idle, when they go old. Age of retirement is influenced by physical factors to some extent, but the greatest factor is whether a man has a son willing to support him.[11] Lastly, in some of the places particularly in Western Cuddapah some weavers have completely withdrawn from weaving and became ordinary workers in the fields like Agriculture, Masonry, Grocers' shops and Cloth Shops. Some looms have become idle mainly due to irregularity in the availability of raw materials required by the Industry. The supply of raw materials, is largely influenced by its prices.

Work Place and Residence

In the sample size of 215 households, except 4, all the households have their places of work in or attached to their residence (*See Table 3.5 on page 96*). By

Table 3.4 : Working Looms and Idle Looms

Area	Number of household	Total Number of looms					
		Working looms	Average of working looms per Household	Idle looms	Average of idle looms per house-hold	Total No. of loom (working+ idle)	Average of total loom per house-hold
West Rural	50	72 (80.90)	1.44	17 (19.10)	0.34	89 (100)	1.78
West Urban	75	99 (85.35)	1.32	17 (14.65)	0.23	116 (100)	1.55
Total West	125	171 (83.42)	1.37	34 (16.58)	0.27	205 (100)	1.64
East Rural	35	44 (88.0)	1.26	6 (12.0)	0.17	50 (100)	1.43
East Urban	55	71 (83.53)	1.29	14 (16.47)	0.25	85 (100)	1.55
Total East	90	115 (85.18)	1.28	20 (14.82)	0.22	135 (100)	1.50
Grand Total	**215**	**286 (84.12)**	**1.33**	**54 (15.88)**	**0.25**	**340 (100)**	**1.58**

Source : Field Survey Data.
Figures in brackets are the percentages to their respective totals.

and large weavers have expressed their reluctance to change their work place to separate premises even if some Government help is provided. The main reason is that if the work place is different from place of residence that would severely restrict the extent of participation of household labour, especially those of women-folk in production activities of the units concerned. It is learnt that short intervals of the time would be profitably used for the production work by women., even engaged in bobbin winding or pirn winding while breast feeding their babies.

It is rather difficult to draw a line between the work place and the residence of a weaver. There are hardly any separate apartments/rooms in a weavers house. The house would be designed and built in such a way that a minimum of 6′×12′ space is made available for a loom to operate in a house.

Table 3.5 : Location of Work Place

Total number of units surveyed	Work place and Residence together		Seperate work place	
	Number of units	2 as a % of 1	Number of units	4 as a % of 1
215	211	98	4	2

Source: Field Survey Data.

Process of Production

To a casual observer, weaving on the handlooms may appear a simple process but in reality it involves a number of laborious preliminary processes before the yarn is put on the loom. When the yarn is purchased from the dealers, it is not in a ready form for weaving. The yarn for Warp and Weft undergo a number of different processes before being actually woven into required fabrics. In actual practice the process is some what complicated. All the weaving processes are briefly described in the following pages.

The cost of the production process is a significant element in the total cost of production of the cloth. For example nearly half of the total labour cost involved in the production of a saree is due to these preliminary processes.[12]

Dyeing

The very first process, which begins after the yarn is received from the Kills, is dyeing of yarn. The process of dyeing is highly skilled. Before the advent of chemical dyes, the indigenous and natural dye-stuffs were used. But with the use of chemical dyes, the process of dyeing poses less number of problems at present than in the past. The dyeing industry in India is an ancient industry which dates back to 3000 B.C.[13] Usually it is the seller in the retail trade and the Master Weavers who get the yarn dyed depending upon the fashion in vogue, prior to sale.

In the field survey it was reported that the Co-operative Societies and the Master Weavers arrange to dye the yarn in their own dye-houses or get the yarn dyed in the private dye-house. From this it is clear that dyeing need not necessarily be a part of the activities of the household handloom units.

Loosening and Unwinding

As soon as the yarn is obtained it has to be loosened and unwound[14]. The yarn so unwound is rewound on the warp bobbins and used for the preparation of warp and weft. The work of winding yarn on Faratis or Reels is almost always given to women workers of the weavng communities, or to the female members of the family. As women have to cook food and look after children, they undertake winding of yarn as a part-time job. The rates of wages varied with the fineness of yarn wound.

Pirn-winding

After the yarn is loosened and unwound, it has to be wound again on the pirns. Pirn winding is done in the case of Weft yarn or breadth-wise yarn. This process is done with the help of a spinning wheel by housewives.

Warping

After the yarn is unwound from the hanks, it has to be Warped. Warping is length-wise yarn preparation. The threads that lie length-wise are called the Warp.[15] When the yarn is warped on the pegs, it is known as Peg Warping.[16] The system of peg-warping is an old and outdated method. During field survey the use of Circular Warping Machine has been noticed. Wages for preparing the Warp vary according to the number (fineness) of yarn.

Sizing

Sizing is necessary for providing strength to the yarn. The Warping and Sizing are often done in open space/area (on road side) for reasons of convenience. Warp is being stretched out on simple trestles, made of bamboos. The water left after boiling rice is (Ganji) is used in Sizing yarn. The water so removed from the boiling of rice is used as a paste in Sizing Warps of Sarees[17].

Fig. 3.3 : Yarn Winding

Fig. 3.4 : Sizing

Fig. 3.5 : Joining and Twisting

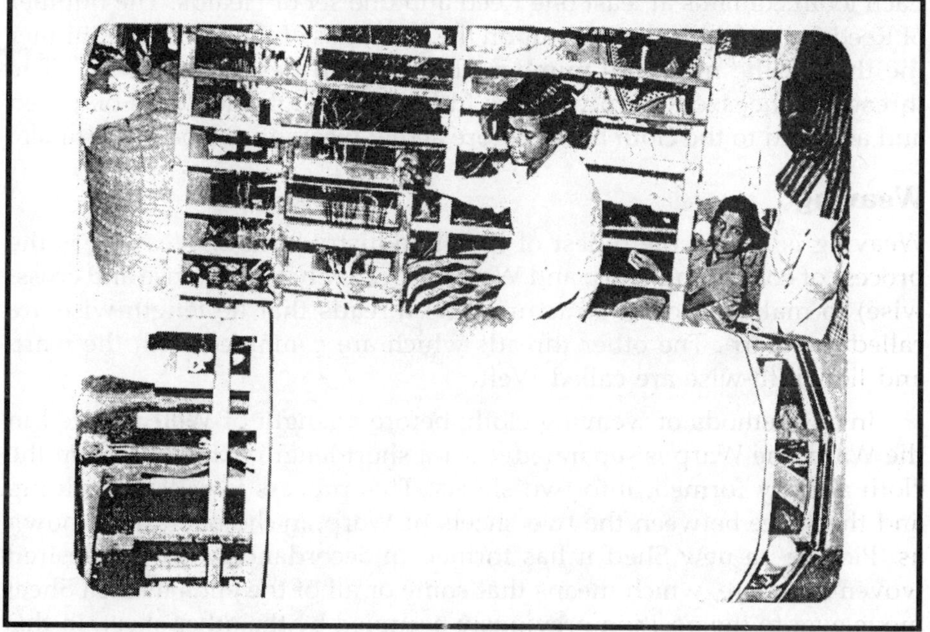

Fig. 3.6 : Beaming

The Sizing is done by two or more persons walking the length of the warp, meanwhile applying sizing paste with brushes made of coir fibre[18]. The warp in such cases is done for no more than 40 yards length generally because of the obvious limitations of the space in public thoroughfares. This method of Warping and Sizing in the open area has other disadvantages also. Apart from obstructing traffic, work is interrupted due to excessive heat in summer and due to rains in the monsoon.

Joining and Twisting

The process of Joining the threads of the new warp to the ends of the warp on the loom is called 'Twisting' or Joining. This is one of the important and delicate processes of weaving. This work is generally done by the adult members of the family.

Beaming

The warp yarn is wound on the wooden beam which is cylindrical in shape and is fixed in front of the loom. Each warp will last for 40 to 50 yards of cloth. After the weaving is done, the cloth thus produced is removed and another warp has to be arranged, which means loss of time and discontinuity in weaving.

Reeding

Each loom contains at least one Reed and one set of Healds. The number of Reeds and Healds depends upon the thickness of the cloth. The thinner the thread, the more the number of reeds and healds required.[19] The threads of the sized warp yarn are Inserted through the Dents of a reed and attached to the cloth beam before actual weaving can be undertaken.

Weaving

Weaving is one of the oldest of man's industrial arts[20]. Weaving is the process of combining Warp and Weft (respectively length-wise and cross-wise) to make a woven structure. The threads that lie length-wise are called the warp. The other threads which are combined with the warp and lie width-wise are called Weft.

In all methods of weaving cloth, before a length of Weft inserted in the Warp, the Warp is separated, over a short length extending from the cloth already formed, into two sheets. This process is called Shedding and the space between the two sheets of Warp, in the operation known as 'Picking', a new Shed it has formed in accordance with the desired woven structure, which means that some or all of the ends in each Sheet move over to the position previously occupied by the other sheet. In this way the Weft is clasped between two layers of Warp.

Since it is possible to lay the Weft close to the junction of the Warp and the cloth already woven, a further operation la necessary known as 'Beating in', or 'Beating up', which consists in pushing the pick to the desired distance away from the last one inserted previously. Although 'Beating in' usually takes place whlle the Shed is changing, it is normally completed before the new Shed is fully formed.

The sequence of primary operations in one weaving cycle are thus 'Shedding', 'Picking' and 'Beating in'. At the time of the cycle the geometrical relation of the Pick to the Warp is the same as it would have been if the pick had been threaded through the spaces between alternative ends, first from one side of the cloth and then from the other as in Darning. For this reason the 'weaving process is often described as 'Interlacing'.

Participation of Family Members in Different Processes of Weaving

The production processes involve Winding, Warping, Sizing, and Weaving. The industry is exclusively a cottage industry and all the members of the family help in the preparation of cloth.[21] All these processes are carried on by some of the members of the family also, and some others get the work done by depending completely on other workers. In some cases members of the family together with the workers do the processes of production. The extent of involvement of either family members, or other workers or both depends on the nature of process and the strength of the family of the household concerned. Certain occupations are exclusively followed by men and others by women. Stated generally, the occupations that demanded certain amount of strength and stamina are followed by men, while others involving less strength are done by women. But there are certain exceptions to the above rule[22].

Besides the participation of adult men and women, children of the weaving households also participate in the different processes of weaving. The wife takes care of the domestic chores and prepares weft threads, the younger children attend to school, the elder children attend to the loom and the husband is weaving full-time.[23]

From Table 3.6 (*See on next page*), it is clear that 73 per cent of the households in the sample do the process of winding through members of the family only, and the remaining get it done either by the outside labour completely or through a combination of family labour and outside labour. 76 per cent of the winding work is done by women, 7 per cent by men, and the remaining 17 per cent by children between the ages of 10 to 15 years. The participation of children in this process is relatively more

Table 3.6 : Participation of Family Members in the Process of Production

Area	Number of Households	Warping			Winding			Sizing		
		Family Members	Other Workers	Family Members & Other workers	Family Members	other Workers	F.M.*& other Workers	Family Members	other Workers	F.M. & other Workers
West Rural	50	43 (86.0)	—	7 (14.0)	37 (74.0)	8 (16.0)	5 (10.0)	46 (92.0)	—	4 (8.0)
West Urban	75	54 (72.0)	—	21 (28.0)	50 (66.67)	12 (16.0)	13 (17.33)	68 (90.67)	—	7 (9.33)
Total West	125	97 (77.6)	—	28 (22.4)	87 (69.6)	20 (16.0)	18 (14.4)	114 (91.2)	—	11 (8.8)
East Rural	35	7 (20.0)	—	28 (80.0)	30 (85.72)	—	5 (14.28)	29 (82.86)	—	6 (17.14
East Urban	55	11 (20.0)	1 (1.82)	43 (78.18)	41 (74.55)	5 (9.09)	9 (16.36)	44 (80.0)	1 (1.82)	10 (18.18)
Total East	90	18 (20.0)	1 (1.11)	71 (78.89)	71 (78.89)	5 (5.55)	14 (15.55)	73 (81.11)	1 (1.11)	16 (17.78)
Grand Total	**215**	**115 (53.49)**	**1 (0.46)**	**99 (46.05)**	**158 (73.69)**	**25 (11.63)**	**27 (14.68)**	**187 (86.98)**	**1 (0.50)**	**27 (13.0)**

Source : Field Survey Data.
Figure in brackets are the percentages to their respective totals.
* Family members

(24 per cent) in Western Cuddapah, than in Eastern Cuddapah (5 per cent), because the winding of yarn of lower Counts needs less skill and hence participation of children is significant in Western Cuddapah. It is also observed that women participation in this process is comparatively less in Western (67%) than in Eastern Cuddapah (92%). This is due to higher percentage of women participation in the process of weaving in Western Cuddapah.

It becomes clear from Table 3.6 that 53 per cent of the total households surveyed involve only members of the family in the process of Warping and the remaining 46 per do it together with the help of the outside workers.

As presented in the Tables 3.7 (*See on page 104*) and 3.7A (*See on page 105*) the involvement of the members of the family in the process of Warping is comparatively more in Western (78%) than in Eastern Cddapah (20%). The involvement of men in this process is 58% women 30%, and children 12 per cent. The participation of men in Western zone is relatively less (47%) than in Eastern zone (74%). This may be due to the fact that in Western region, yarn of lower Counts is used, the warping process of it is relatively easier than in Eastern region, where yarn of higher Counts is used.

Among the households surveyed, 87 per cent do the process of Sizing purely through the members of the family, and the remaining 13 per cent do it together with the help of outside workers. Heavy rains render Sizing in streets difficult[24]. The participation of women in this process is relatively more (58%) than men (42%).

Weaving is an important process in terms of the value added. This process is undertaken only by the members of the family. The percentage of involvement of men, women and the children of the family in the process of weaving is 60, 30, and 10 per cent respectively. The participation of men and women members is almost equal in Western zone, while the men participation is relatively more (77%) than the women (8%) in Eastern zone. The higher Percentage of women participation in Western Cuddapah (46%), compare to women participation in Eastern Cuddapah (8%) is largely due to the fact that weaving of yarn of higher counts in Eastern Cuddapah need more skill and stamina. Apart from this, services of women are constantly required in the process of winding in Eastern region. So women in this region cannot concentrate on weaving.

Mode of Acquisition of Looms

Table 3.8 (*See on page 106*) shows that the general mode of acquisition of looms is through inheritance. It is clear from the table that 67 per cent of the looms in the sample were inherited and the remaining 32 per cent

Table 3.7 : Involvement of Members In Different Processes of Weaving

Area	No. of looms	Winding					Warping				
		Men	Women	Children (10 to 15 years)	Total	Average	Men	Women	Children (10 to 15 years)	Total	Average
West Rural	72	10 (10.53)	66 (69.47)	19 (20.0)	95 (100.0)	1.32	77 (48.73)	62 (39.85)	19 (12.02)	158 (100.0)	2.19
West Urban	99	11 (8.46)	84 (64.62)	35 (26.92)	130 (100.0)	1.31	125 (45.95)	88 (32.36)	59 (21.69)	272 (100.0)	2.7
Total West	171	21 (9.33)	150 (66.67)	54 (24.0)	226 (100.0)	1.32	202 (46.98)	150 (34.88)	78 (18.14)	430 (100.0)	2.51
East Rural	44	—	45 (100.0)	—	45 (100.0)	1.02	80 (72.73)	30 (27.27)	—	110 (100.0)	2.50
East Urban	71	4 (4.60)	76 (87.36)	7 (8.04)	87 (100.0)	1.23	151 (75.12)	46 (22.88)	4 (1.99)	201 (100.0)	2.83
Total East	115	4 (3.03)	121 (91.67)	7 (5.30)	132 (100.0)	1.15	231 (74.28)	76 (24.43)	4 (1.29)	311 (100.0)	2.70
Grand Total	**286**	**25 (7.0)**	**271 (76.0)**	**61 (17.0)**	**357 (100.0)**	**1.25**	**433 (58.0)**	**226 (30.0)**	**82 (12.0)**	**741 (100.0)**	**2.59**

Source : Field Survey Data.

Figures in the brackets are the percentages to their respective totals.

Table 3.7A : Involvement of Members in Different Processes of Weaving

Area	No. of looms	Winding					Warping				
		Men	Women	Children (10 to 15 years)	Total	Average	Men	Women	Children (10 to 15 years)	Total	Averag
West Rural	72	41 (40.59)	59 (58.42)	1 (0.99)	101 (100.0)	1.40	64 (67.37)	26 (27.37)	5 (5.26)	95 (100.00)	1.32
West Urban	99	74 (49.33)	76 (50.67)	—	150 (100.0)	1.52	28 (27.72)	64 (63.37)	9 (8.91)	101 (100.00)	1.02
Total West	171	115 (45.82)	135 (53.78)	1 (0.40)	251 (100.0)	1.47	92 (46.94)	90 (45.92)	14 (7.14)	196 (100.00)	1.15
East Rural	44	27 (38.03)	44 (61.97)	—	71 (100.0)	1.67	24 (80.0)	6 (20.0)	—	30 (100.00)	1.25
East Urban	71	37 (34.26)	69 (63.89)	2 (1.85)	108 (100.0)	1.52	69 (70.41)	7 (7.14)	22 (22.45)	98	1.38
Total East	115	64 (35.75)	113 (63.13)	2 (1.12)	179 (100.0)	1.56	111 (76.55)	12 (8.28)	22 (15.17)	145	1.26
Grand Total	**286**	**179 (41.63)**	**248 (57.67)**	**3 (0.70)**	**430 (100.0)**	**1.50**	**203 (59.53)**	**102 (29.91)**	**36 (10.56)**	**341**	**1.19**

Source : Field Survey Data.

Figures in the brackets are the percentages to their respective totals.

Table. 3.8 : Mode of Acquisition of Looms

Area	Total Looms in the Household	Nature of ownership		New Entrants	5 as % of (2)	Replacement for old and outdated looms	7 as % of (2)
		By inheri tence	Self acquired				
West Rural	89	63 (70. 79)	26 (29.21)	2	2.25	2	2.25
West Urban	116	80 (68.96)	36 (31.04)	2	1.72	2	1.72
Total West	205	143 (69.76)	62 (30.24)	4	1.95	4	1.95
East Rural	50	31 (62.0)	19 (38.0)	3	6.00	8	16.00
East Urban	85	53 (62.35)	32 (37.65)	5	5.88	10	11.76
Total East	135	84 (62.22)	51 (37.78)	8	5.93	18	13.33
Grand Total	**340**	**227 (66. 77)**	**113 (33.24)**	**12**	**3.53**	**22**	**6.47**

Source : Field Survey Data.

Figures in the brackets are the percentages to their respective totals.

had been newly acquired. P.C.Mahapatro's[25] study of handloom industry in Orissa also indicate the same result. However newly acquired loom does not necessarily imply fresh entry into the industry. Out of 113 newly acquired looms 22 looms or 19.47 per cent were mere replacements for the old looms inherited, and only 91 looms or 80.53 per cent were infact newly introduced. Further, out of these 91 newly introduced looms, weavers working in 79 looms were pushed into seperate units with the division of joint families. The owners of the remaining 12 looms only i.e 4 per cent of the total looms, were infact new entrants to the industry.

The obvious inference is that the fresh entry into the industry is almost negligible and inheritance is the general mode of acquisition of looms. This indicates that this industry does not offer any gainful employment or income to those employed in the industry. At the same time, the existing weavers do not leave it as the scope to get lucrative employment is limited. Thus, they have stuck to weaving activity not by choice, but out of compussion and inertia[26].

The inference therefore is that the industry survives largely on hereditary basis and it doesn't offer or present rosy prospects for fresh entrants. However the position is relatively better in Eastern zone than in Western zone of cuddaph district.

Raw Material

It is not the quantity of cloth that is important, but it is the quality that matters much for its marketing. The quality of raw material used determines the quality of finished cloth. The important raw materials used by the handlooms of Cuddapah district are: Cotton yarn, Silk and Zari. Of all the raw materials required, cotton yarn is the most significant. Cotton yarn is the basic raw material of the Handloom Industry[27].

It is clear from Table No. 3.9 (*See on next page*) that 71 per cent of the looms in Western Cuddapah use only cotton as the basic raw material. Silk is the chief raw material for 26 per cent of looms and only 3 per cent of looms are using yarn of higher Counts and Zari together. Unlike the practice in western region, all looms in Eastern region of Cuddapah district use only yarn of higher counts and Zari.

Though Cotton yarn ia the basic raw material required by the industry, yarn of different Counts is used to produce different varieties of cloth. For example, as shown in Table 3.10 (*See on next page*) yarn of 30×40 Counts is used to produce Janata Dhoties, 40×40 Counts for Janata Sarees, 40×60 Counts for Shirting, Lungis; and 100×120 Counts for Pure Zari Sarees.

Table 3.9 : Fineness/Varieties of Yarn Used by Looms

Area	Number of Households	Number of looms	Looms using only cotton	Looms using only silk	Looms using yarn & zari	Warp X Weft (Counts)				
						30x40	40x40	40x60	100x100	100x120
West Rural	50	72	57 (79.17)	15 (20.83)	—	36 (63.16)	11 (19.30)	10 (17.54)	—	—
West Urban	75	99	65 (65.66)	29 (29.29)	5 (5.05)	24 (34.29)	23 (32.86)	18 (25.71)	4 (5.71)	1 (1.43)
Total West	125	171	122 (71.35)	44 (25.73)	5 (2.92)	60 (47.24)	34 (26.77)	28 (22.05)	4 (3.15)	1 (0.79)
East Rural	35	44	—	—	44 (100.0)	—	—	—	—	44 (100.0)
East Urban	55	71	—	—	71 (100.0)	—	—	—	—	71 (100.0)
Total East	90	115	—	—	115 (100.0)	—	—	—	—	115 (100.0)
Grand Total	**215**	**286**	**122 (42.66)**	**44 (15.39)**	**120 (41.95)**	**60 (24.79)**	**34 (14.05)**	**28 (14.57)**	**4 (1.65)**	**116 (47.94)**

Source : Field Survey Data.

Figures in the brackets are the percentages to their respective totals.

Table 3.10 : Fineness of Yarn Used and the Products

Products	Number of Looms	Counts of Yarn used				
		30×40	40×40	40×60	100×100	100×120
Janata dhoties	60 (21.0)	60 (100.0)	—	—	—	—
Janata sarees	27 (9.0)	—	27 (100.0)	—	—	—
Shirting	28 (10.0)	—	—	28 (100.0)	—	—
Lungis	7 (2.0)	—	—	7 (100.0)	—	—
Resham	44 (15.0)	—	—	—	—	—
Pure zari sarees	120 (43.0)	—	—	—	4 (3.33)	116 (96.67)
Grand Total	**286 (100.0)**	**60 (24.79)**	**27 (11.16)**	**35 (14.46)**	**4 (1.65)**	**116 (47.94)**

Source : Field Survey Data.
Figures in the bracketa are the percentages to their respective totals.

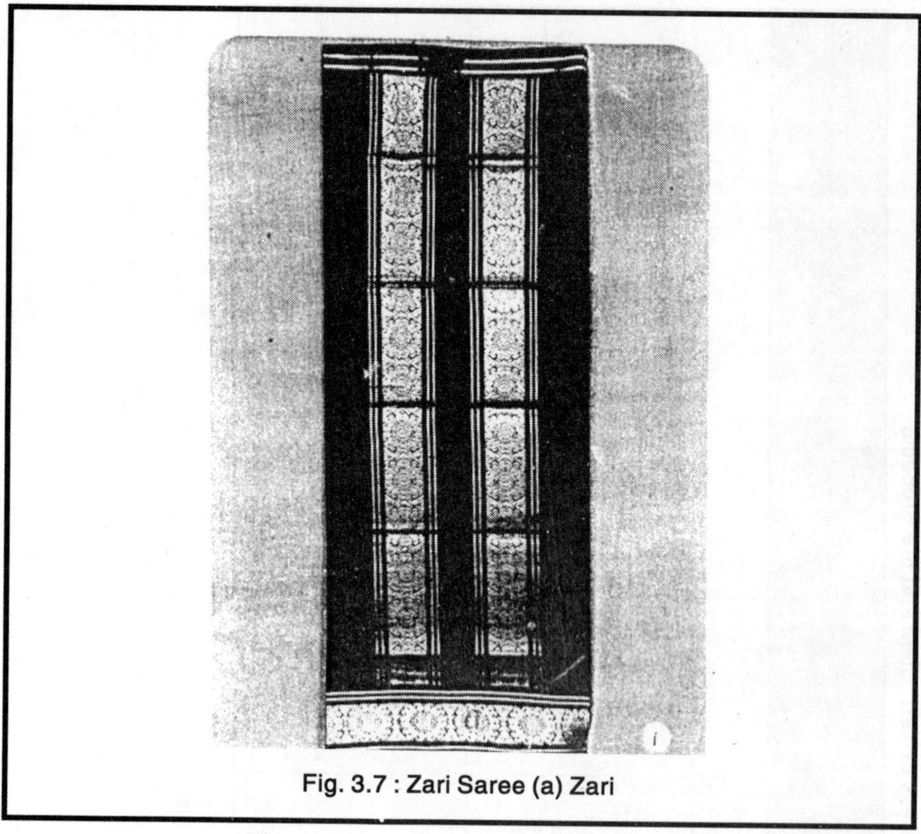

Fig. 3.7 : Zari Saree (a) Zari

Excepting 4 per cent of the looms in the Western zone, all the 96 per cent have been using yarn of lower Counts ranging from 30 to 60 Counts. Of the 4 per cent looms using yarn of higher Counts, 3 per cent are using yarn of 100×100 Counts, and the remaining 1 per cent 100×120 Counts. But all the looms in Eastern Cuddapah are using yarn of higher Counts only i.e. 100×120 Counts. The relative cost of raw material varied with the fineness. As the fineness increases the cost also increases.

Yarn of lower Counts and Silk are the chief raw materials used in Western Cuddapah, while yarn of higher Counts and pure Zari are used in Eastern Cuddapah. Only Coarse varieties are produced in Western region, while Superior varieties of Zari Sarees are produced in Eastern region of Cuddapah district.

Product-wise Distribution of Looms

Table 3.11 (*See on page 111*) shows the important varieties produced in Cuddapah district. They are, Pure Zari Sarees., also known as Venkatagiri Zari Sarees, Janata Sarees, Janata Dhoties, Silk Cloth (Resham), Shirting

Table 3.11 : Product-wise Distribution of Lcoms

Area	Looms Producing						Total Looms
	Zari sarees	Sarees*	Dhoty	Resham	Shirting	Lungis	
West Rural	—	11 (15.28)	36 (50.0)	15 (20.83)	10 (13.89)	—	72 (100.0)
West Urban	5 (5.05)	16 (16.16)	24 (24.24)	29 (29.29)	18 (18.18)	7 (7.07)	99 (100.0)
Total West	5 (2.92)	27 (15.79)	60 (35.09)	44 (25.73)	28 (16.37)	7 (4.10)	171 (100.0)
East Rural	44 (100.0)	—	—	—	—	—	44 (100.0)
East Urban	71 (100.0)	—	—	—	—	—	71 (100.0)
Total East	115 (100.0)	—	—	—	—	—	115 (100.0)
Grand Total	**120 (41.96)**	**27 (9.44)**	**60 (20.98)**	**44 (15.38)**	**28 (9.79)**	**7 (2.45)**	**286 (100.0)**

Source : Field Survey Data.
Figures in the brackets are the percentages to their respective totals.
*Ordinary sarees or cheap varieties like janata sarees

and Lungis. Only coarse varieties are produced in Western Cuddapah, where as Superior Venkatagiri Zari Sarees are produced in Eastern Cuddapah. Out of 286 looms surveyed in the district, 42 per cent are producing pure Zari Sarees. Janata Dhoti is the second important product produced in the district. In Western Cuddapah only 3 per cent of the looms are engaged in producing Zari Sarees. Contrary to this situation, all the looms in Eastern Cuddapah are producing Pure Zari Sarees. The production of Resam Sarees (Silk Sarees) is completely absent in Eastern zone, while 26 per cent of the looms in Western Cuddapah are producing this cloth.

Type of Zari Sarees Produced

Details of Zari Sarees produced in Cuddapah district are presented in Table 3.12 (*See on page 113*). The names of Zari Sarees produced in the district are: 20 laka,[28] 30 laka, 40 laka, 50 laka, 90 laka and 120 laka Zari Sarees. The predominant variety of Zari sarees produced in the district produce 20 Laka Zari product. All the 5 Zari cloth producing looms in Western Cudapah produce 20 laka Zari Saree. Around 41 per cent of the looms in Western Cuddapah produce 20 Laka Sarees only. Larger amount of capital is required to produce higher laka Zari sarees. Hence it is obvious that the handloom industry in western Cuddapah is Capital intensive.

An Organic View of the Handloom Weaving

Under this, we propose to make an organic interpretation of the weaving establishments functioning in Cuddapah district. The main purpose of such analysis is to indicate the personal and human relationship that exists among the various workers engaged in weaving. This relationship is organic rather than mechanical[29] and only by looking at the relationship in this organic form we can derive useful insights into the economics of these units.

Mainly there are four categories of Handloom weavers in the district (*See Tables 3.13, 3.14 and 3.15 on page 115*). Category one consists of Weavers in Co-operative sector and the second category consists of those working under the manufacturers of handloom cloth generally known as 'Master Weavers'. The third category consists of Independent Handloom Weavers who generally purchase yarn and other raw materials in the open market, produce salable cloth and sell it for their own advantage either to the Master Weaver or to the dealers of handloom cloth. The Corporate Sector constitutes the fourth category.

Table 3.12 : Production of Zari Sarees and Their Types

Area	Total Looms	Looms Producing zari sarees	Type of Zari Saree					
			20Laka	30Laka	40Laka	50Laka	90Laka	120Laka
West Rural	72	—	—	—	—	—	—	—
West Urban	99 (100.0)	5 (5.0)	5 (100.0)	—	—	—	—	—
Total West	171 (100.0)	5 (3.0)	5 (100.0)	—	—	—	—	—
East Rural	44 (100.0)	44 (100.0)	20 (45.45)	2 (4.55)	10 (22.73)	— —	10 (22.73)	2 (4.55)
East Urban	71	71	25 (35.21)	2 (2.82)	13 (18.31)	2 (2.82)	24 (33.80)	5 (7.04)
Total East	115	115 (100.0)	45 (39.13)	4 (3.48)	23 (20.0)	2 (1.74)	34 (29.57)	7 (6.08)
Grand Total	**286**	**120 (100.0)**	**50 (41.67)**	**4 (3.33)**	**23 (19.17)**	**2 (1.67)**	**34 (28.33)**	**7 (5.83)**

Source : Field Survey Data.

Figures in the brackets are the percentages to their respective totals.

Table 3.13 : Organisational Distribution—Ownership of Looms

Area	Total Number Looms	Looms Working For			
		Master Weaver	Co-ope-rativea	Indepen-dent	Corpo-ration
West Rural	72 (100.0)	12 (16.67)	47 (65.28)	5 (6.94)	8 (11.11)
West Urban	99 (100.0)	36 (36.36)	39 (39.39)	4 (4.04)	20 (20.20)
Total West	171 (100.0)	48 (28.07)	86 (50.29)	9 (5.26)	28 (16.37)
East.Rural	44 (100.0)	17 (38.64)	10 (22.73)	17 (38.63)	—
East Urban	71 (100.0)	30 (42.25)	14 (19.72)	27 (38.03)	—
Total East	115 (100.0)	47 (40.87)	24 (20.87)	44 (28.26)	—
Grand Total	**286 (100.0)**	**142 (49.65)**	**72 (25.18)**	**56 (19.58)**	**16 (5.59)**

Source : Field Survey Data.
Figures in the brackets are the percentages to their respective totals.

Table 3.14 : Organisational Composition of the Looms

Area	Total Looms in the sample	Looms working for a single organi-sation during the year	Looms working for different Organi-sation during the year
West Rural	72 (100.0)	58 (80.56)	14 (19.44)
West Urban	99 (100.0)	73 (73.74)	26 (26.26)
Total West	171 (100.0)	131 (77.0)	40 (23.0)
East Rural	44 (100.0)	33 (75.0)	11 (25.0)
East Urban	71 (100.0)	60 (84.51)	11 (15.49)
Total East	115 (100.0)	93 (80.87)	22 (19.13)
Grand Total	**286 100.0)**	**224 (78.32)**	**62 (21.68)**

Source: Field Survey Data.
Figures in the brackets are the percentages to their respective totals.

Table 3.15 : Distribution of Looms by Different Organisations and Products

Area	Products Produced																				
	Sarees				Dhoty				Resham				Lungi				Shirting				
	MW	CO-OP	IND	COR	MW	CO-OP	IND	COR	MW	CO-OP	IND	COR	MW	CO-OP	IND	COR	MW	CO-OP	IND	COR	Total
West Rural	—	7	4	—	—	30	—	6	10	4	—	1	—	—	—	—	2	6	1	1	72
West Urban	—	12	—	9	—	16	—	8	19	8	2	—	5	2	—	—	12	1	2	3	99
Total West	—	19	4	9	—	46	—	14	29	12	2	1	5	2	—	—	14	7	3	4	171
East Rural	17	10	17	—	—	—	—	—	—	—	—	—	—	—	—	—	—	—	—	—	44
East Urban	30	14	27	—	—	—	—	—	—	—	—	—	—	—	—	—	—	—	—	—	71
Total East	47	24	44	—	—	—	—	—	—	—	—	—	—	—	—	—	—	—	—	—	115
Grand Total	**47**	**43**	**48**	**9**	**—**	**46**	**—**	**14**	**29**	**12**	**2**	**1**	**5**	**2**	**—**	**—**	**14**	**7**	**3**	**4**	**286**

Source : Field Survey Data.

M= Master Weaver   Ind = Independent

Co-op = Cooperative   Cor = Corporation

Master Weaver Sector

In this sector, the organiser of many looms, known as Master Weaver, supplies the required raw materials and finance to the weavers and the cloth is produced according to the specifications of the Master Weaver. Master Weaver shoulders the responsibility of marketing the products. Master Weaver pay piece-wage to the weavers as per the agreement, entered into. In most of the cases Master Weaver exploits the weavers by paying low wages. The merchant advances small sums of money, provides the silk and buys the fabric from the weaver at a large profit to himself.[30] Daily wage system does not prevail in Cuddapah district. It is the uncertainty of continuous work that acts as a powerful factor for the weavers to cling to the Master weavers.[31]

Co-operative Organisation

In the case of Primary Co-operative Society weavers join together and form a registered organisation. Weavers are the members of it. The Government supplies the required raw material and finance to the Primary Societies. Society, In turn has to supply the raw materials and finance to the weavers and the weaver weave the cloth as per the specifications of the Government agency viz., Andhra Pradesh Co-operative Marketing Society(APCO). The APCO purchases the products from the Societies. The profits thus accrued to the Primary Societies will be evenly distributed to the members of the Society. This organisation was introduced by the Government to protect the small weavers from the xploitation of the Master Weaver. In this system, the weaver members get all the inputs and design patterns from the Society. On completion of the job, they are paid wages after a proper appraisal of their fabric. The quantum of payment of wages is different from one Society to the other.[32] Additional monetary facilities are not provided by the Societies to the weaver members on occasions like the marriage of relatives, construction of house etc., while such facilities are provided by the Master Weavers.[33]

Independent Weaver

An Independent Weaver is one who procures the raw material himself. The earliest stage is that of the Independent Weaver working generally in ordinary coarse cloth, and disposing of his produce locally.[34] He gets no assistance from any agency. He himself has to market the products. Weavers with good financial conditions naturally become Independent Weavers. Independent weaver is seldom a hundred per cent Independent[35]. At times he seeks the help of the Master Weavers to get the raw materials, and weaves for him.

Andhra Pradesh State Textile Development Corporation (APSTDC)

APSTDC was established in 1975. Its main objective is to assist in the development of handloom weavers particularly those weavers who are outside the Co-operative fold. This has also been entrusted with the implementation of special programmes aimed at assisting handloom weavers by imparting training to them in the production of new varieties of cloth by supplying improved types of loom by providing infrastructure facilities and by assisting them in the marketing of their production. Wages paid to the weaver in this sector are fairly better than the wages under the Master Weaver Sector.

Thus all the looms in the district belong to one of the four organisations described above. However the Co operative organisation in Western Cuddapah and the Master weaver sector in Eastern Cuddapah are important. Weavers in the district some times work for more than one organisation.

Holidays

While some households do not work on specified days like Festivals, others abstain from work at will without following any specified time

Table 3.16 : Holidays Observed by The Weaver Households

Area	Number of Households	Fixed Holidays Only	Fixed holidays plus abstaining from work at will	At will only-No fixed holiday
West Rural	50	—	1 (2.0)	49 (98.0)
West Urban	75	—	34 (45.33)	41 (54.67)
Total West	125	—	35 (28.0)	90 (72.0)
East Rural	35	—	35 (100.0)	—
East Urban	55	—	55 (100.0)	—
Total East	90	—	90 (100.0)	—
Grand Total	**215**	—	**125 (58.14)**	**90 (41.86)**

Source : Field Survey Data.

Figures in the brackets are the percentages to their respective totals.

Table 3.17 : Caste Composition of Weaver Households

Area	Dudekula	Padrna Sale	Thogata	Devanga	Muslims	S.C.	Total Households
West Rural	3 (6.0)	6 (12.0)	24 (48.0)	14 (28.0)	2 (4.0)	1 (2.0)	50 (100.0)
West Urban	1 (1.33)	34 (45.33)	37 (49.33)	—	3 (4.0)	—	75 (100.0)
Total West	**4 (3.20)**	**40 (32.0)**	**61 (48.8)**	**14 (11.2)**	**5 (4.0)**	**1 (0.8)**	**125 (100.0)**
East Rural	—	35 (100.0)	—	—	—	—	35 (100.0)
East Urban	—	55 (100.0)	—	—	—	—	55 (100.0)
Total East	**—**	**90 (100.0)**	**—**	**—**	**—**	**—**	**90 (100.0)**
Grand Total	**4 (1.86)**	**130 (60.47)**	**61 (28.37)**	**14 (6.51)**	**5 (2.33)**	**1 (0.46)**	**215 (100.0)**

Source: Field Survey Data.
Figures in the brackets are the percentages to their respective totals.

table. Among the sample of 215 households surveyed, 58 per cent of the weaving households are found to observe holidays on certain fixed days., viz., Festivals, Ceremonies, Amavasya etc., in addition to a few other days at will, while the remaining 42 per cent observe holidays at will only, and they do not have any fixed holidays. Only 2 per cent of households in Rural Western Cuddapah and 28 per cent in the whole of Eastern Cuddapah observe holidays at will in addition to fixed holidays. But all the households in Eastern Cuddapah observe fixed holidays in addition to holidays at will.

From Table 3.16 (*See on page 117*) we can find that there is the influence of Caste on the holidays observed by weavers. Only weavers belonging to 'Padmasale' community were observing holiday on all public holidays specially on Amavasya (New Moon)[36]. Most of the weavers stop the work on every Amavasya day, (New Moon day) and on almost all Hindu Holidays[37].

During the survey it was revealed (*See Tables 3.17 and 3.18 on pages 118 and 119*) that Thogata and Devanga communities in Western Cuddapah were observing holiday on 'Punnam' (Full Moon) but later on they gave up this tradition.

Table 3.18 : Holidays Observed on the Basis of Castes

Castes	Number of Households	Fixed Holidays only	At will in addition to fixed Holidays	At will only Does not have any fixed holidays
Dudekula	4 (2.0)	—	—	4 (100.0)
Padmasale	130 (60.0)	—	125 (96.0)	5 (4.0)
Thogata	61 (28.0)	—	—	61 (100.0)
Devanga	14 (7.0)	—	—	14 (100.0)
Muslims	5 (2.0)	—	—	5 (100.0)
Scheduled Castes	1 (1.0)	—	—	1 (100.0)
Grand Total	**215 (100.0)**	—	**125 (55.14)**	**90 (41.86)**

Source : Field Survey Data.

Figures in the brackets are the percentages to their respective totals.

Summary

1. Handloom Industry in Cuddapah district is a household industry and consists mostly of small household units having one or two looms each.
2. Productivity is related to the age of the weaver. The quantity produced by him and quality of cloth will not be the same all through his life. After certain age the weaver can not even operate the loom. In the survey it was noticed that the maximum weaving capacity of the weaver is for a period of not more than 60 years Weaving of Coarse varieties seems to make the retire early.
3. All the looms in Cuddapah District belong to the category of Fly-shuttle pit looms. Throw Shuttle pit looms came to be replaced from 1950 onwards. Throw shuttle looms were in use upto 1965 in Western Cuddapah and upto 1970 in Eastern Cuddapah.
4. It was found that on an average, 5 households, had a total of 7 looms in Western Cuddapah and 6 looms in Eastern Cuddapah. Idle looms were also in existence. The percentage of idle looms in different regions of ranges between 13 to 21. Replacement outdated looms under modernisation scheme, giving up weaving activity by the artisans with adequate educational background, and the retirement of the weaver because of old age; have been some of the important reasons for leaving the looms idle.
5. The work place is either part of the residence in or attached to the residence. Weavers have expressed reluctance to change their work place to a seperate premises even if some help is provided, because it would severely restrict the extent of participation of household labour especially of the women-folk in production activities.
6. The important processes involved in this industry are winding of yarn, warping, sizing and weaving. Different processes of production are attended to by the family members, and hired workers and at times by both the groups. Even children take part in different processes involved in cloth making.
7. Handloom Industry in Cuddapah district survives on hereditary basis. Inheritance is the general mode of acquisition of handlooms, and fresh entry into this industry is negligible.
8. The industry does not offer any gainful employment to those employed in the industry. At the same time the existing weavers cannot leave the industry, because of the absence of alternate employment opportunities. Hence, efforts are being made seriously by the weaving households to divert their children to

other fields of activity (in fields like education, business, employment etc.,) to enable them to improve their living conditions.

9. The important raw materials used in the handloom industry of Cuddapah are: Cotton Yarn, Silk and Zari. Of all the raw materials required, Cotton yarn is the most important. Yarn of lower Counts is used in Western Cuddapah, while yarn of higher Counts only is used in the Eastern Cuddapah.
10. Pure Zari Sarees, Janata Sarees, Janata Dhoties, Resham Cloth, Shirting and Lungis are the important varieties produced in Cuddapah district. All the looms in Eastern Cuddapah are producing only pure Zari Sarees, and hence the industry in this zone is relatively Capital intensive.
11. Weavers of Cuddapah district can be classified into four broad categories. They are: (1) Weavers working for the Master Weavers; (2) Weavers working for the Cooperative Sector; (3) Independent workers not working for any one; (4) Weavers working for the Corporate Sector. The Co-operative organisation in the Western zone and the Master Weaver in Eastern zone are dominating the scene of the handloom industry in the district. Weavers have been some times found to be working for more than one organisation.
12. Caste affiliation is very much prevalent in the industry. Padmasale, Devanga and Thogata Communities are the important traditional weaving communities in Cuddapah district. Non-weaving communities viz., Muslims and Scheduled Castes are also involved in this industry.
13. Weavers have the tradition of observing important public (Govt.) holidays in addition to abstaining from work. Most of the weavers in Western Cuddapah do not observe public holidays, but unlike this, in the Eastern Cuddapah weavers do observe certain days as public holidays. The most important among them is Amavasya day (New Moon).

REFERENCES

1. G.Subramanyam, 'A Survey of Handloom Weavers in East Godavari District'. *Chenetha*, a monthly journal, May 1982, p. 4.
2. Cuddapah District Gazetteer, 1967, p. 367.
3. The Fact Finding Committee Report, Govt. of India, 1942, p. 32.
4. *Ibid.*, p. 31.

5. Fact Finding Committee, *Op.cit.,* p. 33
6. Patel, R.B. Handloom Industry in India 1906, p. 31.
7. Kulkarni.R.S., Khadi Gramodyog, July 1978, p. 508.
8. Looms remain idle permanently are considered as idle looms. Looms which lie idle occasionally are not idle looms.
9. Report of the Fact Finding Committee, *op.cit.,* p.29.
10. The Report of the Textile Enquiry Report, Govt. of India, 1952, p. 123.
11. Yvonne J.Arterburn 'The Loom of Interdependence', Hindustan Publishing Corporation (India), 1982, p. 41.
12. Angadi—Handloom Industry in Karnataka, Ph.D Thesis, p. 100
13. O.Sadasiva Rao., Chenetha, Dt.29/7/91.
14. R.G.Kakade., A Socio-economic Survey of Weaving Communities in Sholapur, p. 24.
15. Encyclopaedia of Britanica 23 Volume, p. 1968.
16. Peg warping: Only one thread is warped at a time in case of peg warping. On warping machine 40 threads are warped at a time.
17. Kakade R.G., Socio-economic Survey of Weaving Communities In Sholapur, p. 158.
18. Textile Enquiry Committee Report, *op.cit.,* p. 11.
19. Encyclopaedia of Britannica 23 V., p. 1968.
20. Idem.
21. M.P. Gandhi 'The Indian Cotton Textile Industry—Its Past, Present and Future', The Book Company Limited, Calcutta, 1930, p. 7.
22. Kakade—*Op.cit.,* p. 139.
23. Yvonne J.Arterburn, 'The Loom of Interdependence', Hindustan Publishing Corporation (India), 1982, pp. 35-36.
24. Kakade, *op.cit.,* p. 23
25. Mahapatro.P.C., Economics of Cotton Handloom Industry—Ashish Publishing House, New Delhi-1986, p. 65.
26. *Ibid.*, p. 66.
27. Surendra, S.T. 'Co-operatives in Andhra Pradesh' An Unpublished Thesis, July 1984, p. 59.
28. Four threads of Zari in the border of the saree is equivalent to one laka.
29. Dr.Satyanarayana, 'A Case Study of Silk Handloom Weaving Industry of Rayadurg, Unpublished Dissertation, July 1982, p. 30.
30. D.R. Gadgil An Evolution of Industries, Oxford University Press 1985, p.189
31. Ansari-Indian Co-operative Review-Jan 1970, pp. 259-64.
32. Dr. B.Sudhakar Rao and Others—'Employment Factor in Handlooms' NIRD, 1986, p.19.
33. Ansari-*Ibid.*, pp. 259-64.

34. D.R.Gadgil., The Industrial Evolution of India in Recent Times, Oxford University Press, 1985, p. 185.
35. The Textile Enquiry Committee, *Op.cit.,* 1952, p. 12.
36. R.G.Kakade, *Op.cit.,* p. 50.
37. At the time of survey it was revealed by the 'Padmasale' community people that 'Moon' will suffer from severe stomachache if the weavers touch the loom on 'Amavasya'. This tradition of observing holiday is passed on from generation to generation.

4

Socio-economic Conditions of Handloom Weavers in Cuddapah District

The involvement of the 'Human factor' and the dependence of millions of people on the handloom industry make it obligatory to preserve and encourage the handloom industry not only in Andhra Pradesh but also throughout the country. Even in the age of machinery handloom has to be protected not for its own sake but for the sake of vast weaving population that depend upon it for their livelihood. A survey of the socio-economic problems of the weavers illustrates the point. The survey helps in understanding the problems of a vital segment of the society in the country. The present chapter attempts to describe the socio-economic conditions of handloom weavers in Cuddapah district of Andhra Pradesh.

Before we go deep into the study, relating to the socio-economic conditions of handloom weavers in Cuddapah district, let us have a look into the profile of the district.

Cuddapah District Profile

Cuddapah district is one of the four districts of Rayalaseema region in Andhra Pradesh. Cuddapah district is situated within the geographical co-ordination of 13°-43° and 15°-14° of northern longitude and 77°-55° and 79° -29° of eastern longitude. The altitude varies from 259' to 3787' above sea level. The district is bounded on north by Kurnool on the south by Chittor, on the west by Anantapur and on the east by Nellore districts. The total geographical area of the district is 15,359 sq.kms., consisting of 980 villages. The total population of the district as per 1991 census is 22.59 lakhs which the rural population accounts for

75.92 per cent and the remaining 24.08 per cent is urban population. The female population is 957 for every 1000 males. The density of population of the district is 147 persons per square kelometre as against the state average of 241 persons per sq.km.

The important soils are black and red. The important economic minerals that occur in the district are 'Asbestos' Barites and lime stone. The total forest area in the district is 5,05,496 hectares forming 32.87 per cent of total geographical area of the district. The important rivers in the district are Pennar, Kundu, Papagni, Chitravathi, Sagileru, Cheyyeru and Pincha. All these rivers are the tributaries of the river Pennar. According to the census of land holdings, in 1980-81, there are about 2.42 lakh land holders operating an area of about 5.01 lakh hectares. The district gets the benefit of both the monsoon periods. The annual normal rainfall of the district is 680.9 mm which is 215 mm less than the state average. The net area sown in the district during 88-89 is 18,29,513 acres which accounts for 57.08 per cent of the total geographical area. The main source of irrigation in the district is ground water exploited through the tube wells and open wells. The total length of the road in the district is 4204 kms out of which 10 kms cement concrete, 78 kms black-top, 2365 kms metalled road and 1871 kms unmettled road.

Caste Affiliation to the Industry

In the olden days the weavers used to supply cloth to the farmers in exchange for the foodgrains. This exchange more often had been a matter of mutual obligation set by the social structure than of economic motivation of making a profit. In course of time, the caste affiliation for the industry took firm roots. This affiliation over time led to a rigid and rather inflexible division and segregation of the spheres of activity by caste categories.[1] Days have changed. Commercialisation has made in roads into the industry. Education is spreading in the villages. Consequently the association between caste and occupation got loosened[2]. It is now found that other non traditional weaving communities like Muslims, Scheduled Castes, and Dudekula also entered into the industry.

In Cuddapah district the weaving activity is, mostly being carried out by the two prominent communities namely 'Padmasale' and 'Thogata'. Of the 215 sample respondents as many as 130 respondents, representing 60.47 per cent belonged to Padmasale, and 61 representing about 28.37 per cent belong to Thogata. The artisans who belonged to Castes such as, Dudekula, Devanga, Muslim and Scheduled Castes constitute the remaining 11.16 per cent of the weavers in the industry.

It is quite clear from the Table 4.1 that 'Padmasale' the dominating weaving community concentrating on the handloom weaving followed by 'Thogata' Community. It may be seen from Table 4.2 that Padmasale concentration is there in the eastern part of the district, while the 'Thogata' concentration is there in the western part of Cuddapah.

Table 4.1 : Castes Involved in the Handloom Industry

Castes	Number of Households	2 as % of Total No. of Households
Padmasale	130	60.47
Thogata	61	28.37
Devanga	14	6.51
Dudekula	4	1.86
Muslim	5	2.33
Scheduled Castes	1	0.46
Total	**215**	**100.00**

Source: Field Survey Data.

As is observed from the Table 4.2 weaving is largely a caste-based profession of 'Sale' Community in Cuddapah district. As a whole,

Table 4.2 : Caste Composition of Weaving Households

Regions	Category of Caste						
	Dudekula	Padmasale	Thogata	Devanga	Muslims	Scheduled Caste	Total
West rural	3 (6.0)	6 (12.0)	24 (48.0)	14 (28.0)	2 (4.0)	1 (2.0)	50 (100.0)
West urban	1 (1.33)	34 (45.33)	37 (49.33)	—	3 (4.0)	—	75 (100.0)
Total west	4 (3.20)	40 (32.0)	61 (48.8)	14 (11.2)	5 (4.0)	1 (0.8)	125 (100.0)
East rural	—	35 (100.0)	—	—	—	—	35 (100.0)
East urban	—	55 (100.0)	—	—	—	—	55 (100.0)
Total east	—	90 (100.0)	—	—	—	—	90 (100.0)
Total	**4 (1.86)**	**130 (60.47)**	**61 (28.37)**	**14 (6.51)**	**5 (2.33)**	**1 (0.46)**	**215 (100.0)**

Source : Field Survey Data.
Figures in brackets are percentages to their respective totals.

'Padmasale' caste dominates among all other weaving communities[3]. Strangely, members of a family that belonged to Scheduled Caste in the western part of the district also took up weaving as their profession.

Age of Population

The Table 4.3 shows that females, in the age group of 0 to 5 years, out number the males of the same age group. Whil the reverae in trend is observed in the case of males of the age group of 5 to 10 years. Except in the age group of 40-50 years and 50-60 years, in all other age groups men outnumber female population.

Table 4.3 : Members of Sample Families Classified According To Age

Age (in Years)	Male	Female	Total
0 – 5	41	48	89
5 – 10	64	54	118
10 – 15	52	45	97
15 – 20	49	52	101
20 – 30	115	106	221
30 – 40	74	69	143
40 – 50	53	54	107
50 – 60	36	38	74
60 and above	41	35	76
Total	**525 (51.17)**	**501 (48.83)**	**1026 (100.0)**

Source: Field Survey Data.

Age of Weavers

It may be observed from Table 4.4 that one fourth of the weavers are in the age group of 15-20 years. And nearly 50 per cent of the weavers fall in the age group of 20-40 years. It is clear from the table that middle aged involved in are weaving activity. Of the total 286 weavers that belongs to 215 households or 81.47 per cent are men, and the remaining are women. On the whole, the women weavers are significantly less in number. The participation of women workers in western Cuddapah is relatively more when compared to their counterparts in the eastern zone of Cuddapah.

Table 4.4 : Age-wise Distribution of Weavers In Cuddapah

Age (in Years)	Male	Female	Total	Percentage
10 – 15	22	8	30	10.49
15 – 20	53	15	68	23.78
20 – 40	117	23	140	48.95
40 – 60	28	7	35	12.24
Above 60	13	—	13	4.54
Total	**233 (81.47)**	**53 (18.53)**	**286 (100.0)**	**100.0**

Source: Field Survey Data.

Classification of Families According to Their Size

As shown in Table 4.5 (*See on next page*) the average size of a sample household is 4.77, which is less than the average size of households which belonged to Muslim, Padmasale and Dudekula communities. Thogata, Devanga and Scheduled Castes households have nuclear families as per the survey.

The average size of Padmasale families was about 5.42 and in the case of Dudekula the average was 5.0. The average size of the Muslim family was 5.8, higher by 1.03, than the average and largest in the sample. It means that 26 per cent of the families had less than 4.77 members each and the remaining 74 per cent had more than 4.77 members.

One may here try to correlate (*See Table 4.6 on page 130*) the size of the family with the income of the family. Here we find that the increase in the size of the family the average income level of the individual members also has increased. Since a handloom product is a function of the Co-operation among several individuals larger sized families have the opportunity to produce larger number of pieces per capita than in the case of smaller sized families i.e., the productivity of the weaver in large sized families is more an the productivity of weaver in smaller sized families.

Sex Composition

The distribution of population of households in different ares of Cuddapah district is presented in Tables 4.7A and 4.7B (*See on pages 131 and 132*). The average number of boys (below 16 years of age), per household is one in the western Cuddapah where as it is less than one in the eastern Cuddapah. However, 10 households have 10 boys in the western zone and 9 boys in the eastern zone of Cuddapah district. The average number of girls per household in both the western and eastern Cuddapah is not even one each.

Table 4.5 : Families Classified According to Number of Members

Members in the Family	Number of Families according to Castes						Total Families
	Padraasale	Dudekula	Thogata	Devanga	Muslim	Scheduled Caste	
1 Member	5	—	3	2	—	—	10
2 Members	3	—	20	—	—	—	23
3 Members	13	1	13	2	—	—	29
4 Members	33	—	11	3	1	1	49
5 Members	15	1	7	7	2	—	32
6 Members	17	2	3	—	—	—	22
7 Members	18	—	2	—	1	—	21
8 Members	17	—	1	—	1	—	19
9 Members	7	—	—	—	—	—	7
10 Members	1	—	—	—	—	—	2
Above 10	1	—	1	—	—	—	1
Total Families	130	4	61	14	5	1	215
Total Population:	705 (68.7)	20 (1.95)	212 (20.66)	55 (5.4)	29 (2.83)	4 (0.39)	1026 (100.0)
Average Population per Household:	5.42	5.0	3.48	3.93	5.8	4.0	4.77

Source: Field Survey data.
Figures in brackets are percentages to their respective totals.

The average size of children per household for the western part of Cuddapah and for the district as a whole is 1.87.

Table 4.6 : Number of Members in the Family and the Income of the Family

Members in the Family	Total Families	Total income of the families	Average income of the families
1 Member	10	77219	7722.00
2 Members	23	178270	7751.00
3 Members	29	228636	7884.00
4 Members	49	394936	8060.00
5 Members	32	255320	7979.00
6 Members	22	181180	8235.00
7 Members	21	177676	8461.00
8 Members	19	161552	8503.00
9 Members	7	69908	9987.00
10 Members	2	21824	10912.00
Above 10	1	12229	12229.00

Source: Field Survey data.

The Value of Correlation between total families (r) = 0.7464 and average income of the families.

Sex ratio is defined as a number of females per thousand male population. The sex ratio in Cuddapah district has been always adverse to women as has been the case in most of the districts in the state and in the country as a whole i.e. the number of women per thousand men has always been less than one thousand. In the sample selected, the sex ratio is 950 as against the district figure of 957 for the district on the whole[4].

The adult population in the sample constitutes the 'work force' of the handloom industry. The distribution of adult population per household is 3.0 in the western Cuddapah and less than 3 in the eastern Cuddapah.

As is already pointed out that the participation of adult population is significant in the handloom industry. The number of adult persons in the family decides the number of looms in the household. In order to study the strength of relationship between the number of adults per household and the number of looms the value of Co-efficient of Correlation is calculated and shown in Table 4.8 (*See on page 133*). The value of coefficient of Correlation (r = 0.9996) implies the fact that the two variables are perfectly Correlated and the relationship is positive.

Table 4.7A : Sex Composition and Sex Ratio in Different Areas of the Sample

Regions	Number of households	CHILDREN (Below 18 Years)						ADULTS (Above 18 Years)			
		Boys		Girls		Total		Men		Women	
		Number	Average per household	Number	Average per household	Number	Average per household	Number	Average per household	Number	Average per household
West Rural	50	59 (64.0)	1.18	33 (36.0)	0.66	92 (100.0)	1.84	78 (50.0)	1.56	77 (50.0)	1.54
West Urban	75	67 (47.0)	0.89	75 (53.0)	1.00	142 (100.0)	1.89	115 (52.0)	1.53	106 (48.0)	1.41
Total West	125	126 (54.0)	1.00	108 (46.0)	0.86	234 (100.0)	1.87	193 (51.0)	1.54	183 (49.0)	1.46
East Rural	35	29 (51.0)	0.83	28 (49.0)	0.80	57 (100.0)	1.63	48 (51.0)	1.37	46 (49.0)	1.31
East Urban	55	51 (46.0)	0.93	61 (54.0)	1.11	112 (100.0)	2.04	78 (52.0)	1.42	73 (48.0)	1.33
Total East	90	80 (47.0)	0.89	89 (53.0)	0.99	169 (100.0)	1.88	126 (51.0)	1.40	119 (49.0)	1.32
Total	**215**	**206 (51.0)**	**0.96**	**197 (49.0)**	**0.92**	**403 (100.0)**	**1.87**	**319 (51.0)**	**1.48**	**302 (49.0)**	**1.40**

Source: Field Survey Data.
Figures in brackets are percentages to their respective totals.

Table 4.7B : Sex Composition and Sex Ratio in Different Areas of the Sample

Region	Adults		Total Population (Children & Adults)						Total females for every 1000 males
	Total		Male		Female		Total		
	Number	Average	Number	Average	Number	Average	Number	Average	
West Rural	155	3.10	137 (55.0)	2.74	110 (45.0)	2.20	247 (100.0)	4.94	803
West Urban	221	2.95	182 (55.0)	2.43	181 (50.0)	2.41	363 (100.0)	4.84	995
Total West	376	3.01	319 (52.0)	2.55	291 (48.0)	2.33	610 (100.0)	4.88	912
East Rural	94	2.69	77 (51.0)	2.20	74 (49.0)	2.11	151 (100.0)	4.31	961
East Urban	151	2.75	129 (49.0)	2.35	134 (51.0)	2.44	263 (100.0)	4.78	1039
Total East	245	2.72	206 (50.0)	2.29	208 (50.0)	2.31	414 (100.0)	4.60	1010
Grand Total	**621**	**2.89**	**525 (51.0)**	**2.44**	**499 (49.0)**	**2.32**	**1024 (100.0)**	**4.76**	**951**

Source: Field Survey Data.

Figures in brackets are percentages to their respective totals

Table 4.8 : Details of Adult Population and Number of Looms in the Household

Regions	Number of Households	Total Looms	Total Adults	Looms per Household(Y)	No. of Adults per Household(X)	No. of Adults per Loom
West Rural	50	72	155	1.44	3.10	2.15
West Urban	75	99	221	1.32	2.95	2.23
Total West	125	171	376	1.37	3.01	2.20
East Rural	35	44	94	1.26	2.69	2.14
East Urban	55	71	151	1.29	2.75	2.13
Total East	90	115	245	1.28	2.72	2.13
Grand Total	**215**	**2186**	**621**	**1.33**	**2.89**	**2.17**

Source: Field Survey Data.

Figures in brackets are percentages to their respective totals

The Value of Co-efficient of

Correlation between X & Y (r) = 0.9996

Regression of Y on X Y = 0. 3371 + 0.3495(X)

The regression equation of $Y = 0.3371 \pm 0.3495(x)$ explains that about 2 adults on an average bring one additional loom into operation.

Literacy

Data pertaining to literacy of the children and adults are shown in Tables 4.9A, 4.9B, 4.9C (See on pages 135, 136 and 137. Irrespective of age and sex, 458 out of 920 persons, or about 50 per cent of the population of over 5 years of age, were illiterate and only 462 persons or 50 per cent of the population were literates. The level of education that they possess enables them to write letters to friends and relatives besides carrying on correspondence with the parties. Of the 462 literates, 79 per cent had primary level education, 12.55 per cent had secondary level education, 4.55 per cent had education upto Intermediate level, 1.95 per cent had degree level education, 0.65 per cent are post-graduates and the remaining 1.30 per cent had Technical education.

Among the females of 5 years of age and above only 30 per cent have been recorded as literate as against 70 per cent among males of the corresponding age. It is noticed that 41 per cent of the total adult men were illiterates, as against 83 per cent among women. 35 per cent men adults were illiterate in western Cuddapah as against 50 per cent in eastern Cuddapah. It is 78 per cent in case of women in western Cuddapah as against 91 per cent in eastern zone.

In case of Children, 9.3 per cent of boys were illiterate as against 42.7 per cent for girls. The percentage of illiteracy for boys in western Cuddapah was 6 as against 10 in eastern Cuddapah. For girls it was 39 per cent in western Cuddapah, as against 19 per cent in eastern Cuddapah. The percentage of illiterates in Cuddapah district as a whole was 58.48 per cent in total, 45.78 per cent in case of men and 71.73 per cent in case of women according to 1991 census[5].

It is clear from Tables 4.9A, 4.9B and 4.9C that adult illiteracy is more in eastern Cuddapah than in western Cuddapah. Contrary to this, illiteracy among children is more in western Cuddapah than in eastern Cuddapah. But in all the areas, irrespective of age, the female illiteracy is significantly more than the male illiteracy.

Educational Background of the Heads of the Households

Information relating to the educational background of the heads of the household is presented in Table 4.10 (*See on page 138*). Out of 215 heads of the households, 107 heads or 49.77 per cent were illiterate 75 heads or 45 per cent had primary level of education; 31 heads or 14.42 per cent

Table 4.9A : Educational Status of Children of the Sample Households

Levels of Exucation	West Rural(150)			West Urban(75)			Total West (125)			East Rural (35)			East Uraban (55)			Total East (90)			Grand Total (215)		
	Boys	Girls	Total	Boys	Girls	Total	Boys	Girls	Total	Boys	Girls	Total	Boys	Girls	Total	Boys	Girls	Total	Boys	Girls	Total
Not Yet Admitted	15 (25)	7 (21)	22 (24)	13 (19)	15 (20)	28 (20)	28 (22)	22 (20)	15 (21)	10 (35)	14 (50)	24 (42)	7 (23)	23 (77)	30 (100)	17 (21)	37 (42)	54 (32)	45 (32)	59 (30)	104 (26)
Illiterate	4 (7)	11 (33)	15 (16)	7 (11)	27 (36)	34 (24)	7 (6)	42 (39)	49 (21)	2 (7)	4 (14)	6 (11)	6 (32)	13 (68)	19 (100)	8 (10)	17 (19)	25 (9)* (15)	15 (43)* (7)	59 (25)* (30)	74 (18)
Primary	26 (44)	12 (36)	38 (41)	41 (62)	33 (44)	74 (52)	71 (56)	41 (38)	112 (48)	11 (38)	9 (32)	20 (55)	33 (58)	24 (42)	57 (100)	44 (55)	33 (37)	77 (46)	116 (56)	74 (38)	189 (47)
SSC	9 (15)	2 (6)	11 (12)	6 (9)	—	6 (4)	15 (12)	2 (2)	17 (7)	4 (14)	1 (4)	5 (9)	—	1 (100)	1 (100)	4 (5)	2 (2)	6 (4)	19 (9)	4 (2)	23 (6)
Intermediate	3 (5)	1 (3)	4 (5)	—	—	—	3 (3)	1 (1)	4 (2)	2 (7)	—	2 (4)	3 (100)	—	3 (100)	5 (6)	—	5 (3)	8 (4)	1 (1)	9 (2)
Degree	1 (2)	— —	1 (1)	—	—	—	1 (1)	—	1 (1)	—	—	—	2 (100)	—	2 (100)	2 (3)	—	2 (2)	3 (2)	— —	3 (1)
Post Graduation	—	—	—	—	—	—	—	—	—	—	—	—	—	—	—	—	—	—	—	—	—
Technical	1	—	1	—	—	—	1	—	1	—	—	—	—	—	—	—	—	—	1	—	1
Total	**59** (100)	**33** (100)	**92** (100)	**67** (100)	**75** (100)	**142** (100)	**126** (100)	**108** (100)	**234** (100)	**29** (100)	**28** (100)	**57** (100)	**51** (100)	**61** (100)	**112** (100)	**80** (100)	**89** (100)	**169** (100)	**206** (100)	**197** (100)	**403** (100)

Source: Field Survey data.

* Percentage of illiteracy after ignoring the number not yet admitted to the school.

** Belongs to Children Below 5 years only.

Table 4.9B : Educational Status of Adult Population of Weavers in Cuddapah District

Levels of Exucation	West Rural(150)			West Urban(75)			Total West (125)			East Rural (35)			East Uraban (55)			Total East (90)			Grand Total (215)		
	Men	Women	Total	Men	Women	Total	Men	Women	Total	Men	Women	Total	Men	Women	Total	Men	Women	Total	Men	Women	Total
Illiterate	26 (33)	58 (75)	84 (54)	42 (36)	86 (81)	128 (57)	68 (35)	144 (78)	212 (56)	22 (45)	41 (89)	63 (67)	39 (50)	70 (95)	109 (72)	63 (50)	109 (91)	172 (70)	131 (41)	253 (83)	384 (61)
Primary	30 (38)	16 (21)	26 (30)	52 (45)	20 (19)	72 (33)	82 (42)	36 (20)	118 (31)	22 (46)	5 (11)	27 (29)	28 (36)	3 (4)	31 (20)	38 (38)	10 (9)	58 (24)	130 (41)	46 (15)	176 (28)
SSC	10 (13)	2 (3)	12 (8)	14 (12)	—	14 (6)	24 (12)	2 (1)	26 (7)	4 (8)	—	4 (4)	5 (6)	—	5 (3)	9 (7)	—	9 (4)	33 (10)	2 (0.7)	35 (6)
Intermediate	2 (3)	1 (1)	3 (2)	7 (6)	—	7 (3)	9 (5)	1 (0.6)	10 (3)	—	—	—	2 (3)	—	2 (1)	2 (2)	—	2 (1)	11 (4)	1 (0.3)	12 (2)
Degree	4 (5)	— —	4 (3)	—	—	—	4 (3)	—	4 (2)	—	—	—	2 (3)	—	2 (1)	2 (2)	—	2 (1)	6 (2)	—	6 (1)
Post-Graduation	1 (1)	—	1 (1)	—	—	—	1 (0.52)	1 (0.27)	—	—	—	—	2 (2.6)	—	2 (1.32)	2 (1.6)	—	2 (0.82)	3 (0.94)	—	3 (0.48)
Technical	5 (6.4)	—	5 (3.23)	—	—	—	5 (2.59)	—	5 (1.33)	—	—	—	—	—	—	—	—	—	5 (1.57)	—	5 (0.81)
Total	**78** (100)	**77** (100)	**155** (100)	**115** (100)	**106** (100)	**221** (100)	**193** (100)	**183** (100)	**376** (100)	**48** (100)	**46** (100)	**94** (100)	**78** (100)	**73** (100)	**151** (100)	**126** (100)	**119** (100)	**245** (100)	**319** (100)	**302** (100)	**621** (100)

Source: Field Survey data.

Figures in brackets are percentages to their respective totals.

Table 4.9C : Educational Status of Total Population of Weavers in Cuddapah District

Levels of Exucation	West Rural(50)			West Urban(75)			T otal West (125)			East Rural (35)			East Uraban (55)			Total East (90)			Grand Total (215)		
	Men	Women	Total	Men	Women	Total	Men	Women	Total	Men	Women	Total	Men	Women	Total	Men	Women	Total	Men	Women	Total
Not Yet** Admitted	15 (11)	7 (6)	22 (9)	13 (7)	15 (8)	28 (8)	28 (9)	22 (8)	50 (8)	10 (13)	14 (19)	24 (16)	7 (5)	23 (17)	30 (11)	17 (8)	37 (18)	54 (13)	45 (9) (31)*	59 (12) (70)*	104 (10) (50)*
Illiterate	30 (22)	69 (63)	99 (40)	49 (27)	113 (62)	162 (45)	79 (25)	182 (63)	261 (43)	24 (31)	45 (61)	69 (46)	45 (35)	83 (62)	128 (49)	69 (34)	128 (62)	197 (48)	148 (28)	310 (62)	458 (45)
Primary	56 (41)	28 (26)	84 (34)	93 (51)	53 (29)	146 (40)	149 (47)	81 (24)	230 (38)	33 (43)	14 (19)	47 (31)	61 (47)	27 (20)	88 (34)	94 (46)	41 (20)	135 (33)	243 (46)	122 (25)	365 (36)
S3C	19 (14)	4 (4)	23 (9)	20 (11)	—	20 (6)	39 (12)	4 (1)	43 (7)	8 (10)	1 (1)	9 (6)	5 (4)	1 (1)	6 (2)	13 (6)	2 (1)	15 (4)	52 (10)	6 (1)	58 (6)
Intermediate	5 (4)	2 (2)	7 (3)	7 (4)	—	7 (2)	12 (4)	2 (1)	14 (2)	2 (3)	—	2 (1)	5 (4)	—	5 (2)	7 (3)	—	7 (2)	19 (4)	2 (0.4)	21 (2.1)
Degree	5 (4)	—	5 (2)	—	—	—	5 (2)	—	5 (1)	—	—	—	4 (3)	—	4 (2)	4 (2)	—	4 (1)	9 (2)	—	9 (1)
Post-Graduation	1 (1)	—	1 (0.4)	—	—	—	1 (0.31)	—	1 (0.16)	—	—	—	2 (1.6)	—	2 (0.76)	2 (0.97)	— —	2 (0.48)	3 (0.6)	— —	3 (0.3)
Technical	6	—	6	—	—	—	6	—	6	—	—	—	—	—	—	—	—	—	6 (1.14)	— (0.6)	6
Total	137 (100)	110 (100)	247 (100)	182 (100)	181 (100)	363 (100)	319 (100)	291 (100)	610 (100)	77 (100)	74 (100)	151 (100)	129 (100)	134 (100)	263 (100)	206 (100)	208 (100)	414 (100)	525 (100)	499 (100)	1024 (100)

Source: Field Survey Data.

* Percentage of illiteracy after ignoring the number not yet admitted to the school.

** Belongs to Children Below 5 years only.

had Secondary education and the remaining 2 heads of households or 0.93 per cent had technical qualification.

From the Table 4.10 we can understand that around 50 per cent of the heads of the households were illiterates in the district as a whole.

Table 4.10. Educational Background of the Head of the Household

Regions	Literacy Levels				
	Illiterate	Primary	SSC	Technical	Total
West Rural	18 (36.0)	28 (50.0)	4 (14.0)	—	50 (100.0)
West Urban	43 (57.0)	26 (35.0)	4 (5.0)	2 (3.0)	75 (100.0)
Total West	61 (49.0)	54 (43.0)	8 (6.0)	2 (2.0)	125 (100.0)
East Rural	18 (51.0)	11 (31.0)	6 (18.0)	—	35 (100.0)
East Urban	28 (51.0)	10 (18.0)	17 (31.0)	—	55 (100.0)
Total East	46 (51.0)	21 (23.0)	23 (26.0)	—	90 (100.0)
Grand Total	**107 (49.77)**	**75 (44.88)**	**31 (14.42)**	**2 (0.93)**	**215 (100.0)**

Source: Field Survey Data.

Figures in brackets are percentages to their respective totals

Civil Conditions

Tables 4.11-A & 4.11-B reveal a number of interesting facts. Firstly in the group of non-adults, i.e., between 10-15 years of age, while all the males were unmarried, the percentage of unmarried females was 72 per cent. This percentage was the highest in eastern Cuddapah at 74.60 per cent and lowest in western Cuddapah at 69.09 per cent. No female in this group was recorded as a widow. In the western Cuddapah among illiterate weaver families 33 per cent of girls were married before they attained the age of 15. Among adults of 20 years, however, 27 per cent of men and 5 per cent of women were unmarried. Here again, 72 per cent of women were married and the rest were widowed.

The corresponding figures for western and eastern Cuddapah were 70 per cent and 75 per cent respectively. As regards widows, western Cuddapah stood at the top with 26 per cent, eastern Cuddapah at

Table 4.11A : Educational Status of Adult Population of Weavers in Cuddapah District

Age Group	Total								Eastern Cuddapah							
	Male				Female				Male				Female			
	Married	Unmarried	Widower	Total	Married	Unmarried	Widow	Total	Married	Unmarried	Widower	Total	Married	Unmarried	Widow	Total
10 to 15 years	—	70	—	70	17	38	—	55	—	54	—	54	16	47	—	63
Percentage	—	100.0	—	100.0	30.9	69.09	—	100	—	100	—	100	25.4	74.6	—	100
15 years & above	77	28	8	113	102	5	38	145	45	18	6	69	46	5	10	61
Percentage	68.14	24.78	7.08	100	70.34	3.45	26.21	100	65.2	27.3	8.71	100	75.41	8.20	16.39	100
Total	**77**	**98**	**8**	**183**	**119**	**43**	**38**	**200**	**45**	**72**	**6**	**123**	**62**	**52**	**10**	**124**
Percentage	**42.08**	**53.55**	**4.37**	**100**	**59.5**	**21.5**	**19.0**	**100**	**36.5**	**958.54**	**4.87**	**100**	**50.0**	**41.9**	**8.1**	**100**

Source : Field Survey Data

Table 4.11.B : Members of Sample Families Classified According to Marital Conditions

Age	Total							
	Male				Female			
	Married	Unmarried	Widower	Total	Married	Unmarried	Widow	Total
10 to 15 years	—	124	—	124	33	85	—	118
Percentage	—	100	—	100	27.97	72.03	—	100
15 years & above	122	46	14	182	148	10	48	206
Percentage	67.03	25.27	7.70	100	71.84	4.85	23.31	100
Total	**122**	**170**	**14**	**306**	**181**	**95**	**48**	**324**
Percentage	**39.87**	**55.56**	**4.57**	**100**	**55.86**	**29.33**	**14.81**	**100**

Source : Field Survey Data.

16 per cent. Comparatively, there were fewer widowers than widows in every class. Further, out of the total 265 unmarried persons, 170 persons or 64 per cent were males and 95 or 46 per cent were females. But they did not belong to the same age group. Most of the unmarried males were adults.

In the case of widowed persons, however, 14 persons or 23 per cent were males and the remaining 48 members or 77 per cent were females. Out of 630 total members, in the age group of above 10 years, 303 or 48 per cent were married; 265 or 42 per cent were unmarried, and the remaining 14 persons or 2 per cent were widowers; and 48 persons or 8 per cent were widows.

Age of the Couple When Married

The composition of married couples according to their age at the time of their marriage is presented in Table 4.12 (*See on next page*). At the age of 20 years or above 91 per cent of the men were married and the remaining before 20 years of age. The percentage of men married below 20 years of age is more in rural areas (14%) than in urban areas (2%) of western Cuddapah. Among the total male population, the average of men at the time of marriage is 22.3 years. The median age group work out to 20 to 25 years.

It may be seen from the table that about 96 per cent of women had 15 years of age or above, at the time of their marriage. Only 9 women or 4 per cent, had the age of below 15 years at the time of their marriage. The percentage of women married below 15 years is relatively more in the rural areas of western Cuddapah. No woman in urban areas of eastern Cuddapah got married below 15 years of age. Only 10 women or 5 per cent got married at the age of over and above 20 years. The percentage of women married after 20 years of age is more in rural areas of western Cuddapah (8%) and less in urban areas of eastern Cuddapah (2%). The average age of marriage for women is 17.5 years. The median age group work out to 15 to 20 years.

Composition of Households as per the Couple Size

Contrary to the expectation of their parents, Sons get separated from their parents and form a new family for themselves after the marriage. A few couples however do not get separated from their joint families even after marriage. Marriages, death of the parents, anticipated family burdens, lack of adequate housing facilities are some of the reasons for the break up of the joint families.

Table 4.13 (*See on page 143*) shows that 165 households out of 215 households or 77 per cent had only one couple in the house and the

Table 4.12 : Age-wise Distribution of Couple at the Time of Their Marriage

Regions	Age groups of Males at the time of their Marriage					Age group of Females at the time of their Marriage				
	Below 20	20-25	Above Years	Total years	Average Age 25 Years	Below 20	20-25	Above years	Total	Average Age at Marriage
West Rural	5 (10.0)	44 (88.0)	1 (2.0)	50 (100.0)	22.1	4 (8.0)	42 (84.0)	4 (8.0)	50 (100.0)	17.5
West Urban	9 (13.0)	55 (77.0)	7 (10.0)	71 (100.0)	22.4	3 (4.0)	64 (90.0)	4 (6.0)	71 (100.0)	17.6
Total West	14 (12.0)	99 (82.0)	8 (6.0)	121 (100.0)	22.3	7 (6.0)	106 (88.0)	8 (6.0)	121 (100.0)	17.5
East Rural	5 (14.0)	30 (87.0)	0	35 (100.0)	21.8	2 (6.0)	32 (91.0)	1 (3.0)	35 (100.0)	17.4
East Urban	1 (2.0)	52 (95.0)	2 (3.0)	55 (100.0)	22.6	0	54 (98.0)	1 (2.0)	55 (100.0)	17.6
Total East	6 (7.0)	82 (91.0)	2 (2.0)	90 (100.0)	22.3	2 (2.0)	86 (96.0)	2 (2.0)	90 (100.0)	17.5
Grand Total	**20 (9.0)**	**181 (86.0)**	**10 (5.0)**	**211 (100.0)**	**22.3**	**9 (4.0)**	**192 (91.0)**	**10 (5.0)**	**211 (100.0)**	**17.5**

Source : Field Survey Data.

Figures in brackets are percentages to their respective totals.

Table 4.13 : Distribution of Households as per the Couple Size

Regions	Total No. of Household holds.	Number of couples in the households				Total No. of couples	Couple per Houawhols
		Zero	One	Two	Three		
West Rural	50 (100.0)	4 (8.0)	35 (70.0)	8 (16.0)	3 (6.0)	60	1.20
West Urban	75 (100.0)	7 (9.0)	53 (71.0)	11 (15.0)	4 (5.0)	87	1. 16
Total West	125 (100.0)	11 (9.0)	88 (70.0)	19 (15.0)	7 (6.0)	147	1. 18
East Rural	35 (100.0)	1 (3.0)	33 (94.0)	1 (3.0)	—	35	1.00
East Urban	55 (100.0)	3 (5.0)	44 (80.0)	6 (11.0)	2 (4.0)	62	1.13
Total East	90 (100.0)	4 (4.0)	77 (86.0)	7 (8.0)	2 (2.0)	97	1.08
Grand Total	**215 (100.0)**	**15 (7.0)**	**165 (77.0)**	**26 (12.0)**	**9 (4.0)**	**244**	**1. 14**

Source: Field Survey Data.

Figures in brackets are percentages to their respective totals.

remaining 26 households or 12 per cent had two couples each and only 9 households or 4 per cent had three couples each. The situation was same both in the western zone and eastern zone of Cuddapah and in the rural and urban areas also. Yet the average number of couples per household is a little more in the western Cuddapah (1.18) than in the eastern Cuddapah (1.08). For every 100 households in western Cuddapah there were 118 couples, whereas in eastern Cuddapah it was 108 couples. The attitude of the married couple in eastern Cuddapah appears to be more in favour of small or nuclear family.

Marriage among Close Relatives

Weavers have a tradition of marrying among their own relatives. They marry others, only when they do not have suitable matches among their relatives. Table 4.14 (*See on next page*) shows that 91 out of 244 couples interviewed (37 per cent) were married with in their close relatives, and the remaining 63 per cent had married new persons. The percentage of marriages among close relatives is more (45%) in the rural areas of western Cuddapah than in urban areas of eastern Cuddapah (32%).

Marrying the daughter of Father's sister is a more common practice (35%) than the daughter of mother's brother (27%), Sisters' Daughters (27%) and other relatives (10%).

Break-up of the Joint Family

As already stated weavers get themselves separated from the joint families usually after marriage. Of the sample size of 215 households 165 households or 68 per cent got separated after marriage and the rest of households 79 or 32 per cent did not continue as the members of the joint family. The percentage of newly married couples living with the joint families is more in western Cuddapah than in eastern Cuddapah.

Like all others, the weavers, also, think that there is no need to get themselves separated from the parents, if they have no brothers and sisters.

We may now look at the duration of the joint families. Nearly 153 families or 93 per cent got divided from the joint families with in 5 years of their married life. Only 5 per cent of married couple lived within the joint families for 5 to 10 years, and the remaining 2 per cent for about 10 years or above. The situation is almost same in all the regions of Cuddapah district.

It may be noted that the weavers do not have generally immovable properties like lands and building. The major part of the property of the weaver is his loom and some accessories. So, division from the joint family is very easy in case of weavers and it can be done over night.

Table 4.14 : Married Couples—type of Relationship Before Marriage

Regions	Number of Households	Total Number of Couples	Marriage with		Type of Relationship in case of marriage among relatives			
			New Persons	Relatives	MBD	FSD	SD	Others
West Rural	50	60 (100.0)	33 (55.0)	27 (45.0)	8 (30.0)	13 (48.0)	5 (19.0)	1 (4.0)
West Urban	75	87 (100.0)	57 (66.0)	30 (34.0)	7 (23.0)	7 (23.0)	11 (37.0)	5 (17.0)
Total West	125	147 (100.0)	90 (61.0)	57 (39.0)	15 (26.0)	20 (35.0)	16 (28.0)	6 (11.0)
East Rural	35	35 (100.0)	21 (60.0)	14 (40.0)	6 (43.0)	5 (36.0)	3 (21.0)	0
East Urban	55	62 (100.0)	42 (68.0)	20 (32.0)	4 (20.0)	7 (35.0)	6 (30.0)	3 (15.0)
Total East	90	97 (100.0)	63 (65.0)	34 (35.0)	10 (29.0)	12 (35.0)	9 (26.0)	3 (9.0)
Grand Total	**215**	**244 (100.0)**	**153 (63.0)**	**91 (37.0)**	**25 (27.0)**	**32 (35.0)**	**25 (27.0)**	**9 (10.0)**

Source : Field Survey data.

Figures in brackets are percentages to their respective totals.

FIBD = Daughter of Mother's Brother.

FSD = Daughter of Father's Sister.

FSD = Sister's Daughter.

Table 4.15 : Area-wise Distribution of Joint Family Households and Duration of Living Together

Regions	Number of Households holds	Total Number of Couples	No. of Couples sepered from joint families after Marriage	No. of Couples living in the joint family even after marriage	Duration of the joint family			Average size of the joint family	S.D	C.V
					0-5	5-10	above 10			
West Rural	50 (100.0)	60 (58.0)	35 (42.0)	25 (86.0)	30 (11.0)	4 (1.0)	1	3.36	4.03	119.90
West Urban	75	87 (100.0)	53 (61.0)	34 (39.0)	52 (98.0)	1 (2.0)	0	2.59	2.68	103.47
Total West	125	147 (100.0)	88 (60.0)	59 (40.0)	82 (93.0)	5 (6.0)	1 (1.0)	2.90	3.29	113.0
East Rural	35	35 (100.0)	33 (94.0)	2 (6.0)	30 (91.0)	2 (6.0)	1 (3.0)	3.11	3.72	119.61
East Urban	55	62 (100.0)	44 (71.0)	18 (29.0)	41 (93.0)	2 (5.0)	1 (2.0)	2.96	3.45	116.55
Total East	90	97 (100.0)	77 (79.0)	20 (21.0)	71 (92.0)	4 (5.0)	2 (3.0)	3.02	3.57	118.21
Grand Total	**215**	**244 (100.0)**	**165 (68.0)**	**79 (32.0)**	**153 (93.0)**	**9 (5.0)**	**3 (2.0)**	**2.96**	**3.42**	**115.54**

Source: Field Survey Data.

Figures in brackets are percentages to their respective totals.

Pespondents Attitude Towards Allowing Their Children to Take-up the Same Occupation

Information pertaining to attitude of the respondents to allow their children to take up weaving as their occupation is presented in Table 4.16 (*See on next page*). Most of the weavers do not like to see their children in the handloom industry for different reasons. The reasons are varied and many. They feel that their children's dependence on the industry would put them in troubles. Many felt, that the handloom industry did not help them to improve their living standards.

As many as 126 respondents or 59 per cent have expressed the opinion that they do not want their children to work in the handloom industry, 22 per cent or 48 respondents are interested and the remaining 19 per cent or 41 respondents are indifferent. The percentage of respondents not interested in making this a hereditary industry was more in the eastern Cuddapah(78%), than in western Cuddapah(45%). The percentage of weavers interested in the continuance of their Children in the handloom industry is relatively more in western Cuddapah (33%), than in the eastern zone (8 per cent).

From the calculated values of Chi-Square (X^2), as presented in Table 4.16, one may arrive at the conclusion that there is significant difference in the attitude of parents in allowing their children to continue in the Handloom Industry in different regions of Cuddapah. In eastern Cuddapah where the literacy levels are low parents however seem to be largely indifferent.

Rationale for Allowing Their Sons Taking to Weaving

Of the 215 total households, 22 per cent were interested in allowing their sons work on looms; 59 per cent were not interested and the remaining 19 per cent were indifferent.

The reasons expressed in supporting of their willingness to make this a hereditary occupation is presented in Table 4.17 (*See on page 149*). About 58 per cent of the respondents felt that there was no other alternative. Around 29 per cent attribute their willingness for fear of unemployment while the rest felt they run short of finance to take up any other remunerative work.

Respondents gave the following reasons for not being interested to rope in their children into the industry. 62 per cent of the 215 households attributed it for the non-remunerative nature of the industry, 19 per cent of them felt that the profession is highly difficult, 14 per cent felt that the industry was subject to constant fluctuations in marketing conditions and availability of raw materials etc.

Table 4.16 : Respondents' Attitude in Allowing Their Children to Continue in Handloom Sector

Regions	No. of Respondents	Attitude towards allowing their children to continue in the Handloom Industry		
		Interested	Not Interested	Indifferent
West rural	50	3 (6.0)	27 (54.0)	20 (40.0)
West urban	75	38 (51.0)	29 (39.0)	8 (10.0)
Total west	125	41 (33.0)	56 (45.0)	28 (22.0)
East rural	35	3 (9.0)	25 (71.0)	7 (20.0)
East urban	55	4 (7.0)	45 (82.0)	6 (11.0)
Total east	90	7 (8.0)	70 (78.0)	13 (14.0)
Grand total	**215**	**48 (22.0)**	**126 (59.0)**	**41 (19.0)**

Source: Field survey Data.

Figures in brackets are percentages to their respective totals.

X^2 for,

West-East = 25.51

Rural-Urban = 27.26

West Rural-West Urban = 31.32

East Rural-East Urban = 1.5412 *

*Significant at 5% level of significance

Nearly 63 per cent of the respondents, who were indifferent, about the continuance in handloom industry expressed the view that they couldn't predict the future; 17 per cent of them had no children; and the remaining 17 per cent left the decision for their children.

From the values of X^2 presented in Table 4.18 (*See on page 150*) we find that there was no significant difference in the opinions expressed by the respondents about the future of their children-(Interested to Continue/Not interested to/Indifferent) among all the different regions of Cuddapah district. It means that all the weavers in different regions were of the same opinion about the future of their children.

Table 4.17 : Reasons for Allowing Childeren to Continue in the Handloom Industry

Regions	No. of Respon-dents	Reasons for being interested			Reasons for Not being interested				Reasons for Indifference			
		A	B	C	D	E	F	G	H	I	J	K
West Rural	50	3 (100.0)	— —	— —	3 (11.1)	6 (22.2)	15 (55.5)	3 (11.2)	3 (15.0)	12 (60.0)	4 (20.0)	1 (5.0)
Weat Urban	75	20 (52.6)	12 (31.6)	6 (15.8)	2 (6.9)	6 (20.7)	19 (65.5)	2 (6.9)	—	8 (100.0)	—	—
Total West	125	23 (56.1)	12 (29.3)	6 (14.6)	5 (8.9)	12 (21.4)	34 (60.7)	5 (3.9)	3 (10.7)	20 (71.4)	4 (14.3)	1 (3.6)
East Rural	35	2 (66.6)	1 (33.4)	—	3 (12.0)	4 (16.0)	17 (68.0)	1 (4.0)	2 (28.6)	3 (42.9)	2 (28.5)	—
East Urban	55	3 (75.0)	1 (25.0)	—	9 (20.0)	8 (17.7)	27 (60.0)	1 (2.3)	2 (33.3)	3 (50.0)	1 (16.7)	—
Total East	90	5 (71.4)	2 (28.6)	—	12 (17.0)	12 (17.0)	44 (62.9)	2 (2.9)	4 (30.8)	6 (46.2)	3 (23.0)	—
Grand Total	**215**	**28 (58.3)**	**14 (29.2)**	**6 (12. 5)**	**17 (13.5)**	**24 (19.0)**	**78 (61.9)**	**7 (5.6)**	**7 (17.1)**	**26 (63.4)**	**7 (17.0)**	**1 (2.5)**

Source : Field Survey Data.

Figures in brackets are percentages to their respective totals.

A. No Alternative
B. Fear of Unemployment
C. Other Reasons
D. Constant Fluctuations
E. Highly difficult.
F. Not Remunerative
G. Other Reasons
H. No Children
I. Cannot Predict the Future
J. Left to the Children
K. Other Reasons

Table 4.18 : X^2, Values for Attitudes of the Respondents to Allow their Children in the Handloom Industry

X^2 between	Interested	Not Interested	Indifferent
West-East	1.4917*	1.5390*	0.8298*
Rural-Urban	2.1933*	0.8262	2.3643*
West Rural West Urban	2.0385*	0.8211*	4.5295*
East Rural East Urban	0.0000*	4.1823*	0.0000*

*Significant both at 1% and 5% levels of significance
X^2 = chi-square.

Agencies or Persons Motivated to Enter into Handloom Industry

The persons or agencies that motivated the persons to take up the weaving profession are presented in Table 4.19 (*See on next page*). According to the information recorded, out of 215 households interviewed 87 or 40 per cent of the weaving households were motivated by the family members; and the 68 or 32 per cent households by the Master Weavers; 37 or 17 per cent by the Friends and Relatives; 13 or 6 per cent by the Government agencies; and the remaining 10 or 5 per cent by the local merchants. The table makes us to understand that a higher percentage of weavers in eastern Cuddapah were motivated by the family members; while the Master weavers persuaded them to take up weaving as their occupation in the western region.

The values of X^2 (Chi-Square) relating to the persons that motivated a person to enter Into the handloom industry explains that between the areas of eastern and western Cuddapah, there is significant difference in the influencing agencies or persons enter the handloom industry.

But in other areas (rural-urban; west rural-west urban; east rural-east urban) the difference in the influencing agencies or persons motivation, is not significant.

Organisational Factors Influencing the Weavers to Take-up Wraving as a Profession

Information is presented in Table 4.20 (*See on page 152*) which facilitates one to know the organisational factors influencing the weavers to join the industry. Weaver working under the Mlaster weaver would very much be influenced by the members of the families concerned to join the industry, and the influence cast by the Master weaver himself.

Table 4.19. Agencies/Persons that Motivated than to Enter the Handloom Industry

Regions	Family Members	Influencing Agencies/Persons				Total
		Friends and Relatives	Local Merchants	Master Weaver	Govt. Agency	
West Rural	6 (12.0)	12 (24.0)	3 (6.0)	28 (56.0)	1 (2.0)	50 (100.0)
West Urban	16 (21.0)	12 (16.0)	7 (9.0)	28 (38.0)	12 (16.0)	75 (100.0)
Total West	22 (18.0)	24 (19.0)	10 (8.0)	56 (45.0)	10 (13.0)	125 (100.0)
East Rural	26 (74.0)	6 (17.0)	—	3 (9.0)	—	35 (100.0)
East Urban	39 (71.0)	7 (13.0)	—	9 (16.0)	—	55 (100.0)
Total East	65 (72.0)	13 (14.0)	— —	12 (14.0)	—	90 (100.0)
Grand Total	**87 (40.0)**	**37 (17.0)**	**10 (5.0)**	**68 (32.0)**	**13 (6.0)**	**215 (100.0)**

Source: Field Survey Data.

Figures in brackets are percentages to their respective totals.

*Significant at 5% and 1% levels of significance.

X^2. Values for

West-East	= 79.08
Rural-Urban	= 7.8017*
West Rural-West Urban	= 7.1702*
East Rural East Urban	= 1.7614*

The Independent weavers too, are also motivated by the members of the family, friends, relatives and Local merchants to enter into the weaving profession.

It is observed that 75 per cent of the weavers who were working under the Co-operative Societies were influenced by the local merchants. On the whole, weavers are largely influenced by the family members, followed by the Master weavers, local merchants, friends and relatives to take up weaving as their occupation/profession.

From the calculated values of X^2 (Chi-Square) relating to the Organisational factors that influence the weavers to join the industry, we may infer that there is no significant difference in the strength of factors responsible for the weavers to enter the handloom industry viz., Co-operative and Corporate Sectors. If we take the case of Independent weavers and those that are working under the. Master Weaver the strength of the influencing factors is different in different sectors.

Table 4.20 : Factors Influencing The Choice of Organisation

Organisations	Influencing Factors				
	Family Members	Friends Relatives	Local Merchants	Master Weavers	Total No. of looms
Master weaver	72 (51.0)	2 (1.0)	—	68 (48.0)	142 (100.0)
Independent weaver	48 (76.0)	15 (21.0)	9 (12.0)	—	72 (100.0)
Co-operatives	6 (11.0)	8 (14.0)	42 (75.0)	—	56 (100.0)
Corporation	4 (25.0)	2 (13.0)	10 (62.0)	—	16 (100.0)
Total	**130 (45.0)**	**27 (9.0)**	**61 (21.0)**	**68 (25.0)**	**286 (100.0)**

Source: Field Survey Data.

Figures in brackets are percentages to their respective totals.

*Significant at 5 per cent and 1 per cent levels of signi ficance.

X^2 Values for:

Master weaver-independent	=	53.019
Master weaver-co-operative	=	159.48
Master weaver-corporation	=	21.49
Independent-co-operative	=	56.58
Independent-corporation	=	15.8264
Cooperative-corporation	=	3.5333*

Housing Conditions

Next to food and clothes, housing occupies the most important place in deciding the standard of living of the people. Generally a good house reflects good socio-economic background of the household. Information relating to housing conditions of the weavers is collected and presented in Table 4.21.

Description of Thatched Houses

Thatched hut is made of mud walls, largely with a single room that can accommodate a loom. One has to enter it only by lowering one's head, as the door is of four or five feet high. The house is normally rectangular in shape, about 20 feet length and 8 feet width. This area is sufficient to set a loom to work. The rest of the house is dumped with fuel (twigs and dung) and utensils, a tall grain urn, torn mats folded away, a few other household belongings, a wall shelf with comb and oil and old powder tin, framed photographs of the weaver with his wife and child (Caught in stiff self-conscious expression) and from vail to wall, diagonally, a clothes line hung with used and unwashed clothes. Turn to the loom and turn back the soft cotton cloth that covers the fabric on the loom and to help of the light that comes from the only window of the hut (cut low in the wall to allow sun light to fall on loom) and from naked electric bulb that hangs low over frontage of the loom.

Here, in his hut the weaver pursues his exacting craft; working to the percussion sound of wooden loom frame and clinking needles, a 9 hour day almost round the year.

It may be noted from table 4.21 that a large number of weavers in the western Cuddapah have been living in the thatched-houses, where as most of their counterparts in the eastern Cuddapah have been living in semi-permanent houses. The percentage of weavers living in the permanent houses is more in the western zone (17 per cent) than in the eastern zone (14 per cent), and as such it may be inferred that economic inequalities are more in the western region than in the eastern region of Cuddapah district. All the rented houses, except 3 households or 6 per cent, were thatched houses. The position is the same both in the eastern and in western zones of Cuddapah district.

It is understood from the values of X^2 (Chi-Square) presented in Table 4.22 (*See on page 155*) that there is a significant deference in the housing conditions of the handloom households in eastern and western zones of Cuddapah district at 5 per cent and 1 per cent levels of significance. This difference between the areas of rural-urban, west rural-west urban and east rural-east urban is not significant at 1 per cent level of sifinificance.

Table 4.21 : Housing Conditions

Regions	No. of Households Living in		Description of own houses			Description of Rented Houses			Description of all Houses			
	Own House	Rented House	Thatched	Semi-Perma-nent	Perma-nent	That ched	Semi erma nent	Perma-nent	That ched	Semi perma-nent	Perma-nent	Total No. of respo-ndent
West Rural	41 (82.0)	9 (18.0)	30 (73.0)	3 (7.0)	8 (20.0)	9 (100.0)	—	—	39 (78.0)	3 (6.0)	8 (16.0)	50 (100.0)
West Urban	40 (53.0)	35 (47.0)	29 (73.0)	5 (13.0)	6 (14.0)	33 (94.0)	2 (6.0)	—	62 (83.0)	7 (9.0)	6 (8.0)	75 (100.0)
Total West	81 (65.0)	44 (35.0)	59 (73.0)	8 (10.0)	14 (17.0)	42 (95.0)	2 (5.0)	—	101 (81.0)	10 (8.0)	14 (11.0)	125 (100.0)
East Rural	32 (91.0)	3 (9.0)	12 (38.0)	13 (41.0)	7 (21.0)	3 (100.0)	—	—	15 (43.0)	13 (37.0)	7 (20.0)	35 (100.0)
East Urban	51 (93.0)	4 (7.0)	11 (22.0)	35 (69.0)	5 (9.0)	3 (75.0)	1 (25.0)	—	14 (25.0)	36 (66.0)	5 (9.0)	55 (100.0)
Total East	83 (92.0)	7 (8.0)	23 (28.0)	48 (58.0)	12 (14.0)	6 (86.0)	1 (14.0)	—	29 (33.0)	49 (54.0)	12 (13.0)	90 (100.0)
Grand Total	**164 (76.0)**	**51 (24.0)**	**82 (50.0)**	**56 (34.0)**	**26 (16.0)**	**48 (94.0)**	**3 (6.0)**	—	**130 (61.0)**	**59 (27.0)**	**26 (12.0)**	**215 (100.0)**

Source : Field Survey Data.
Figures in brackets are percentages to their respective totals.

The X^2 (Chi-Square) value for tented houses, shows that the difference is not significant at 1 per cent and 5 per cent levels of significance in all the areas of the district.

Table 4.22 : X^2 Values for the Housing Conditions of the Handlooh Households

Sl.No.	X^2 values for	Owned Houses	Rented Houses	Total
1.	West-East	45.2230*	1.4006*	59.9365*
2.	Rural-Urban	8.7040*	1.6179*	7.8444*
3.	West Rural West Urban	0.7857**	0.5303*	1.6247*
4.	East Rural- East Urban	6.1505**	0.7753*	6.8096**

*Significant at 5% and 1%, level of significance.

**Significant at 1% level of significance.

The variation in the housing conditions (Owned and Rented) is significant in the areaa of eastern and western Cuddapah and it is not significant in the case of west rural-west urban; east rural-east urban areas at 5 per cent and 1 per cent levels of significance. Similarly for areas of rural-urban Cuddapah also the variation in housing condition is not significant at 1 per cent level of significance.

Migration

The notable characteristic feature of the industrial labour in India has been its migratory nature indicating that a majority of the industrial workers are immigrants from the nearby and adjoining rural areas. Immigration is the result of prolonged unemployment in ones own place. Often Marriages also cause the weavers to migrate-Either the bride's parents move out and settle in the bridegroom's native place or vice-versa. It depends upon the economic factors. Information relating to migration of handloom weavers is presented in Table 4.23.

From the table it is clear that 21 per cent households have migrated from one place to another. The Percentage of weaving households that migrated is relatively ffiore in western zone (26%) than in eastern zone (14%) of Cuddapah district.

It is also clear from the table that higher percentage of weavers are migrated from rural to urban areas (72%).

Table 4.23 : Details Relating to Migration

Regions	No. of Households			Type of Migration			
	Migrated	Not Migrated	Total	Rural to Urban	Rural to Rural	Urban Rural	Urban to Urban.
West Rural	6 (12.0)	44 (88.0)	50 (100.0)	—	5 (83.0)	1 (17.0)	—
West Urban	27 (36.0)	48 (64.0)	75 (100.0)	24 (89.0)	—	—	3 (11.0)
Total West	33 (26.0)	92 (74.0)	125 (100.0)	24 (73.0)	5 (15.0)	1 (3.0)	3 (9.0)
East Rural	1 (3.0)	34 (97.0)	35 (100.0)	—	1 (100.0)	—	—
East Urban	12 (22.0)	43 (78.0)	55 (100.0)	9 (75.0)	—	—	3 (25.0)
Total East	13 (14.0)	77 (86.0)	90 (100.0)	9 (69.0)	— (8.0)	—	3 (23.0)
Grand Total	**46 (21.0)**	**169 (79.0)**	**215 (100.0)**	**33 (72.0)**	**6 (13.0)**	**1 (2.0)**	**6 (13.0)**

Source : Field Survey Data.

Figures in brackets are percentages to their respective totals.

Diseases or Occupational Hazards

Health is wealth, that too, in the case of workers who get succour just by selling their labour. Health is a key factor to progress; for it supplies energy to do work. Health supplies necessary amount of will to work and a healthy attitude towards life. The health of the weavers is of immense importance not only for themselves but also in relation to general progress of the Nation. In case of handloom weavers, health is an important determinant of the productivity of labourers. In an under developing country like India, handloom weavers are caught in a vicious circle of nutritional deficiency, ill-health, low-productivity, low earnings-etc. The breaking of this vicious circle can release untapped human energies which give a big boost to economic growth. The health problems of the handloom workers are dichotomous in nature. It is so because the workers are very often exposed to occupational risks in their work places in addition to the health hazards common to the community as a whole[6]. The weavers have to strain their eyes hence they suffer from eye diseases viz., Short-Sightedness or Blindness. It is the interaction of man and his environment which determines the incidence of disease[7]. A majority (nearly 75%) of the weavers smoke Beedis and work in closed and congested environment as such, the workers would be affected by Asthma.

In Cuddapah district 14 per cent of the total sample surveyed were suffering from diseases. As shown in table 4.24 (See on next page), 57 per cent of the adults were affected with the Short-Sightedness; 21 per cent from Asthma; 12 per cent from Tuberculosis; 6 per cent from Paralysis; 3 per cent from high Blood Pressure and 1 per cent from Cancer.

Monthly Earnings

The monthly earnings of the weavers' family is a good indicator of the economic condition and the standard of living of the weaver and his family. Therefore information was collected on this important aspect from the weavers and presented in Tables 4.25 and 4.25A (*See on page 159 and 160*).

The average monthly income per household is the lowest in urban ares of western Cuddapah where as it is the highest in urban areas of estern Cuddapah. The value of Co-efficient of Variation and Standard Deviation pertaining to monthly earnings of the weavers families is the highest for urban areas of western Cuddapah, while it is the lowest in urban parts of eastern Cuddapah. It is clear from the table that the variation in the monthly earnings of the weavers is lower in eastern zone than in western zone of Cuddapah district. Around 42 per cent of the weaving households are getting less than ₹ 500/- of income per month,

Table 4.24 : Disease-wise Distribution of Respondents

Regions	Short Sight	Asthma	Paralysis	T.B	Cancer	B.P.	Total Diseased	Total Adults	% of Total diseased in the total adult population
West Rural	13 (59.0)	3 (14.0)	1 (5.0)	3 (14.0)	—	2 (8.0)	22 (100.0)	155	14
West Urban	16 (55.0)	8 (28.0)	2 (7.0)	2 (7.0)	—	1 (3.0)	29 (100.0)	221	13
Total West	29 (57.0)	11 (22.0)	3 (6.0)	5 (10.0)	—	3 (5.0)	51 (100.0)	376	14
East Rural	6 (46.0)	2 (15.0)	2 (15.0)	3 (24.0)	—	—	13 (100.0)	94	14
East Urban	14 (64.0)	5 (23.0)	— —	2 (9.0)	1 (4.0)	—	22 (100.0)	151	15
Total East	20 (57.0)	7 (20.0)	2 (6.0)	5 (14.0)	1 (3.0)	—	35 (100.0)	245	14
Grand Total	**49 (57.0)**	**18 (21.0)**	**5 (6.0)**	**10 (12.0)**	**1 (1.0)**	**3 (3.0)**	**86 (100.0)**	**621**	**14**

Source : Field Survey Data.

Figures in breckets are percentages to their respective totals.

Table 4.25 : Monthly Earnings of the Weaving Families

Areas	Income Levels (Rs)					Total No. of Households	Total Income	Average income per household	C.V.	S. D.
	Below 250	251-500	501 750	751-1000	Above 1000					
West Rural	1 (2)	21 (42)	18 (36. 00)	6 (12.00	4 (8.0)	50 (100.0)	28643	573	41.58	238
West Urban	4 (5.0)	27 (36.0)	28 (37.0)	8 (11.0)	8 (11.0)	75 (100.0)	49192	523	49.85	261
Total Uest	5 (4.0)	48 (38.0)	46 (37.0)	14 (11.0)	12 (10.0)	125 (100.0)	67834	543	46.41	252
East Rural	—	10 (29.0)	15 (43.0)	4 (11.0)	6 (17.0)	35 (100.0)	28300	809	31.85	258
East Urban	—	11 (20.0)	13 (24.0)	21 (38.0)	10 (18.0)	55 (100.0)	50428	917	27.37	251
Total East	—	21 (23.0)	28 (31.0)	25 (28.0)	16 (18.0)	90 (100.0)	78728	875	29.45	258
Grand Total	**5 (2.3)**	**69 (32.1)**	**74 (34.4)**	**39 (18.1)**	**28 (13.0)**	**215 (100. 0)**	**146563**	**682**	**38.70**	**264**

Source : Field Survey Data.

Figures in brackets are percentages to their respective totals.

Table 4.25A : Yearly Earnings of the Weaving Families

Areas	Income Levels (Rs.)					Total No. of Households	Total Income	Average income per Year per household	P.C.I.	S.D.	C.V.
	Below 3000	3001-6000	6001-9000	9001-12000	Above 12000						
West Rural	1 (2.0)	21 (42.0)	18 (36.0)	6 (12.0)	4 (8.0)	50 (100.0)	343710	6874	1391.54	2858	41.58
West Urban	4 (5.0)	27 (36.0)	28 (37.0)	8 (11.0)	8 (11.0)	75 (100.0)	470300	6271	1295.59	3126	49.85
Total West	5 (4.0)	48 (38.0)	46 (37.0)	14 (11.0)	12 (10.0)	125 (100.0)	814010	6512	1334.44	3022	46.41
East Rural	—	10 (29.0)	15 (43.0)	4 (11.0)	6 (17.0)	35 (100.0)	339600	9703	2249.00	3090	31.85
East Urban	—	11 (20.0)	13 (24.0)	21 (38.0)	10 (18.0)	55 (100.0)	605140	11003	2300-91	3012	27.37
Total East	—	21 (23.0)	28 (31.0)	25 (28.0)	16 (18.0)	90 (100.0)	944740	10497	2281.98	3092	29.45
Grand Total	**5 (2.0)**	**69 (32.0)**	**74 (34.0)**	**39 (18.0)**	**28 (14.0)**	**215 (100.0)**	**1758750**	**8180**	**1717.53**	**3166**	**38.70**

Source : Field Survey Data.

Figures in brackets are percentages to their respective totals.

Table 4-25B : Per Capita Income of the Weavers' Household

Areas	Per Capita Income (Rs)						Total No. of Households.	Total population	Total Income	Average household Income	Per Capita Income
	Below 1000	1001-1500	1501-2000	2001-2500	2501-3000	Above 3001					
West Rural	8 (16.0)	16 (32.0)	14 (28.0)	2 (4.0)	8 (16.0)	2 (4.0)	50 (100.0)	247	343710	6874	1392
West Urban	14 (18.67)	27 (36.0)	15 (20.0)	11 (14.67)	1 (1.33)	7 (9.33)	75 (100.0)	363	470300	6271	1296
Total West	22 (17.6)	43 (34.4)	29 (23.2)	13 (10.4)	9 (7.2)	9 (7.20)	125 (100.0)	610	814010	6512	1334
East Rural	2 (5.71)	7 (20.0)	3 (8.57)	11 (31.43)	2 (5.71)	10 (28.58)	35 (100.0)	151	339600	9703	2249
East Urban	2 (3.64)	13 (23.64)	13 (23.64)	8 (14.55)	10 (18.18)	9 (16.35)	5 (100.0)	263	605140	11003	2301
Total East	4 (4.44)	20 (22.23)	16 (17.78)	19 (21.11)	12 (13.33)	19 (21.11)	90 (100.0)	414	944740	10497	2282
Grand Total	**26 (12.09)**	**63 (29.30)**	**45 (20.93)**	**32 (14.88)**	**21 (9.77)**	**28 (13.03)**	**215 (100.0)**	**1024**	**1758780**	**8180**	**1718**

Source : Field Survey Data.

Figures in brackets are percentages to their respective totals.

contrary to this, in eastern zone 23 per cent of the weaving households are getting less than ₹ 500 per month, and the rest are getting over and above ₹ 500 income. In sum, the average income of the weaving household is ₹ 682; and all the areas in western Cuddapah are getting only less than the average income of the district and all areas in eastern Cuddapah were getting over and above the district average. Around 35 per cent of the weaving households are setting ₹ 500 or less and the rest are earning over and above ₹ 500.

Since the per capita income gives a better insight into the economic conditions of the weavers, these figure worked out and presented in Table 4.26 (*See on next page*). The average per capita income of all the categories put together is ₹ 143 and this will not be sufficient even to provide two aquare meals a day. The average Per Capita Income of the weavers in western Cuddapah is much lower (₹ 111) than their counterparts in eastern Cuddapah. (₹ 190).

Yearly Earnings of Weavers Families

The average yearly income per household is the highest for eastern Cuddapah than in western Cuddapah. All the households in western Cuddapah are getting less than the average income of the district as a whole. The per capita income is also highest in eastern Cuddapah than in western Cuddapah. The per capita income is ₹ 1334 in western Cuddapah, ₹ 1718 for the district as a whole; as against ₹ 3934 for the state of Andhra Pradesh in 1989-90.

Per Capita Income of Weavers' Household

In terms of per capita income, west urban Cuddapah has the lowest and east urban Cuddapah has the highest per Capita income. An attempt is made to establish Correlation between per capita income and average population per household, as these two are interdependent. The value of Co-efficient of Correlation is Calculated and it is inferred that these two variables are perfectly correlated in all the areas.

Per Capita Income Range of Weavers' Household

Table 4.27 (*See on page 164*) shows that monthly earnings of different categories of weavers that range from ₹ 53.30 to ₹ 500.00. The average earning of a weaving family is ₹ 682 and needless to say, majority of the weavers in western Cuddapah, constituting 58.1 per cent, earn less than this average. This indicates that the average has been largely influenced by the higher income groups in eastern Cuddapah, whose income is high, compared to that of weavers of western Cuddapah (*See Table 4.28 on page*

Table 4.26 : Per Capita Income of the Weaving Families (Per Month)

Areas	Per Capita Income								Total House-holds	Total Population	Total income of the House-hold	Average income of the House-hold	Per Capita Income	Average population per House-hold	C.V.	S.D.
	Below 100	101-150	151-200	201-250	251-300	301-350	351-400	Above 400								
West Rural	8 (16.0)	16 (32.0)	14 (28.0)	2 (4.0)	8 (16.0)	—	1 (2.0)	1 (2.0)	50 (100.0)	247	28643	573	116	4.94	65.25	65.3
West Urban	14 (19.0)	27 (36.0)	15 (20.0)	11 (15.0)	1 (1.0)	—	3 (4.0)	4 (5.0)	75 (100.0)	363	39192	523	108	4.84	14.40	75.3
Total West	22 (18.0)	43 (34.0)	29 (23.0)	13 (10.0)	9 (7.0)	— —	4 (3.0)	5 (5.0)	125 (100.0)	610	67834	543	111	4.88	13.41	72.8
East Rural	2 (6.0)	7 (20.0)	3 (9.0)	11 (31.0)	2 (6.0)	—	3 (9.0)	7 (19.0)	35 (100.0)	151	28300	809	187	4.31	11.78	95.3
East Urban	2 (4.0)	13 (24.0)	13 (24.0)	8 (15.0)	10 (18.0)	— —	(7.0)	5 (8.0)	55 (100.0)	263	50428	917	192	4.78	8.85	81.2
Total East	4 (4.0)	20 (22.0)	16 (18.0)	19 (21.0)	12 (13.0)	— —	7 (8.0)	12 (14.0)	90 (100.0)	414	78728	875	190	4.60	10.00	87.5
Grand Total	**26 (12.09)**	**63 (29.30)**	**45 (20.93)**	**32 (14.88)**	**21 (9.77)**	—	**11 (5.12)**	**17 (7.91)**	**215 (100.0)**	**1024**	**146563**	**682**	**143**	**4.76**	**12.14**	**82.8**

Source : Field Survey Data.

Figures in brackets are percentages to their respective totals.

Co-efficence of Correlation between per Capita income and Average Population per Household

West Rural (r_l) = 0.930
West Urban(r_2) = 0.930
Total West(r_3) = 0.930
East Rural(r_4) = 0.986
East Urban(r_5) = 0.987

165)). Out of 17 weavers who earn more than ₹ 400 per moth, there are 2 weavers working for the Master weaver; 5 weavers working for the Co-operatives, 2 weavers as Independents and the remaining 8 weavers working for more than one organisation. No weaver under the Corporate sector earns over and above ₹ 300.

Sources of Income

Weaving is the primary occupation of all the weaving households surveyed in Cuddapah district. Hence the major source of income is weaving. A few weavers were reported to be doing agriculture, business and other remunerative works. In order to meet the deficit, weavers used to work as agricultural coolies during seasons or keep their children in fair price shops as clerks etc. Some with a fair financial background are doing business. The income that weavers get from other sources is subsidiary income to them. As shown in Table 4.29 (*See on page 166*), 91 per cent of the income earned by the waving households is purely from weaving and the remaining 9 per cent is from subsidiary occupations. Dependence on subsidiary occupations is less in eastern zone, than in western zone of Cuddapah district. For example, 85 per cent of the total income is from weaving in western zone, while it is 96 per cent in eastern zone. The remaining 15 per cent of income in western zone and 4 per cent in eastern zone is from other occupations.

Table 4.27 : Per Capita Income Range of the Weavers' Families

Areas	Per Capita income Range		Average per Capita Income ₹
	₹	₹	
West Rural	53.30	416.65	116.00
West Urban	55.00	406.25	108.00
Total West	53.30	416.65	111.00
East Rural	66.60	450.00	187.00
East Urban	83.30	500.00	192.00
Total East	66.60	500.00	190.00
Grand Total	**53.30**	**500.00**	**143.00**

Source : Field Survey Data.
Figures in brackets are percentages to their respective totals

Weavers Attending Other Works Besides Weaving

Depending on the convenience, one or all members completely or partially work in other fields of activities beside weaving. In order to make both

Table 4.28 : Monthly Earnings of the Weaving Households

Monthly Earnings (₹)	Number of Weaving Families					Total
	Master Weaver	Co-operative	Indepan-dent.	Corrpo-ration	Working for more than one organisation	
Less then 100	9 (34.62)	4 (15.38)	5 (19.23)	1 (3.85)	7 (26.92)	26 (100.0)
101-150	24 (38.10)	10 (15.87)	15 (23.81)	2 (3.17)	12 (19.5)	63 (100.0)
151-200	25 (55.56)	2 (4.44)	6 (13.33)	1 (2.22)	11 (24.44)	45 (100.0)
201-250	15 (46.88)	12 (37.5)	2 (6.25)	1 (3.13)	2 (6.25)	32 (100.0)
251-300	13 (61.90)	3 (14. 22)	2 (9.52)	1 (4.76)	2 (9.53)	21 (100.0)
301-350	—	—	—	—	—	—
351-400	3 (27. 27)	2 (18. 18)	1 (9.09)	—	5 (45.46)	11 (100.0)
Above 400	2 (11.76)	5 (29. 41)	2 (11.77)	— —	8 (47.06)	17 (100.0)
Grand Total	**91 (42.33)**	**38 (17.67)**	**33 (15.35)**	**6 (2.79)**	**47 (21.86)**	**215 (100. 0)**

Source : Field Survey Data.

Figures in brackets are percentages to their respective totals.

Table 4.29 : Sources of Income of the Weaving Households

Areas	Annual Income				Total	No.of House-holds	No.of Looms	Average income per household	Average income per loom	No.of persons in the family	Per Capita income
	Weaving	Agricu-lture	Other Business	Any other							
West Rural	343710 (87.0)	600	16200 (4.0)	34800 (9.0)	39310 (100)	50	72	7906	4774	247	1600.45
West Urban	470300 (84.0)	—	6120 (1.0)	83000 (15.0)	559420 (100.0)	75	99	7459	4751	363	1514.10
Total West	814010 (85.0)	600	22320 (2.0)	117800 (13.0)	954730 (100)	125	171	7638	4760	610	1565.13
East Rural	339600 (92.0)	2160 (1.0)	26900 (7.0)	—	368660 (100)	35	44	10533	7718	151	2441.46
East Urban	605140 (99.0)	4600 (0.75)	2400 (0.25)	— —	612140 (100.0)	55	71	11130	8523	263	2327.53
Total East	944740 (96.0)	6760 (1.0)	29300 (3.0)	—	980800 (100.0)	90	115	10898	8215	414	2369.08
Grand Total	**1758750 (91.0)**	**7360 (0.38)**	**51620 (3.0)**	**117800 (5.0)**	**1935530 (100.0)**	**215**	**286**	**9002**	**6149**	**1024**	**1890.17**

Source : Field Survey Data.

Figures in brackets are percentages to their respective totals.

ends meet, weavers, whose income is not sufficient would work in other fields. Table 4.30 (*See on page 168*) shows that in addition to weaving they also work as agricultural laborers, coolies on daily wage basis, Masonry laborers, Warpers[9] etc. In the sample, out of 215 households surveyed 77 per cent of weaving households are completely dependent on weaving only and for the remaining 23 per cent weaving is the main occupation, besides many subsidiary occupations. The weavers depending on other occupations besides weaving is relatively more in western Cuddapah than in eastern Cuddapah. For instance in western zone only 65 per cent of the weavers take weaving as only occupation, while it is 93 per cent in eastern Cuddapah. The remaining 35 per cent in western zone and 7 per cent in eastern region take part in other remunerative works.

The situation is almost same in rural and urban centres of eastern Cuddapah. But the percentage of weavers dependent purely on agriculture is relatively more (70%) in rural areas than in urban places of western Cuddapah. During the survey it is observed that the weavers in western region have good alternative sources of employment. The rural areas in western Cuddapah chosen for the study, are closely situated to the urban and industrially developed ares viz., Proddatur and Jammalamadugu. Hence, weavers during slack season prefer to work in other fields also. In eastern Cuddapah, where the industry is sound and employment is secure throughout the year, weavers are less dependent on other activities.

Of the 215 households surveyed, 50 households or 23 per cent of the weavers' households have subsidiary occupations. Of them, 12 constitute agricultural labourers, 34 per cent are coolies, 2 per cent are industrial labourers, 10 per cent are working in Government or Private establishments as employees on fairly good remunerative basis, 8 per cent are doing business, 6 per cent engaged on preparation of warps 6 per cent on tailoring and the remaining 8 per cent in other works viz., as clerks in fair shops, Cloth shops etc.

Income Distribution based on Organisation and Product

In order to know the influence of organisations, (viz Master weaver, Co-operative Societies, Corporations, dependent) and production of different varieties produced in the district on the income earned by the weavers, information is collected on these aspects and presented in Tables 4.31 and 4.31A (*See on pages 169 and 170*). Zari Sarees, Cotton Sarees (Janata), Cotton Dhoties (Janata), Cotton Lungis, Resham Sarees and Shirting are the important items produced on the looms.

Table 4.30 : Details of Weavers Attending to other Works besides Weaving

Areas	No. of House-holds	House-holds doing only Weaving	House-holds attending other works	Details ofother works the weavers are attending								
				Agricu-lture	Cooly	Masonry	Labour	Employee	Busi-ness	Warping	Tailo-ring	Others
West Rural	50	35 (70.0)	15 (30.0)	2 (13.0)	4 (27.0)	7 (60.0)	1	1	—	—	—	—
West Urban	75	46 (61.0)	29 (39.0)	1 (3.0)	13 (45.0)	—	—	4 (14.0)	4 (14.0)	1 (3.0)	3 (10.0)	3 (11.0)
Total West	125	81 (65.0)	44 (35.0)	3 (7.0)	17 (39.05)	7 (16.0)	1 (2.0)	5 (11.0)	4 (9.0)	1 (2.0)	3 (7.0)	3 (7.0)
East Rural	35	32 (91.0)	3 (9.0)	—	—	—	—	—	—	2 (66.67)	—	1 (33.33)
East Urban	55	52 (95.0)	3 (5.0)	3 (100.0)	—	—	—	—	—	—	—	—
Total East	90	84 (93.0)	6 (7.0)	3 (50.0)	—	—	—	—	—	2 (33.33)	—	1 (16.67)
Grand Total	**215**	**165 (77.0)**	**50 (23.0)**	**6 (12.0)**	**17 (34.0)**	**7 (14.0)**	**(2.0)**	**5 (10.0)**	**4 (8.0)**	**3 (6.0)**	**3 (6.00)**	**4 (8.0)**

Source : Field Survey Data.

Figures in brackets are percentages to their respective totals.

Table 4.31 : Income Distribution Based on Organisation and Product

Areas	Type of Products																			
	Zari Saree					Cotton Saree					Cotton Dethi					Cotton Lungi				
	MW	CO-OP	CORP	IND	Total	MW	CO-OP	CORP	IND	Total	MW	CO-OP	CORP	IND	Total	MW	CO-OP	CORP	IND	Total
West Rural	—	—	—	—	—	—	7 23820 (3403)	4 21670 (5418)	—	11 45490 (4135)	—	30 138590 (4620)	6 31680 (5280)	—	36 170270 (4730)	—	—	—	—	—
West Urban	—	1 5400 (5400)	4 20160 (5040)	—	5 25560 (5112)	—	11 51600 (4691)	5 28800 (5760)	—	16 80400 (5025)	—	16 63120 (3945)	8 42680 (5335)	—	24 105800 4408)	5 11800 (2360)	2 4800 (2400)	—	—	7 16600 (2371)
Total West	—	1 5400 (5400)	4 20160 (5040)	—	5 25560 (5112)	— —	18 75420 (4190)	9 50470 (5608)	—	27 125890 (4663)	—	46 201710 (4385)	14 74360 (5311)	—	60 276070 (4601)	5 11800 (2360)	2 4800 (2400)	—	—	7 16600 (2371)
East Rural	17 167460 (8728)	10 67200 (7817)	—	17 104940 (8661)	44 339600 (8523)	—	—	—	—	—	—	—	—	—	—	—	—	—	—	—
East Urban	30 261840 (8728)	14 109440 (7817)	—	27 233860 (8661)	71 605140 (8523)	—	—	—	—	—	—	—	—	—	—	—	—	—	—	—
Total East	47 429300 (9134)	24 176640 (7360)	—	44 338800 (7700)	115 944740 (8215)	—	—	—	—	—	—	—	—	—	—	—	—	—	—	—
Grand Total	51 449460 (8813)	25 182040 (7282)	— —	44 338800 (7700)	120 970300 (8086)	—	18 75420 (4190)	9 50470 (5608)	— —	27 125890 (4663)	— —	46 201710 (4385)	14 74360 (5311)	—	60 276070 (4601)	5 11800 (2360)	2 4800 (2400)	—	—	7 16600 (2371)

Source: Field Survey Data.

Figures in brackets are averages to their above totals.

MW = Master Weaver

Co-op = Co-operative Societies

Corp = Corporation

Ind = Independent

Table 4.31A : Income Distribution Based on Organisation and Product

Areas	Type of Products														Total
	Resham					Shirting					Grand Total				
	MW	CO-OP	CORP	IND	Total	MW	CO-OP	CORP	IND	Total	MW	CO-OP	CORP	IND	
West Rural	10 55800 (5580)	4 14400 (3600)	—	2 13200 (6600)	16 83400 (5213)	2 6400 (3200)	6 21270 (3545)	1 3200 (3200)	—	9 30870 (3430)	12 62200 (5183)	47 198080 (4215)	11 56550 (5141)	2 13200 (6600)	72 330030 (4584)
West Urban	19 19600 (6295)	8 36480 (4560)	—	2 13200 (6600)	29 16980 (5837)	12 40380 (3365)	1 3540 (3540)	3 11840 (3947)	2 16440 (8220)	18 72200 (4011)	36 171780 (4772)	39 164940 (4229)	20 103480 (5174)	4 29640 (7410)	99 469840 (4746)
Total West	29 175400 (6048)	12 50880 (4240)	—	4 26400 (6600)	45 252680 (5615)	14 46780 (3341)	7 24810 (3544)	4 15040 (3760)	2 16440 (8220)	27 103070 (3817)	48 233940 (4875)	86 363020 (4221)	31 160030 (5162	7 42480 (6120)	171 799870 (4678)
East Rural	—	—	—	—	—	—	—	—	—	—	17 167460 (9851)	10 67200 (6720)	— (6173)	17 104940 (7718)	44 339600
East Urban	—	—	—	—	—	—	—	—	—	—	30 261840 (8728)	14 109440 (7817)	—	27 233860 (8662)	71 605140 (8523)
Total East	—	—	—	—	—	—	—	—	—	—	47 429300 (9134)	24 176640 (7360)	—	44 338800 (7700)	115 944740 (8215)
Grand Total	**29 175400 (6048)**	**12 50880 (4240)**	—	**4 26400 (6600)**	**45 252680 (5615)**	**14 46780 (3341)**	**7 24810 (3544)**	**4 15040 (3760)**	**2 16440 (8220)**	**27 103070 (3817)**	**95 663280 (6982)**	**110 539660 (4906)**	**31 160030 (5162)**	**51 381604 (7483)**	**286 1744610 (6100)**

Source: Field Survey Data.

Figures in brackets are averages to their above figure.

MW = Master Weaver

Co-op = Co-operative societies.

Corp = Corporation.

Ind = Independent.

Out of 125 looms producing Zari Saree 120 looms or 96 per cent are in eastern Cuddapah and the remaining 5 looms or 4 per cent are in western Cuddapah. Zari Sarees are not produced in west-rural Cuddapah. All these 5 looms (one in Co-operative sector and the remaining 4 looms in Corporate sector) are in urban centres of western Cuddapah. Every weaver on an average is earning ₹ 5112 in the western Cuddapah.

Out of 120 weavers producing zari sarees in eastern Cuddapah, 51 weavers or 43 per cent are under the Master weaver sector; 25 weavers or 21 per cent are under Co-operative sector and the remaining 44 weavers or 37 per cent are working under Independent sector. Weavers under Master weaver sector, Co-operative sector and Independent sectors were earning ₹ 8813, ₹ 7282 and ₹ 7700 respectively, on an average per year. Weavers producing Zari Sarees in eastern Cuddapah are better off than their counterparts in western Cuddapah.

Cotton Sarees are produced only in western Cuddapah. Out of 27 looms product Cotton Sarees 18 loom or 67 per cent were in the Co-operative sector and the remaining 9 looms or 33 per cent were under Corporate sector. Every weaver producing this product, earning ₹ 4663, on an average, per year.

Out of 60 weavers producing Cotton Dhoties. 46 weavers or 77 per cent are in Co-operative sector and the remaining 14 weavers or 23 per cent were in Corporate sector. Every weaver producing Cotton Dhoties on an average is earning ₹ 4601 per year.

Of the total 206 looms surveyed, in the district, 7 looms or 2.4 per cent are producing Cotton Lungis. Of the total 7 looms 5 looms or 71 per cent are working under Master weaver sector and the regaining 2 looms or 29 per c.nt vere under Co-operative sector. Looms producing Cotton Lungis are completely absent in Corporate and Independent sector. 16 per cent (45 looms) of the total looms surveyed produce Resham cloth in the district. All these looms are concentrated in western Cuddapah only. Of these 45 looms 29 or 64 per cent are underMaster weaver sector, 27 per cent are under Co-operative sector and the remaining 9 per cent are under Independent sector. Every weaver producing Resham earns ₹ 5615 on an average in one year.

27 looms or 9 per cent are producing Shirting Cloth of these looms 14 or 52 per cent were under Master weaver sector; 7 looms or 26 per cent were under Co-operative Sector; 4 looms or 15 per cent were under Corporate sector; and the remaining 2 looms or 7 per cent were under the Independent sector. Looms working under Master weaver sector, Co-operative sector, Corporate sector and Independent sectors were

earning ₹ 3341, ₹ 3544, ₹ 3760, and ₹ 8220 respectively on an average per one year.

On the whole the position of the Independent weaver is better off in western zone while the position of the Master weaver is better off in the eastern zone of Cuddapah district. Weavers producing zari sarees are getting the highest income where as the weavers producing Cotton Lungis were getting the lowest income in the district. The income earning capacity of the weaver in eastern zone is better than in the western zone of Cuddapah. Unequal earnings are, in turn due to unequal opportunities, unequal abilities, unequal ownership of assets and a host of other institutional factors[10].

Details of Poverty among Households

Based on the Per Capita Income of the weaving households poverty line[11] has been constructed and presented in Table 4.32 (*See on next page*). According to which 20 per cent in west rural Cuddapah, 44 per cent in west urban Cuddapah were living below the poverty line. In all, 34 per cent of the weaving population in western zone were below the Poverty Line. In eastern zone the percentage of population below poverty line is just 14 per cent in rural parts of eastern Cuddapah, 13 per cent in urban centres of eastern Cuddapah and 13 per cent in the total eastern Cuddapah. Around 26 per cent of the weaving households were found living below the Poverty line in Cuddapah district as a whole. In contrast, we find that the percentage of people living below the poverty line is more in western Cuddapah (34%) than in eastern Cuddapah(13%).

Results of Regression Analysis—for per Capita Income and Other Related Variables

Generally, the per capita income of the household depends on the size of the household, men and women participation rates in weaving, average production per loom per month, average wage per unit of cloth produced per month. With a view to knowing the strength of relationship and nature of relationship between the independent variables viz., Size of household, average production per loom per month, Participation of men and women in weaving activity, average wage and dependent variable-per capita income, Multiple Regression technique is employed for the different areas in the district and for the whole district separately. We may write the per capita income function as follows.

$$Y = f(Xl, X2, X3, X4, X5)$$

Where,

Y = Annual per capita income in Rupees.

X_1 = Size of the household.

X_2 = Male participation rate in weaving.

X_3 = Female Participation rate in weaving.

X_4 = Average production per loom per month (in Mtrs)

X_5 = Average wage per unit of cloth produced (in ₹)

Table 4.32 : Details of Poverty among Households (Poverty Line = ₹ 1320, 1989-90)

Areas of Cuddapah Dt.	Number below Poverty line	Number Above Poverty line	Total households
West Rural	10 (20.0)	40 (80.0)	50 (100.0)
West Urban	33 (44.0)	42 (56.0)	75 (100.0)
Total West	43 (34.0)	82 (66.0)	125 (100.0)
East Rural	5 (14.0)	30 (86.0)	35 (100.0)
East Urban	7 (13.0)	48 (87.0)	55 (100.0)
Total East	12 (13.0)	78 (87.0)	90 (100.0)
Grand Total	**55 (26.0)**	**160 (74.0)**	**215 (100.0)**

Source : Field Survey Data.

Figures in brackets are percentages to their respective totals

Multiple linear regression models are used to specify the functional relationship and computer help is taken to estimate the regression Co-efficients. The following is the regression model employed in the survey.

$$Y = b_0 + b_1 \times 1 + b_2 \times 2 + b_3 \times 3 + b_4 \times 4 + b_5 \times 5$$

The parameter b_1 is expected to have a negative sign since there exists an inverse relationship between size of the household and per capita income. The other parameters b_2,b_3,b_4 and b_5 are expected to have positive signs as both household and per capita income levels improve with increase in participation rates, average production and average wage rate.

Regression equations are worked out for different regions in the district. To facilitate comparison, regression results of the different regions are presented in a tabular form. Table 4.32-A presents estimated regression Co-efficients for the variables included in the model with respect to the regions.

The following inferences can be drawn on the basis of the regression results presented in Table 4.32A (*See on page 176*).

1. The Co-efficients relating to the variables included in the model have the expected signs in all the categories of household.
2. There are inter-Centre variations in the magnitude of the Co-efficients relating to the explanatory variables included In the model.

For example, the estimated Co-efficient of the variable X1 i.e. size of the household found to be highly significant for the sample households in eastern Cuddapah. But it is comparatively less significant in case of western Cuddapah. The variation in this respect is highly significant between rural and urban areas of western Cuddapah; while there was no significant difference for the sample households in the urban and rural areas of western Cuddapah and total western Cuddapah district. For instance the per capita income is altered by 45 units in eastern Cuddapah for a unit change in the size of the household, in western Cuddapah the change will be only 10 units.

The per capita income is altered by 20 units in rural and urban centres of western Cuddapah and 24 units in total vestern Cuddapah with one unit change in Male Participation rate in weaving. The variation in the values of Co-efficients influencing the per capita income is more significant in case of rural and urban centres of eastern Cuddapah. The change in per capita income is 14 units for rural areas of eastern Cuddapah, 77 units for urban areas of estern Cuddapah with one unit change in Male participation rate.

The Co-efficient values pertaining to Female participation rate in weaving also show significant difference. For instance, per capita income is altered by 10 units in case of rural centres of western Cuddapah, 20 units in case of urban centres of western Cuddapah and only 9 units in case of total western Cuddapah with one unit change in female participation rate. A unit change in the female participation rates in handloom industry increases the Per capita income of households in rural and urban centres of eastern Cuddapah by 49 units and 62 units respectively. For the whole of eastern Cuddapah it is 51 units.

The Co-efficient values of average production per loom per month show no significant impact on per capita income in both western region and eastern zones of Cuddapah district.

Table 4.32A : Estimated Regression Co-efficients of the Variables Involved in the Model by Centre of Production

Areas	Per Capita income(Y)	Constant (bo)	Size of the household ($b_1 \times 1$)	Male Participation rate in weaving ($b_2 \times 2$)	Female Participation rate in weaving ($b_3 \times 3$)	Average production per loom per month ($b_4 \times 4$)	Average wage per unit of cloth produced ($b_5 \times 5$)	R^2
West Rural	—	125.54 (55.33)	–10.28 × 1 (3.96)	27.98 × 2 (15.45)	10.22 × 3 (15.45)	0.02 × 4 (0.0047)	2.98 × 5 (4.476)	0.429028
West Urban	—	61.86 (57.25)	–10.11 × 1 (3.10)	27.49 × 2 (11.53)	20.38 × 3 (35.34)	0.030 × 4 (0.005)	0.24 × 5 (1.59)	0.518268
Total West	—	101.27 (57.33)	–10.32 × 1 (2.37)	24.28 × 2 (8.43)	9.16 × 3 (14.00)	0.019 × 4 (0.003)	0.58 × 5 (1.42)	0.445651
East Rural	—	114.30 (73.63)	–31.98 × 1 (10.09)	13.63 × 2 (41.15)	49.02 × 3 (34.37)	0.00 × 4 (0.00)	14.74 × 5 (3.98)	0.57
East Urban	—	102.31 (60.37)	–55.35 × 1 (6.67)	77.06 × 2 (20.10)	62.44 × 3 (10.12)	0.007 × 4 (0.006)	13.62 × 5 (2.85)	0.7337
Total East	—	94.32 (64.70)	–44.53 × 1 (5.11)	57.28 × 2 (17.24)	50.69 × 3 (15.46)	0.003 × 4 (0.001)	15.44 × 5 (1.79)	0.650348
Grand Total	—	**126.92 (76.01)**	**–9.17 × 1 (1.62)**	**0.04 × 2 (0.14)**	**2.34 × 3 (1.35)**	**0.01 × 4 (0.00)**	**7.77 × 5 (1.34)**	**0.39**

Source : Field Survey Data.

The difference between the values of Co-efflcients pertaining to western Cuddapah and eastern Cuddapah is significant. While average wage per unit of cloth produced show no significant impact on the per capita income in western Cuddapah, per capita income is altered by 15 units with one unit change in average wage per unit of cloth produced in eastern Cuddapah.

The above results clearly bring to light the absolute differences in the magnitude of Co-efficients relating to the variables included in the model and the differences in the estimated income functions for the major categories of the weavers.

However, the absolute differences in the Cofficients relating to variables included in the model, will make it difficult to arrive at a uniform solution for improving the levels of living of handloom weavers in all the categories. Yet, we can identify X_2, X_1 and X_3 variables in western Cuddapah, X_1, X_2, X_3, and X_5 variables in eastern Cuddapah i.e. Male participation rate, Size of household, Female participation rate and average wage per unit of cloth produced, as the roost influencing variables. Thus an increase in Male and female participation rates, average wage per unit of cloth and reduction in the size of population would help the sample unit to improve their levels of living.

The average wage among other things, depends upon the counts of yarn used, texture, design of the fabric, other qualitative inputs like zari and silk used. An improvement in all the above will enable the weaver to get more remuneration and thus his per capita income will increase. Moreover, the fabrics will have greater consumer acceptability. Thus there is a strong case for better varieties and quality fabrics both for improving the lot of the weavers and capturing the market for cloth.

Expenditure Details of the Households

In a socio-economic survey of the weavers not only income should be considered but expenditure should also be taken into account as ultimate solvency and even survival depends on this. Expenditure figures are presented in Table 4.33 (*See on next page*).

The percentage of weavers that spent more than ₹ 7000 or more per annum was less in rural centres of eastern cuddapah than in other areas. In terms of average household expenditure too, rural centres of eastern Cuddapah is lagging behind with ₹ 4470 compare to other areas viz., rural, urban centres of western Cuddapah and urban centres of eastern Cuddapah where average household expenditure is ₹ 7781, ₹ 7544 and ₹ 7434 respectively. An important observation in this table is that the Standard Deviation of expenditure in rural centres of western Cuddapah

Table 4.33 : Total Expenditwe of the Household in a Year

Areas	Expenditure					Total Expenditure	Total No. of House holds	Average Household Expenditure	Total Members in the family	Per Capita Expenditure	S.D.	C.V.
	Below 2500	2501-4000	4001-5500	5501-7000	Above 7000							
West Rural	—	2 (4.0)	9 (18.0)	13 (26.0)	26 (52.0)	389059	50	7781	247	1575.14	1338	17.20
West Urban	2 (3.0)	4 (5.0)	15 (20.0)	18 (24.0)	36 (48.0)	553908	75	7385	363	1525.92	1591	21.54
Total West	2 (2.0)	6 (5.0)	24 (19.0)	31 (25.0)	62 (49.0)	942967	125	7544	610	1545.85	1500	19.88
East Rural	17 (49.0)	5 (14.0)	3 (9.0)	1 (3.0)	9 (25.0)	156458	35	4470	151	1036.15	2518	56.00
East Urban	—	2 (4.0)	2 (4.0)	15 (27.0)	36 (65.0)	517930	55	9417	263	1969.32	1082	11.48
Total East	17 (19.0)	7 (8.0)	5 (6.0)	16 (18.0)	45 (50.0)	674388	90	7493	414	1628.96	2366	31.58
Grand Total	**19 (9.0)**	**13 (6.0)**	**29 (13.0)**	**47 (22.0)**	**107 (50.0)**	**1617355**	**215**	**7523**	**1024**	**1579.45**	**1936**	**21.73**

Source : Field Survey Data.

Figures in brackets are percentages to their respective totals.

is absolutely less with ₹ 1338 where household average income was less compare to other areas. Average household expenditure is highest in rural centres of eastern Cuddapah with ₹ 2518. In terms of household average expenditure we can observe that the consumption standards are the same in western zone and eastern zones of Cuddapah district.

Distribution of Households by Per Capita Expenditure

The details of per capita expenditure are presented in Table 4.34 (*See on page 179*). Contrary to the situation in regard to total expenditure of households, in terms of per capita expenditure the standard of consumption is relatively better in eastern Cuddapah than in western Cuddapah. The per capita expenditure of handloom weaver is lower in rural areas of eastern Cuddapah and higher in urban areas of eastern Cuddapah.

Per Capita Expenditure Range of Households

The range pertaining to per capita expenditure of different categories of weavers is given in Table 4.35 (*See on page 180*).

The average per capita expenditure of all the categories put together is ₹ 131.50 per month and that of the averages pertaining to rural centres of eastern Cuddapah, urban centres of western Cuddapah have lower per capita expenditure than the general average. The average per capita expenditure of all categories of weavers, except the above two categories, is a little higher than the average per capita expenditure. These figures of expenditure both total and per capita speak of the poor standard of living maintained by a majority of weavers covered by our study in Cuddapah district.

Expenditure Pattern

A study of the expenditure pattern of the weaving community of Cuddapah district could be of great interest in the context of the study of the socio-economic aspects of the weavers. The data in this regard were collected from the weavers studied and presented in Table 4.36 (*See on page 181*).

As expected the expenditure on food forms a major part of the total expenditure with 75 per cent in the case of all categories. The percentage of expenditure on food is highest in the case of weavers in rural centres of western Cuddapah with 82 per cent where as it is relatively less in case of rural and urban centres of eastern Cuddapah with 71 per cent and 73 per cent respectively. Thus it is proves Engel's law of consumption which states that the proportion of expenditure on food decreases with the increase in income.

Table 4.34: Distribution of Table of Households by Per Capita Expenditure

Areas	Per Capita Expenditure						No. of House-holds	Per Capita Expen-diture	S.D.	C.V.
	Below 500	501-1000	1001-1500	1501-2000	2001 2500	Above 2500				
West Rural	—	2 (4.0)	21 (42.0)	14 (28.0)	10 (20.0)	3 (6.0)	50 (100.0)	1575	497	31.56
West Urban	—	10 (13.0)	31 (41.0)	17 (23.0)	12 (16.0)	5 (7.0)	75 (100.0)	1526	553	36.24
Total West	—	12 (10.0)	52 (42.0)	31 (25.0)	22 (18.0)	8 (5.0)	125 (100.0)	1546	534	34.54
East Rural	—	1 (3.0)	10 (29.0)	9 (26.0)	11 (31.0)	4 (11.0)	35 (100.0)	1036	532	51.35
East Urban	—	—	16 (29.0)	20 (36.0)	8 (15.0)	11 (20.0)	55 (100.0)	1969	541	27.48
Total East	—	1 (1.0)	26 (29.0)	29 (32.0)	19 (21.0)	15 (17.0)	90 (100.0)	1629	538	33.03
Grand Total	**—**	**13 (6.0)**	**78 (36.0)**	**60 (28.0)**	**41 (19.0)**	**23 (11.0)**	**215 (100.0)**	**1579**	**552**	**34.96**

Source : Field Survey Data.

Figures in brackets are percentages to their respective totals.

Table 4.35 : Per Capita Expenditure Range of the Weavers' Families

Areas	Per Capita Expenditure Range		Average per Capita Expenditure
	₹	₹	₹
West Rural	72.50	395.80	131.25
West Urban	55.00	320.80	127.15
Total West	55.00	395.80	128.80
East Rural	101.40	300.00	86.30
East Urban	100.00	354.15	164.00
Total East	100.00	354.15	135.75
Grand Total	**55.00**	**395.80**	**131.50**

Source : Field Survey Data
Figures in brackets are percentages to their respective totals

The proportion of expenditure on clothing is more than 10 per cent in the case of weavers in urban centres of western Cuddapah, rural and urban centres of eastern Cuddapah and it is 11 per cent, 13 per cent and 12 per cent respectively. It is 8 per cent in the case of weavers in rural centres of western Cuddapah.

Most of the weavers in eastern Cuddapah have their own houses hence weavers living in rented houses are less. There fore only 1 per cent of the expenditure is made for the payment of house rents. In western Cuddapah 3 per cent of the expenditure is going for the payment of house rents.

Expenditure on medical expenses also is higher in case of weavers in eastern region, compared to their counter parts in western regions of Cuddapah district.

The proportion of expenditure on children's education is low in all areas of the district with 1 per cent of expenditure each, except in rural centres of western Cuddapah, where it is 2 per cent of expenditure only.

The proportion of expenditure on personal expenses and miscellaneous expenses viz. smoking, drinking etc., is higher in rural centres of eastern Cuddapah with 11 per cent. In other parts of the district viz., rural and urban centres of western Cuddapah and urban centres of eastern Cuddapah the Proportion of expenditure on this head is 5 per cent, 5.36 per cent and 6 per cent respectively. Although the respondents do not come out openly, It was felt that the expenditure on this account is higher than what is stated. Working male members of the weaving families usually take tea in nearby stalls once or twice regularly.

Table 4.36 : Expenditure Details of the Households

Region	Total income	Details of Expenditure							Total Expendi-ture.	Total Members of the family	Per Capita Expen-diture	Per Capita Income
		Food	Clothing	House Rent	Medical	Education	Personel Expenditure	Miscella-neous				
West Rural	395310	318800 (82.0)	29500 (8.0)	3604 (1.0)	11150 (3.0)	8375 (2.0)	2330 (1.0)	15300 (4.0)	389059 (100.0)	247	1575	1600.45
West Urban	559420	409640 (74.0)	62350 (11.0)	22888 (4.0)	21790 (4.0)	4500 (1.0)	2000 (0.36)	30740 (4.0)	553908 (100.0)	363	1526	1541.10
Total West	954730	728440 (77.0)	91850 (10.0)	26492 (3.0)	32940 (3.0)	12875 (1.0)	4330 (0.46)	46040 (5.0)	942967 (100.0)	610	1546	1565.13
East Rural	368660	202500 (71.0)	37000 (13.0)	2540 (1.0)	11300 (4.0)	1550 (1.0)	23740 (8.0)	7170 (3.0)	285800 (100.0)	151	1036	2441.46
East Urban	612140	376600 (73.0)	63100 (12.0)	5800 (1.0)	18290 (4.0)	8650 (2.0)	23150 (4.00)	12340 (2.0)	517930 (100.0)	263	1969	2327.53
Total East	980800	579100 (72.0)	100100 (12.0)	8340 (1.0)	29590 (4.0)	10200 (1.0)	46890 (6.0)	19510 (2.0)	803730 (100.0)	414	1629	2369.08
Grand Total	**1935530**	**1307540 (75.0)**	**191950 (11.0)**	**34832 (2.0)**	**62530 (4.0)**	**23075 (1.0)**	**51220 (3.0)**	**65550 (4.0)**	**1746697 (100.0)**	**1024**	**1579**	**1890.17**

Source : Field survey data.

Figures in brackets are percentages to their respective totals.

Respondents have not revealed about their drinking habits. But, it is a fact that most of the weavers are addicted to liquors during evening times.

Savings

A corollary of the study of income and expenditure is the study of monthly savings and indebtedness. Table 4.37 (*See on next page*) gives the monthly savings of different categories of weavers.

Out of 215 households studied, only 68 households constituting 32 per cent have savings ranging from ₹ 20 to ₹ 600 per month. A majority of those who save i.e. 21 out of 68 save more than ₹ 500 and the remaining less than ₹ 500. If we look into the region-wise savings of the weaving households it appears that the economic position of the weaver is not sound in western Cuddapah as around 78 per cent of the weavers are not at all saving. While it is 54 per cent in the eastern Cuddapah. Weavers saving more than ₹ 500 per month were also more in eastern Cuddapah with 21.11 per cent than in western Cuddapah with 1.60 per cent. The amount of saving per month is the highest for rural centres of eastern Cuddapah and it is lowest for rural centres of western Cuddapah. The average savings range between ₹ 121 to ₹ 227 and ₹ 448 to ₹ 601 for western and eastern regions respectively. The average amount of savings per month is more in eastern Cuddapah with ₹ 508 while it is ₹ 176 for western Cuddapah.

Distribution of Savings According to Organisation

In order to find out the impact of organisation on the savings of the weaving households information was collected from the weaving households and presented in Table 4.38 & 4.38-A (*See on pages 184 and 185*). Weavers working independently are having the highest saving with an average of ₹ 563 per month. Out of 6 households weaving for the Corporate sector only 1 household is saving and the amount of saving is ₹ 167 per month, which is the lowest amount in the sample. Weavers working for the Master weaver, Co-operative, have got the second and third positions in terms of Savings, with ₹ 364 and ₹ 284 respectively. Weavers working for more than one organisation are saving ₹ 214 per month.

Monthly Savings of Weaving Families

Except in the case of Independent weavers, in all other organisations, weavers saving are larger in percentage in urban centres of western Cuddapah than in rural centres of western Cuddapah. The proportion of weavers saving money is comparatively more in eastern Cuddapah in

Table 4.37 : Monthly Savings of the Weaving Families

Regions	No. of House-holds	No. of House-holds Not Saving	No. of House-holds Saving	Monthly Savings							Total Saving	Average Savings of house-holds Saving
				Nil	Less than 100	101-200	201-300	301-400	401-500	500& Above		
West Rural	50	37 (74.0)	13 (26.0)	37 (74.0)	6 (12.0)	6 (12.0)	—	—	—	1 (2.0)	1570	121
West Urban	75	61 (81.33)	14 (18.67)	61 (81.33)	4 (5.33)	—	7 (9.33)	2 (2.67)	—	1 (1.33)	3176	227
Total West	125	98 (78.4)	27 (21.6)	98 (78.4)	10 (8.0)	6 (4.80)	7 (5.60)	2 (1.60)	—	2 (1.60)	4746	176
East Rural	35	19 (54.29)	16 (45.71)	19 (54.29)	—	—	—	1 (2.86)	1 (2.85)	14 (40.0)	9611	601
East Urban	55	30 (54.55)	25 (45.45)	30 (54.55)	2 (3.64)	7 (12.73)	4 (7.27)	—	7 (12.73)	5 (9.09)	11208	448
Total East	90	49 (54.44)	41 (45.56)	49 (54.44)	2 (2.22)	7 (7.78)	4 (4.44)	1 (1.11)	8 (8.88)	19 (21.11)	20819	508
Grand Total	**215**	**147 (68.37)**	**68 (31.63)**	**147 (68.37)**	**12 (5.58)**	**13 (6.05)**	**11 (5.12)**	**3 (1.40)**	**8 (3.72)**	**21 (9.77)**	**25565**	**376**

Source: Field Survey Data.

Figuere in brackets are percentages to their respective totals.

Table 4.38 : Distribution of Saving According to Organisation

Region	Master Weaver				Co-operative				Independent				Corporation			
	No.of House-holds.	No. Sav-ing	Total Savi-ngs.	Average Savings holds.	No.of House-ing	No. Sav-ngs.	Total Savi-	Average Savings holds.	No.of House-ing	No. Sav-ngs	Total Savi-holds	Average Savings ing.	No.of House-ng	No. Sav-	Total Savi-	Average Savings
West Rural	24	3 (12.5)	290	96.65	—	—	—	—	15	7 (46.67)	867	123.85	1	— (0)	—	—
West Urban	37	3 (8.11)	670	223.30	13	3 (23.08)	626	108.65	1	1 (100)	720	720.00	5	1 (20.0)	167	167
Total West	61	6 (9.84)	960	160.00	13	3 (23.08)	626	208.65	16	8 (50.0)	1587	198.35	6	1 (18.67)	167	167
East Rural	11	3 (27.27)	824	291.00	6	1 (16.67)	1224	1125.00	9	7 (77.78)	18063	1151.86	—	—	—	—
East Urban	19	10 (52.63)	5131	513.10	19	3 (15.79)	1175	301.67	8	7 (87.5)	2744	392.00	—	—	—	—
Total East	30	13 (43.33)	5955	458.10	25	4 (16.0)	1399	349.75	17	14 (82.35)	10807	772.00	—	—	—	—
Grand Total	**91**	**19 (20.88)**	**6915**	**363.95**	**38**	**7 (18.42)**	**2025**	**289.30**	**33**	**22 (66.67)**	**12394**	**563.35**	**6**	**1 (16.67)**	**167**	**167**

Source: Field Survey Data.

Figuere in brackets are percentages to their respective totals.

case of weavers working for Master weavers, Independent weavers and wavers working for all organisations. In case of Co-operative organisation and Corporate sectors the proportion of weavers saving in western Cuddapah is more than their counterparts in eastern Cuddapah. From this, it is clear that Co-operative system is relatively better in western Cuddapah than eastern Cuddapah.

Table 4.38A : Distribution of Saving According to Organisation

Regions	Working for all organisations				Total House-holds
	No. of House-holds	No. of Saving	Total Saving	Average Saving	
West Rural	10	3 (3.0)	413	137.65	50
West Urban	19	6 (31.38)	993	165.50	75
Total West	29	9 (31.03)	1406	152.25	125
East Rural	9	5 (55.56)	505	100.00	35
East Urban	9	5 (55.56)	2158	431.60	55
Total East	18	10 (55.56)	2658	265.80	90
Grand Total	**47**	**19 (40.43)**	**4064**	**213.90**	**217**

Source: Field Survey Data.
Figuere in brackets are percentages to their respective totals.

Details of Savings

Information, pertaining to organisations in which weavers have saved their savings is given in Table 4.40 (*See on page 187*). According to the information available in the table the major amount of money is saved with private Chit fund companies. About 60 per cent of the money saved In western region and 52 per cent in eastern region of Cuddapah district is kept in Chits. Commercial Banks are the second important source of savings for the weavers in both the regions. The savings of weavers are normally kept in Co-op Bank, Co-operative Society and post-offices also.

Table 4.39: Monthly Savings of the Weaving Families

Organisation	No. of House-holds not saving	No. of House-holds	Total No. of House-holds	Total Savings							Total Savings	Average Savings
				Nil	Less than 100	101-200	201-300	301-400	401-500	500& Above		
Master weaver	19 (20.88)	72 (72.12)	91 (100.0)	72 (79.12)	3 (3.30)	2 (2.20)	4 (4.40)	—	3 (3.29)	7 (7.69)	6915	364
Co-operative	7 (18.42)	31 (81.58)	38 (100.0)	31 (81.68)	—	2 (5.23)	1 (2.64)	—	2 (5.23)	2 (5.23)	2025	289
Independent	22 (66.67)	11 (33.33)	33 (100.0)	11 (33.33)	1 (3.03)	5 (15.5)	3 (3.03)	1 (6.07)	2 (30.30)	10	12394	563
Corporation	1 (16.67)	5 (83.33)	6 (100.0)	5 (83.33)	—	1 (16.67)	—	—	—	—	167	167
Weavers working for more than one organisation	19 (40.43)	28 (59.57)	47 (100.0)	28 (59.57)	6 (12.77)	3 (6.33)	2 (4.26)	— —	— —	8 (17.02)	4064	214
Total	**68 (31.63)**	**147 (68.37)**	**215 (100.0)**	**147 (68.37)**	**10 (4.65)**	**13 (6.05)**	**10 (4.65)**	**1 (0.47)**	**7 (3.26)**	**27 12.56**	**25565**	**376**

Source : Field Survey Data.

Figures in brackets are percentages to their respective totals.

Table 4.40: Particulars of Savings

Regions	No. of Households Saving	No. of Househol Not Saving	Total House holds	Datails of Saving					Total Saving	Average Saving
				Commercial Banks	Co-op Banks	Co-op Society	Post Office	Chits		
West Rural	13	37	50	490 (31.21)	—	—	40 (2.55)	1040 (66.24)	1570 (100.0)	121
West Urban	14	61	75	828 (26.07)	296 (9.32)	225 (7.08)	—	1827 (51.53)	3176 (100.0)	227
Total West	27	98	125	1318 (27.77)	296 (6.24)	225 (4.74)	40 (0.84)	2867 (60.41)	4746 (100.0)	176
East Rural	16	19	35	5708 (59.39)	—	—	1313 (13.66)	2590 (26.95)	9611 (100.0)	601
East Urban	25	30	55	3041 (27.13)	—	—	— —	8167 (72.87)	11208 (100.0)	448
Total East	41	49	90	8749 (42.02)	—	—	1313 (6.31)	10757 (51.67)	20819 (100.0)	508
Grand Total	**68**	**147**	**215**	**10067 (39.38)**	**296 (1.56)**	**225 (0.88)**	**1353 (5.29)**	**13624 (53.29)**	**25565 (100.0)**	**376**

Source : Field Survey Data.

Figures in brackets are percentages to their respective totals.

Indebtedness

Table 4.41 (*See on page 189*) gives details of indebtedness of various categories of weavers as on the date of survey. A majority of the weavers i.e. 149 out of 215 households constituting 69.30 per cent are indebted. The debts are ranging from ₹ 50 to ₹ 10000.

Purpose and Source of Borrowing

The sources of borrowing, for the weavers are Master weavers, Traders, Co-operative societies Commercial Banks and Relatives etc. Out of 149 households who have, taken loans 107 households constituting 71.89 per cent have taken from the Master weavers and the second important source of borrowing is the local traders and moneylenders. Bank financing is very insignificant with only 3 per cent. Master weaver himself is the principal lender not only for weavers working under him, but also for all other weavers working for different organisations except those under Co-operative sector. Weavers working under Co-operative sector are getting loans from the Cooperative Society or the Co-operative Bank. Only the Independent weavers availed themselves loans of Commercial Banks.

Master weavers establish long-term economic relationship with weavers by giving them large sums as advances or personal-interest free loans which are deducted in small amounts from the weavers wages. A weaver thus obliged is unlikely to leave without repaying the debt for two reasons. First, a Master weaver is more likely to resort to Court action to recover a large amount of money and a weaver may lose his house, looms and all other personal assets. Second, the grape wine is a rapid means of communication. A weaver leaving a Master weaver while still owning him a large amount of money finds that the other Master weavers have already heard of this and are unwilling to take the financial risk involved in hiring him. Thus once weavers borrow money from Master weavers always find themselves caught in the debt trap for ever.

Purpose and Source of Borrowing Based on Organisation

Table 4.43 (*See on page 191*) shows that obviously the Sowcar-weaver is the major source of loans and advances. He supplies loans advances for both productive and unproductive purposes.

Advances for productive purposes include raw materials supplied to the weavers and wages given in advance.

The Co-operatives supply raw materials to the weavers, But such supply of raw materials is not treated as advance as at no stage the

Table 4.41 : Details of Loan Borrowed by the Weaving Households

Regions	No.of House-holds	No.of House-holds Borro-wed loan	House-holds without any loan	Amount of Loan borrowed. (In ₹)						Loan House-hold)	Total Loan	Average Looms	No.of Loan Looms	Average per	S.D.
				Below 1000	1001-2000	2001-3000	3001-4000	4001-5000	Above 5000						
West Rural	50	30 (60.0)	20 (40.0)	16 (53.0)	5 (17.0)	4 (13.0)	3 (10.0)	1 (3.0)	1 (4.0)	54500	1090	72	757	1378	182
West Urban	75	42 (56.0)	33 (44.0)	22 (52.0)	8 (19.0)	5 (12.0)	1 (5.0)	2 (10.0)	4	95000	1267	99	960	1632	170
Total West	125	72 (58.0)	53 (42.0)	38 (53.0)	13 (18.0)	9 (13.0)	4 (6.0)	3 (4.0)	5 (6.0)	149500	1196	171	874	1533	175
East Rural	35	31 (89.0)	4 (11.0)	12 (39.0)	11 (35.0)	—	1 (3.0)	3 (10.0)	4 (13.0)	81000	2314	44	1841	1794	97.6
East Urban	55	46 (84.0)	9 (16.0)	5 (11.0)	17 (37.0)	2 (4.0)	4 (9.0)	3 (7.0)	15 (32.0)	185900	3380	71	2618	1928	73.6
Total East	90	77 (86.0)	13 (14.0)	17 (22.0)	28 (36.0)	2 (3.0)	5 (6.0)	6 (8.0)	19 (25.0)	266900	2966	115	2321	1955	84.2
Grand Total	**215**	**149 (69.0)**	**66 (31.0)**	**55 (37.0)**	**41 (28.0)**	**11 (7.0)**	**9 (6.0)**	**9 (6.0)**	**23 (16.0)**	**416400**	**1937**	**286**	**1456**	**1827**	**125.5**

Source : Field Survey Data.

Figures in brackets are percentages to their respective totals.

Table 4.42 : Purpose and Source of Borrowing of the Households

Regions	No. of House-holds	No. Borro-wed Loan	Purpose of Borrowing							Source of Borrowing				
			Produ-ction	Consump-tion	Housing	Marke-ting	Functi-ons	Busi-ness	Others	Bank	Co-op Society	Master Weaver	Traders	Others
West Rural	50	30	—	26 (87.0)	—	—	3 (10.0)	—	1 (3.0)	—	—	24	5	1
West Urban	75	42	3 (7.0)	28 (66.0)	4 (10.0)	—	5 (12.0)	2 (5.0)	—	2 (5.0)	3 (7.0)	28 (67.0)	6 (14.0)	3 (7.0)
Total West	125	72	3 (4.0)	54 (75.0)	4 (6.0)	—	8 (19.0)	2 (5.0)	1 (2.0)	2 (3.0)	3 (4.0)	52 (72.0)	11 (15.0)	4 (6.0)
East Rural	35	31	6 (19.0)	16 (52.0)	— —	4 (13.0)	3 (10.0)	— —	2 (6.0)	1 (3.0)	1 (3.0)	22 (71.0)	5 (16.0)	2 (7.0)
East Urban	55	46	6 (13.0)	29 (63.0)	2 (4.0)	3 (7.0)	6 (13.0)	—	—	2 (4.0)	1 (2.0)	33 (72.0)	7 (15.0)	3 (7.0)
Total East	90	77	12 (16.0)	45 (58.0)	2 (3.0)	7 (9.0)	9 (12.0)	—	2 (3.0)	3 (4.0)	2 (3.0)	55 (71.0)	12 (16.0)	5 (6.0)
Grand Total	**215**	**149**	**15 (10.0)**	**99 (66.0)**	**6 (4.0)**	**7 (5.0)**	**17 (11.0)**	**2 (1.0)**	**3 (2.0)**	**5 (3.0)**	**5 (3.0)**	**107 (72.0)**	**23 (15.0)**	**9 (6.0)**

Source : Field Survey Data.

Figures in brackets are percentages to their respective totals.

Table 4.43: Purpose and Source of Borrowing based on Organisation

Organisations	No. of House-holds	No. Borro-wed Loan	Purpose of Borrowing							Source of Borrowing				
			Produ-ction	Consump-tion	Housing	Marke-ting	Functi-ons	Busi-ness	Others	Bank	Co-op Society	Master Weaver	Traders	Others
Master weaver	91	91	4 (4.0)	79 (87.0)	—	—	8 (9.0)	—	—	—	—	85 (93.0)	4 (4.0)	2 (3.0)
Co-operatives	38	15	5 (33.0)	6 (40.0)	—	—	3 (20.0)	—	1 (7.0)	—	5 (33.0)		5 (33.0)	5 (34.0)
Independent	33	14	5 (36.0)	2 (14.0)	2 (14.0)	2 (14.0)	—	2 (14.0)	1 (8.0)	4 (29.0)	— —	— —	8 (57.0)	2 (14.0)
Corporation	6	4	1 (25.0)	1 (25.0)	1 (25.0)	—	1 (25.0)	—	—	—	—	2 (50.0)	2 (50.0)	—
Working for more than one organisations	47	25	—	11 (44.0)	3 (12.0)	5 (20.0)	5 (20.0)	— —	1 (4.0)	1 (4.0)	— —	20 (80.0)	4 (16.0)	—
Total	**215**	**149 (69.3)**	**15 (10.0)**	**99 (66.0)**	**6 (4.0)**	**7 (5.0)**	**17 (11.0)**	**2 (1.0)**	**3 (3.0)**	**5 (3.0)**	**5 (3.0)**	**107 (72.0)**	**23 (15.0)**	**9 (7.0)**

Source : Field Survey Data.

Figures in brackets are percentages to their respective totals.

weavers become their owners. Besides most of the Co-operatives do not give credit for unproductive purposes. These two reasons explain the low share of Co-operatives in the total amount of loans and advances obtained by the sample units. The poor performance of banking institutions as sources of credit to the weavers indicate that these institutions have to go a long way to emerge as important sources of credit to the weavers. The weavers have little to offer as securities which the banks demand against credit facilities. In the course of informal interview it is learnt that where ever Banks adopted a liberal credit policy on a trail basis, there was non-payment of loans by weavers. This therefore discouraged the Banks from adopting such a policy.

On the other hand the weavers view is that inadequate funds supplied to them by the Banks could not help them to increase their repaying capacity. Many of them however admitted the misuse of credit money for unproductive purposes.

On the whole, the Master weaver and the private moneylenders taken together constitute the main source of loans and advances. Hence they are in a position to control most of the units, irrespective of whether they work directly for them or for the Co-operatives or the Corporation. The Co-operatives do not meet all types of credit requirements of the weavers working for them and also do not function as effectively as they ought to do. The Corporations and Banks are yet to gain a foothold in the field.

Only about 10 per cent of the total borrowings of the sample units was meant for productive purposes. That is to say, the low Co-operative coverage and reluctance or inability of the Co-operatives to accommodate the weavers for unproductive loans and advances are mainly responsible for the strangle-hold of the Sowcar weavers in the industry.

The average debt burden per unit was worked out to be ₹ 1937. The low amount of debt should not at any rate be considered as a reflection of the sound economic condition of the units. On the contrary, this is an indicator of the lack of credit worthiness of the units, their small-scale operation and non-availability of adequate amount of credit on suitable terms and conditions. It cannot be denied that credit worthiness depends on the general economic status of any borrower. Obviously the poor weaver does not satisfy the aforesaid condition.

Volume of debt by itself may not indicate precisely the economic condition of the borrower. If a household incurs debt for consumption or ceremonial purposes and the loan doesn't help any productive effort, then, even a small loan necessarily becomes a burden. That is, the purpose for which credit is used is very important. Further the burden of loan, very largely, depends on the conditions on which it is borrowed. These again depend on the sources of credit. Judged from these points of view, the weavers have a smaller volume of debt which does not necessarily that they are in a position of advantage. On the contrary, this indicates that their scale of operation is : small they do not have credit worthiness and adequate quantity of credit is not available to them on suitable terms and conditions. They are poor and therefore, they borrow to meet their consumption needs and ceremonial expenses, the Master-weavers and private moneylenders are the main sources of credit and the terms and conditions on which credit is available further Indicates the extent of the debt burden.

Interest on Borrquings

Table 4.44 (*See on next page*) explains the interest paid on the borrowings. The amount of interest paid ranges between 0-40 per cent per annum. Of the 72 households that borrowed loan in western Cuddapah 68 per cent of them are not paying interest, 10 per cent of them pay 12 per cent of interest and the remaining 16 households or 22 per cent pay interest at the rate of 24 per cent. No household in western Cuddapah pays over and above 24 per cent rate of interest. The percentage of weavers that pay interest charges 24 per cent and more constitute large proportion in Cuddapah.

On the basis of data collected it may be noted, that amount of borrowings outstanding against 215 sample household units was ₹ 4,16,400 and tho average worked out to ₹ 1937. The percentage of households that borrowed loan is relatively less(58%) in western Cuddapah, while it is more (86%) in eastern Cuddapah. The average amount of loan is the highest at ₹ 2652 in eastern Cuddapah as against ₹ 1146 in western Cuddapah.

Properties Owned

A study of the total assets owned by the weaving communities would be of interest in the overall context of the study of the socio-economic aspects of the weaver, as it gives an indication of the socio-economic status of the weaver in the society. The data collected are presented in Tables 4.45 and 4.46 (*See on page 195 and 196*).

The value of property ranges from ₹ 1500 to ₹ 85000 per household and the asset consist mainly of houses and looms. Very few of them own landed property.

An analysis of the data reveals that those who do not own any property at all comprise mostly of weavers working under Master weavers, Co-operatives and weavers working for more than one

Table 4.44 : Details of Interest Paid by the Households

Regions	No. of House-holds	Total amount of loan	Average Loan per Household	Amount of loan repaid during 1988	Amount of loan outsta-nding	Average amount of loan outsta-nding	Rate of Interest paid: Nil	12%	24%	Above 24%.	Total No. borrowed Loan	Average Rate of interest
Rural	50	54500	1090	—	54500	1090	19 (63.0)	3 (10.0)	8 (27.0)	—	30 (100.0)	19.5
West Urban	75	95000	1267	6200	88800	1184	30 (71.0)	4 (10.0)	8 (19.0)	—	42 (100.0)	20.0
Total West	125	149500	1196	6200	143300	1146	49	7	16	—	72	20.0
East Rural	35	81000	2314	5550	75450	2156	17 (55.0)	—	12 (39.0)	2 (6.0)	31 (100.0)	26.5
East Urban	55	185900	3380	22700	163200	2967	12 (26.0)	—	23 (50.0)	11 (24.0)	46 (100.0)	29.0
Total East	90	266900	2966	28250	238650	2652	29		35	13	77	28.0
Grand Total	**215**	**416400**	**1937**	**34450**	**381950**	**1777**	**78 (53.0)**	**7 (5.0)**	**51 (34.0)**	**13 (9.0)**	**149**	**24.0**

Source : Field Survey Data.

Figures in brackets are percentages to their respective totals.

Table 4.45 : Assets Distribution of the Households

Regions	Distribution of Assets					No. of House-holds	Total Value of Assets	Average	S.D.	C.V.
	Below 5000	5001-10000	10001-20000	20001-30000	Above 30000					
West Rural	16 (32.0)	12 (24.0)	15 (30.0)	3 (6.0)	4 (8.0)	50 (100.0)	859500	17190	10913	63.48
West Urban	35 (46.67)	10 (13.33)	8 (10.67)	8 (10.67)	14 (18.66)	75 (100.0)	1250500	16673	13557	81.31
Total West	51 (40.80)	22 (17.60)	23 (18.40)	11 (8.80)	18 (14.4)	125 (100.0)	2110000	16880	12602	74.66
East Rural	4 (11.43)	4 (11.43)	13 (37.14)	2 (5.71)	12 (34.29)	35 (100.0)	946200	27034	10762	39.81
East Urban	7 (12.72)	5 (9.09)	19 (34.55)	13 (23.64)	11 (20.0)	55 (100.0)	1257200	22858	9510	41.60
Total East	11 (12.22)	9 (10.0)	32 (35.56)	15 (16.67)	23 (25.56)	90 (100.0)	2203400	24482	10078	41.16
Grand Total	**62 (28.84)**	**31 (14.42)**	**55 (25.58)**	**26 (12.09)**	**41 (19.07)**	**215 (100.0)**	**4313400**	**20540**	**12207**	**59.43**

Source : Field Survey Data.

Figures in brackets are percentages to their respective totals.

Table 4.46 : Assets of the Households

Reoions	No. Owning Houses	No. not having houses	Value of housing property	Average value of housing property	Details of agricultural land				Fixed capital sunk in hand-looms	Any other	Total value	Average	S.B.	C.V.
					No. with land	Extent (acres)	Value	No. with-out land						
West Rural	41 (82.0)	9 (18.0)	783500	19110	2 (4.0)	3.25	29000	48 (96.0)	46000	1000	859500	17190	7175	41.74
West Urban	40 (53.33)	35 (46.67)	1160000	29000	2 (2.67)	2.00	3000	73 (97.33)	87500	—	1250500	16673	1856	11.13
Total West	81 (64.80)	44 (35.20)	1943500	23994	4 (3.20)	5.25	32000	121 (96.80)	133500	1000	2110000	16880	5300	31.39
East Rural	32 (91.43)	3 (8.57)	742200	23194	1 (2.86)	1.50	30000	34 (97.14)	44000	130000	946200	27034	1798	6.65
East Urban	51 (92.73)	4 (7.27)	1094700	21465	3 (5.46)	3.00	64000	52 (94.54)	75000	23500	1257200	22858	2835	12.40
Total East	83 (92.225)	7 (7.88)	1836900	22131	4 (4.44)	4.50	94000	86 (95.56)	119000	153500	2203400	24482	3338	13.60
Grand Total	**164 (76.28)**	**51 (23.72)**	**3780400**	**23051**	**8 (3.72)**	**9.75**	**126000**	**207 (96.28)**	**252500**	**154500**	**4313400**	**20062**	**5534**	**27.58**

Source : Field Survey Data.

Figures in brackets are percentages to their respective totals.

organisation. Assets worth ₹ 20000 and above, on an average, are owned by the Independent weavers, and weavers working for more than one organisation. Weavers working for Master weavers, Co-operative Societies and Corporations have assets worth ₹ 19836, ₹ 15969 and ₹ 9043 respectively on an average.

Of the 125 households, 81 households or 65 per cent in western Cuddapah another 83 households or 92 per cent of 90 households in eastern Cuddapah live in their own houses and the rest do not have house of their own. Among the sample households, 76 per cent have their own houses and the rest do not have houses at all.

The average value of the house is a little more in western Cuddapah at ₹ 23994 and in eastern Cuddapah it is around ₹ 22131, on an average.

Only 8 households of 215 or 4 per cent have landed property, the rest do not have any agricultural property. The percentage is 3 in western Cuddapah and 4 in eastern Cuddapah. The average value of landed property owned by a household is ₹ 32000 in western Cuddapah, while it is ₹ 94000 in eastern Cuddapah. The Co-efficient of variation, in the value of property owned, is the highest in rural areas of western Cuddapah at 41.74; while it is lowest in rural areas of eastern Cuddapah at 6.65. For urban areas of western Cuddapah the value of C.V is 11.13; while it is 12.40 for urban areas of eastern Cuddapah. We may thus find that the value of C.V is more for western Cuddapah at 31.39; while it is less for eastern Cuddapah at 13.63. It is quite clear from the foregoing that the level of variation, in the value of properties possessed is the highest in rural areas of western Cuddapah and urban areas of eastern Cuddapah while it is less in urban areas of western Cuddapah and rural areas of Eastern Cuddapah. The variation appears to be significantly more in western Cuddapah than in eastern Cuddapah.

Value of Property Owned by the Households

The area-wise distribution of assets is presented in Table 4.47 (*See on next page*). This table gives a clear picture of the distribution of assets in different areas of the district.

Employment

The handloom industry provides employment on such a large scale that it ranks next only to agriculture. A study of this aspect is however, beset with many difficulties. Unlike the organised industries, there is no discipline in the household industries, like the present one under study with regard to hours of work. Further, the main worker in this industry is assisted by other members of the household in the different processes

Table 4.47 : Values of Properties Owned by the Weaving Families

Value of properties owned	Number of weaving families					Total
	Master weaver	Co-operatives	Corporation	Independent	Woeking for more than one organisation	
Nil	8	7	1	—	8	24
Less than 5000	4	10	2	9	13	38
5001-10000	16	5	—	5	5	31
10001-20000	28	8	1	9	9	55
20001-30000	15	1	1	6	3	26
30001-50000	18	7	1	4	7	37
Above 50000	2	—	—	—	2	4
Total No. of Households	91	38	6	33	47	215
Total value of assets	1805115	606810	54260	825820	1021395	4313400
Average value of assets	19836	15969	9043	25025	21732	20062

Source : Field Survey Data.

of manufacture. This pattern of employment is further complicated by the absence of rigid specialisation of work. The workers in this industry attend to more than one process of work and thus generally enjoy a multi-activity status. It becomes difficult for these reasons to gauge the nature and magnitude of employment in this industry.[12] However, an attempt has been made to examine the employment aspects of the handloom industry, in this section.

Nature of Employment

Cotton handloom weaving is carried on mainly on a household basis, primarily using household labour and very little of hired labour. This characteristic of the industry has some times been advanced as a strong argument in favour of its protection and development. The argument is that it is the beat form of decentralised production, and the self-employment provided by this industry, is the best form of employment giving opportunities for the full development of the personality of the worker[13].

Size of Employment

Table 4.48 and 4.48-A (*See on pages 200 and 201*) show that the total number of persons employed, among the sample units, was 739. This represents about 2.77 employed persons per unit. Of this total number of employed 289 or 39.11 per cent were men, 285 or 38.57 per cent were women and 165 or 22.33 per cent were child labourers. Obviously, the high percentage of women labour in the sample units indicates its importance in this household industry. In fact, women are considered as an economic asset to weavers families in Cuddapah district.

Members of the Family and Generation of Employment

The units are run primarily by the household labourers. Table 4.49 (*See on page 202*) shows that out of a total of 898 workers 739 or 82.29 per cent were household members and only 159 or 17.71 per cent were outside workers. That is to say on an average, a unit of the sample employed 3.14 persons, of whom only 0.56 were hired workers and 2.77 workers were household members. The household characteristic of the units is thus clear. This in turn influences the number of looms. A household with a larger number of workers can maintain a more looms and vice versa.

In rural parts of western Cuddapah out of 95 men adults in the family 65 or 68 per cent were engaged in the handloom industry. Around 78 women members or 94 per cent of the total women members in the family

Table 4.48 : Details of Employment Generation in the Handloom Industry

Regions	No. of Looms	Family aembers								Others							
		Full-Time				Part-Time				Full-Time				Part-Tiitie			
		Men	Women	Children	Total	Men	Women	Children	Total	Men	Women	Children	Total	Men	Women	Children	Total
West Rural	72	49 (44.0)	56 (50.0)	6 (6.0)	111 (100.0)	16 (23.0)	22 (32.0)	31 (45.0)	69 (100.0)	1 (50.0)	—	1 (50.0)	2 (100.0)	22 (88.0)	3 (12.0)	—	25 (100.0)
West Urban	99	57 (31.0)	78 (43.0)	46 (26.0)	181 (100.0)	43 (49.0)	13 (15.0)	31 (36.0)	87 (100.0)	—	—	—	—	28 (88.0)	4 (12.0)	—	32 (100.0)
Total West	171	106 (36.0)	134 (46.0)	52 (18.0)	292 (100.0)	59 (38.0)	35 (22.0)	62 (40.0)	156 (100.0)	1 (50.0)	—	1 (50.0)	2 (100.0)	50 (88.0)	7 (12.0)	—	57 (100.0)
East Rural	44	44 (50.0)	41 (47.0)	3 (3.0)	88 (100.0)	2 (13.0)	2 (13.0)	12 (74.0)	16 (100.0)	—	—	—	—	35 (92.0)	3 (8.0)	—	38 (100.0)
East Urban	71	74 (49.0)	73 (48.0)	4 (3.0)	151 (100.0)	4 (11.0)	—	32 (89.0)	36 (100.0)	—	—	—	—	50 (78.0)	13 (20.0)	1 (2.0)	64 (100.0)
Total East	115	118 (49.0)	114 (48.0)	7 (3.0)	239 (100.0)	6 (12.0)	2 (4.0)	44 (84.0)	52 (100.0)	—	—	—	—	85 (83.0)	16 (16.0)	1 (1.0)	102 (100.0)
Grand Total	**286**	**224 (42.0)**	**248 (47.0)**	**59 (11.0)**	**531 (100.0)**	**65 (31.0)**	**37 (18.0)**	**106 (51.0)**	**208 (100)**	**1 (50.0)**	**—**	**1 (50.0)**	**2 (100.)**	**135 (85.0)**	**23 (14.0)**	**1 (1.0)**	**159 (100.0)**

Source : Field Survey Data.

Figures in brackets are percentages to their respective totals.

Table 4.48A : Details of Employment Generation In the Handloom Industry

Regions	No. of Looms	Total Employment								Average Employment							
		Full-Time				Part-Time				Full-Time				Part-Titie			
		Men	Women	Children	Total	Men	Women	Children	Total	Men	Women	Children	Total	Men	Women	Children	Total
West Rural	72	50 (44.0)	56 (50.0)	7 (6.0)	113 (100.0)	38 (40.0)	25 (27.0)	31 (33.0)	94 (100.0)	0.69	0.78	0.10	1.57	0.53	0.35	0.43	1.31
West Urban	99	57 (31.0)	78 (43.0)	46 (26.0)	181 (100.0)	71 (60.0)	17 (14.0)	31 (26.0)	119 (100.0)	0.58	0.79	0.46	1.83	0.71	0.17	0.31	1.20
Total West	171	107 (36.0)	134 (46.0)	53 (18.0)	204 (100.0)	109 (51.0)	42 (20.0)	62 (29.0)	213 (100.0)	0.63	0.78	0.31	1.72	0.64	0.25	0.36	1.25
East Rural	44	44 (50.0)	41 (47.0)	2 (3.0)	88 (100.0)	37 (69.0)	5 (9.0)	12 (22.0)	54 (100.0)	1.00	0.93	0.07	2.00	0.84	0.11	0.27	1.23
East Urban	71	74 (49.0)	73 (48.0)	4 (3.0)	151 (100.0)	54 (54.0)	13 (13.0)	33 (33.0)	100 (100.0)	1.04	1.03	0.06	2.13	0.76	0.18	0.46	1.41
Total East	115	118 (49.0)	114 (48.0)	7 (3.0)	239 (100.0)	91 (59.0)	18 (12.0)	45 (29.0)	154 (100.0)	1.03	0.99	0.06	2.08	0.79	0.16	0.39	1.34
Grand Total	**286**	**225 (42.0)**	**248 (47.0)**	**60 (11.0)**	**533 (100.0)**	**200 (54.0)**	**60 (16.0)**	**107 (30.0)**	**367 (100.0)**	**0.79**	**0.87**	**0.21**	**1.86**	**0.70**	**0.21**	**0.37**	**1.28**

Source : Field Survey Data.

Figures in brackets are percentages to their respective totals.

Table 4.49 : Members of the Family and Employment Generation

Regions	No. of Looms	Total Family Members				No. Employed (Full-Time)				No. Employed (Part-Time)				Grand Total Employed				Average Employed per loom
		Men	Women	Children	Total	Men	Women	Children	Total	Men	Women	Children	Total	Men	Women	Children	Total	
West Rural	72	95	83	70	248	49	56	6	111	16	22	31	69	65 (68.0)	78 (94.0)	37 (53.0)	180 (73.0)	2.50
West Urban	99	135	137	91	373	57	78	46	181	43	13	31	87	100 (74.0)	91 (66.0)	77 (85.0)	268 (72.0)	2.71
Total West	171	230	220	161	621	106	134	52	202	59	35	62	156	165 (72.0)	169 (77.0)	114 (71.0)	443 (72.0)	2.62
East Rural	44	52	52	47	151	44	41	3	88	2	2	12	16	46 (88.0)	43 (83.0)	15 (32.0)	104 (69.0)	2.36
East Urban	71	84	83	87	254	74	73	4	151	4	—	32	36	78 (92.0)	73 (88.0)	36 (41.0)	187 (74.0)	2.63
Total East	115	136	135	134	105	118	114	7	239	6	2	44	52	124 (91.0)	116 (86.0)	51 (38.0)	291 (72.0)	2.53
Grand Total	**286**	**366**	**355**	**295**	**1026**	**224**	**248**	**59**	**531**	**65**	**37**	**106**	**208**	**289 (79.0)**	**285 (80.0)**	**165 (56.0)**	**739 (72.0)**	**2.77**

Source : Field Survey Data.

Figures in brackets are percentages to their respective totals.

and 53 per cent of children were reported to be employed in the handloom industry of rural parts of western Cuddapah.

In urban parts of western Cuddapah district, of the total household population, 74 per cent of men 66 per cent of women and 85 per cent of children were employed in the industry. In the western zone of Cuddapah district 72 per cent of men, 77 per cent of women and 71 per cent of children were employed in the industry.

In rural centres of eastern Cuddapah 88 per cent of men, 83 per cent of women and 32 per cent of children were employed in the industry. In urban areas of eastern Cuddapah 92 per cent of Men, 88 per cent of women and 41 per cent of Children were engaged in the handloom industry. If we take the whole of eastern Cuddapah 91 per cent of men, 86 per cent of women and another 38 per cent of Children (1-15 years of age) were found engaged in the handloom industry.

Generation of Employment According to Products

Information pertaining to employment generating capacity of different handloom products in the district is presented in Table 4.50 (*See on page 204*). Janata Dhoties, Janata Sarees, Shirting, Lungis, Resham, 20 Laka, 30 laka, 40 Laka, 50 Laka, 90 Laka, 120 Laka and 150 laka pure zari sarees provide employment at the rate of 2.88; 2.89; 2.93; 2.86; 3.00; 3.33; 3.39; 3.50; 3.44; 4.00 and 3.00 persons per unit respectively. From this we can understand that superior varieties like Resham and zari cloth sarees provide more employment than coarse varieties of cloth viz., Janata Dhoties, Janata Sarees, Shirting and Lungis.

From the foregoing we may come to the conclusion that the participation of adult men is more in eastern zone and that of adult women and children participation is relatively more in western zone of Cuddapah district. The industry in western zone can manage with simple skills and hence children participation rate in the industry is significant. Another important reason is that for the weavers in eastern Cuddapah the main source of livelihood is weaving; hence almost all the adult men participate in the handloom industry. Unlike this adult men in western Cuddapah engage themselves in other works—masonry, coolies, clerks in kirana shops etc. Hence their participation in the weaving industry is less in western Cuddapah. So, in order to compensate for the absence of adult men in the industry of western Cuddapah; women and children take active part in the industry.

Table 4.50 : Generation on Employment According to Products

Regions	No. of Looms	Total Employment								Average Employment							
		Full-Time				Part-Time				Full-Time				Part-Time			
		Men	Women	Children	Total	Men	Women	Children	Total	Men	Women	Children	Total	Men	Women	Children	Total
Janta Dhoties	60	37	46	19	102	36	13	22	71	0.62	0.77	0.32	1.70	0.60	0.22	0.37	1.18
Janta Sarees	27	16	20	8	44	17	7	10	34	0.59	0.74	0.30	1.63	0.63	0.26	0.37	1.26
Shirting	28	17	21	9	47	18	7	10	35	0.61	0.75	0.32	1.68	0.64	0.25	0.36	1.25
Lungies	7	4	5	2	11	4	2	3	9	0.57	0.71	0.29	1.57	0.57	0.29	0.43	1.29
Resham	44	31	37	14	82	30	13	16	59	0.70	0.84	0.32	1.86	0.68	0.30	0.36	1.34
20 Laka P.Z.S.	48	48	44	3	95	38	8	19	65	1.00	0.92	0.06	1.98	0.79	0.17	0.40	1.35
30 Laka P.Z.S.	3	3	3	—	6	2	1	1	4	1.00	1.00	—	2.00	0.67	0.33	0.33	1.33
40 Laka P.Z.S.	23	24	23	—	47	18	4	9	31	1.04	1.00	—	2.04	0.78	0.17	0.39	1.35
50 Laka P.Z.S.	2	2	2	—	4	2	—	1	3	1.03	1.00	—	2.00	1.00	—	0.50	1.50
90 Laka P.Z.S.	34	35	35	2	72	27	5	13	45	1.03	1.03	0.06	2.12	0.79	0.15	0.38	1.32
120 Laka P.Z.S.	9	12	11	1	24	7	1	4	12	1.22	1.22	0.11	2.67	0.78	0.11	0.44	1.33
150 Laka P.Z.S.	1	1	2	—	3	—	—	—	—	1.00	2.00	—	3.00	—	—	—	—
Total	**286**	**230**	**249**	**58**	**537**	**199**	**61**	**108**	**368**	**0.80**	**0.87**	**0.20**	**1.88**	**0.70**	**0.21**	**0.38**	**1.29**

Source: Field Survey Data.
P.Z.S. = Pure Zari Sarees.

Summary and Conclusions on the Basis of Survey

The weaving activity in Cuddapah district is being mostly shared by Padmasale and Thogata castes that belong to traditional weaving communities.

The involvement of middle aged persons in the handloom industry is very significant. The participation of men population in the weaving activity is more (81.47%) than the women (18.53%).The women participation in the western zone is relatively more compared to the eastern zone of Cuddapah district.

Since a handloom product is a function of the co-operation among several individuals larger sized families have the opportunity to produce larger number of pieces per capita than in the case of smaller sized families. Here we find that the increase in the size of the family the average income level of the individual members also has increased.

The number of adult persons in the family influences the number of handlooms in the household and about 2 adults are bringing one additional loom into operation.

Adult illiteracy is more in eastern Cuddapah than in the case of children, illiteracy is more in the western zone than in the eastern zone of Cuddapah district. In all the areas, irrespective of age, women illiteracy is significant.

Nearly fifty per cent of the heads of households were illiterate.

The average age of marriage for females is 17.5 years and for men 22.3 years.

Weavers have a tendency generally to separate themselves after marriage from the joint family. The attitude of the married couples in eastern Cuddapah appears to be more in favour of nuclear family, and it was relatively less in western zone of Cuddapah district.

Weavers in this district have a tradition of marrying among their own relatives. They marry others only when they do not find suitable matches among the relatives.

Most of the weavers do not like their children to work or continue to work, in the handloom industry. Many weavers felt that the handloom industry did not help to improve their living standards. Significant differences exist in the attitude of the parents regarding the continuance of their children in handloom industry between eastern and western Cuddapah and between rural and urban areas 62 per cent of the respondents attributed their unwillingness to make weaving a hereditary one to non remunerative nature of the industry; 19 per cent of them felt that the profession is highly difficult; and 14 per cent have been apprehensive of the constant fluctuations in the industry. The respondents willing to allow their children to continue in the industry stated that they had no other alterative except weaving.

The higher percentage of weavers in eastern Cuddapah were motivated by members of the family. The influence of Master Weaver in the western Cuddapah is predominant in motivating the weavers to take up the job of weaving. For example in western Cuddapah the influence of Master Weaver is high while in eastern Cuddapah the influence of family members is high.

The influence of family members and in some cases the influence of Master Weaver seem to be responsible for the entry and continuance of different persons in the Handloom Industry. We may infer that there is no significant difference in the strength of factors responsible for the weavers to enter the handloom industry viz., Co-operative and Corporate sectors.

Housing next to food and clothes occupies the most important place in deciding the standard of living of the people. Almost all the weavers in western Cuddapah live in thatched houses, where as a majority of their counterparts in eastern Cuddapah have been living In semi-permanent houses. Majority (92%) of the weavers in the western Cuddapah have been living in their own houses., but in the western Cuddapah only 65 per cent have been living in their own houses. The percentage of weavers having own houses is relatively more in the rural areas(82%) than in urban areas (53%).

Industrial labour in India has a migratory nature, indicating that majority of the industrial workers are immigrants from the nearby and adjoining rural areas. From the present study it may be observed that 21 per cent of the weaving households have migrated to nearby villages and have settled. Migrant labourers were found in handloom weaving centres of Cuddapah. Weavers have migrated from rural to urban areas.

Health is wealth to workers who get succour just by selling their physical labour. But handloom weavers are caught in a vicious circle of nutritional deficiency, ill-health, and are subjected to professional hazards such as, Short-sightedness, Asthma, Tuberculosis, Paralysis and high Blood Pressure are some of the diseases prevalent among the handloom weavers in Cuddapah.

Average income per household at ₹ 6271 is the lowest in urban parts of western Cuddapah while it is the highest in urban parts of eastern Cuddapah at ₹ 11003.

The monthly earnings of different categories of weavers studied ranges from ₹ 53.30 to ₹ 500 and the average income has been largely influenced by the higher income groups in eastern Cuddapah whose income is high compare to that of weavers of other income groups in western Cuddapah.

Weaving is the principal occupation of all the households surveyed. Besides this, a few weaving households also take up agriculture, business and other remunerative works.

91 per cent of the total income is from weaving and the remaining 9 per cent comes from other subsidiary occupations.

Dependence on other occupations is relatively more in western Cuddapah region than in eastern Cuddapah region.

The income earning capacity of the Independent weaver is better in western Cuddapah, while it is the is the Master weaver in eastern Cuddapah.

Weavers producing pure zari sarees get the highest income where as the weavers producing lungis were getting the lowest income in the district and thus the income earning capacity of the weaver in eastern region is greater than western region of Cuddapah district.

The percentage of weavers living below the poverty line is more in western zone of Cuddapah at 34 per cent than in eastern zone.

The type of raw material used is one of the important factors that determines the income of the household. Weavers using only cotton yarn as the raw material get less income than weavers using zari along with yarn.

Rural centres of eastern Cuddapah urban centres of western Cuddapah have lower per capita expenditure at ₹ 1525.92 than the general average of ₹ 1579.45.

Expenditure on food at 75 per cent forms a major part of the expenditure. The proportion of expenditure is more where average household income is less, and vice versa. Thus the Engel's Law of consumption which states that proportion of expenditure on food decreases with the increase in income, seems to be in operation.

The number savers and the amount of saving are significantly more in eastern region than for their counter parts in western zone of Cuddapah district.

Independent weavers have the highest savings in the sample followed by weavers, working for the Master weavers, and Co-operative sector.

A major part of the money saved is invested in private chits. Savings kept with Commercial Banks and Post offices constitutes only 43.5 per cent.

'Sowcar-weaver' (one who deals in handloom cloth marketing) is the major source of loans and advances. Institutional finance is not made available to the weaving industry. The Banking institutions have to go a long way to emerge as important sources of credit to the weaver.

Average debt of the Household at ₹ 1937 should not at any rate be considered as a reflection of the sound economic condition of the units. On the contrary, this is an indicator of the lack of credit worthiness of the units concerned.

The percentage of households that borrowed is relatively less (58%) in western region of Cuddapah than in eastern region of Cuddapah district. The average amount of borrowing at ₹ 2966 is highest in eastern Cuddapah. It is due to credit worthiness of the weaver in eastern Cuddapah.

The value of assets range from ₹ 1500 to ₹ 85000 per household and properties consist mainly of houses and looms. Very few of them own landed property.

The variation in the value of properties owned is significantly more in western Cuddapah than in eastern Cuddapah. The degree of variation in the value of properties possessed is the highest in rural zones of western Cuddapah and urban centres of eastern Cuddapah district while it is lower in urban centres of western Cuddapah and rural centres of eastern Cuddapah.

Weavers who do not own any property at all comprise mostly weavers working under Master weavers, Co-operatives and weavers working for more than one organisations. Properties worth ₹ 20000 and above on an average are owned by Independent weavers.

The average value of property owned is relatively less in western region compared to eastern region of Cuddapah district.

REFERENCE

1. T.S. Papola 'Rural Industrialisation (Approach and Potential), Himalayan Publishing House, Bombay, 1982, p. 25.
2. T.S. Papola, *op.cit.,* p.15.
3. S.T. Surendra—'Some Aspects of the Gadwal Handloom Industries' Chenetha, a monthly journal, Oct 1983, p. 7.
4. R.P. Singh, Director of Census Operations, Andhra Pradesh, Provisional Population Totals, Series 2, p. 22.
5. R.P. Singh-Provisional Population Totals, Director of Census operation, Andhra Pradesh, Series-2, Paper 1 of 1991, Table 4, p. 25.
6. Indian Labour Year Book-1984-Labour Bureau, Ministry of Labour, Govt. of India, p.144.
7. Gerald M.Heir., Leading issues in Economic development, Third Edition-1976-p. 496 & 97.

8. Survey of Economic Trends and State Plan 1992-93, Govt.of Andhra Pradesh, Hyderabad.March 1992, p. 31.
9. Labourers participate in the process of warping.
10. Thimmaiah, G(1983)-Inequality and Poverty, Himalayan Publishing House, Bombay, p. 7.
11. The Poverty line determined by the Government, has been corrected for the year 1989-90 using price index.
12. Report of the working group(Study Team) for the Handloom Industry, Bombay: Ministry of Commerce and Industry, Govt. of India, 1959, p. 42.
13. Report of the village and Small Scale Industries (Second Five-year Plan) Committee, New Delhi,Planning Commission, Govt. of India-1956, p. 22.

5

Costs, Prices and Capacity Utilisation

Utilisation of Capacity

There are many factors which hinder industrial growth. One such factor is the under-utilisation of capacity. In a capital scarce economy it is imperative that capacity is fully utilised, to achieve the targeted rates of production. Idle capacity aggravates many problems in a developing economy. It directly depresses the growth of production, increases the capital output ratio, reduces employment, and increases the cost of production. Capacity utilisation is one of the important indicators among the available tools for measuring the efficiency of operation of manufacturing enterprises. If the installed capacity is not utilised fully, the capacity unutilised therein would be dead or idle to the extent of non-utilisation[1].

The volume of actual production depends on the utilisation of installed capacity. Therefore, output-variations in production among different size-groups of establishments, can be better studied in the context of the existing 'Maximum Capacity' of different establishments, with a view to finding out not only the capacity of each group of establishments to give out the maximum value of output, but also to visualise the rates of 'Utilised Capacity' and 'Idle Capacity' of these establishments.

Maximum Capacity

Maximum Capacity (or installed capacity) is the production or output potential of a unit of production with its existing set of machinery and equipment, assuming that the operation conditions of the unit such as the availability of raw materials, credit, demand for its products etc., are normal and that the unit operates uninterrupted through out the year. The aggregate volume of production thus turned out during 300 days (the normal production period in a year), working one shift per day of 8 hours each, is reckoned as the maximum capacity of a unit[2].

However, unlike the organised sector, the unorganised industries, especially those of household type like the one under survey, where the production potential is related more to the uncertain human capacities and dispositions than to the working of the plant and machinery, encounter a lot of difficulties for the measurement of 'maximum capacity'. Since human capacities depend on a number of variable factors like social and economic conditions, health, disposition, skill, training and other day-to-day living conditions etc., of each individual, no satisfactory method can be devised to overcome the uncertanities or to isolate these variables. Any attempt to account for these variables will, therefore be arbitrary. To overcome this problem of measnrement, the maximum capacity has been related only to the existing equipment (looms and tools, which are more or less of identical capacity in this industry) and the normal duration and period of working, assuming other conditions auch as mentioned above, as given. Thus, the figures of maximum capacity have been worked out for an average of 300 days of 8 hours duration (or 2,400 hours a year), working with the existing looms and tools, at the existing hourly rate of output. The figures of 'Utilised Capacity' are the total annual output actually obtained during the year by different groups of establishments.

Idle Capacity

Table 5.1 gives details of maximum capacity, utilised capacity and idle capacity of the different size groups of establishments under survey. A study of these figures shows that in the smaller size-groups, utilised capacity is substantially low as compared with that in the larger groups. Thus, households with 1 loom, 2 looms, 3 looms and 4 looms have on an average idle capacity to the extent of 18.68 per cent, 12.38 per cent, 9.77 per cent and 6.55 per cent respectively. However, none of the looms have utilised on an average, their maximum capacity in full and have suffered from the presence of unutilised capacity at one time or the other during the year. As a matter of fact, during the busy seasons all the establishments work to more than full capacity, during normal periods they are not able to utilise their total capacities. During slack season, the situation in respect of capacity utilisation is still worse. Smaller establishments are as usual the worst sufferers in this period.

Table 5.1 : Utilisation of Capacity by Size of Establishments

Size groups	Maximum Capacity in value per year (₹)	Actual Capacity in value per year (₹)	Idle capacity in % (per establishments)
1 Loom	3261527	2652261 (81.32)	18.68
2 Looms	2489012	2180751 (87.62)	12.38
3 Looms	21457	19360 (90.23)	9.77
4 Looms	364824	340928 (93.25)	6.55
Total	**6136820**	**5193300 (84.63)**	**15.37**

Source: Field Survey Data.
Note: Figures in brackets are percentages of capacity utilised.

Table 5.2 (*See on next page*) gives details of capacity utilised in different areas of the district. In rural parts of western Cuddapah about 74.01 per cent of the capacity of the handlooms is utilised and in urban centres of western Cuddapah it is 66.63 per cent. In case of the whole western Cuddapah the percentage of capacity utilised is 69.20.

Compared to western Cuddapah, the capacity utilised in eastern Cuddapah is relatively better, where it is 84.63 per cent. In rural areas of eastern Cuddapah it is 83.72 per cent and urban areas of eastern Cuddapah the percentage of Capacity utilised is 85.21.

In Table 5.3 (*See on page 214*) product-wise capacity utilisation is presented. The amount of capacity utilised is less for coarse varieties and it is the highest for superior varieties of handloom products. The percentage of capacity utilised for Janata Dhoties, Janata Sarees, Shirting and Resham is 42.54; 47.23; 46.67; 49.39; and 49.00 respectively. For zari cloth producing handlooms, the Percentage of capacity utilised is more. For example, in the case of 20 laka sarees, capacity utilisation is 59.02 cent., for 30 laka, 40 laka, 50 laka, 120 laka and 150 laka zari sarees the capacity utilised is 60.19 percent; 82.88 per cent; 64.90 per cent; 97.57 per cent; 98.48 per cent; and 100.0 per cent respectively. The percentage of capacity utilised for the whole district works to 59.21 cent.

Table 5.2 : Capacity utilisation of the Handloom Industry

Villages	No.of looms	No.of looms working		Actual production during 1988 (₹)	Maximum productive capacity (₹)	Average Actual production during 1988 (₹)	Averate Maximum production during 1988 (₹)	percentage of capacity utilisation	Loss of produ-ction due to working below cap-acity	percentage of loss of production to the total pro-duction due to working below capacity
		below capacity	Full Capacity							
West Rural	72	57 (79.0)	15 (21.0)	2351705	3177500	32663	44132	74.01	825795	35.12
West Urban	99	81 (82.0)	18 (18.0)	3966795	5953311	40069	60135	66.63	1986516	50.08
Total West	171	138 (81.0)	33 (19.0)	6318500	9130811	36950	53397	69.20	2812311	44.51
East Rural	44	32 (73.0)	12 (27.0)	2003100	2392700	45525	54380	83.72	389600	19.00
East Urban	71	45 (63.0)	26 (37.0)	3190200	3744120	44932	52734	85.21	553920	17.0
Total East	115	77 (67.0)	38 (33.0)	5193300	6136820	45159	53364	84.63	943520	18.00
Grand Total	**286**	**215 (75.0)**	**71 (25.0)**	**11511800**	**19431630**	**40251**	**67943**	**59.24**	**7919830**	**68.80**

Source: Field Survey Data.

Note: Figures in brackets are percentages to their respective totals.

Table 5.3 : Product-wise Capacity Utilisation of Looms

Products	No. of looms	No. of looms working		Actual production during 1988 (₹)	Maximum productive capacity (₹)	Average Actual production during 1988 (₹)	Averate Maximum production during 1988 (₹)	percentage of capacity utilisation	Loss of production due to working below capacity	percentage of loss of production to the total production due to working below capacity
		below capacity	Full Capacity							
Janata Dhoties	60	58(97.0)	2(3.0)	876000	2012000	14600	33533	43.54	1136000	129.68
Janata Sarees	27	22(81.0)	5(19.0)	408240	864420	15120	32016	47.23	456180	111.74
Shirting	28	25(89.0)	3(11.0)	356160	763200	12720	27257	46.67	407040	114.29
Lungis	7	5(71.0)	2(29.0)	81200	164400	11600	23486	49.39	83200	102.46
Resham	44	23(52.0)	21(48.0)	4439400	9060480	100895	205920	49.00	4621080	104.09
20 Laka Z.S	48	43(90.0)	5(10.0)	1284500	2176500	26760	45344	59.02	892000	69.44
30 Laka Z.S	3	2(67.0)	1(33.0)	89200	148200	29733	49400	60.19	59000	66.14
40 Laka Z.S	23	16(70.0)	7(30.0)	828000	999000	36000	43435	82.88	171000	20.65
50 Laka Z.S	2	2(100.0)	—	49000	75500	24500	37750	64.90	26500	54.08
90 Laka Z.S	34	15(44.0)	19(56.0)	2254970	2311200	66323	67976	97.57	56230	2.49
120 Laka Z.S.	9	4(44.0)	5(56.0)	750130	761730	83348	84637	98.48	11600	1.55
150 Laka Z.S.	1	—	1(100.0)	95000	95000	95000	95000	100.00	0	0
Total	**286**	**215(75.0)**	**71(25.0)**	**11511800**	**19431630**	**40251**	**67943**	**59.24**	**7919830**	**68.80**

Source: Field Survey Data.

Note: Figures in brackets are percentages of respective totals.

Z.S. = Zari Saree.

Reasons for Idle Capacity

Reasons for the existence of the idle capacity are many, such as difficulties in the procurement of raw materials, lack of demand, lack of capital resources, problems of labour and others. Some of these problems are. inter-linked and so their intensity cannot be gauged correctly and separately. So, with a view to assess the reasons with which the looms are working below capacity, information is collected on these aspects and presented in Table 5.4 (*See on next page*). Shortage of raw materials (79%) and lack of demand (17%) are by far the most important reasons for under utilisation of capacity in rural areas of western Cuddapah. But in urban areas of western Cuddapah the Important reasons for under utilisation of capacity are shortage of raw materials (79%) and labour problems (12%). For western Cuddapah as a whole, major reasons for under utilisation of capacity are shortage of raw materials (79%) and lack of demand for the products (11 per cent).

For the whole district the important reasons for under utilisation of capacity were shortage of raw materials (58%) and labour problems (27%). However lack of adequate supply of required raw materials to the looms seems to be an important deterrent to the utilisation of capacity than labour demand problems.

The reasons for product-wise under utilisation of capacity are given in Table 5.5 (*See on page 217*). Shortage of raw material is the basic problem for coarse varieties like Janata Dhoties, Sarees, Shirting and Lungis. For the superior varieties of handloom products viz., Zari Cloth Sarees, shortage of finance and labour problems are the most significant factors influencing under utilisation of capacity of the handlooms.

'Labour Problems' hererefer mainly to marked absenteeism of the hired workers. In a large number of cases, these workers usually absent themselves for an extra day (or at least half a day) immediately following important holidays for festivals. In many cases, it has also been reported that the workers often run away after collecting wages and /or raw materials in advance, resulting in not only considerable loss to the owners but also in the loss of loom-hours.

Other reasons, resulting in idle capacity, include enforced idleness due to illness, visits of guests, religious or social ceremonies and weather conditions etc. Since Sizing and Beaming of the Warp are usually done in the open fields or lanes, the work is often interrupted during the rainy season or due to excessive heat during the summer.

In conclusion, it may be observed that the existence of (to some degree) idle capacity in the handloom establishments in the smaller size-

Table 5.4 : Reasons for Working Below Capacity

Areas	No. of loon working below capacity	No.working full capacity	Total Lqoms	Reasons for working below capacity				Other reasons
				Shortage of Raw material	Shortage of Finance	Labour problems	Lack of Demand	
West Rural	57 (79.0)	15 (21.0)	72 (100.0)	45 (79.0)	—	2 (4.0)	10 (17.0)	—
West Urban	81 (82.0)	18 (18.0)	99 (100.0)	64 (79.0)	2 (2.0)	10 (12.0)	5 (7.0)	—
Total West	138 (81.0)	33 (19.0)	171 (100.0)	109 (79.0)	2 (1.0)	12 (9.0)	15 (11.0)	—
East Rural	32 (73.0)	12 (27.0)	44 (100.0)	4 (13.0)	6 (19.0)	20 (61.0)	2 (7.0)	—
East Urban	45 (63.0)	26 (34.0)	71 (100.0)	11 (24.0)	6 (13.0)	26 (58.0)	2 (5.0)	—
Total East	77 (67.0)	38 (33.0)	115 (100.0)	15 (19.0)	12 (16.0)	46 (60.0)	4 (5.0)	—
Grand Total	**215 (75.0)**	**71 (25.0)**	**286 (100.0)**	**124 (58.0)**	**14 (7.0)**	**58 (27.0)**	**19 (8.0)**	—

Source: Field Survey Data.

Note: Figures in brackets are percentages to their respective totals.

Table 5.5 : Looms Working Below Capacity—Product-wise Analysis

Verities of product	No.working below capacity	No.working full capacity	Total Looms	Reasonsfor working below capacity				
				Shortage of Raw material	Shortage of Finance	Labour problems	Lack of Demand	Other reasons
Janata Doties	58	2	60	50 (86.0)	—	3 (5.0)	5 (9.0)	—
Janata Sarees	22	5	27	15 (68.0)	—	2 (9.0)	5 (23.0)	—
Shirting	25	3	28	15 (60.0)	2 (8.0)	4 (16.0)	4 (16.0)	
Lungis	5	2	7	4 (80.0)	—	—	1 (20.0)	—
Resham	23	21	44	20 (87.0)	—	3 (13.0)	—	—
20 Laka Z.S.	43	5	48	2 (5.0)	2 (5.0)	37 (86.0)	2 (4.0)	—
30 Laka Z.S.	2	1	3	—	—	2 (100.0)	—	—
40 Laka Z.S.	16	7	23	8 (50.0)	4 (25.0)	4 (25.0)	—	—
50 Laka Z.S.	2	—	2	1 (50.0)	—	1 (50.0)	—	—
90 Laka Z.S.	15	19	34	7 (47.0)	4 (27.0)	2 (13.0)	—	—
120 Laka Z.S.	4	5	9	2 (50.0)	2 (50.0)	—	—	—
150 Laka Z.S.	—	1	1	—	—	—	—	—
Total	**215**	**71**	**286**	**124**	**14 (7.0)**	**58 (27.0)**	**19 (8.0)**	—

Source: Field Survey Data.

Note: Figures in brackets are percentages to their respective totals.

groups which form the bulk in the industry, is one among the many reasons weakening the competitive capacity of these establishments vis-a-vis their larger counter parts. Apart from directly raising the unit cost of their products. This also impinges adversely on the overall productivity and the net earnings of these establishments as well as of their hired labour force.

For How Long the Same Variety is Produced

Information partaining to duration for which the present cloth is woven is presented in Table 5.6 (*See on next page*). As discussed earlier that weavers weaving superior varieties of cloth are able to increase their income. The scope for shifting the weaver from producing the coarse variety to superior variety is almost absent in western Cuddapah. In eastern Cuddapah there has been constant encouragement from the organisations concerned to switch over to produce superior varieties of cloth. But weavers are reluctant for such a switch over. It is disheartening to know that handloom weavers are most reluctant to adopt modern techniques. This has inevitably come in the way of an improvement in productivity and the pattern of production[3]. One major problem in the handloom industry is the persistence of a general resistance to the adoption of improved technology[4]. The weavers reluctance to accept new designs, whether in respect of sizing, warping, pirn winding or weaving has been one of the major causes to keep handlooms sluggish, thereby stunting their growth and development on the right lines[5].

Weavers are afraid of going in for production of superior varieties because it may take many years for them to improve their skills to produce such varieties. Manufacturing defects if any, may cause severe deterioration in the living standards, as the weaver has to bear the loss in such case. The Institute of Handloom Technology, Varanasi has expressed the view that handloom operators are conservative by nature and therefore the introduction of new tools and improved techniques is far from easy[6].

The resistance to change emanates out of their unwillingness to take risks despite their awareness that production of the same traditional varieties would lead to stagnation and accumulation of stocks. Similarly there has also been resistance to introduction of new technology as weavers feel sophistication would mean more work[7].

Consequently traditional designs and techniques continue to exist without any change. Host of the weavers are accustomed to produce traditional varieties and even resist any changes. At the same time the capacity of the handloom sector to produce a good number of varieties

Table 5.6 : Duration for Which Present Cloth is Woven

Areas	No.of Households	No.of looms	No.of using Dobbis	looms making designed cloth	No.of looms	No.of years the present cloth is woven			
					1 Year	2 Years	3 Years	4 Years	5Years
West Rural	50	72	—	—	13 (18.0)	18 (25.0)	19 (26.0)	10 (14.0)	12 (17.0)
West Urban	75	99	18 (18.0)	18 (18.0)	24 (24.0)	10 (10.0)	27 (28.0)	26 (26.0)	12 (12.0)
Total West	125	171	18 (11.0)	18 (11.0)	37 (22.0)	28 (16.0)	46 (27.0)	36 (21.0)	24 (14.0)
East Rural	35	44	32 (72.0)	32 (72.0)	12 (27.0)	14 (32.0)	10 (23.0)	8 (18.0)	—
East Urban	55	71	52 (73.0)	52 (73.0)	15 (21.0)	26 (37.0)	12 (17.0)	7 (10.0)	11 (15.0)
Total East	90	115	84 (73.0)	84 (73.0)	27 (23.0)	40 (35.0)	22 (19.0)	15 (13.0)	11 (10.0)
Grand Total	**215**	**286**	**102 (36.0)**	**102 (36.0)**	**64 (22.0)**	**68 (24.0)**	**68 (24.0)**	**51 (18.0)**	**35 (12.0)**

Source: Field Survey Data.

Note: Figures in brackets are percentages to their respective totals.

with varied designs cannot be matched by Mills and Powerlooms though the productivity of handlooma is the lowest. However, practically no new varieties are manufactured in many units. Another reasons for the resistance to change is the low wages paid to the weavers, during the change over time. Payment of normal wages for such periods would encourage the introduction of newer designs[8].

Number of Times the Weavers Go to the Suppliers for Raw Materials

Table 5.7 (*See on next page*) gives details pertaining to the number of times that weavers have to visit the suppliers of raw materials to get the raw materials required. Most of the weavers (58.0%) see the suppliers of raw materials once in a week. Around 21 per cent of the respondents have the habit of visiting the raw material supplier once in a fortnight, and around 16 per cent go twice in a week to the suppliers of raw materials. Only 5 per cent go to the suppliers of raw materials once in a month. Weavers, in their efforts to get the required raw materials lose much of their precious time.

General Problems with Regard to Raw Materials

As already pointed out, Yarn is the chief raw material required by the handloom industry of Cuddapah district. It is reported during the field survey that the difficulty, the handloom weavers are facing, in getting the required raw materials on time, is one of the important reasons for the under utilisation of their capacity. In order to know the details pertaining to general difficulties in securing raw material, an attempt has been made in this direction to collect the relevant information from the respondents. The information thus collected is presented in Table 5.8 (*See on page 222*).

Poor quality of raw materials supplied to the handloom weavers (43%) is an important problem faced in all parts of the district. High price paid for getting the raw material is another important problem faced by the weavers in eastern Cuddapah. Adulteration is another important problem experienced more in eastern Cuddapah than in western Cuddapah. The problem of non-availability of Yarn of specified Counts is equally felt in both the western and eastern zones of Cuddapah district.

Table 5.9 (*See on page 223*) gives details of the organisations facing difficulties in securing raw materials. Poor quality of raw material is the first important difficulty felt by the Master weavers, followed by the non-availability of raw materials in required quantities. Independent weavers felt that the problem is of high prices and adulteration. Weavers

Table 5.7 : Number of Times the Weaers Have to Visit the Suppliers for Raw Materials

Areas	No. of Households	Daily	Once in a week	Twice in a week	Once in a Fornight	Once in a Month
West Rural	50	—	34 (68.0)	4 (8.0)	10 (20.0)	2 (4.0)
West Urban	75	—	44 (59.0)	15 (20.0)	16 (21.0)	—
Total West	125	—	78 (62.0)	19 (15.0)	26 (21.0)	2 (2.0)
East Rural	35	1 (3.0)	25 (71.0)	4 (11.0)	5 (15.0)	—
East Urban	55	—	21 (38.0)	11 (20.0)	14 (25.0)	9 (17.0)
Total East	90	1 (1.0)	46 (51.0)	15 (17.0)	19 (21.0)	9 (10.0)
Grand Total	**215**	**1 (0.5)**	**124 (58.0)**	**34 (16.0)**	**45 (21.0)**	**11 (5.0)**

Source: Field Survey Data.

Note: Figures in brackets are percentages to their respective totals.

Table 5.8 : General Difficulties in Securing the Raw Material

Areas	No. of Looms	Common difficulties, in securing raw materials					
		Not available on time	Not Available in required quantities	High Price	Adulte-ration	Poor Quality	Yarn of required counts not available
West Rural	72	14 (19.0)	19 (26.0)	3 (4.0)	9 (13.0)	27 (38.0)	—
West Urban	99	12 (12.0)	21 (21.0)	6 (6.0)	2 (2.0)	57 (58.0)	1 (1.0)
Total West	171	26 (15.0)	40 (23.0)	9 (5.0)	11 (6.0)	84 (49.0)	1 (2.0)
East Rural	44	3 (7.0)	9 (20.0)	12 (27.0)	5 (11.0)	14 (32.0)	1 (3.0)
East Urban	71	3 (4.0)	8 (11.0)	25 (35.0)	10 (14.0)	25 (35.0)	—
Total East	115	6 (5.0)	17 (15.0)	37 (32.0)	15 (13.0)	39 (34.0)	1 (1.0)
Grand Total	**286**	**32 (11.0)**	**57 (20.0)**	**46 (16.0)**	**26 (9.0)**	**123 (43.0)**	**2 (1.0)**

Source: Field Survey Data.

Note: Figures in brackets are percentages to their respective totals.

Table 5.9 : Difficulties Faced In Securing Rau Materials by Different Organisations

	No. of Looms	Difficulties in securing raw materials					
		Not available on time	Not available in required quantities	High Price	Adulte-ration	Poor Quality	Yarn of required counts not available
Master weaver	142	—	19 (13.0)	—	—	123 (87.0)	—
Independent	72	—	—	46 (64.0)	26 (36.0)	—	—
Co-operative	56	32 (57.0)	24 (43.0)	—	—	—	—
Corporation	16	—	14 (88.0)	—	—	—	2 (12.0)
Grand Total	**286**	**32 (11.0)**	**57 (20.0)**	**46 (16.0)**	**26 (9.0)**	**123 (43.0)**	**2 (1.0)**

Source: Field Survey Data.

Note: Figures in brackets are percentages to their respective totals.

working for Co-operative organisation felt difficulty with respect to availability of raw materials on time, and the required quantities. Weavers working for Corporations also felt that the non-availability of raw materials in required quantities is an important difficulty.

Poor quality of yarn is another important problem faced by all in the district.

From the foregoing analysis one can understand that weavers in western and eastern zones of Cuddapah are not supplied qualitative inputs. Consequently weavers have to spend more hours per piece of cloth. It reduces the earning capacity of the weaver and helps to increase the profit of the merchant or organisation.

The problem of non-availability of raw material in required quantities when needed is more intensely felt in western Cuddapah than in eastern Cuddapah. This can be attributed to the role played by the organisations concerned. From this it can be inferred that, the organisational efficiency in western region is less compared to its counter part in eastern region of Cuddapah.

Quality and Value of Raw Material on the Loom

Table 5.10 (*See on next page*) gives the details relating to the quantity and value of raw material available on the loom at the time of survey. Yarn and Resham are the chief raw materials used in western Cuddapah. Yarn and Zari are the important raw material required by industry of eastern Cuddapah. Every loom on an average, has raw material worth of ₹ 198 in rural centres of western Cuddapah ₹ 252 in urban centres of western Cuddapah. For the whole of western Cuddapah, it comes to ₹ 229. In rural centres of eastern Cuddapah each loom has raw materials worth ₹ 883 on the loom. In the total district it is ₹ 528 per loom.

From the foregoing it is clear that the handloom industry in eastern Cuddapah is more capital intensive compared to the industry in western Cuddapah.

Weavers Willingness towards Superior Varieties

With a view to understanding whether the weavers desire to improve their living standards by going in for the production of superior varieties, an attempt has been made to collect the information in this respect and the information thus collected is presented in Tables 5.11 and 5.12 (*See on page 226*). A majority of the weavers in western Cuddapah are in favour of producing superior varieties of cloth to improve their living standards. But organisational problems, such as, lack of dynamic entrepreneurship,

Table 5.10 : Quantity and Value of Raw Material on the Loom

Areas	Yarn			Zari			Resham			Total		
	No.of Looms	Value	Average	No.of Looms	Value	Average	No. of Looms	Value	Average	No.of Looms	Value	Average
West Rural	57	7395	130	—	—	—	15	6825	455	72	14220	198
West Urban	70	9570	137	5	2700	540	29	12709	438	99	24979	252
Total West	127	16965	134	5	2700	540	44	19534	444	171	39199	229
East Rural	44	9850	224	44	29000	604	—	—	—	44	38850	883
East Urban	71	17880	252	71	55200	777	—	—	—	71	73080	1029
Total East	115	27730	241	115	84200	732	—	—	—	115	111930	973
Grand Total	**242**	**44695**	**185**	**120**	**86900**	**724**	**44**	**19534**	**893**	**286**	**151129**	**528**

Source: Field Survey Data.

Note: Figures in brackets are percentages to their respective totals.

Table 5.11 : Difficulties in Modernisation

Areas	No.of Looms	Lack of Finance	Lack of Technical Knowledge	Indifference	Any other
West Rural	50	8 (16.0)	19 (38.0)	23 (46.0)	—
West Urban	75	19 (25.33)	14 (18.67)	40 (53.33)	2 (2.67)
Total West	125	27 (21.6)	33 (26.4)	63 (50.4)	2 (1.6)
East Rural	35	8 (22.86)	3 (8.57)	24 (68.57)	—
East Urban	55	16 (29.09)	3 (5.45)	36 (65.45)	—
Total East	90	24 (26.67)	6 (6.67)	60 (66.67)	—
Grand Total	**215**	**51 (23.72)**	**39 (18.14)**	**123 (57.21)**	**2 (0.93)**

Source: Field Survey Data.

Note: Figures in brackets are percentages of capacity utilised.

Table 5.12 : Willingness of Weavers to Go in for Superior Varieties

Areas	No.of respon-dents	Willingness to produce superior varieties	Not wiling	Indifferent
West Rural	50	40 (80.0)	3 (6.0)	7 (14.0)
West Urban	75	67 (89.33)	3 (4.0)	5 (6.67)
Total West	125	107 (85.6)	6 (4.8)	12 (9.6)
East Rural	35	9 (25.71)	22 (62.86)	4 (11.43)
East Urban	55	10 (18.18)	39 (70.91)	6 (10.91)
Total East	90	19 (21.11)	61 (67.78)	10 (11.11)
Grand Total	**215**	**126 (58.60)**	**67 (31.16)**	**22 (10.23)**

Source: Field Survey Data.

Note: Figures in brackets are percentages to their respective totals.

lack of skills and techniques, motivation are responsible for the present plight of weavers in western Cuddapah. Weavers have expressed their reluctance to leave their places and go to other areas where superior varieties are produced. Hence there is every need to take steps to transfer the weaving techniques practised in eastern Cuddapah to western Cuddapah. The willingness of the weavers in eastern Cuddapah to produce superior varieties of cloth is insignificant, as such they are content with the production of the present cloth.

Working Capital Requirements of the Industry

Out of 286 looms surveyed in the district only 122 looms or 42.65 per cent are using yarn as the chief raw material. Another 120 looms or 41.96 per cent are using both zari and yarn as the raw materials and the remaining. 44 looms or 15.38 per cent use Resham as the raw material.

Table 5.13 shows that every loom on an average requires yarn worth ₹ 3980 per year in western Cuddapah, where as it is ₹ 8292 for eastern Cuddapah. As far as the requirement of zari product is concerned, every loom on an average requires ₹ 14880 per year in western Cuddapah, while it is ₹ 17377 in eastern Cuddapah. Every loom on an average needs ₹ 17780 per year to get the required Resham or Silk. Looms using Resham are completely absent in eastern Cuddapah. Yarn, zari and Resham put together, every loom on an average needs raw material worth ₹ 7966 per year in western Cuddapah, while it is ₹ 25678 in eastern Cuddapah.

While yarn and Resham are the important raw materials required by the industry in western Cuddapah. Zari is the next important raw materials (after yarn) required in eastern Cuddapah. The difference in the average value of raw material of the handloom industry, between eastern and western Cuddapah is due to use of superior or superfine raw material by the industry of eastern Cuddapah. But its counterpart is using only cheap raw material to produce coarse varieties viz., Janata Sarees, Janata Dhoties, Lungia and Shirting. For instance yarn of 40 × 80 Counts is used in western region while 100 - 120 Counts of yarn is used in eastern regions of Cuddapah district.

Table 5.14 (*See on page 229*) provides an insight into the working capital requirements of the handloom industry. About 71 per cent of the handlooms require less than ₹ 10,000 of working capital in western Cuddapah. But in eastern region only 10 per cent of the looms require less than ₹ 10000 of working capital per year and the remaining 90 per

Table 5.13 : Requirement of Working Capital for One Year

Areas	Yarn Requirement			Zari Requirement			Reshant			Grand Total		
	No.of Looms	Total Value	Average Value	No.of Looms	Total Value	Average Value	No.of Looms	Total Value	Average Value	No.of Looms	Total Value	Average Value
West Rural	57	239460	4201	—	—	—	15	360450	24030	72	599910	8332
West Urban	70	265980	3800	5	74400	14880	29	421860	14547	99	762240	7699
Total West	127	505440	3980	5	74400	14800	44	782310	17780	171	1362150	7966
East Rural	44	366000	3980	5	644260	14642	—	—	—	44	1010260	22960
East Urban	71	588700	8292	71	1354060	19071	—	—	—	71	1942760	27363
Total East	115	954700	8302	115	1998320	17377	—	—	—	115	2953020	25678
Grand Total	**242**	**1460140**	**6034**	**120**	**2072720**	**17273**	**44**	**782310**	**17780**	**286**	**4315170**	**15088**

Source: Field Survey Data.

Note: Figures in brackets are percentages to their respective totals.

Table 5.14 : Working Capital Requirement of Looms

(In ₹)

Areas	Requirement of working capital						Total Capital Required	No.of Looms	Average	S.D.
	Below 10000	10001-20000	20001-30000	30001-40000	40001-50000	Above 50001				
West Rural	53 (74.0)	4 (6.0)	14 (19.0)	1 (1.0)	—	—	599910	72	8332	3465
West Urban	68 (69.0)	29 (29.0)	2 (2.0)	—	—	—	762240	99	7699	130
Total West	121 (71.0)	33 (19.0)	16 (9.0)	1	—	—	1362150	171	7966	2452
East Rural	11 (25.0)	16 (36.0)	9 (20.0)	4	—	4	1010260	44	22960	574
East Urban	— (41.0)	29 (11.0)	8 (37.0)	26 (4.0)	3 (7.0)	5	1942760	71	27363	1947
Total East	11 (10.0)	45 (39.0)	17 (15.0)	30 (26.0)	3 (3.0)	9 (7.0)	2953020	115	25678	2391
Grand Total	**132 (46.0)**	**78 (27.0)**	**33 (12.0)**	**31 (11.0)**	**3 (1.0)**	**9 (3.0)**	**4315170**	**286**	**15088**	**8886**

Source: Field Survey Data.

Note: Figures in brackets are percentages to their respective totals.

cent of the looms require more than ₹ 10,000 per year. This again indicates that the handloom industry in eastern Cuddapah is more capital intensive than the industry in western Cuddapah. Co-efficient of Correlation is calculated for the two variables viz., Working Capital requirement and income of the weaver in Table 5.15 (*See on next page*). The value of Correlation works out to be 0.8404. Thus there is a perfect positive correlation between the amount of working capital used and the generation of income. Looms that use more working capital are able to fetch the weaver more income. To ascertain the amount of working capital required to fetch a given amount of income to the weaver and vice versa, regression equation of X on Y and Y on X have been fitted.

Production Pattern

Distribution of Looms by the Type of Fabrics Produced

Table 5.16 (*See on page 232*) gives a clear picture of the distribution of looms producing different products in different areas. Technically speaking it is possible for a weaver to weave all kinds of fabrics, but due to a natural and long term evolution of preferences and specialisations, different centres tend to specialise in the production of particular varieties. Dhoties production is an important item produced in western Cuddapah, where as only zari cloth sarees are produced in eastern Cuddapah. In western Cuddapah along with Dhoties, Resham, Shirting; Cotton Lungis and Cotton Sarees are also produced. But in eastern region the only item produced is zari cloth of superfine varieties.

Distribution of Looms According to Production of Cloth

Information relating to the value of cloth produced in different areas in the district, is collected and presented in table 5.17 (*See on page 233*). About 52 per cent of the looms in western Cuddapah and 68 per cent of the looms in eastern Cuddapah produced cloth worth ₹ 30,000 or above during the year 1988, on an average. The average production of cloth was ₹ 37,000 in western region; while it was ₹ 45,000 in eastern region of Cuddapah district. Looms in eastern Cuddapah produced superior varieties and hence the values of cloth in money terms was highest in that area. The per capita production of cloth (in Meters) was the highest in western Cuddapah, with 1586 mtrs per loom per year and it was only 960 mtrs in eastern Cuddapah. Weavers in western Cuddapah produced only coarse varieties with yarn of lower counts.

Table 5.15 : Working Capital Requirement of Looms and Income

Income (Y)	Working Capital (X)						Total Looms
	Below 10000	10001-20000	20001-30000	30001-40000	40001-50000	Above 50001	
Below 3000	45 (100.0)	—	—	—	—	—	45 (100.0)
3001 - 6000	76 (93.0)	6 (7.0)	—	—	—	—	82 (100. 0)
6001 - 9000	11 (21.0)	42 (79.0)	—	—	—	—	53 (100.0)
9001 - 12000	—	21 (48.0)	18 (41.0)	5 (11.0)	—	—	44 (100.0)
Above 12000	—	9 (15.0)	6 (10.0)	35 (56.0)	3 (5.0)	9 (14.0)	62 (100.0)
Grand Total	**132 (46.0)**	**78 (27.0)**	**24 (8.0)**	**40 (14.0)**	**3 (1.0)**	**9 (4.0)**	**286 (100.0)**

Figures in brackets are precentages to their respectie totals

Source: Field Survey Data.

Correlation r = 0.8404

Regression of *Y* on *X* $Y = -1724 + 0.2693(X)$

Regression of X on Y $X = 14610 + 2.6248(Y)$

Table 5.16 : Production-wise Distribution of Looms

Areas	Type of Products						Total
	Zari Saree	Cotton Saree	Cotton Dhoty	Cotton Lungis	Resham	Shirting	
West Rural	—	11 (15.28)	36 (50.0)	—	16 (22.22)	9 (12.50)	72 (100.0)
West Urban	5 (5.05)	16 (16.16)	24 (24.24)	7 (7.07)	29 (29.29)	18 (18.18)	99 (100.0)
Total West	5 (2.92)	27 (15.79)	60 (35.09)	7 (4.09)	45 (26.32)	27 (15.79)	171 (100.0)
East Rural	44 (100.0)	—	—	—	—	—	44
East Urban	71 (100.0)	—	—	—	—	—	71
Total East	115 (100.0)	—	—	—	—	—	115
Grand Total	**120 (41.96)**	**27 (9.44)**	**60 (20.98)**	**7 (2.45)**	**45 (15.73)**	**27 (9.44)**	**286 (100.0)**

Source: Field Survey Data.

Note: Figures in brackets are percentages to their respective totals.

Table 5.17 : Distribution of Looms According to Production of Cloth

Areas	No. of Looms	Production of Cloth in a Year (In ₹)							Average Value of Production	Average Quantity of Production
		Below 10000	10001-15000	15001-20000	20001-25000	25001-30000	30001 35000	Above 35000		
West Rural	72	1 (1.39)	2 (2.78)	23 (31.94)	3 (4.17)	5 (6.94)	30 (41.47)	8 (11.11)	32663	113616
West Urban	99	—	1 (1.01)	5 (5.05)	8 (8.08)	33 (33.33)	26 (26.26)	26 (26.26)	40069	157600
Total West	171	1 (0.59)	3 (1.75)	28 (16.37)	11 (6.43)	38 (22.22)	56 (32.75)	34 (19.88)	36950	271200
East Rural	44	1 (2.27)	3 (6.82)	—	8 (18.18)	4 (9.09)	5 (11.36)	23 (52.27)	45525	43200
East Urban	71	—	6 (8.45)	3 (4.23)	1 (1.41)	11 (15.49)	11 (15.49)	39 (54.93)	44932	67400
Total East	115	1 (0.87)	9 (7.83)	3 (2.61)	9 (7.83)	15 (13.04)	16 (13.91)	62 (53.91)	45159	110400
Grand Total	**286**	**2 (0.70)**	**12 (4.20)**	**31 (10.34)**	**20 (6.99)**	**53 (18.53)**	**72 (25.18)**	**96 (33.57)**	**33689**	**381600**

Source: Field Survey Data.

Note: Figures in brackets are percentages to their respective totals.

Number of Looms and Production of Cloth

Information relating to the influence of the number of looms on the cloth produced, is collected and presented in table 5.18 (*See on next page*). The difference in the quantity of cloth produced between the two regions of Cuddapah i.e., western and eastern is quite significant-with 7.93 Mtrs per day in western region and 4.80 Mtrs per day in eastern region of Cuddapah district. The difference in the quantity of cloth produced is due to the difference in the number of looms in the household. For instance households with one loom produced 8.51 Mtrs in western Cuddapah, and 5.14 Mtrs in eastern Cuddapah. But households with two looms produced 7.41 Mtrs in western Cuddapah and 4.39 Mtrs in eastern Cuddapah and the households with four looms produced 6.5 Mtr's per day per loom in western Cuddapah and 3.75 Mtrs per day per loom in eastern Cuddapah district.

It is clear from Table 5.19 (*See on page 236*) there is association between the number of looms in the household and the production of cloth. It is found out that the increase in number of looms in the households decreases the average production of cloth per weaver. This has been attributed to the delay in pre-looming processes and supply of raw materials for the looms on time and organisational problems.

Details of production of different products are presented in Tables 5.20, 5.21 and 5.22 (*See on page 237, 238 and 239*). The number of looms producing Resham cloth' increased from 30 in 1987 to 44 in 1988. There was a significant fall in the number of looms producing Janata Dhoties, Janata Sarees, Shirting and Lungia. There is therefore the variation in the production of cloth between 1987 and 1988. In the case of Janata Dhoties, Janata Sarees, Shirting and 20 laka zari Sarees value of cloth production came down but in other areas of production there is a significant increase in the value of production.

Why do different areas specialise in the production of different products? Information on this is collected and presented in Tables 5.23 (*See on page 240 and 241*) and 5.24. 43 per cent of the respondents attributed this for the specialisation in the production of the handloom products. The next important reason according to them was the remunerative nature of the handloom industry. Other reasons are the availability of ready market, lack of tools to produce other products, Habit and the importance of the area for the production of those products etc. The value of handloom cloth produced in different areas is presented in table 5.22. In all the areas there was a significant improvement in the value of cloth produced between 1987 and 1988. The average increase in the production was the highest in eastern Cuddapah at ₹ 7523 and the lowest in western Cuddapah at ₹ 4176.

Table 5.18 : Average Production of Household and the No.of Looms in the Household

Areas	No.of House-Holds	No.of Looms	House-holds with one loom	Total Produ-ction of (4)	Average Produ-ction of (5)	House-holds with two looms	Total Produ-ction of(7)	Average Produ-clion of (8)	House-holds with three looms	Total Produ-ction of (10)	Average Produ-ction of (11)	House-holds with four looms	Total produ-ction of (13)	Average Produ-ction of (14)	Total Produ-ction by all looms	Average produ-ction of(16)
West Rural	50	72	30 (60.0)	250 (44.0)	8.33	19 (38.0)	288 (51.0)	7.58	—	—	—	1 (2.0)	30 (5.0)	7.5	568 (100.0)	7.89
West Urban	75	99	54 (72.0)	465 (59.0)	8.61	19 (25.0)	275 (35.0)	7.24	1 (2.0)	22 (3.0)	7.33	1 (1.0)	26 (3.0)	6.50	788 (100.0)	7.96
Total West	125	171	84 (67.0)	715 (53.0)	8.51	38 (30.0)	563 (42.0)	7.41	1 (1.0)	22 (2.0)	7.33	2 (2.0)	56 (4.0)	7.00	1356 (100.0)	7.93
East Rural	35	44	26 (74.0)	139 (65.0)	5.35	9 (26.0)	76 (35.0)	4.22	—	—	—	—	—	—	215 (100.00)	4.89
East Urban	55	71	43 (78.0)	216 (64.0)	5.02	10 (18.0)	91 (27.0)	4.55	—	—	—	2 (4.0)	30 (9.0)	3.75	337 (100.0)	4.75
Total East	90	115	69 (77.0)	355 (64.0)	5.14	19 (21.0)	167 (30.0)	4.39	—	—	—	2 (2.0)	30 (6.0)	3.75	552	4.80
Grand Total	**215**	**286**	**153 (71.0)**	**1070 (56.0)**	**6.99**	**57 (27.0)**	**730 (38.0)**	**6.40**	**1 (0.46)**	**22 (1.0)**	**7.33**	**4 (2.0)**	**86 (5.0)**	**5.38**	**1908 (100.0)**	**6.67**

Source: Field Survey Data.

Note: Figures in brackets are percentages to their respective totals.

Table 5.19 : Production of Cloth Per Day

Areas	No.of House-Holds	No.of Looms	Per Day Production of Cloth								Total Production per day in Mtrs	Average Production
			3 Yards	4 Yards	5 Yards	6 Yards	7 Yards	8 Yards	9 Yards	10 Yards		
West Rural	50	72	—	—	4 (6.0)	12 (17.0)	12 (17.0)	18 (25.0)	12 (17.0)	14 (19.0)	568	7.89
West Urban	75	99	—	—	3 (3.0)	12 (12.0)	17 (17.0)	34 (35.0)	20 (20.0)	13 (13.0)	788	7.96
Total West	125	171	—	—	7 (4.0)	24 (14.0)	29 (17.0)	52 (30.0)	32 (19.0)	27 (16.0)	1356	7.93
East Rural	35	44	4 (9.0)	10 (23.0)	17 (39.0)	13 (30.0)	—	—	—	—	215	4.89
East Urban	55	71	5 (7.0)	22 (31.0)	30 (42.0)	14 (20.0)	—	—	—	—	337	4.75
Total East	**90**	**115**	**9 (8.0)**	**32 (28.0)**	**47 (41.0)**	**27 (23.0)**	—	—	—	—	**552**	**4.80**

Source: Field Survey Data.

Note: Figures in brackets are percentages to their respective totals.

Table 5.20 : Production of Handloom Cloth

Areas	No. of Looms	Total Production		Net increas in total production	Average production		Net Increase in average production
		1988	1989		1988	1989	
West Rural	72	2340742	2351705	10963	32510	32663	152.26
West Urban	99	3263618	3966795	703177	32966	40069	7103
Total West	171	5604360	6318500	714140	32774	36950	4176
East Rural	44	1886000	2003100	117100	42864	45525	2661
East Urban	71	2442170	3190200	748030	34397	44932	10535
Total East	115	4328170	5193300	865130	37636	45159	7523
Grand Total	**286**	**9932530**	**11511800**	**1195842**	**29508**	**33689**	**4181**

Source: Field Survey Data.

Note: Figures in brackets are percentages to their respective totals.

Table 5.21 : Product-wise Production

Products	No. of Looms in 1987	No. of Looms in 1988	Total Production in		Net increase in total production	Average Production in		Net increase - in Average production
			1987	1988		1987	1988	
Janata doties	64	60	932400	876000	–56400	14569	14600	–940
Janata sarees	30	27	456200	408240	–47960	15207	15120	–1776
Shirting	36	28	459920	356160	–103760	12776	12720	–3706
Lungis	6	7	72600	81200	8600	12100	11600	1229
Resham	30	44	3538220	4439400	901180	117941	100895	20481
20 Laka Z.S.	59	48	1336650	1284500	–52150	22655	26760	4105
30 Laka Z.S.	3	3	78300	89200	10900	26100	29733	3633
40 Laka Z.S.	20	23	585000	828000	243000	25435	36000	10565
50 Laka Z.S.	2	2	49000	49000	—	24500	24500	—
90 Laka Z.S.	30	34	1940000	2254970	314970	64667	66323	1656
120 Laka Z.S.	6	9	484240	750130	265890	80707	83348	2641
150 Laka Z.S.	0	1	—	95000	—	—	95000	—
Total	**276**	**286**	**9932530**	**11511800**	**1579270**	**35987**	**40251**	—

Source: Field Survey Data.

Table 5.22 : Distribution of Looms According to Production of Cloth

Regions	No.of Looms	Production of Cloth in a year 1989 (In ₹)							Total produ-ction in (₹)	Average produc-tion (₹)	Tolal produ-ction (Mtrs)	Average production (in Mtrs)
		Below 10000	10001-15000	15001-20000	20001-25000	25001-30000	30001-35000	Above 35000				
West Rural	72	1 (1.39)	2 (2.78)	23 (31.94)	3 (4.17)	5 (6.94)	30 (41.47)	8 (11.11)	2351705	32663	113600	1578
West Urban	99	—	1 (1.01)	5 (5.05)	8 (8.08)	33 (33.33)	26 (26.26)	26 (26.26)	3966795	40069	157600	1592
Total West	171	1 (0.59)	3 (1.75)	28 (16.37)	11 (6.43)	38 (22.22)	56 (32.75)	34 (19.88)	6318500	36950	271200	1586
East Rural	44	1 (2.27)	3 (6.82)	—	8 (18.18)	4 (9.09)	5 (11.36)	23 (52.27)	2003100	45525	43200	982
East Urban	71	—	6 (8.45)	3 (4.23)	1 (1.41)	11 (15.49)	11 (15.49)	39 (54.93)	3190200	44932	67400	949
Total East	115	1 (0.87)	9 (7.83)	3 (2.61)	9 (7.83)	15 (13.04)	1 (13.91)	62 (53.91)	5193300	45159	110400	960
Grand Total	**286**	**2 (0.70)**	**12 (4.20)**	**31 (10.34)**	**20 (6.99)**	**53 (18.53)**	**72 (25.18)**	**96 (33.57)**	**11511800**	**33689**	**381600**	**1334**

Source: Field Survey Data.

Note: Figures in brackets are percentages to their respective totals.

Table 5.23: Reasons for Producing the Products

Areas	No. of Looms	Reasons for producing the products					
		Remune-rative	Ready Market	Lack of tools to produce	Specialised in these products other products	Habituated	Area is famous for the products
West Rural	72	15 (10.0)	15 (10.0)	—	57 (40.0)	—	57 (40)
West Urban	99	32 (16.0)	32 (16.0)	—	67 (34.0)	—	67 (34.0)
Total West	171	47 (14.0)	47 (14.0)	—	124 (36.0)	—	124 (36.0)
East Rural	44	31 (35.0)	13 (15.0)	—	—	—	44 (50.0)
East Urban	71	55 (39.0)	16 (11.0)	—	—	—	71 (50.0)
Total East	115	86 (37.0)	29 (13.0)	—	—	—	115 (50.0)
Grand Tota	**286**	**133 (23.0)**	**76 (13.0)**	**—**	**124 (22.0)**	**—**	**239 (42.0)**

Source: Field Survey Data.

Note: Figures in brackets are percentages to their respective totals.

Table 5.24 : Reasons for Producing the Products

Areas	No. of Respondents (or looms) in	Reasons for producing the products					
		Remune-rative	Ready Market	Lack of tools to produce other products	Specialised in these products	Habituated	Area is famous for the products
Janata dhoties	60	—	—	—	60 (50.0)	28 (23.0)	32 (27.0)
Janta sarees	27	—	—	—	27 (50.0)	7 (13.0)	20 (37.0)
Shirting	28	—	—	4 (7.0)	24 (43.0)	23 (41.0)	5 (9.0)
Lungis	7	—	—	—	7 (50.0)	—	7 (50.0)
Resham	44	44 (50.0)	—	—	44 (50.0)	—	—
20 laka Z.S.	48	—	48 (50.0)	—	48 (50.0)	—	—
30 laka Z.S.	3	3 (50.0)	—	—	3 (50.0)	—	—
40 laka Z.S.	23	20 (43.0)	3 (7.0)	—	—	2 (9.0)	21 (41.0)
50 laka Z.S.	2	2 (50.0)	—	—	—	2 (50.0)	—
90 laka Z.S.	34	34 (50.0)	—	—	25(37.0)	9 (13.0)	—
120 Laka Z.S.	9	9 (50.0)	—	—	7(39.0)	2 (11.0)	—
150 Laka Z.S.	1	1 (50.0)	—	—	—	1 (50.0)	—
Total	**286**	**113 (20.0)**	**51 (9.0)**	**4 (1.0)**	**245 (43.0)**	**74 (13.0)**	**85 (15.0)**

Source: Field Survey Data.

In order to assess the influence of raw materials used on the quantity of production of handloom cloth, information is collected and presented in Table 5.25. Janata Dhoties using yarn of 30×40 Counts are produced at the rate of 8.92 Mtrs per day. The average production of Janata Sarees using yarn of 40×40 Counts is 8.22 Mtrs per day. In case of Shirting, Lungis, Resham and Pure Zari Sarees the average amount of cloth produced per day is 7.89 Mtrs, 7.43 Mtrs, 6.70 Mtrs and 4.86 Mtrs respectively. The average quantity of all types of cloth produced per day is 6.67 Mtrs. In the case of pure zari sarees only 100×120 counts of yarn is used. In all other items only lower Counts of yarn (i.e from 40 to 80 Counts) is used. The higher the fineness or the counts of yarn used, the lower would be the average quantity of cloth produced.

Table 5.25 : Counts of Yarn Used and Average Production

Products	No. of Looms	Fineness of Yarn used	Total Production per year (Yds)	Average per day (Yds)
Janata dhoties	60	30×40	535	8.92
Janata sarees	27	40×40	222	8.22
Shirting	28	40×60	221	7.89
Lungis	7	40×60	52	7.43
Resham	44	—	295	6.70
Pure Z. S.	120	100×100=4 100x120=116	583	4.86
Total	**286**		**1908**	**6.67**

Source: Field Survey Data.

Note: Figures in brackets are percentages to their respective totals.

Information pertaining to different items of cloth produced and the per day production of cloth is presented in Tables 5.26 and 5.27 (*See on pages 243, 245*). For the remaining products their respective averages falls between 3.0 and 8.9 Mtrs. The table makes it clear that the average production of looms producing coarse varieties like Janata Dhoties, Janata Sarees, Shirting and Lungis is significantly more than the other zari cloth producing handlooms.

Cost of Production

Production in the organised Industries is carefully planned by calculating the costs before hand. It is possible to find out the exact cost of a metre of cloth produced and the different elements that go to make it up, by

Table 5.26 : Production of Cloth Per Day on the Basis of Products

Products	No. of Looms	Per day production of Cloth								Total Production per day (Yds)	Average Production per day (Yds)
		3 Yards	4 Yards	5 Yards	6 Yards	7 Yards	8 Yards	9 Yards	10 Yards		
Janata doties	60	—	—	—	—	2(3.0)	22(37.0)	15(25.0)	21(35.0)	535	8.92
Janata sarees	27	—	—	—	—	3(11.0)	17(63.0)	5(19.0)	2(7.0)	222	8.22
Shirting	28	—	—	1(4.0)	5(18.0)	6(21.0)	4(14.0)	8(29.0)	4(14.0)	221	8.07
Lungis	7	—	—	—	1(14.0)	3(43.0)	2(29.0)	1(4.0)	—	52	7.43
Resham	44	—	—	7(16.0)	12(27.0)	15(34.0)	7(16.0)	3(7.0)	—	295	6.70
20 Laka Z.S.	48	—	5(10.0)	12(25.0)	31(65.0)	—	—	—	—	266	5.54
30 Laka Z.S.	3	—	1(33.0)	—	2(67.0)	—	—	—	—	16	5.33
40 Laka Z.S.	23	—	12(52.0)	11(48.0)	—	—	—	—	103	4.48	
50 Laka Z.S.	2	—	—	2(100.0)	—	—	—	—	—	10	5.00
90 Laka Z.S.	34	5(15.0)	8(24.0)	21(61.0)	—	—	—	—	—	152	4.47
120 Laka Z.S.	9	3(33.0)	6(67.0)	—	—	—	—	—	—	33	3.67
150 Laka Z.S.	1	1(100.0)	—	—	—	—	—	—	—	3	3.00
Total	**286**	**9(3.0)**	**32(11.0)**	**54(19.0)**	**51(18.0)**	**29(10.0)**	**52(18.0)**	**32(11.0)**	**27(9.0)**	**1908**	**.67**

Source: Field Survey Data.

Table 5.27 : Production-wise Distribution of Looms

Areas	Zari Sarees	Cotton Sarees	Cotton Dhoties	Cotton Lungis	Resham	Shirting	Total
West Rural	—	11 (15.28)	36 (50.0)	—	16 (22.22)	9 (12.50)	72 (100.0)
West Urban	5 (5.05)	16 (16.16)	24 (24.24)	7 (7.07)	29 (29.29)	18 (18.18)	99 (100.0)
Total West	5 (2.92)	27 (15.79)	60 (35.09)	7 (4.09)	45 (26.82)	27 (15.79)	171 (100.0)
East Rural	44 (100.0)	—	—	—	—	—	44 (100.0)
East Urban	71 (100.0)	—	—	—	—	—	71 (100.0)
Total East	115 (100.0)	—	—	—	—	—	115 (100.0)
Grand Total	**120 (41.96)**	**27 (9.44)**	**60 (20.98)**	**7 (2.45)**	**45 (15.73)**	**27 (9.44)**	**286 (100.0)**

Source: Field Survey Data.

Note: Figures in brackets are percentages to their respective totals.

referring to their account books. But the handloom weaver, whether he works independently or for the weavers Co-operative Society or for the Corporation or for the Sowcar Weaver does not worry about the Costing. The Independent weaver purchases his yarn on the basis of some crude calculations. He seldom keeps any accounts. In the case of non-independent weavers the account of yarn supplied to them is maintained by the sowcar weavers, weavers' Co-operative Societies and the Corporation, as the case may be. The weaver is mainly concerned about the amount of wages which he receives for his work. Further more different weavers produce different types of cloth. Even in the case of an individual weaver the cost of each piece of fabric woven may be different from the other. Any proper cost accounting, under these circumstances can only be carried out by some experienced and specialist investigator in the field daily watching and recording the various items of cost incurred by the weaver[9]. This is obviously a difficult task for an individual investigator like the present one. Consequently the present study is not concerned with costs to such an extent as to undertake a very minute study. Nevertheless, it is necessary to know what are the different items of cost in handloom production and what is their relative importance.

Yarn is by far the most Important input entering into the cost of production. The cost of silk, zari, Starching, Winding, Warping and Dyeing charges are the other items that enter into cost of production. The labour cost includes preparation as well as weaving. 'Before it is estimated as to what the weaver actually gets, it is necessary to take into account how much is paid in preparatory charges. The field survey reveals that usually preparatory charges do not exceed 10 per cent of the total cost of production. Though these charges are included under the head—labour cost, weaver may not get the whole or part of these, if hired labour is employed to assist him in preliminary processes. But in general the preparatory processes are performed by the weaver himself assisted by the household members. In such cases the labour charges for weaving as well as for pre-weaving activities are earned by the weaver and his family. Thus raw materials and labour charges are the two main components of the cost of production of handloom fabrics as noticed in the sample survey. In an industry like handloom weaving, where heterogeneity of product is the rule the proportion of the aforesaid elements in the total cost of production can not be expected to conform to any uniform pattern. On the other hand these proportions vary from place to place, from one type of fabric to another and from one range of Counts to another[10].

Tables 5.28 and 5.29 illustrates the variation in the relative position of labour charges and the cost of raw materials in the cost structure of

Table 5.28 : Cost of Production for a Set of Product

(Cost in ₹)

Productions	No.of Looms	Yarn	Average	Zari	Average	Silk	Average	Total value of raw material	Average	Weaving	Average	Total	Average
West Rural	72	762	13.37	—	—	952	63.46	1714	23.81	442.92	6.15	2157.95	29.97
West Urban	99	987	14.10	—	—	1840	63.45	2527	28.56	663.90	6.71	3491.00	35.26
Total West	171	1749	13.77	—	—	2792	63.45	4541	26.56	1108.00	6.40	5648.95	33.03
East Rural	44	1898	43.13	5374	122.13	—	—	7272	165.30	2474.00	56.20	9746.00	221.50
East Urban	71	3088	43.49	10543	148.49	—	—	13631	192.00	4670.00	66.00	18301.00	253.00
Total East	115	4986	43.36	15917	138.40	—	—	20903	182.00	7144.00	62.12	28047.00	240.00
Grand Total	**286**	**6735**	**27.83**	**15917**	**138.40**	**2792**	**63.45**	**25444**	**88.97**	**8252.00**	**28.85**	**33697.00**	**118.00**

Source: Field Survey Data.

Table 5.29 : Product-wise Cost of Production

Products	No. of Looms	Average amount of Yarn/Silk used per product	Average Value of zari used per product	Wage per unit of production	Total Average Value of Cost of production
Janata Doties	60	9.45(58.33)	—	3.75(41.67)	16.20(100.0)
Janaia Sarees	27	15.50(16.51)	—	9.70(38.49)	25.20(100.0)
Shirting(IMt)	28	10.13(75.71)	—	3.25(24.29)	13.38(100.0)
Lungis(2Mtrs)	7	12.75(57.30)	—	9.50(42.70)	22.25(100.0)
Resham	44	42.50(74.24)	—	14.75(25.76)	57.25(100.0)
20 laka p.z.s.	48	30.50(24.40)	52.83(42)	41.67(33.34)	125.00(100.0)
30 laka p.z.s.	3	30.50(21.79)	59.50(42)	50.00(35.71)	140.00(100.0)
40 laka p.z. s.	23	31.40(17.44)	73.60(40)	75.00(41.67)	180.00(100.0)
50 laka p.z.s.	2	31.40(15.86)	87.20(44)	79.40(40.10)	198.00(100.0)
90 laka p.z.s.	34	33.30(9.79)	223.37(65)	83.33(24.51)	340.00(100.0)
120 laka p.z.s.	9	33.30(7.43)	314.70(70)	100.0(22.32)	448.00(100.0)
150 laka p.z.s.	1	33.30(6.97)	336.37(70)	108.33(22.66)	478.00(100.0)

Source: Field Survey Data.

Note: Figures in brackets are percentages to their respective totals.

some typical varieties of handloom products, depending on the fineness of yarn used and the design of the fabrics.

As may be seen from the table the total cost of production as well as the absolute amounts of both the cost of raw materials and labour charges increase for fabrics with the fineness of (higher counts) yarn and designs. But the percentage of labour cost involved is higher in fabrics with yarn of higher Counts and better designs; consequently the percentage of cost of raw materials is correspondingly lower and vice versa.

The Marketing Organisation

The problem of marketing of handloom products is intricately mixed up with those not only of the supply of yarh but also with these of finance and it is difficult to deal with it separately. It may also be said that the agencies of marketing besides being diverse are also far too numerous to leave much margin of earnings for the weavers. By comparing the position of the milk industry in this respect one can understand how the handloom weavers are seriously handicapped in the sale of that goods. This diversity of the marketing agencies chiefly arises from the unorganised condition of the industry itself.

Thus the Independent weaver may sell his products either direct to the consumer or to the Master-weaver and other intermediaries prior to its sale to the final consumer. If the weaver is bound by any contractual relationship with the middleman, he is, of course, to that extent relieved of his responsibility for marketing the cloth. But in this case the Master-weaver will be called upon to seek the assistance of wholesalers or retailers in the rural or urban areas. The wholesaler, again may pass on the goods to retailers and petty shopkeepers in the final market.

Further, one has to consider the degree of dependence of the weaver upon these marketing agencies for the sale of his cloth. In this context the general conclusion is that, in roost places, he is at the mercy of the cloth dealer. Even an Independent weaver is not always able to dispose of his products directly to the consumer in the retail market and he has to approach the cloth dealer, who generally charges a substantial commission for selling the cloth. The case of the weaver who works for the master weaver is definitely worse. In the first place, he is probably indebted to the latter and is dependent upon him for his day to day livelihood. Secondly, his staying-power is hopelessly poor and he is not in a position to hold on even for a few days. His problem is not merely how to dispose of his cloth, but also to obtain further raw material in the shape of yarn for the next days work, and all the while he must also worry about the provision of food for his family. Thus, if he is an independent weaver he wanders from shop to shop offering his goods and finally selling them off at any price that can be obtained. The labourer weaver too has to accept whatever terms are offered by the Master weaver for fear of having to face starvation in the event of his refusal to accept a low offer. Sometimes the weaver can go in for borrowing further yarn on his own credit for the next days work, but thus he may be only postponing his difficulties. If the situation doesn't improve he has to sell his products at low prices all the same.

One of the important agencies of marketing are the moneylenders. There are various classes of professional money-lenders, who combine money lending business with the sale of a number of articles including handloom cloth and sundry necessaries of life. These moneylenders no doubt exploit the needy condition of the weaver. It would be a desirable reform, if in the labour centres this agency of marketing handloom cloth is replaced by a more suitable one, such as installment credit shops, run by Co-operative Societies[11].

There is no doubt that on the whole, the present system of marketing of handloom products is a very expensive one and that the high cost of marketing impinges upon the residual income of the weaver. The prices of handloom products are,in the ultimate analysis, fixed by the entire cloth market and the pace of these prices is set to a large extent by the prices of mill made piece goods. Thus to arrive at the residual income of the weaver, we have to deduct from the final price, the cost of the raw material, the cost of preparation of yarn for weaving, the interest charges directly or indirectly imposed by the middle men, the cost of marketing including the middlemen's profits, transport charges etc. From the weavers point of view, again, the loss of time involved in disposing of the goods in the markets is also to be considered. Where the weaver is an independent one, he has to spend a day or two or even more in finding a purchaser for his goods. It is to be noted that the competitive position of the handloom industry is seriously affected by the fact that the marketing cost is far more heavy in the case of its products than in that of mill made goods[12]. The main conclusion that emerges is that the cost of marketing the handloom fabrics is prohibitively high. It may appear that the middlemen are largely to be blamed for the high cost of marketing. We are not sure, however, that in every case the middlemen are reaping huge profits at the expense of the weaver[13]. At the same time there are many middlemen who appear to be keeping their heads above water by taking proportionately higher share of the gross profits of the industry than the weaver himself.

Against this background an attempt has been made to find out the cost of production of handloom products in the district, and the respective price spread, when the products make a move from one establishment to another before they ultimately reach the consumer, (Tables 5.30, 5.31, 5.32, 5.33 and 5.34).

In the case of Janata Dhoties the Cost of Production is ₹ 16.20. It is sold at the rate of ₹ 14.00. The loss of ₹ 2.20 is compensated by the Govt. assistance. The cost of Janata Saree is ₹ 25.20 and it is marketed at the rate of ₹ 19/-, the loss thua incurred viz., ₹ 6.20 is borne by the Government. The coat of production of Shirting of 1 Mtr is 13.38 and it ia sold for ₹ 16.00 and the profit thus earned i.e ₹ 2.62 per meter goes to the organisation concerned. The consumer is purchasing the cloth for ₹ 19.50. Thus the price spread between the trader and consumer is Ra.3.50. The total price spread between the cost of production and the final consumer with respect to shirting is about ₹ 6.12.

Resham cloth is manufactured at the cost of ₹ 57.25 per meter and sold to the trader at the value of ₹ 67.50 and thus the concerned organisation is making a profit of ₹ 12.50. It reaches the final consumer at a price of ₹ 98.00. Hence the price spread between cost of production and the price paid by the final consumer is ₹ 40.75 or 71.18 per cent of the total cost of production.

Other varieties (*See Table 5.35 on next page*) viz., 20 laka, 30 laka, 40 laka, 50 laka, 90 laka, 120 laka and 150 laka pure zari sarees are manufactured at the cost of ₹ 125,140, 180, 198, 340, 448 and 478 respectively. The products are sold by different organisations to the traders at the average price of ₹ 145,175, 225, 250, 420, 550 and 600 respectively and thus the organisations are making a profit of ₹ 20 on 20 laka saree; ₹ 35 on 30 laka Sarees; ₹ 45 on 40 laka sarees; ₹ 52 on 50 laka Sarees; Ra.80 on 90 laka sarees; ₹ 102 on 120 laka sarees, and Ra.122 on 150 laka pure zari sareea. The trader is selling these products at the price of ₹ 162.75; ₹ 210.00; ₹ 300.00; ₹ 340.00; ₹ 575.00; Re.725.00; and Ra.800 reapectively to the final consumer, and thus trader is making a profit of ₹ 17.25 on selling 20 laka pure zari saree, ₹ 35 from 30 laka; ₹ 75 from 40 laka; ₹ 90 from 50 laka; ₹ 155 from 90 laka; ₹ 175 from 120 laka; and ₹ 200 from 150 laka sarees. The total price spread between the cost of production and the price paid by the consumer is ₹ 37.25 for 20 laka; ₹ 70 for 30 laka; ₹ 120 for 40 laka; ₹ 142 for 50 laka; ₹ 235 for 90 laka; ₹ 227 for 120 laka; and ₹ 322 for 150 laka zari sarees. Thus higher the quality of cloth, higher would be the price spread.

From the above analysis one can understand that the organiser[14] who is responsible for manufacturing the handloom cloth is not paid in

Table 5.30 : Product-wise Price Spread under Different Organisations

Products	No. of Looms	Cost of Production(₹)					Price of the Product(₹)					Price Spread (₹)				
		MW	Co-op	Ind.	Corp.	Average	MW	Co-op	Ind.	Corp.	Average	MW	Co-op	Ind.	Corp.	Average
Janata Doties	60	—	16.20	—	16.20	16.20	—	14.00	—	14.00	14.00	—	–2.20	—	–2.20	–2.20
Janata Sarees	27	—	25.20	—	25.20	25.20	—	19.00	—	19.00	19.00	—	–6.20	—	6.20	–6.20
Shirting (1Mt)	28	14.50	12.50	14.00	12.50	13.38	16.00	16.00	16.00	16.00	16.00	1.50	3.50	2.00	3.50	2.63
Lunfia (2Mtrs)	7	22.00	22.50	22.00	22.50	22.25	23.00	23.00	23.00	23.00	23.00	1.00	0.50	0.50	0.50	0.83
Resham	44	55.00	60.00	54.00	60.00	57.25	67.00	68.00	67.00	68.00	67.50	12.00	13.00	12.00	13.00	12.50
20 laka p.z.s.	48	127.00	127	121	—	125	150	150	135	—	145	23	23	14	—	20
30 laka p.z.s.	3	142	142	136	—	140	178	177	170	—	175	36	35	34	—	35
40 laka p.z.s.	23	183	183	174	—	180	240	235	200	—	225	57	52	26	—	45
50 laka p.z.s.	2	202	202	190	—	198	265	265	220	—	250	63	63	30	—	52
90 laka p.z.s.	34	343	342	335	—	340	445	435	380	—	420	102	93	45	—	80
120 laka p.z.s.	9	452	452	449	—	448	590	580	480	—	550	138	128	40	—	102
150 laka p.z.s.	1	485	485	465	—	478	625	625	550	—	600	140	141	85	—	122

Source: Field Survey Data.

Note: Figures in brackets are percentages to their respective totals.

MW = Waster Weaver, Co-op = Co-operatives, Ind = Independent, Corp = Corporation.

p.z.s = Pure Zari Sarees.

Table 5.31 : Product-wise Price Spread (Between Cost of Production and Price Paid by the Consumer)

Products	No.of Looms	Total Cost of Production(I)					Price paid Consumer (II)	Price Spread between I and II (₹)				
		MW	Co-op	Ind.	Corp.	Average		MW	Co-op	Indp.	Corp.	Average
Janata Duties	60	—	16.20	—	16.20	16.20	14.00	—	–2.20	—	–2.20	–2.20
Janata Sarees	27	—	25.20	—	25.20	25.20	19.00	—	–6.20	—	–6.20	–6.20
Shitting (1Mt)	28	14.50	12.50	14.00	12.50	13.38	19.50	5.00	7.00	5.50	7.00	6.13
Lungis (2Mtrs)	7	22.00	22.50	22.00	22.50	22.25	32.00	10.00	9.50	10.00	9.50	9.75
Resham	44	55.00	60.00	54.00	60.00	57.25	98.00	43.00	38.00	44.00	38.00	40.75
20 laka p.z.s.	48	127.00	127	121	—	125	162.25	35.35	35.35	41.25	—	37.25
30 laka p.z.s.	3	142	142	136	—	140	210.00	68.00	68.00	74.00	—	70.00
40 laka p.z.s.	23	183	183	174	—	180	300.00	117.00	117.00	126.00	—	120.00
50 laka p.z.s.	2	202	202	190	—	198	340.00	138.00	138.00	150.00	—	142.00
90 laka p.z.s.	34	343	342	335	—	340	575.00	232.00	233.00	240.00	—	210.00
120 laka p.z.s.	9	452	452	449	—	448	725.00	273.00	273.00	285.00	—	277.00
150 laka p.z.s.	1	485	484	465	—	478	800.00	315.00	316.00	335.00	—	322.00

Source: Field Survey Data.

MW = Master Weaver, Co-op = Co-operatives, Ind = Independent, Corp = Corporation.

p.z.s = Pure Zari Sarees.

Table 5.32 : Total Price Spread

Product	Price Spread (between cost and price paid by the trader)	Price Spread (between trader and consumer)	Total Price spread
Janata Doties	–2.20 (100.0)	0	–2.20
Janata Sarees	–6.20 (100.0)	0	–6.20
Shirting (1Mt)	2.63 (42.90)	3.50 (57.10)	6.13 (100.0)
Lungis(2Mtrs)	0.83 (8.44)	9.00 (91.56)	9.83 (100.0)
Resham	12.50 (39.68)	19.00 (60.32)	31.50 (100.0)
20 laka p.z.s.	20.00 (53.69)	17.25 (46.31)	37.25 (100.0)
30 laka p.z.s.	35.00 (50.0)	35.0 (50.0)	70.00 (100.0)
40 laka p.z.s.	45.00 (37.50)	75.00 (62.50)	120.00 (100.0)
50 laka p.z.s.	52.00 (36.62)	90.00 (63.38)	142.00 (100.0)
90 laka p.z.s.	80.00 (34.04)	155.00 (65.96)	235.00 (100.0)
120 laka p.z.s.	102.00 (36.82)	175.00 (63.18)	277.00 (100.0)
150 laka p.z.s.	122.00 (37.89)	200.00 (62.11)	322.00 (100.0)

Source: Field Survey Data.

Note: Figures in brackets are percentages to their respective totals.

Table 5.33 : Product-wise Price Spread (Between Price Paid by the Trader and Price Paid by the Consumer)

Products	No. of Looms	Price paid by the trader					Price paid by the consumer	Price Spread				
		MW	Co-op	Ind.	Corp	Average		MW	Co-op	Ind.	Corp.	Average
Janata Doties	60	—	14.0	—	14.0	14.0	14.0	—	0	00		
Janata Sarees	27	—	19.0	—	19.0	19.0	19.0	—	0	—	0	0
Shirting(1Mt)	28	16.00	16.0	16.0	16.0	16.0	19.50	3.50	3.50	3.50	3.50	3.50
Lungist(2Mtrs)	7	23.00	23.0	23.0	23.0	23.0	32.00	9.00	9.00	9.00	9.00	9.00
Resham	44	80.00	78.0	80.0	·78.0	79.0	98.0	18.0	20.0	18.0	20.0	19.0
20 laka p.z.s.	48	150	150	135	—	145	162.25	12.25	12.25	27.25	—	17.25
30 laka p.z.s.	3	178	177	170	—	175	210.00	32.00	33.00	40.00	—	35.00
40 laka p.z.s.	23	240	235	200	—	225	300	60.00	65.00	100.0	—	75.00
50 laka p.z.s.	2	265	265	220	—	250	340.00	75.00	75.00	120.0	—	90.00
90 laka p.z.s	34	445	435	380	—	420	575.00	130.0	140.0	195.0	—	155.00
120 laka p.z.s	9	590	580	480	—	550	725.00	135.0	145.0	245.0	—	175.00
150 laka p.z.s.	1	625	625	550	—	600	800.00	175.0	175.0	250.0	—	200.00

Source: Field Survey Data.
MW = Master Weaver

Table 5.34 : Average Price Spread—Product-wise

Areas	No. of Looms	Zari Sarees		Sarees (Ordinary)		Dothi		Reshara		Shirting		Lungis	
		No. of looms	Average price spread	No. of looms	Average price spread	No. of looms	Average price spread	No. of looms	Average price spread	No. of looms	Average price spread	No. of looms	Average price spread
West Rural	72	—	—	11	–6.20	36	–2.20	15	19.0	10	6.13	—	—
West Urban	99	5	37.25	16	–6.20	24	–2.20	29	40.75	18	6.13	99	9.75
Total West	171	5	37.25	27	–6.20	60	–2.20	44	40.75	28	6.13	171	9.75
East Rural	44	44	69.60	—	—	—	—	—	—	—	—	—	—
East Urban	71	71	80.20	—	—	—	—	—	—	—	—	—	—
Total East	115	115	74.90	—	—	—	—	—	—	—	—	—	—
Grand Total	**286**	**120**	**56.08**	**27**	**–6.20**	**60**	**–2.20**	**44**	**40.75**	**28**	**6.13**	**117**	**9.75**

Source: Field Survey Data.

Table 5.35 : Price Spread on Zari Product

Products	No.of Looms	Average Cost of production value	Average Price paid by the traders	Average Price paid by the traders	Price Spread between trader and the Cost of production	Price spread between the the Trader consumer	Price Spread between the of production and consumer
20 Laka Zari Saree	48	125	145	162.25	20	17.25	37.25
30 Laka Zari Saree	3	140	175	210.00	35	35.00	70.00
40 Laka Zari Saree	23	180	225	300.00	45	75.00	120.00
50 laka Zari Saree	2	198	250	340.00	52	90.00	142.00
90 Laka Zari Saree	34	340	420	575.00	80	155.00	210.00
120 Laka Zari Saree	9	448	550	725.00	102	175.00	277.00
150 laka Zari Saree	1	478	600	800.00	122	200.00	322.00
Total	**120**	**272.70**	**337.86**	**444.60**	**65.14**	**106.04**	**168.04**

Source: Field Survey Data.

Average Increase in Price paid by Consumer with the increase in cost of Production $\Big\} \frac{168.04}{272.70} = 0.6162$ for 1 Rupee proportion to his service. But the trader, whose contribution is nil for the manufacturing of the handloom cloth, is making much profit out of his sales. Higher the price of the product, higher would be the profit to the trader. The trader gets more than 50% of the total value added or price spread out of his sales.

From the simple linear regression equations of Y(price spread) on X (Cost of Production) and X on Y it is possible to assess the relationship existing between the variables. It helps us to calculate the amount of price spread with the given amount of cost value and vice versa. From the tables (*see Tables 5.36 and 5.37 on pages 258 and 259*) it is estimated that for every ₹ 100 amount of cost the price spread would be ₹ 18,76, and every ₹ 100 of price spread, the expected value of cost of production is ₹ 503.78.

Details of Weaving Households Using Diffcrent Raw Materials and Their Respective Incomes

To ascertain the effect of different types of raw materials used on the incomes of the weaving households, information pertaining to these variables is collected and presented in Table 5.38 (*See on page 260*). 122 looms or 43 per cent, of the total surveyed, are using only Cotton as the chief raw material; 15 per cent of the looms are using only silk as the raw material and the remaining 120 looms are using both yarn and zari as the raw material. In western Cuddapah cotton is used as the chief raw material. Around 71 per cent of the looms in western Cuddapah are using yarn as the chief raw material; 26 per cent are using only silk; and the remaining 3 per cent are using both yarn and zari as the raw materials. All the 120 looms in eastern Cuddapah are using both yarn and zari as the raw materials to their looms.

Table 5.38 shows the influence of the different raw materials used on the income of the weaver. From the table, it may be noted that each weaver who uses only cotton yarn as the raw material, earns ₹ 4308 per year. Weavers using

Silk as the chief raw material get ₹ 5970 on an average per year; and those who are using yarn and zari as the raw materials earn ₹ 8088 on an average per year. From this, one can draw an inference that the raw material used has influence on the income of the household and that the weavers who use cotton yarn as the only raw material get less income, compared to the others using silk and yarn with zari. Weavers using zari along with the cotton yarn earn more income than the other two categories of weavers. Weavers using only silk stand between the other two categories of weavers. It can be concluded that introducing zari cloth varieties in those places where only cotton is used would help the weavers to increase their Income.

Table 5.36 : Price Spread Between Cost of Production and the Sale Price of the Product

Value of Cost of production(X)	(Y) Price Spread between the Cost of Production and the sale Price of the Product							Total Looms
	Below 10	11-20	21-30	31-40	41-50	51-60	Above 60	
0-50	122	—	—	—	—	—	—	122
51 - 100	—	44	—	—	—	—	—	44
101 - 150	—	48	—	3	—	—	—	51
151 - 200	—	—	—	—	23	2	—	25
201 - 250	—	—	—	—	—	—	—	—
251 - 300	—	—	—	—	—	—	34	34
301 - 351	—	—	—	—	—	—	—	—
351 - 400	—	—	—	—	—	—	9	9
401 - 450	—	—	—	—	—	—	1	1
451 - 500	122	92	—	3	23	2	44	286

Source: Field Survey Data.

Correlation(r) = 0.9574

Regression of Y on X $\quad Y = 0.76 + 0.1803\,x$

Regression of X on Y $\quad X = 7.63 + 4.9615\,y$

Table 5.37 : Product-wise Price Spread Between Price Paid by the Trader and Price Paid by the Consumer

Products	No.of Looms	Total Cost of Production(I)					Price paid by the consumer (II)	Price Spread between I & II				
		MW	Co-op	Ind.	Corp	Average		MW	Co-op	Ind.	Corp.	Average
Janata Doties	60	—	16.20	—	16.20	16.20	14.0	—	–2.20	—	–2.20	–2.20
Janata Sarees	27	—	25.20	—	25.20	25.20	19.0	—	–6.20	—	–6.20	–6.20
Shirting(1Mt)	28	14.50	12.50	14.0	12.50	13.38	19.50	5.00	7.00	5.50	7.00	6.13
Lungis(2Mtrs)	7	22.00	22.50	22.00	22.50	22.25	32.00	10.00	9.50	10.00	9.50	9.75
Resharn	44	55.00	60.00	54.00	60.00	57.25	98.00	43.00	38.0	44.0	38.0	40.75
20 laka p.z.s.	48	127.00	127.0	121.0	—	125.00	162.25	35.25	35.25	41.25	—	37.25
30 laka p.z.s.	3	142.00	142.0	136.0	—	140.00	210.00	68.00	68.00	74.00	—	70.00
40 laka p.z.s.	23	183.00	183.0	174.0	—	180.00	300.00	117.00	117.0	126.0	—	120.00
50 laka p.z.s.	2	202.0	202.0	190.0	—	198.00	340.00	138.00	138.0	150.0	—	142.00
90 laka p.z.s	94	343.0	342.0	335.0	—	340.00	575.00	232.0	233.0	240.0	—	210.00
120 laka p.z.s	9	452.0	452.0	440.0	—	448.0	725.0	273.0	273.0	285.0	—	277.00
150 laka p.z.s	1	485.0	484.0	465.0	—	478.0	800.00	315.0	316.0	335.0	—	322.00

Source : Field Survey Data.

MM = Master Weaver, Co-op=Co-operatives, Indp = Independent, Corp = Corporation.

Table 5.38 : Use of Different Raw Materials and Incomes There on

(Income in ₹)

Regions	Looms Using											
	Only Cotton			Only Silk			Yarn and Zari			Total Looms	Total Income	Average Income
	No.of Looms	Total Income	Average Income	No.of Looms	Total Income	Average Income	No.of Looms	Total Income	Average Income			
West Rural	57	250890	4402	15	92820	6188	—	—	—	72	343710	4774
West Urban	65	274680	4226	29	169860	5857	5	25760	5152	99	470300	4751
Total West	122	525570	4308	44	262680	5970	5	25760	5152	171	814010	4760
East Rural	—	—	—	—	—	—	44	339600	7718	44	339600	7718
East Urban	—	—	—	—	—	—	71	605140	8523	71	605140	8523
Total East	—	—	—	—	—	—	115	944740	8215	115	944740	8215
Grand Total	**286**	**525570**	**4308**	**44**	**262680**	**5970**	**120**	**970500**	**8088**	**286**	**1758750**	**6114**

Source: Field Survey Data.

Summary and Conclusions

There are many factors which hinder industrial growth. One such factor is the under-utilisation of capacity. During the busy seasons all the handloom establishments work to more than full capacity; during normal periods they are not able to utilise their total capacities. During slack season, the situation in respect of capacity utilisation is still worse. Capacity utilisation of handloom is more in eastern Cuddapah at 84.63 per cent, compared to western Cuddapah with 69.20 per cent.

The percentage of capacity utilisation is low where coarse varieties are made and it is the highest where superior varieties of handloom products are made. Reasons for the existence of idle capacity are many-such as, raw material difficulties, lack of demand, lack of capital resources, problems of labour etc. Other reasons, resulting in idle capacity, include enforced idleness due to illness, visits of guests, religious and social ceremonies and weather conditions etc.

It may be observed that the existence of considerable degree of idle capacity in the establishments with less number of looms which form the bulk of the industry, is one important reason weakening the competitive position of these establishments vis-a-vis their larger counterparts.

The scope for shifting the weaver from the production of coarse variety to superior variety is almost absent in western Cuddapah. In eastern Cuddapah there was constant encouragement from the organisations concerned to switch over to superior varieties of cloth production. Though weavers are aware of the fact that it is desirable, necessary and profitable to introduce new technology and shift the line of production from coarse varieties to superior varieties, they are afraid of taking risks involved in the process and are unwilling to put in the necessary extra work. As a result Stagnation and poverty exist.

Poor quality of raw materials supplied to the handloom weavers is an important problem faced equally by the weavers in all parts of Cuddapah district. Handloom industry in eastern Cuddapah is more capital intensive than its counter part in western Cuddapah.

Further, lack of dynamic entrepreneurship, lack of skills and techniques, lack of capital, lack of motivation are responsible for the poverty of weavers in western Cuddapah. Hence there is every need to take steps to mobilise the weaving techniques practised in eastern zone to western zone of Cuddapah district. Weaving training camps must be organised at the backward weaving centres to update their productive techniques. The technology that is being developed by the Handloom Research Institutes should be immediately passed on to the handloom centres. Government should stand by the weavers until they realise the usefulness of such techniques and practice them.

There is a posltive Correlation between the amount of working capital used and the income generated. Increase in the number of looms in the household decreases the average production of cloth. This is because of internal dis-economies. The weavers have to depend upon the persons involved in the preparatory activities to get the required inputs. At times, weavers have to stop weaving, due to inadequate supply of inputs. Introduction of mechanisation in the preparatory activities would help the weavers to increase their productivity.

Charges involved in the preparation of cloth do not exceed 10 per cent of the total cost of production. The higher the fineness of yarn used i.e. the greater the number of counts of yarn used and better the designs introduced greater is the increase in the total cost including labour costs and raw material costs. If the weavers are helped to switch over from the use of cheaper raw material to that of superior raw material and produce fine varieties, the remuneration to the weavers also increases and the demand for such products is better.

The present system of marketing of handloom products is a very costly one and this impinges upon the residual income of the weaver. Neither the weaver nor the organiser, who is responsible for manufacturing the handloom cloth, is paid adequately. The trader, whose contribution is absolutely nil for the manufacturing of the handloom cloth, is making undeservedly large profit. Higher the price of the product, higher would be the profit to the trader.

For every piece of cloth whose cost of production is ₹ 100 the consumer pays around ₹ 118.76, So the price spread is 18.76 per cent. Weavers that use zari along with the cotton yarn earn more Income than the other categories of weavers. Introducing production of zari cloth varieties in those places where only cotton is used would help the weavers to increase their income.

REFERENCES

1. Dr. Nageswara Rao & O. Gupta-Capacity Utilisation in Textile Industry-Productivity, 1987-July-Sep., pp.119-126.
2. M.C.Shetty, Small Scale and Household Industries in a Developing Economy. Bombay,1963, p. 72.
3. *Financial Express*, Strategy for Handlooms, Editorial, 10/1/80, p. 4.
4. Editorial, *The Hindu*, 2 Oct, 1981.

5. *Indian Cotton Mills Federation Journal*, 15(9) Jan 79, Notes and Comments, p. 593.
6. Editorial, *Financial Express*, Strategy for Handlooms, 10/1/80, p. 4.
7. *The Hindu*, Special Report, 29/9/1981, p. 17.
8. *Indian Cotton Mills Federation Journal*, Jan 1979, Notes and Comments, p. 595.
9. The Fact Finding Committee Report, *op.cit.,* p. 32.
10. The Fact Finding Committee Report, *op.cit.,* p. 134.
11. The Fact Finding Committee Report, p. 138.
12. The Fact Finding Committee Report, p. 139.
13. *Ibid.*, p.141.
14. Organiser is one who brings factors of production to a particular place and starts production.

6

Nature and Structure of Handloom Industry in Cuddapah District

Change is a universal phenomenon. Change in customs and traditions bring about changes in the habits and living conditions of the people. In the same way, the tastes and preferences of the consumers also change. The change in the preference of the consumer will automatically bring change in the pattern of production. For instance, we preferred to wear Khadi or cotton varieties in olden days. At present a majority of the people are wearing synthetic fabrics., instead of Cotton varieties. Over a period of time, this process may be reversed.

In the way the other industries have evolved in their own way to meet the changing preferences and tastes of the consuming public, the handloom industry in Cuddapah district also acquired its own uniqueness in the process of its change over a period of time. This change is different in different areas of the district. The present Chapter makes an attempt to study whether the handloom industry in Cuddapah has undergone any process of change? If so, has the evolution of the industry helped to improve the productivity of the weaver or does it help to introduce new products in the handloom industry? If the industry had really undergone a change, what has been the effect of any such change in the quantity or productivity of the loom and the value of production in different areas of Cuddapah district? How far the evolution of the handloom industry helped the weaving communities to improve their economic position?

We do not have precise official, published information about the number of looms, the various types of handlooms, quantity and varieties of production and employment etc., in India[1]. Regrettably, we do not have time series data on the handloom industry, with respect to its production, employment, raw material used etc. So, in order to fill this gap an attempt has been made, in the present study, to construct a time series data, by private effort, to understand the changes that took place in the industry over a period of time in Cuddapah district of Andhra Pradesh.

Objectives

1. To prepare time series data to understand the problems of the industry in the right way.
2. To know whether the handloom industry has undergone any change during the last 20 years period.
3. Has the evolution or change of the industry brought any significant improvement in the economic conditions of the handloom weaver.

With the objectives stated above data have been collected from the private records of the Master Weavers in Cuddapah district. Weavers concerned have also been interviewed for cross checking the data and to fill up certain data gaps. The district of Cuddapah has been divided into two parts viz., East and West, and 50 handloom weavers from each part of the district have been selected for purposes of this study.

The researcher went through the ledgers maintained by the Master Weavers to collect the information pertaining to the sample. As a native of the district and as a traditional weaver the researcher had easy access to the local Handloom Cloth manufacturers and the weavers, made his task relatively easy.

The first problem, the researcher had to face was with regard to the weavers who change organisations quite frequently. As already explained in Chapter-4, weavers are in the habit of moving from one organisation to another. In such cases continuous information is not available with the organisation concerned. In order to tide over this problem, all the information available from the ledgers of the organiser concerned, have been recorded, and data gaps were filled in by consulting the weaver concerned. Thus the data had been collected for about 20 years from 1970 to 1990, personally by the researcher by going from one organisation to another from one employer to another.

Another problem the researcher had to face was with regard to non-availability of relevant records in western Cuddapah district. The data are available only from 1986 in western Cuddapah. In order to bridge this gap, 50 handloom weavers in West were selected at random and information was collected from them, from private records and the data thus collected are presented in the following tables.

Limitations

1. One of the limitation of the study is with to the size of sample.
2. The study has largely relied upon the accuracy and authenticity of the records maintained by the organisations concerned. Of course whereever possible, cross checking was also done.
3. In order to meet the exigencies of circumstances, or commitments made to other business men, weavers sometimes work for a number of organisations without the knowledge of the regular employer/ organisation under whom the weaver normally works. Such production outside the regular employment thus cannot be accounted. However the quantum of this type of production is negligible. This factor therefore does not influence much in the total, quantity of production of the weaver concerned.
4. In order to meet the clothing requirements of his own family, the weaver sometimes, makes use of the raw-materials saved over a period of time to produce cloth. The amount of cloth thus produced for self consumption in this respect is not normally added to the total quantity.

Hypotheses

1. The industry has not undergone any specific change, both in terms of quantity and quality of production.
2. The change in the quantity and value of production is not significant.
3. The evolution or change, the handloom industry had undergone, did not bring any significant improvement in the economic conditions of the weaver.

Varieties of Handloom Products Produced in Cuddapah District

In the year 1970-71, only ordinary varieties of Sarees called 'Amarasilpi Jakkanna' Sarees of 8 yards, 'Piping' Sarees of 7yards, 'Maheswari' Sarees of 9 yards were produced in western Cuddapah district. All these products were marketed in the neighbouring States of Karnataka, Orissa and Madhya Pradeah. In eastern Cuddapah, 'Dhoties' and 'Kanduvas', for men, and 'Gunavathi' Sarees 'Devata Border' Sarees, 'Kanchukota Sarees', 'Kaddianchu Sarees' 'Lakkanchu' Sarees, 'One side Border Sarees', for women were produced. The major source of market for the varieties produced in eastern Cuddapah was Telangana, Coastal districts of Andhra Pradesh State, and neighbouring States of Karnataka and Tamilnadu.

Varieties of Handloom Products Produced in Cuddapah District During 1970-90

Table 6.1 (*See on next page*) shows that among sample weavers in western Cuddapah all the respondents were found producing ordinary varieties of Sarees of 60×60, 40×40, 30×30 Counts in 1970-71. In eastern Cuddapah as many as 14 looms or 28 per cent of the respondents were producing Dhoties and the rest viz., 72 per cent of looms were producing Sarees in 1970-71. Of the 36 looms producing Sarees, 24 per cent were producing Sarees without 'Zari'[2]. Sarees with Simple Size Zarl Border, Medium Size Zari Border, and Big Size Zari Border were 28 per cent, 14 per cent and 6 per cent respectively in eastern Cuddapah.

In the year 1975-76, production of Shirting was introduced in western Cuddapah. This was an export variety marketed in America. As many as 37 looms or 74 per cent were producing ordinary Sarees and the remaining 13 looms or 26 per cent of the sample were producing 'Check' shirting.

In eastern Cuddapah district improvement in the number of looms producing Medium and Big Zari Border Sarees, can be seen between 1970-90. For instance, the per centage of looms producing Medium and Big Border Zari Sarees has gone upto 36 and 16 respectively during 1970-71 and 75-76 from 14 and 6 in 1970-71. Significant fall in the production of Dhoties from 28 per cent in 1970-71, to 6 per cent in 1975-76 also can be observed from Table 6.1. The percentage of looms producing Sarees without Zari and Sarees with Simple Zari Border has declined to 22 per cent and 20 per cent respectively in 1975-76; from 24 per cent and 28 per cent in 1970-71.

There was a fall in the number of looms, producing Ordinary Sarees during the period 1975-76 and 1980-81., in western Cuddapah district. The percentage of looms producing Ordinary Sarees came down to 26 per cent in 1980-81, from 74 per cent in 1975-76. Significant progress in the number of looms producing Shirting cloth may also be observed by 1980-81. The percentage of looms producing Shirting cloth was 26 in 1980-81, while it is not at all produced in 1970-71. The scheme for production of 'Janata Sarees' and 'Janata Dhoties' was introduced in 1977 for mass consumption by the Government of India. About 22 per cent of the looms were producing these varieties in 1980-81 in western Cuddapah district.

There was a big increase in the percentage of looms producing Sarees with Big Border Zari in eastern Cuddapah district. The percentage of Sarees produced with Big Zari Border was just 16 in 1975-76 and it increased to 44 per cent by 1980-81. It is largely because of the increase In demand for Superior varieties.

Table 6.1 : Varieties of Handloom Cloth Produced in Cuddapah District

Years	Western Cuddapah						Eastern Cuddapah					
	No.of looms producing						No.of looms producing					
	Ordinary Sarees	Shirting	Janata Sarees	Resham Shirting	Sarees with Simple zari Border	Total looms	Dothies	Sarees without zari	Sarees with simple Zari Border	Sarees with Medium Zari Border	Sarees with Big Zari Border	Total looms
1970-71	50 (100.0)	—	—	—	—	50 (100.0)	14 (28.0)	12 (24.0)	14 (28.0)	7 (14.0)	3 (6.0)	50 (100.0)
1975-76	37 (74.0)	13 (26.0)	—	—	—	50 (100.0)	3 (6.0)	11 (22.0)	10 (20.0)	18 (36.0)	6 (16.0)	50 (100.0)
1980-81	13 (26.0)	26 (52.0)	11 (22.0)	—	—	50 (100.0)	—	7 (14.0)	8 (16.0)	13 (26.0)	22 (44.0)	50 (100.0)
1985-86	—	31 (62.0)	11 (22.0)	8 (16.0)	—	50 (100.0)	—	5 (10.0)	10 (20.0)	27 (54.0)	6 (16.0)	50 (100.0)
1989-90	3 (6.0)	4 (8.0)	16 (32.0)	23 (46.0)	4 (8.0)	50 (100.0)	—	1 (2.0)	8 (16.0)	15 (30.0)	26 (52.0)	50 (100.0)

Source: Field Survey Data.

Figures in brackets are percentages to their respective totals.

By 1985-86 the number of looms producing Shirting cloth reached its peak, in western Cuddapah district. As many as 62 percentage of looms were producing Shirting in 1985-86. The percentage of looms, producing Janata Sarees and Dhoties remained the same during the period 1980-85 at 22 per cent Production of 'Resham'[3] cloth was introduced in western Cuddapah in 1983 for the first time. The percentage of looms producing Resham cloth was 16 in 1985-86.

In eastern Cuddapah district, during 1985-86 as many as 27 looms or 54 per cent were producing Sarees with Simple Zari Border and the looms producing (*a*) Sarees without zari, (*b*)Sarees with Simple Zari Border and (*c*) Sarees with Big Zari Border were about 10 per cent, 20 per cent and 16 per cent respectively. There was a big fall in the looms producing Big Zari Border Sarees from 44 in 1980-81 to 16 per cent in 1985-86. Significant increase in the number of looms producing Sarees with Medium Zari Border may be observed from Table 6.1. Number of looms- producing Sarees with Medium Zari Border increased from 26 per cent in 1980-81 to 54 per cent in 1985-86. The reduction in the looms producing Medium Zari Border Sarees was due to the fact that 'Pure Zari' was introduced in the industry in a big way, in the place of Half Fine and Art Powder Zari. Pure Zari is expensive compared to Art Powder and Half Fine Zari. To ascertain the acceptability of Pure Zari Sarees in the market low priced Pure Zari Sarees with Medium and Simple Borders were introduced in the beginning. Looms producing Sarees with Simple Border Zari and without Zari were 20 per cent and 10 per cent respectively.

The number of looms producing 'Resham' cloth showed a significant increase from 16 per cent in 1985-86, to 46 per cent in 1988-89 in western Cuddapah. Increase in the number of looms producing Janata Sarees and Dhoties also took place during this period in eastern Cuddapah—the percentage of which increased from 22 in 1985-86 to 32 in 1989-90. As many as 4 looms or 8 per cent of the total looms were producing Sarees exclusively with Simple Zari Border. Significant fall In the number of looms producing Shirting is observed during this period. The percentage of looms producing Shirting came down to 8 in 1989-90 from 62 in 1985-86.

In western Cuddapah, a significant increase in the number of looms producing Sarees with Big Zari Border may be observed during the period 1985-89. From 16 per cent in 1985-86, it rose to 52 per cent in 1989-90. As a result the quantum of production of other items shows a significant fall.

Item-wise details of changes in the production of different items indicates that the percentage of looms producing ordinary sarees came down to 6 per cent in 1989-90 from 100 per cent in 1970-71 in western Cuddapah. The trend in the looms producing 'Shirting' is not uniform. It has been subject to fluctuations. The percentage of looms producing Shirting cloth was just 26 in 1975-76 and it was 52 per cent, 62 per cent and 8 per cent respectively in 1980-81, 85-86 and 1989-90.

The progress of the looms producing Janata Sarees and Dhoties was slow but steady in western Cuddapah. Its percentage did not change during the period 1980-86, but by 1989-90 it reached 32 per cent figure from 16 in 1985-86. Sarees with Simple Zari Border (8%) were introduced only in 1989-90 in this region.

In eastern Cuddapah, Production of Dhoties was carried out in 1970 and 1976. But the relative Importance of Dhoties production came down from 28 per cent in 1970-71 to 6 per cent in 1975-76., as the production of Lungis was at an increasing trend.

The relative importance of looms producing Sarees without Zari and Sarees with Simple Zari Border had a significant decline in eastern Cuddapah. In the case of Sarees without Zari, the decline was from 24 per cent in 1970-71 to 2 per cent in 1989-90. It was from 28 per cent to 16 per cent for Sarees with Simple Border Zari.

Considerable increase in the number of looms producing Sarees with Medium and Big Zari Borders may be observed during the period 1970-75 in eastern Cuddapah. The percentage of looms producing Sarees with out Zari Border was 14 in 1970-71 and it increased to 30 by 1989-90. In the case of Sarees with Big Zari Border, the percentage of looms producing this variety was just 6 in 1970-71 and it increased to 52 in 1989-90.

We may conclude that the handloom Industry in Cuddapah made rapid strides in introducing new items of production of Superior varieties of cloth. In western Cuddapah the handloom industry was concentrating on the production of only Ordinary Sarees in 1970-71. By 1989-90 Resham(46%) Cloth production was given the highest preference after Janata Dhoties and Sarees (32%). In eastern Cuddapah district, while the concentration was on the production of ordinary varieties like Dhoties and Sarees in 1970-71, by 1989-90 the concentration shifted to the production of Big Zari Border Sarees.

Handloora products with Zari are of superior quality and costlier. Only skilled persons can weave with Zari. The industry in eastern Cuddapah district gradually changed from Producing Coarse varieties to Superior Zari cloth production between 1970 and 1990. It can, therefore, be concluded that a significant improvement in the qualitative improvement in the production of handloom cloth is felt in eastern

Cuddapah. But no significant improvement in the qualitative Production of cloth is felt in western Cuddapah.

Raw Materials Used by the Handloom Industry

From Table 6.2 (*See on next page*) it may be noted that yarn is the chief raw-material used in the handloom industry of Cuddapah district. In western Cuddapah, Resham was introduced in 1985-86 and as such the industry in this area uses both yarn and Resham to produce clothes. In the year 1970-71, yarn of 30×30, 40×40, 60×60 Counts were used to produce sarees. The percentage of looms using yarn of 40×40 Counts[4] was the highest with 58 per cent in western Cuddapah.

In 1970-71, yarn of 60×60, 60×80, 80×80, 80×100 and 100×100 Counts were used in eastern Cuddapah. The percentage of looms using yarn of 100×100 Counts was the highest at 46 per cent in 1970-71. Prior to 1970, most of the looms were producing coarse varieties by using 60×60 yarn of Counts.

Looms in western Cuddapah began to use yarn of 20×20 Counts in the year 1975-76, and it was discontinued there after. In eastern Cuddapah yarn of 60×60 and 60×80 counts were used only in 1970-71 and discontinued thereafter.

Table 6.2 clearly explains that the percentage of looms in western Cuddapah using 40×40 yarn significantly fell down from 58 in 1970-71 to 20 in 1975-76. It was due to switch over of looms from using 40×40 Counts to 60×60 counts. It is largely due to increase in demand for these products. Since then, a slow and steady progress in the use of 60×60 Counts can be seen. But in 1989-90, the percentage of looms using 40×40 Counts was 32. All the looms producing Janata Cloth are using yarn of 40×40 Counts.

In the case of looms using 60×40 and 60×60 yarn there is no steady trend In western zone of Cuddapah district. The percentage of looms using 60×60 Counts was 18 in 1970-71 and it increased to 48 in 1975-76. From there, it declined to 18 per cent in 1980-81, increased to 28 per cent in 1985-86 but came down to mere 8 per cent in 1989-90.

The percentage of looms using the yarn of 60×40 counts was 8 in 1975-76 and it jumped upto 60 by 1980-81., but then it came down to 34 per cent in 1985-86 and finally reached 6 per cent in 1989-90.

Significant progress has been made in the production of Resham cloth during the period 1985 and 1990 in western Cuddapah. The percentage of looms producing Resham cloth was 16 in 1985-86 and 46 in 1989-90. As many as 4 looms out of 50 looms were found using yarn of 100×100 counts in 1989-90 only in western Cuddapah.

Table 6.2 : Raw Material Used by the Handloom Industry

Years	Western Cuddapah								Eastern Cuddapah						
	20x20 Counts	30x30 Counts	40x40 Counts	40x60 Counts	60x60 Counts	100x100 Counts	Resham	Total Looms	60x60 Counts	60x80 Counts	80x80 Counts	80x100 Counts	100x100 Counts	100x120 Counts	Total Looms
1970-71	—	12 (24.0)	23 (26.0)	—	9 (18.0)	—	—	50 (100.0)	3 (6.0)	3 (6.0)	9 (18.0)	12 (24.0)	23 (26.0)	—	50 (100.0)
1975-76	12 (24.0)	— (20.0)	10	4 (8.0)	24 (48.0)	—	—	50 (100.0)	—	—	3 (6.0)	5 (10.0)	42 (84.0)	—	50 (100.0)
1980-81	—	—	11 (22.0)	30 (60.0)	9 (18.0)	—	—	50 (100.0)	—	—	8 (16.0)	3 (6.0)	39 (78.0)	—	50 (100.0)
1985-86	—	—	11 (22.0)	17 (34.0)	14 (28.0)	—	8 (16.0)	50 (100.0)	—	—	5 (10.0)	2 (4.0)	33 (66.0)	10 (20.0)	50 (100.0)
1989-90	—	—	16 (32.0)	3 (6.0)	4 (8.0)	4 (8.0)	33 (66.0)	50 (100.0)	—	—	2 (4.0)	3 (6.0)	7 (14.0)	38 (76.0)	50 (100.0)

Source: Field Survey Data.

Figures in brackets are percentages to their respective totals.

In eastern Cuddapah, the relative importance of Yarn of 80×80, 80×100, 100×100 came down significantly from 18 per cent to 4 per cent, 24 per cent to 6 per cent and 46 per cent to 14 per cent respectively during 1970-71 and 89-90. The decline in these varieties waa sufficiently compensated by the increase in use of 100×120 yarn of Counts. In 1985-86 yarn of 100×120 Counts was used to manufacture Superior Zari Sarees. To start with, only 20 per cent of looms were using yarn of 100×120 Counts and it increased to 76 per cent by 1989-90.

From the foregone we conclude that the handloom industry in western Cuddapah has evolved from the use of lower Counts of yarn to Resham that produces Resham Shirting. In western Cuddapah, a steady progress towards the use of higher Counts of yarn and Zari can be observed.

Handlooms using Different Kinds of Zari

Zari is one of the important raw material used in the handloom industry. This is brought from Surat of Gujarat State. There are 3 varieties of zari. They are: (1) Art powder Zari; (2) Half Fine Zari; and (3) Pure Zari. Zari is used for the borders in Sarees. It brings about artistic appearance and look in the texture.

Art-powder Zari is the cheapest form of Zari used in the handlooms industry. The cost of each bundle of zari weighing about 245 grams, ranged from ₹ 50 to ₹ 75 in 1990. The next best quality of Zari is Half-Fine Zari. Copper is used to produced this type of Zari. The price of each bundle was between ₹ 550 and ₹ 650 in 1990 (each bundle weighing about 245 grains).

The super fine Zari used in the handloom cloth is called 'Pure Zari'. This ls a highly expensive form of Zari. The share of this item in the total cost of production is large and as such the handloom products with Pure Zari are highly expensive. Its share in the total cost of production ranges between 10 per cent to 80 per cent. Pure Silver and gold are used in the making of Pure Zari. The cost of each bundle, weighing about 245 grams, ranged between ₹ 1250 to ₹ 1500 in 1990. The ratios of the prices of zari products are about 1:9:20.

How to Know the Quality of Zari

All the three types of Zari products described above look alike. It is not easy to distinguish one produce from another, by looking at the product, unless one is experienced and possesses the requisite skill in this field. So consumers of handloom products using Zari are likely to be cheated.

However simple tests can help us to identify the type of Zari a fabric has. Two or three threads of zari may be picked up from the cloth, normally embedded at the end of the piece, as such the texture of the Saree will not be disturbed. Ue have to tie up these threads to match stick and burn them completely. After a while, we have to examine the final remains of Zari. If we do not find any metal, except the ash, we can decide that it as 'Art Powder Zari' or Zari of inferior quality.

On the other hand if we find a metal after the Zari has been thus burnt, it may be either Half-Fine Zari or 'Pure Zari'. We have to rub the metal thus acquired, on a clean slate or on the floor. Then we have to examine the colour of the metal. If the colour is like silver it is Pure Zari. If it resembles Copper colour the Zari is Half-Fine Zari.

Different Kinds of Zari Used in Cuddapah District

Different types of Zari were used in different periods in the district. Changes in the tastes of the consumers, bring about changes in the varieties of Zari used in the industry. For instance, at the beginning of 1970-71, Half-Fine Zari was used to a large extent in eastern Cuddapah. As much as 40 per cent of looms in the district were using Half-Fine Zari in 1970-71. 56 per cent of looms, were not using any Zari at all. Looms using Art-Powder Zari and Pure Zari constituted 2 per cent each in 1970-71 in this region.

The proportion of looms not using Zari in eastern Cuddapah district came down from 56 per cent in 1970-71 to 2 per cent in 1990-91. The use of Art Powder Zari in this region, has significantly increased from 2 per cent in 1970-71 to 30 per cent in 1985-86; since then it came down to 10 per cent in 1990-91.

Half-Fine Zari ruled the industry during 1977-80. After this period it declined. In the year 1970-71 about 40 per cent of handlooms were using Half-Fine Zari. The proportion of looms using Half-Fine Zari In 1975-76 and 1980-81 were 60 per cent and 66 per cent respectively.

After 1980-81, the increase in number of looms using Art-powder Zari, reduced the relative importance of looms using Half-Fine Zari. The proportion of looms using Half-Fine Zari reached 48 in 1985-86 and then decreased to 6 per cent in 1990-91.

A steady growth in the number of looms using Pure Zari Sarees can be observed from Table 6.3. Only 2 per cent of the looms were using Pure Zari in the year 1970-71. In 80-81, 85-86, 90-91 the proportion of looms using Pure Zari stood at 10 per cent, 10 per cent, 12 per cent and 82 per cent respectively. A sudden jump in the proportion of looms using

Pure Zari can be observed between 1985-90. Pure Zari is thus largely used in the handloom industry of eastern Cuddapah district at present.

Thus for a period of 20 years the handloom industry used Half-Fine., Art-powder Zaries and finally started using Pure Zari in making Sarees. The introduction of Pure Zari in the making of cloth thus replaced Half-Fine and Art Powder Zari Sarees.

In western Cuddapah, looms were not using any kind' of Zari upto 1988. It was only in 1989-90 that 4 out of 50 looms surveyed are reported to have started using Pure Zari in the making of Zari Sarees.

Table 6.3 : Handlooms using Different Kinds of Zari

Years	Looms Not using zari	Looms Using Art Powder zari	Looms Using Half fine zari	Looms Using Pure zari	Total Looms
1970-71	28 (56.0)	1 (2.0)	20 (40.0)	1 (2.0)	50 (100.0)
1975-76	12 (24.0)	3 (6.0)	30 (60.0)	5 (10.0)	50 (100.0)
1980-81	7 (14.0)	5 (10.0)	33 (66.0)	5 (10.0)	50 (100.0)
1985-86	5 (10.0)	15 (30.0)	24 (48.0)	6 (12.0)	50 (100.0)
1989-90	1 (2.0)	5 (10.0)	3 (6.0)	41 (82.0)	50 (100.0)

Source : Field Survey Data.
Figures in brackets are percentages to their respective totals.

Production of Handloom Cloth

Since we have analysed the type of cloth produced and the types of raw material used in the handloom industry, we may now study the quantity of cloth produced in eastern and western Cuddapah and the changes in real value of production over a period of 20 years since 1970-71.

Productivity Trends

Every weaver on an average was able to produce 1365 metres of cloth in the year 1970-71 in western Cuddapah. It was only 829 metres in eastern Cuddapah. This shows that the productivity of handloom weaver in western Cuddapah was more than his counter part in eastern Cuddapah. In western Cuddapah the productivity of loom per year gradually increased upto 1985, and then it came down slightly. In eastern Cuddapah, the trend in productivity is not uniform. It was 829 metres per weaver per year in 1970-71, and it came down to 794 meters in 1975-76, again it increased upto 810 metres in 1980-81, then decreased to 735 metres in 1985-86 and again increased upto 748 metres in 1989-90. Between 1970-71 and 1990-91 the increase in the real productivity has been to the extent of 10.65 per cent in western Cuddapah. The fluctuations in the productivity of cloth was due to frequent switch over of weavers from production of one type of cloth to another.

However, in eastern Cuddapah productivity, measured in terms of quantity, declined by roughly 10 per cent between 1970 and 1990. The average productivity per weaver increased at the annual growth rate of 0.5 per cent in western Cuddapah and it declined at the same rate in eastern Cuddapah. The apparent decline in productivity in eastern Cuddapah has been due to switch over of the weaver to the production of Superior varieties with Zari. This naturally decreases the quantity of production.

The average value of production shows significant improvements in both eastern and western Cuddapah. The average value of production increased in western and eastern Cuddapah at the rate of 19 per cent and 46 per cent respectively.

In order to know whether the increase in the value of production has been due to inflation and the average values of production are deflated to 1970-71 prices.

The value of the cloth is fixed by taking into account the contribution of different factors of production. The value of the raw material and the profit to the producer concerned, together decide the value of the cloth. The method of fixing the value of cloth is explained in detail in the Chapter-5.

In terms of 70-71 prices, the average money value of production in western Cuddapah declined upto 1985-86, and then it made a significant progress. In western Cuddapah the average value of production in 1970-71 prices declined only upto 1975-76. From this period onwards, the average money value in terms of 1970-71 prices increased by leaps and bounds. The average money value of production in western and eastern Cuddapah increased at an annual rate of 1 per cent and 8 per cent respectively during 1970-90.

The difference in the annual growth rates of average production in western and eastern Cuddapah signifies that the eastern Cuddapah had made considerable progress in introducing Super-fine and costly products. But in western Cuddapah It could not make auch progress largely due to weak entrepreneurs.

Table 6.4 : Production of Handloom Cloth in Cuddapah District

Years	Quantity (Mtrs)	Average Quantity (Mtrs)	Value of production (in Rs.)	Average value of production (in Rs.)	Index of Average Value of production	Average production in 70-71 prices (in Rs.)	Index of iten No.7	Quatity (in Mtrs)	Average Quantity (Mtrs)	Value of production (in Rs.)	Average Value of production (in Rs.)	Index of Average Value of production	Average production in 70-71 Prices	Index of item No. 14
1970-71	68253	1365.06	743958	14879.16	100.00	14879.16	100.00	41472	829.44	429228	8584.56	100.0	8584.56	100.0
1975-76	69450	1389.00	762403	15248.06	102.48	8813.91	59.24	39718	794.36	542144	10842.88	126.31	6267.56	126.31
1980-81	79408	1588.16	774248	15484.96	104.07	6044.09	40.62	40542	810.84	1223662	24473.24	285.08	9552.40	285.08
1985-86	80400	1608.00	1342680	26853.60	180.48	7505.00	50.44	36758	735.16	1729637	34592.74	402.96	9668.18	402.96
1989-90	75523	1510.46	3580954	71619.08	481.34	18116.74	121.76	37379	747.58	4355600	87112.00	1014.75	22035.82	1014.75

Source : Field Survey Data.

Figures in brackets are percentages to their respective totals.

From a look at the Tables 6.5A and B (*See on pages 279 and 280*) we can understand that real productivity, in terms of quantity of cloth produced per year, was increasing in western Cuddapah, while it showed a declining trend in eastern Cuddapah. It is largely due to the fact that weavers in western Cuddapah were continuously engaged in producing coarse varieties and as such because of sheer practice the productivity of a weaver in terms of quantity increased. In eastern Cuddapah weavers have switched over from producing cheap varieties which were using Art-Powder and Half-Fine Zari to super fine Pure Zari sarees with artistic designs. Hence in terms of quantity of cloth the productivity of such weavers declined as weaving superior varieties takes relatively more time than weaving coarse varieties. But the value of superior varieties is higher than those of Coarse varieties.

Distribution of Income

From the foregoing, we can understand the significant changes that took place in the handloom industry over a period of 20 years. In order to ascertain whether the structural changes in the handloom industry contributed to improve the economic position of the handloom weaver, information is collected and presented in Tables 6.5A&B.

While the 28 per cent of weavers had been getting ₹ 1500 and below, in western Cuddapah, it was 90 per cent in eastern Cuddapah. Similarly 10 per cent of weavers had been getting ₹ 1501-2000, in eastern Cuddapah, while it was 64 per cent in western Cuddapah. While weavers getting income upto ₹ 2500 is 8 per cent in western Cuddapah in 1970-71, it was completely absent in eastern Cuddapah.

The percentage of weavers getting income (at constant prices) over and above ₹ 1500/- gradually increased over a period of time. As much as 58 per cent in 1975-76, 82 per cent in 1980-81, 92 per cent in 1985-86, 98 per cent in 1989-90 were getting income of ₹ 1500 or above in western Cuddapah district. In eastern Cuddapah the percentage of weavers getting over and above ₹ 1500/- in 1970-71, 75-76, 80-81, 85-86, 89-90 were 10 per cent, 21 per cent, 78 per cent, 80 per cent and 90 per cent respectively. As a result of it, the average income (in current prices) increased very significantly during 1970-71 and 1989-90 in western and eastern Cuddapah.

The average income per year per weaver was only ₹ 1671 in 70-71 in western Cuddapah, and it increased to ₹ 4326 by 1989-90. In other words the average income (in constant prices) in western Cuddapah increased at the annual growth rate of 8 per cent per year. In eastern Cuddapah, average Income of ₹ 1067 in 70-71 increased upto ₹ 5621 in 89-90. It means

Table 6.5A : Income Distribution of Weavers Western Cuddapah

Years	Income in Rupees							Total income earned by looms per year	Average income	Average income in 70-71 prices	S.D	C.V.	Index of item No. 10	Index of item No. 11
	1-500	501-1000	1001-1500	1501-2000	2001-2500	2501-3000	Above 3000							
1970-71	1 (2.0)	3 (6.0)	10 (20.0)	32 (64.0)	4 (8.0)	—	—	83550	1671.00	1671.00	1739.25	104.08	100.00	100.0
1975-76	2 (4.0)	5 (10.01)	2 (4.0)	12 (24.0)	26 (26.0)	2 (4.0)	1 (2.0)	99250	1985.00	965.90	2000.63	100.79	118.79	57.80
1980-81		3 (6.0)	2 (4.0)	4 (58.0)	27 (54.0)	12 (24.0)	2 (4.0)	113565	2271.30	886.53	2304.89	101.48	135.93	53.05
1985-86	—	—	2 (4.0)	2 (4.0)	29 (58.0)	14 (28.0)	3 (6.0)	164938	3298.76	921.96	2423.32	73.46	197.41	55.17
1989-90	—	—	1 (2.0)	—	25 (50.0)	18 (36.0)	6 (12.0)	216293	4325.86	1094.27	2559.79	59.17	258.88	65.49

Source : Field Survey Data.

Figures in brackets are percentages to their respective totals.

that the average income in eastern Cuddapah increased at the annual growth rate of 21 per cent per year.

In order to know whether the increase in value has brought any significant changes in the standard of living of the people, we have deflated the Income figures in terms of 70-71 prices, by using whole sale price index numbers. The average income of the weaver in 70-71 prices shows a significant decline in western Cuddapah, while it increased in eastern Cuddapah, after initial decline during the period 1975-81.

In western Cuddapah the average income per weaver (in 70-71 prices) declined from ₹ 1671 in 70-71, to ₹ 720 in 1975-76 and ₹ 669 in 1980-81. Since then, it started rising. The average income in 70-71 prices touched ₹ 1422 in 1989-90. It shows that the average income of the weaver in eastern Cuddapah Increased at an annual growth rate of 1.66 per cent in terms of 70-71 prices.

The foregoing account indicates that the changes in the handloom industry did not help to improve the income position of the handloom weaver in western Cuddapah. The situation is entirely different in eastern Cuddapah where the income earning capacity of the handloom weaver improved a lot both in money terms and in real terms.

The average income of the weaver alone can not give a clear picture about the economic conditions of the handloom weavers. In general terms it is an important index. So, with a view to finding out whether the income is evenly distributed among the sample units of the weavers, simple tools like Standard Deviation (S.D) and Co-efficient of Variation (C.V) were worked out. Accordingly values of S.D and C.V are presented in Table 6.5 (*See on next page*). Income inequalities seem to be increasing in both western and eastern Cuddapah with increase in the money income. The highest value of C.V(136.95) in 1980-81 for eastern Cuddapah and western Cuddapah and lowest value (44.26) for 89-90, show that the degree of inequality in the distribution of income was the highest in 80-81, and lowest in 1989-90 for both western and eastern parts of Cuddapah district.

Distribution of Looms According to Their Debts

Details pertaining to Debt position of the weavers have been collected and are presented in Tables 6.6A&B. From the table it is clear that the debt burden of the weaver was increasing. The average amount of debt in 1970-71 was ₹ 188.36 paise in western Cuddapah and ₹ 299.10 in eastern Cuddapah. The debt gradually increased to ₹ 1360.76 in western Cuddapah

Table 6.5B : Income Distribution of Weavers

Years	Income in Rupees							Total income earned by looms per year	Average income	Average income in 70-71 prices	S.D	C.V.	Index of item No. 10	Index of item No. 11
	1-500	501-1000	1001-1500	1501-2000	2001-2500	2501-3000	Above 3000							
1970-71	5 (10.0)	20 (40.0)	20 (40.0)	5 (10.0)	—	—	—	53362	1067.24	1067.24	1078.19	101.03	100.00	100.00
1975-76	5 (10.0)	10 (20.0)	23 (46.0)	12 (24.0)	—	—	—	62248	1244.96	719.63	1253.99	100.73	116.65	67.43
1980-81	—	3 (6.0)	11 (22.0)	7 (14.0)	7 (14.0)	11 (22.0)	11 (22.0)	85640	1712.80	668.54	2345.74	136.95	160.49	62.64
1985-86	—	3 (6.0)	7 (14.0)	10 (20.0)	11 (22.0)	7 (14.0)	12 (24.0)	197100	3942.00	1101.73	2360.61	59.88	369.36	103.23
1989-90	—	—	5 (10.0)	9 (18.0)	10 (20.0)	10 (20.0)	14 (28.0)	281063	5621.26	1421.95	2487.97	44.26	526.71	133.23

Source : Field Survey Data.

Figures in brackets are percentages to their respective totals.

Table 6.6A : Distribution of Weavers According to Debts

Years	Western Cuddapah										
	Amount of Debt in Rupees				Total	Average	Index of item No.7	Average Debt in 70-71 prices	Index of item No.9	S.D.	C.V.
	1-250	251-500	501-1000	Above 1000							
1970-71	32 (64.0)	16 (32.0)	2 (4.0)	—	9418	188.36	100.0	188.36	100.0	265.75	141.09
1975-76	3 (6.0)	12 (24.0)	31 (62.0)	4 (8.0)	31725	634.50	336.86	366.76	191.74	713.05	112.38
1980-81	3 (6.0)	7 (14.0)	38 (72.0)	2 (4.0)	34935	698.70	370.94	272.72	144.79	714.58	102.27
1985-86	3 (6.0)	8 (16.0)	32 (64.0)	7 (14.0)	59125	1182.50	627.79	330.49	175.46	776.01	65.63
1989-90	1 (2.0)	9 (18.0)	28 (56.0)	12 (24.0)	68038	1360.76	722.43	344.22	182.75	845.95	62.17

Source: Field Survey Data.

Figures in brackets are percentages to their respective totals.

Table 6.6B : Distribution of Weavers According to Debts

Years	Eastern Cuddapah										
	Amount of Debt in Rupees				Total	Average	Index of item No.7	Average Debt in 70-71 prices	Index of item No.9	S.D.	C.V.
	1-250	251-500 1000	501-1000	Above							
1970-71	25 (50.0)	19 (38.0)	6 (12.0)	—	14955	299.10	100.00	299.10	100.0	358.82	119.97
1975-76	7 (14.0)	16 (32.0)	21 (42.0)	6 (12.0)	29180	583.60	195.12	337.34	112.79	686.25	117.59
1980-81	5 (10.0)	9 (18.0)	31 (62.0)	5 (10.0)	36874	737.48	246.57	287.85	96.23	729.30	98.89
1985-86	3 (6.0)	5 (10.0)	20 (40.0)	22 (44.0)	61778	1235.56	413.09	345.32	115.45	963.07	77.95
1989-90	—	8 (16.0)	14 (28.0)	28 (56.0)	96250	1925.00	643.60	486.95	162.81	1027.13	53.36

Source: Field Survey Data.

Figures in brackets are percentages to their respective totals.

and ₹ 1925 in eastern Cuddapah by 1989-90. In all the 20 year period the debt burden of the handloom weaver was more in western Cuddapah than in eastern Cuddapah.

The average amount of debt (in current prices) increased at an annual rate of 31 per cent during the 20 year period in western Cuddapah district and at 27 per cent in eastern Cuddapah.

In terms of 70-71 prices, significant increase in the average amount of debt may be observed. The debt increased by 183 per cent during 1970-90 in western Cuddapah, and by 163 per cent in eastern Cuddapah. In other words the average amount of debt (70-71 prices) was growing at an annual growth rate of 4 per cent per year in western Cuddapah and at 3 per cent in eastern Cuddapah.

Distribution of Looms According to Organisation

Table 6.7 (*See on next page*) shows the distribution of handlooms in different organisations. In the year 1970-71 the number of looms under the control of Master Weaver was less in western Cuddapah than in eastern Cuddapah. As many as 24 per cent or 12 looms out of 50 looms in western Cuddapah and 60 per cent or 30 looms out of 50 in eastern Cuddapah were working for the Master Weaver in 1970-71. As many as 56 per cent of looms in western Cuddapah and 38 per cent in eastern Cuddapah had been under Co-operative organisation. The remaining 8 per cent of looms in western Cuddapah and 2 per cent of looms in eastern Cuddapah were reported to be working for more than one organisation in 1970-71. The number of looms working for the Master Weaver gradually increased from 24 per cent in 70-71 to 46 per cent in 89-90 in eastern Cuddapah. The relative importance of the Master Weaver, in terms of looms under his control, declined in western Cuddapah and the Co-operative Sector improved significantly. The percentage of weavers working for the Master Weaver was 60 in 70-71 and it came down to 24 by 89-90. The looms under Co-operative fold were 38 per cent in 1970-71, which increased to 44 per cent in 1989-90. The Corporate Sector also made a significant progress during this period. From 8 per cent in 75-76, the percentage of weavers under Corporate Sector increased to 32 in 89-90 in western Cuddapah.

Independent Sector gained momentum in 75-76 in western Cuddapah and made considerable progress there after. Its share was 18 per cent in 1989-90. But steady progress was not made with respect to the number of weavers under Independent Sector in eastern Cuddapah.

Table 6.7 : Distribution of Looms According to Organisation

Years	Eastern Cuddapah					Western Cuddapah					
	Loons working for/as				Total No. of looms surveyed	Looms working for/as					Total No. of looms surveyed
	Master Weaver	Indepen-dent	Co-ope-ratives	More than one orga-nisation		Master Weaver	Indepen-dent	Co-ope-ratives	Corpora-tion	More than one orga-nisation	
1970-71	12 (24.0)	—	28 (56.0)	4 (8.0)	50 (100.0)	30 (60.0)	—	19 (38.0)	—	1 (2.0)	50 (100.0)
1975-76	19 (38.0)	2 (4.0)	26 (52.0)	3 (6.0)	50 (100.0)	22 (44.0)	2 (4.0)	20 (40.0)	4 (8.0)	2 (4.0)	50 (100.0)
1980-81	19 (38.0)	6 (12.0)	17 (34.0)	8 (16.0)	50 (100.0)	28 (56.0)	1 (2.0)	9 (18.0)	12 (24.0)	—	50 (100.0)
1985-86	21 (42.0)	7 (14.0)	20 (40.0)	2 (4.0)	50 (100.0)	22 (44.0)	3 (6.0)	18 (36.0)	5 (10.0)	2 (4.0)	50 (100.0)
1989-90	23 (46.0)	9 (18.0)	15 (30.0)	3 (6.0)	50 (100.00)	12 (24.0)	— —	22 (44.0)	16 (32.0)	—	50 (100.0)

Source : Field Survey Data.

Figures in brackets are percentages to their respective totals.

Summary and Conclusions

Significant progress was made by the handloom industry in Cuddapah district in the production of superior varieties of cloth. Coarse varieties were largely produced in 70-71 both in western and eastern Cuddapah district. The production of the coarse varieties already in existence were substituted by the production of Resham cloth in western Cuddapah and Super Fine Zari Sarees in eastern Cuddapah. Thus there was a move towards production of Resham cloth in western Cuddapah and Zari Sarees in eastern Cuddapah.

The evolution of the handloom industry in western Cuddapah took the form of a movement from the production of cloth of lower Counts to Resham. In eastern Cuddapah steady progress is visible in the production of textiles with yarn of higher Counts and Pure Zari.

Three kinds of Zari products are in existence viz., Art Powder, Half-Fine, and Pure Zari. Most of the looms in western Cuddapah do not use Zari, where as all the looms in eastern Cuddapah use Zari. The advantage of using zari is steadily recognised by the industry in eastern Cuddapah.

Productivity in terms of the quantity of cloth produced in a year has been on the increase in western Cuddapah, while it has shown a declining trend in eastern Cuddapah. Increase in productivity in western Cuddapah has been largely due to the constant involvement of weavers largely in the production of Coarse varieties. In the production of superior varieties of Zari Sarees, with artistic designs, there would naturally be delay and hence reduction in absolute numbers in eastern Cuddapah.

The value of production (in current prices), in both western and eastern Cuddapah district increased by nearly 481 per cent and 1015 per cent respectively.

The average value of production per loom in western Cuddapah district declined upto 1985-86 in Constant prices., since then it progressed well. In eastern Cuddapah the average money value (in terms of 70-71 prices) increased from 75-76.

Higher growth rate in terms of the value of cloth produced in eastern Cuddapah was largely due to the introduction of Superior varieties of cloth by the dynamic entrepreneurs.

The significant changes that took place in introducing new products in the handloom industry helped to improve the money income of the handloom weaver in western and eastern zones of Cuddapah district.

The average real income of the weaver (in 90-91 prices) decreased at an annual rate of 1.73 in western Cuddapah during 1970-90. But in western part income increased at an annual rate of 1.66 per cent during 1970-90.

The debt burden on the handloom weaver has been increasing constantly. The extent of increase in the debt burden, on the handloom weaver has been more in western Cuddapah than in eastern Cuddapah during 1970-90.

The Master Weaver sector in eastern Cuddapah Co-operative and Corporate sectors in western Cuddapah made a steady progress in terms of the number of looms working under them.

The handloom weavers who produce superior varieties of cloth normally need have no fear about marketing the product and their earnings also are high.

Technology transfers between contiguous areas seem to be easier. As such, while the influence of Venkatagiri Zari Sarees of Nellore district is greater in eastern Cuddapah. The influence of the neighbouring Anantapur district where production of Resham cloth takes place, is greater in the western Cuddapah.

Without too much of prompting and prop from other sources adoption of new technology and production techniques took place much more smoothly and quickly in eastern Cuddapah than in western Cuddapah. As such any help from governmental agencies in the transfer of technology would accelerate the pace of progress, particularly in western Cuddapah.

Market research regarding the demand for different varieties of cloth and dissemination of such information would greatly help the weavers particularly of western Cuddapah.

REFERENCE

1. Editorial-Commerce, May 19, 1979, p. 847.
2. Silver Zari is an important raw material, which is used in the borders of superior varieties of Handloom Sarees.
3. Resham cloth is a type of shirting cloth made out of pure silk.
4. 40 × 40 Counts = Warp × Weft – Warp is length-wise yarn and Weft is width wise yarn. Higher counts are used to produce superior varieties and lower counts are used for coarse varieties.

7 Summary and Conclusions

Handloom industry is the oldest industry in India. Since time immemorial handloom industry has been an integral part of India's economy. This industry, by far the largest in the unorganised sector, ranks next only to agriculture in terms of income and employment, it generates. There are over 3 million handlooms in India employing more than 10 million persons. Of this, Andhra Pradesh State has nearly 18 per cent of the total handlooms in the country.

On such an ancient and important industry like this, there are very few studies that deal with its different aspects like the history of the industry, the structure of the industry, socio-economic relations of the workers, inter-regional, inter-state, and intra-state variations. So the present study is aimed at examining the socio-economic conditions of the handloom weavers in Cuddapah district of Andhra Pradesh and compare them with those of others. It also tries to find out the reasons for variations in the socio-economic status of weavers in different parts of Cuddapah district. Attempt is also made to identify the factors that can make the industry less dependent on Government help and acquire self reliance.

Andhra Pradesh state consists of three distinct regions viz Coastal Andhra, Telangana and Rayalaseema. Studies were undertaken on the living conditions of handloom weavers of coastal Andhra and Telangana. However for Rayalaseema region no such study has been undertaken. Particularly for Cuddapah district of Andhra Pradesh no integrated survey on the living conditions of handloom weavers has been undertaken ao far, though this district ranks first among the four districts of

Rayalaseema in Andhra Pradesh State in the concentration of handlooms. Though Rayalaseema region is a predominantly drought prone area it is well known for handloom industry.

Another important reason for the selection of the present problem is that in Cuddapah district there are two distinct regions, namely eastern and western regions. In one region i.e., western region the industry has not prospered well while in the other region i.e. eastern Cuddapah the industry has prospered well. So, it is necessary to ascertain the reasons that influenced the progress of the industry in one region, and impeded the progress in other region. The present study tries to examine the reasons for these variations with in the district.

While the main purpose of the study is an examination of the socio-economic conditions of the handloom weavers in Cuddapah district, the following are the specific objectives of the study:

1. To examine the evolution of the handloom industry in Cuddapah district.
2. To identify the general characteristics of the handloom industry.
3. To examine whether there has been an improvement in the socio-economic status of weavers.
4. To observe the changes that took place in the income employment and indebtedness of the persons employed in the industry during the last 20 years (i.e. 1970-90).
5. To ascertain whether handloom industry in Cuddapah district has undergone any structural changes during the last 20 years including improvement in the skills of the workers.
6. To examine the problems and prospects of handloom industry in general and particularly in relation to Cuddapah district.

The present study is based both on Primary and Secondary data. Secondary data have been collected mainly from the records available with the offices of the Asst. Director of Handlooms and Textiles, Cuddapah; Director of Handlooms and Textiles, Hyderabad and the Commissioner for Handlooms and Textiles, Ministry of Industries, New Delhi. Different types of statistical tools such as Regression 2 (both simple and multiple) techniques, Correlation, X^2(Chi-aquare) tests have been used where and when required.

The field survey has been restricted to eight important handloom centres of the district on account of the practical considerations, such as-time and resources constrains, the unorganised nature of the Industry, its wide dispersion in location giving rise to difficulties of coverage.

Cuddapah district has been selected for detailed study, out of the 23 districts of Andhra Pradesh state, as a first stage sampling. With in Cuddapah district, again there are, two distinct parta namely eastern and western parts or regions. Four handloom centres from each part viz., eastern and western at the rate of 2 urban and 2 rural centres each have been selected. Thus, 8 handloom centres (4 urban and 4 rural) in all have been selected for the purpose of data collection. Multi-stage, purposive sampling technique has thus been used in the selection of sample units for the collection of data.

The period of the present study is 1970-90. Primary data have been collected through canvassing the schedule during the year 1989-90.

Handloom industry in Cuddapah district is a household industry and consists mostly of small household units having one or two looms each. Inheritance is the general method of acquisition of handlooms. The pattern of ownership of looms is generally characterised by individual ownership. Thus weaver is the owner of fixed capital. But he can not get the full quantum of benefit accruing to the units of production, thanks to the unfortunate operating conditions prevailing in the industry.

Mere ownership of tools does not make a weaver an independent entrepreneur. His position is that of a wage-earning artisan. Similarly, the household units are working at their own premises. This, however does not indicate their sound economic conditions.

The work place is attached to the residence of the handloom weavers for reasons of convenience. But the nature of manufacturing needs a separate work place. However, the weaver does not have the required resources for the purpose. Even if the resources are made available, the weaver is reluctant to shift the work place away from the residence because it would severely restrict the participation of household labour, 'especially the labour of Women and children in production activities of the units concerned.

Handloom industry in Cuddapah district survives on a hereditary basis and on the caste-occupation nexus. Caste affiliation to the industry is prevalent. 'Padmasale', 'Devanga' and 'Thogata' Communities are the important weaving communities in Cuddapah district. Traditionally non-weaving communities, like Muslims and Scheduled Castes are also engaged in this industry to some extent. While handloom industry in the eastern zone of Cuddapah district offers prospects for fresh entry, the industry in western zone does not offer any such prospects.

Weavers have stuck to weaving activity not as a matter of choice but out of compulsion. They continue to be In this industry because they can not be else where. The economic inability of the weavers to educate their children and the availability of opportunities for child labour, indicate that the hereditary factor in the industry would continue to operate in the near future. However, serious efforts are being made to encourage the weavers' children to take up other fields of activities like education, business, employment etc., so that they can improve their living conditions.

Age is an important factor that influences the productivity. The weaver can neither produce the same quantity nor quality of cloth all through his life. After a certain age, the weaver can not even operate the loom. In the survey it was noticed that a weaver can remain active in the industry for not more than 60 years in his life. Weaving, of Coarse varieties, seems to make the weaver to retire early.

The much debated inefficiency of the handloom industry is closely linked to the prevailing production processes in the manufacturing activity and the equipment used by the weavers. Winding of yarn, warping, sizing and weaving are the important processes involved in this industry and family labour or hired workers, and at times both are used depending on convention and availability. Even children take part in different processes involved in cloth making.

Drudgery is the basic characteristic of all the processes of production. The slow production process adds to monotony. There is scope for reducing the drudgery element in the processes of production and thereby improving efficiency. Of all the processes of production involved in hand-weaving, weaving part is the most important, from the point of view of value-added. But the fact is that almost equal amount of labour is involved in both pre-weaving and weaving processes as pre-weaving and weaving processes involve almost the same time. The available household work force will be able to devote more time in actual weaving, if the responsibility of pre-loom activity is removed from them. This will also increase their earnings, as the value added of weaving activity is more.

The foregoing account emphasises tho need for mechanisation of pre-weaving operations in centralised workshops. A large proportion of children is now retained now at home to assist in the pro-weaving operations depriving them the opportunity of educating themselves. This is one of the reasons for high rate of dropouts among the school children. Mechanisation and centralisation of pre-weaving operations therefore will go a long way to help the weavers concentrate on weaving and reduce the rate of dropouts from the school. It also helps the households to have greater female participation in weaving.

The looms in Cuddapah District are 'Fly-shuttle pit looms'. 'Throw Shuttle pit looms' were being replaced from 1950. Throw shuttle looms were in uae upto 1965 in western Cuddapah and upto 1970 in eastern Cuddapah. It was found that on an average, 5 households had 7 looms in western Cuddapah and 6 looms in eastern Cuddapah. Idle looms were also in existence. The percentage of idle looms in different regions of Cuddapah district ranges from 13 to 21. Looms are left idle when (*a*) educated weavers leave the industry; (*b*) old weavers retire; (*c*) The head of the family dies.

The important raw materials used by the handlooms of Cuddapah as in other places are: Cotton Yarn, Silk and Zari. Of all the raw materials required, Cotton yarn is the most important. Yarn of lower Counts is used in western Cuddapah, while yarn of higher Counts only is used in the eastern Cuddapah. Pure Zari Sarees, Janata Sarees, Janata Dhoties, Resham Cloth, Shirting and Lungis are the important varieties of cloth produced in Cuddapah district. The looms in eastern Cuddapah district produce only pure Zari Sarees, and hence the industry in this zone is relatively Capital intensive.

Weavers of Cuddapah district may be classified under four broad categories. They are: (1) Weavers working for the Master Weavers; (2) Weavers working for the Co-operative Sector; (3) Independent weavers, not working for any one; (4) Weavers working for the Corporate Sector. The Co-operative organisation in the western zone and the Master Weaver in eastern zone are dominating the scene. Weavers were also found working for different organisations at a time.

Weavers normally do not work on important days of festivals. Further they do not work when ever they have to attend to some other work. Most of the weavers in western Cuddapah do not scrupulously observe public holidays, but unlike this, in the eastern Cuddapah weavers do observe certain days as public holidays. The most Important among them is 'Amavasya day' (New Moon day).

As can be expected, the number of men engaged in weaving is larger than the number of women. The involvement of middle aged persons in the handloom industry is very significant. The participation rate of males in the weaving activity is more (81.17%) than that of* females(18.53%). However the women participation in western zone is significantly more than in eastern zone of Cuddapah district.

The number of adult persons in a family influences the number of handlooms maintained in the house and about two adults on an average bring in one additional loom into operation.

The average age of marriage for females is 17.5 years and for males 22.3 years among weavers in Cuddapah district.

Adult illiteracy is more in eastern Cuddapah than in western Cuddapah. In the case of children, contrary to the above position, illiteracy is more in western zone than in eastern zone of Cuddapah district. In all the areas, irrespective of age, women illiteracy is significantly more than illiteracy among men. Fifty per cent of the heads of households were illiterate.

Weavers in this district have a tradition of marrying their own relatives. They marry others (outsiders) only when they have no suitable grooms/brides among their relatives. Weavers are interested to form nuclear families after their marriage. The attitude of the married couple in eastern Cuddapah appears to be more in favour of forming a nuclear family, but it was relatively less in western zone of Cuddapah district.

Weavers, working under Master weaver and those working as Independent weavers are advised by the members of their respective families not to leave the weaving industry. Unlike this, the weavers working under the Co-operative sector are influenced by the local merchants.

Next to food and clothing, housing occupies the most important place in deciding the standard of living of the people. Almost all the respondents in western Cuddapah live in 'thatched houses', where as in eastern Cuddapah majority of the weavers live in semi-permanent houses. Majority (92%) of the weavers in western zone have been living in their own houses., but in western Cuddapah only 65 per cent have been living in their own houses. The percentage of weavers having own houses is relatively more in the rural 2 areas (82%) than in urban areas (53%), The value of X^2 supports the hypothesis that variation in the housing conditions is significant in western and eastern regions of Cuddapah district.

A notable characteristic of the Industrial labour in India has been its migratory nature, Indicating majority of the industrial workers are immiftrants from the nearby and adjoining rural areas. 21 per cent of the weaving households in our sample have migrated from one area to another. It is relatively more in western zone than in eastern zone of Cuddapah district. Weavers have migrated from rural to urban areas.

Health is wealth to workers particularly to those who get succour just by their physical labour alone. But handloom weavers are caught in a vicious circle of nutritional deficiency, ill-health, low productivity, low earnings etc. 'Short-sightedness', 'Asthma', 'Tuberculosis', 'Paralysis' and 'High Blood Pressure' are some of the diseases/conditions to which handloom weavers are prone.

The average income per household is the lowest in urban areas of western Cuddapah while it is the highest in urban areas of eastern Cuddapah. The monthly earnings of different categories of weavers studied, range from ` 53.30 to ` 500. The average income of Cuddapah district as a whole, has been largely influenced by the higher Income groups in eastern Cuddapah where the average income is relatively high compared to that of weavers in western zone of Cuddapah district. Per capita income is also the highest in eastern Cuddapah than in western Cuddapah. Per capita income is ` 1334 in western Cuddapah, ` 2282 in eastern Cuddapah and ` 1718 for the district as a whole, as against ` 3934 for Andhra Pradesh state as whole in 1989-90.

Besides weaving, which is the primary occupation some have taken up to agriculture, business and other remunerative works. Out of the total income of 265 weaving households, 91 per cent is purely from weaving and the rest of 9 per cent is from other subsidiary occupations. The percentage of weavers that depend on other occupations besides weaving is relatively more in western region than in eastern region of Cuddapah district.

The income earning position is better for the Independent weaver in western Cuddapah, and for the Master Weaver in eastern Cuddapah. Ueavers producing, pure zari saree have beeen earning the highest income where as the the weavers of 'lungis' have been getting the lowest income in the district. As such the income earning capacity of the weaver in eastern region is better than in western region of Cuddapah district. The percentage of weavers living below the poverty line is more in western zone (34%) than in eastern zone of Cuddapah district(13%). It is found that the type of raw material used is one of the important factors that decides the income of the household. Weavers using only cotton yarn as the raw material get less income and weavers using 'zari' along with yarn earn the highest income.

Expenditure on food forms a major part of expenditure. The proportion of expenditure is more where average household income is less and vice versa. Engel's Law of consumption which states that the proportion of expenditure on food decreases with the increase in income finds another piece of evidence. Per capita expenditure is less, in rural centres of eastern Cuddapah and urban centres of western Cuddapah, than the general average.

The number of weavers saving and the amount saved both are significantly more in eastern zone than in western zone of Cuddapah district. Independent weavers have the highest savings in the sample followed by weavers working for the Plaster Weavers, and Co-operative sector. A major portion of the money saved is invested in private Chits.

Very small amount of savings is kept with Commercial Banks and Post offices.

The 'Sowcar-weaver' is the major source of loans and advances. Institutional finance is not available to the weaving industry. The Banking institutions have to go a long way to emerge as important sources of credit to the weaver. The lower amount of debt per unit of household should not at any rate be considered as a reflection of the sound economic condition of the units. On the contrary, this is an indicator of the lack of credit worthiness of the unit concerned. The percentage of households that borrowed loan is relatively less (58%) in western region of Cuddapah while it is more (86%) in eastern region of Cuddapah district. The average amount of loan borrowed is the highest in eastern Cuddapah. It is due to credit worthiness of the weaver in eastern Cuddapah.

The value of property ranges from ` 1500 to ` 85000 per household and properties consist of mainly houses and looms. Very few of them own landed property. The variation in the value of properties owned is significantly more in western Cuddapah than in eastern Cuddapah. The degree of variation in the value of properties possessed is the highest in rural areas of western Cuddapah and urban areas of eastern Cuddapah while it is the lowest in urban areas of western and rural areas of eastern Cuddapah. Weavers who do not own any property at all comprise mostly of weavers that work under Master Weavers, Co-operatives and weavers working for different organisations. Properties worth ` 20000 and above on an average are owned by Independent Weavers. The average value of property owned is relatively less in-western region as compared to eastern region of Cuddapah district.

In the case of households having smaller number of handlooms, utilisation capacity is substantially low as compared with the households that have more looms. Capacity utilisation of handloom is more in eastern Cuddapah at 84.63 per cent, as compared to western Cuddapah with 69.20 per cent. The percentage of capacity utilisation is low where coarse varieties are made and it is the highest where superior varieties of handloom products are made. Reasons for the existence of idle capacity are many, such as—dlfficulties in the procurement of raw material, lack of demand, lack of capital resources, problems of labour. Other reasons, resulting in idle capacity, include enforced idleness due to illness, visits of guests, religious and social ceremonies and weather conditions.

It may be observed that the existence of a considerable degrees of idle capacity in the establishments with less number of looms which form the bulk of the industry, is an important reason weakening the competitive position of these establishments vis-a-vis their larger counterparts.

The scope for shifting the weaver from the production of coarse varieties to superior variety is almost absent in western Cuddapah. In eastern Cuddapah there was constant encouragement from the organisations concerned to switch over to superior varieties of cloth production.

Though weavers are aware of the fact that it is desirable, necessary and profitable to introduce new technology and shift the-line of production from coarse varieties to superior varieties, they are afraid of taking the risks involved in the process and are unwilling to put in the necessary extra work. As a result stagnation and poverty continue to exist.

However Weavers producing coarse varieties like Janata Sarees, Janata Dhoties, Lungis etc., have to work for more hours, where as those that make superior varieties viz., Pure zari sarees, Resham, etc., work for less number of hours.

Poor quality of raw materials supplied to the handloom weavers is an important problem faced equally by the weavers in all parts of Cuddapah district.

Handloom industry in eastern Cuddapah is capital intensive unlike its counterpart in western Cuddapah. Further lack of dynamic entreprenuership, lack of skills and techniques, lack of capital, lack of motivation are responsible for the poverty of weavers in western Cuddapah. Hence there is every need to popularise the weaving techniques practised in eastern zone in western zone of Cuddapah district also. Training camps for weavers must be organised at the backward weaving centres to update their productive techniques. The technology that is being developed by the Handloom Research Institutes should immediately be passed on to the handloom centres. Government should stand by the aide of the weavers until they realise the usefulness of such techniques and practise them.

Charges involved in the preparation of cloth normally do not exceed 10 per cent of the total cost of production. The greater, the fineness of yarn used i.e., the higher the number of counts of yarn used and better the designs introduced, higher is the total cost including labour costs and raw material costs. If the weavers are helped to switch over from the use of cheaper raw material to that of superior raw material and produce fine varieties, the remuneration to the weavers also increases as the demand for such products is better.

The present system of marketing of handloom products is a very costly one and this impinges upon the residual income of the weaver. Neither the weaver nor the organiser, who is responsible for manufacturing the handloom cloth, is paid adequately. The trader, however is making undeservedly large profit.

Higher the price of the product, higher would be the profit to the trader. For every piece the cost of production of which is ` 100, price spread between the cost of production and the amount paid by consumer works out to ` 18.76.

Weavers that use zari along with the cotton yarn earn more income than the other categories of weavers. Introducing production of zari cloth varieties in those places where only cotton is used would help the weavers to increase their income.

Significant progress has been made by the handloom industry in Cuddapah district in the production of superior varieties of cloth. Coarse varieties were largely produced in 70-71 both in western and eastern Cuddapah district. But in course of time the production of coarse varieties yielded place to the production of Resham in western Cuddapah and zari varieties in eastern Cuddapah.

Three kinds of Zari products are in existence viz., Art Powder, Half-Fine, and Pure Zari. Host of the looms in western Cuddapah do not use Zari, where as all the looms in eastern Cuddapah use Zari. The advantage of using zari is steadily recognised by the industry in eastern Cuddapah.

The evolution of the handloom industry in western Cuddapah took the form of a movement from the production of cloth of lower Counts to Resham. In eastern Cuddapah steady progress is visible in the production of textiles with yarn of higher Counts and Pure Zari.

The quantity of cloth produced in a year has been on the increase in western Cuddapah, while it has shown a declining trend in eastern Cuddapah. Increase in the production in western Cuddapah has been largely due to the constant involvement of weavers in the production of Coarse varieties. In the production of superior varieties of Zari Sarees, with artistic designs, there would naturally be delay and hence reduction in the absolute number of pieces produced. The same thing happened in eastern Cuddapah.

The value of production (in current prices), in both western and eastern Cuddapah district Increased by nearly 481 per cent and 1015 per cent respectively between 1970-90. The average value of production per loom in western Cuddapah district declined upto 1985-86 (in Constant prices)., since then it progressed well. In eastern Cuddapah the average money value (in terms of 70-71 prices) increased from 75-76.

Higher growth rate in terms of the value of cloth produced in eastern Cuddapah was largely due to the introduction of Superior varieties of cloth by the dynamic entrepreneurs.

The significant changes that took place through the introduction of new products in the handloom industry helped to improve the money income of the handloom weaver in western and eastern zones of Cuddapah district. But the increase in the income of the weaver in eastern Cuddapah is more than that his counterpart in western Cuddapah.

The debt burden on the handloom weaver has been increasing during 1970-90. The extent of Increase in the debt burden, on the handloom weaver has been more in western Cuddapah than in eastern Cuddapah during 1970-90.

The Master Weaver sector in eastern Cuddapah, Co-operative and Corporate sectors in western Cuddapah made a steady progress in terms of the number of looms working under them. The number of looms working for the Master weaver gradually increased from 24 per cent in 70-71 to 46 per cent in 89-90 in eastern Cuddapah. The looms under Co-operative fold were 38 per cent in 1970-71, which increased to 44 per cent in 1989-90 in western Cuddapah.

The handloom weavers who produce superior varieties of cloth, normally need have no fear about marketing the product and their earnings also are high. Technology transfers between contiguous areas seem to be easier. As such, while the influence of Venkatagiri zari sarees of Nellore district is greater in eastern Cuddapah, the influcence of the neighbouring Anantapur district where production of Resham cloth takes place, is greater in western Cuddapah. Without too much of prompting and prop from other sources adoption of new technology and production techniques took place much more smoothly and quickly in eastern Cuddapah than in western Cuddapah. As such any help from Governmental agencies in the transfer of technology would accelerate the pace of progress, particularly in western Cuddapah.

Market research regarding the demand for different varieties of cloth and dissemination of such information would greatly help the weavers particularly of western Cuddapah.

Handlooms depend upon Hills for their yarn supplies. The Mills supply yarn to the handlooms and then compete with them in the marketing of cloth. Thus the relationship between Hill and handloom sectors is one of structural inequality and is reflected in the dependence and subordination of the latter to the former.

The market for handloom fabric has been shrinking. Shift in the consumer demand in favour of non-cotton and blended fabrics and the continued poaching of mills and powerlooms into the spheres of production reserved for handlooms have greatly affected the market for handloom fabrics.

The staggering growth in the number of power-looms partly because of the differences in the manufacturing costs between mills and powerlooms and partly because of the policy of the Government in treating powerlooms on par with handlooms has resulted in large scale diversion of hank yarn to the powerloom sector.

The shrinkage of market for handloom fabrics, together with yarn shortages, increased the dependence of the weavers on the roaster weavers. In these circumstances, the climatic susceptibility of different processes connected with hand weaving and the necessity of procuring yarn to start the preparatory processes, even before the weaving of one set of fabrics is completed and sold in the market, contributed further to the problems of the weaver.

The policy pursued throughout the colonial period retarded the progress of the handloom sector. At the dawn of independence, as reported by many official committees, a large proportion of handloom weavers were found to be in a state of abject poverty and perpetual dependence on master weavers and middlemen.

After independence, though the problems faced by the handloom sector have been analysed in their right perspective, the policy failed both to protect and promote the interests of handloom weavers. It is disheartening to note hat the successive Five-year Plans listed the same problems of the handloom sector like irregular supply of yarn, inadequate working capital, outdated technology etc., which show that the Governmental measures did not have any impact.

Initially, the policy emphasised protection. Later, the emphasis shifted to promotional measures. But, no significant breakthrough has been achieved in the handloom technology. Sincere attempts were not made to change the production pattern of handlooms in tune with changes in demand pattern. Consequently, handloom weavers are obliged to produce fabrics for which the demand is fast declining, with obsolete forms of technology.

The very low output per unit of time and the high labour intensity of production at each and every stage are the two peculiar features of handloom technology. The former results in an increase in the unit cost of production. To reduce the unit costs of production, the weavers try to economise on paid labour cost by making intensive use of family labour, including children of tender age, since the production process is highly labour intensive.

Given the technology and production pattern, the handloom industry is not in a position to provide adequate productive employment in terms of minimum acceptable level of income. Efforts must be made to improve the technique of production so as to have substantial increases in productivity. In view of the significant association between levels of poverty and production pattern, changes must be brought in the latter, on a priority basis, in favour of modern varieties and fabrics of higher counts. This alone will provide gainful employment to the weavers.

The most serious problem of the handloom industry in Cuddapah district is the defective marketing organisation. It is this problem which handicaps greatly technological progress and competitive strength of the industry. The Fact Finding Committee constituted by the Government of India, aptly pointed out that if the handloom industry requires any help and guidance in any direction, it requires most in solving its marketing problems. Our observations relating to the industry in Cuddapah district are similar and confirm the view that the development of efficient distributive system is the effective remedy to many evils of the handloom industry.

The functions that are involved in the process of distribution are purchasing of raw material, selling the product, planning, contacting consumers, demand creation, negotiations, making contracts, storage, grading, packing and preservation of goods for sale, financing, elaborate organisation to collect information about consumers and their requirements and advertising.

For developing the system of distribution on scientific lines, the first step is to undertake comprehensive market research. The objectives of such research should be to get information regarding the number of consumers, their location, their preferences etc. It should also give a market-schedule of the requisite properties of the handloom products. As any major decisions must be based on the interpretation of available market information, data collected in this behalf should be accurate and adequate. Then the market should be classified into a number of pockets on the basis of tastes and habits of consumers.

Each handloom centre or group of centres should be made to specialise in the production of that type of goods for which it is best suited. This will avoid unnecessary competition between one handloom centre and the other. The goods thus produced are to be marketed, as far as possible, directly to the consumers. This may require the establishment of new sales depots. However in the short run it may not be possible to open adequate number of depots in all commercial centres. It is thus inevitable to market the products through whole-salers and retailers at least in the initial stages. The practice of publishing prices of goods on the packages is very useful and the private sellers should be made to sell at the published prices only. Such prices should include, reasonable profit in addition to other expenses of production and marketing. All this will help to sell the handloom products at reasonable and competitive prices. It will eliminate a large number of middle men and their lucrative profit to a very great extent.

Absence of uniformity and standardisation regarding the quality and price of handloom products is another major defect. Standardisation is absolutely necessary for smooth wholesale trade in the domestic market and also for export trade. Standardisation in a district should involve standardisation of quality, pattern, dimension, measures, colours and prices. An expert agency should be set up under the auspices of the central organisation to implement the programme. The offices of such agencies should be opened in all important handloom centres in the district.

Facilities for giving a finish within the reach of the handloom weavers to make the handloom products more attractive. To cater to modern trends and tastes of consumers good finish should be given to the products. Hence calendering and finishing plants, suitable both for handlooms and powerlooms should be set up in important handloom centres, under the auspices of the central organisation.

The abnormal profit made by the middlemen leads to relatively higher prices of handloom products. Profit margin of middlemen ranges from 15 per cent to 75 per cent depending on the nature of the products. The Fact Finding Committee (1941) observed that the commission charges of middlemen were very high ranging between 10 to 100 per cent. Even now the middlemen's charges are exhorbitant. The competitive position of the handloom industry therefore is seriously affected because the marketing cost is far heavier in the case of handloom products than in the case of mill made goods. Any solution to this problem lies in developing efficient machinery for marketing handloom products, by eliminating middlemen and through establishment of a central organisation in the district.

Demand for handloom products is generally seasonal. For instance, the demand for such products is very great in the marriage and harvest seasons viz., from December to June. During this period of nearly 6 months many important festivals and fairs take place. In the remaining months, the market is practically dull and during this period the products remain as dead-stock. The holding period of handloom products by merchant-cum-master weavers and dealers may, therefore, be upto six months. As there are no warehousing and financing facilities, small merchants, independent weavers and co-operatives are compelled to depend on merchant-cum-master weavers and moneylenders for finance and marketing. The cost of holding this stock is very high since the rate of interest charged by moneylenders is exhorbitant. For this reason also, the small producers and dealers do not take risk of stocking up these products. The merchant cum master weavers who undertake stocking, safeguard themselves against all possible risk of loss arising out of fall in price or accident etc, by cutting down the buying price of goods and wages. Consequently earnings of independent weavers, co-operatives and wage-workers are low during slack season. During slack season production is also cut down considerably. As a result, unemployment is experienced. This situation in the handloom industry emphasises the need for development of an efficient marketing machinery. If there is an agency to purchase the handloom products throughout the year, the fluctuations in income, employment and output can be avoided.

None of the organisations producing handloom cloth in the district has displayed any interest in advertising its products. Majority of them have not even realised the importance of advertisement in modern days. It is amazing to find that Master weavers do not possess even the sample pieces of the type of fabrics they produce. There is certainly scope for pushing up the demand curve upward for handloom products through effective advertisement. Establishment of show-rooms, display centres, Museums, appointment of sales agents, publication of illustrated catalogues, price lists and organisation of film shows, in and outside the country would help the marketing of handloom products. Advertisement through Cinema and T.V. seem to be most effective means for sales promotion.

The Government should open a commercial intelligence Bureau in the district to supply information to the central organisation, regarding the prospective markets and the preferences of the consumers in the existing market. It can also help the producers in getting freight concessions and setting up of Commercial museums.

The marketing system outlined above, for the handloom sector will definitely reduce marketing expenses. The marketing expenses which account on an average for 30 per cent of the final price of the products at present, can be reduced more or less to 10-15 per cent. As the demand is price-elastic, this would mean a larger sale of handloom products. The earnings of handloom weavers will increase. In short, an efficient marketing mechanism would ensure stability and sustained growth of the industry.

Except for minor changes in the designs of sarees old and traditional designs still continue in the handloom industry. To stabilise the existing demand for products and generate additional demand new designs and patterns have to be promoted. If weavers cannot respond to the ever changing demands and tastes of the consumers the marketing organisation, however efficient it might be, will be of little use. Hence there is need for establishing 'Training and Design School' in the district to invent new designs to disseminate information about them and to impart training to weavers.

It is said that it is the inadequacy of finance and not weavers' conservatism, that comes in the way of adoption of improved tools and equipment to a very great extent. As a matter of fact, the shortage of capital is not the only factor that ties down the weavers to the old and obsolete equipment and traditional technique of production. The ignorance and conservative attitude of artisans are equally strong factors which make them adhere to age old equipment and methods of production. The primary survey reveals that besides shortage of finance, the ignorance and conservative attitude of weavers are also responsible for the non-adoption of modern devices.

A majority of the weavers and co-operatives nevertheless experience great difficulty in securing adequate credit at reasonable rate. Consequently they are unable to keep sufficient stocks of raw materials and products. Non utilisation of the available capacity leads to escalation of costs. Under these circumstances actual weavers are exploited by middlemen. Almost all the weavers are in debt. They have to borrow at abnormally high rate of interest which ranges from 25 to 30 per cent. Alternative source of finance is not available even at such a high rate of interest. As a result most of the cooperatives and weavers come under the grip of master weavers.

Some of the Master weavers also borrow from the moneylenders or indigenous bankers, particularly during the slack season. Commercial banks located in the weaving centres are highly reluctant to advance loans to this sector on the security of tools and appliances or the inventories of trade. The net result of all this is slow and unsteady production and higher cost.

The problem of raw-materials arises mainly from the non-availability of yarn of required counts and quality at reasonable rate. The raw material prices in the hand-weaving centres of the district are relatively higher than those in the mill and powerloom sectors. The primary survey shows that weavers have to spend 20 to 30 per cent more for raw-materials than their mill counter parts. The Fact Finding Committee also observed that the presence of a host of middlemen in the raw materials market results in a 'pyramiding' of prices of yarn and deterioration of quality. The weavers have to pay 4 per cent to 25 per cent more on the retail prices of yarn.

The raw material markets are dominated by middlemen. Apart from the profits of the middlemen, there are two other factors which are to be taken into consideration.

The retail yarn dealers in the Centers have the practice of charging retail prices arbitrarily without any relation to market conditions. They not only charge higher prices but also discriminate one person against another. When the yarn is sold on credit both in rural and urban areas there is an addition of 10 per cent to 15 per cent to the usual prices of yarn.

There is another aspect to the problem of raw materials. It arises from the high cost of transportation. This is due to a variety of reasons.

The chief means of transport available in the district are buses and trucks. The bad condition of roads in the rural areas adds to their difficulties. The handloom weavers and dealers in the small centres cannot afford to purchase sufficient raw-materials at a time due to want of finance. Wholesalers also have to depend on distant markets for the supply of raw materials—like Coimbatore, Madras etc., which results in extra transport charges.

Cuddapah district concentrates on the production of coloured sarees. It requires special kinds of dye-stuffs. The dealers in the big centres obtain the 'dye-stuffs' from outside markets through middlemen. Weavers, master-weavers and co-operatives in the big and small centres have to purchase these dye-stuffs at retail prices from the yarn dealers in the local markets or from nearby towns like Proddatur, Venkatagiri, Puttur etc. Dye stuffs supplied to the handlooms are reported to be adulterated also.

The immediate solution to the problem is to establish fair-price shops for the sale of handloom products in important handloom centres. But, in the long run, a permanent solution would lie in the creation of a central organisation for the district to undertake supply of raw materials, production and marketing of handloom products.

The policy of maximising employment in the process of making cloth has been the corner stone of the Textile Policy. Accordingly, handloom Sector was given priority in the successive Five Year Plans. Since

Independence a number of measures have been taken up for the protection and development of the handloom industry. On the organisational side, emphasis is being given to expansion and strengthening of the co-operative sector. Attempts have been made to bring more number of handlooms into co-operative fold, by extending finance and marketing facilities. Efforts have been made to make available institutional finance. The policy to expand the capacity of the Spinning Mills and to set up new ones in the co-operative sector in order to ease the yarn problem, is a step in the right direction. Measures have been taken to protect the handlooms against competition from the mills. A special field in the textile market has been demarcated for the handloom sector through the scheme of reservation. Rebate facility is provided to encourage the demand for handloom cloth. Excise duty is imposed on powerlooms and mill industry for the benefit of the handloom industry.

Government efforts in the direction of increasing the productivity of handlooms did not meet with success. Technology intended for the development of the handloom industry did not reach the weaver. Government efforts to convert the existing handlooms into powerlooms also is a failure because of weavers reluctance. Hence technological development in the handloom industry is a major problem to be solved.

After an analysis of all the Government Plans, any one would be forced to come to the conclusion that serious efforts are not directed towards making the industry economically viable. The industry is made to live on doles and on reservations for years. Consequently, the industry will continue to drain the resources of the public exchequer, and the consumers will continue to pay a high price for cloth. So, the Government Policy must help the industry to stand on its own legs, by producing superior varieties of cloth, which the powerlooms and mills can not produce., and the weavers producing plain varieties of cloth must either be trained to produce artistic varieties of cloth, or they must be engaged in the powerloom industry.

When all is said and done, the Textile Policy of the Government of India of 1985 also is not without deficiencies. Following are the important deficiencies:

The policy does not have a long term and clear perspective for the development of the handloom industry.

The policy does not help improving the technological base of the handloom industry, and hence there is no perceptible progress in increasing the productivity of the handloom weaver. Consequently the competitive ability of the handloom sector has drastically decreased compared to earlier periods.

The policy of treating handlooms on par with powerlooms, has been detrimental to the healthy development of the handloom industry. The advantages that the powerlooms have over the handlooms with their better technology and almost the same level of excise vis-a-vis the handloom sector has to be set right so that the powerlooms are no longer in a position to underbid the handlooms in their legitimate markets.

The policy has seriously neglected the private sector whose role is vital to the industry, which controls about 80 per cent of the total looms in the country. There are large concentrations of looms outside the effective co-operative fold and the Master Weaver fold for which an effective rehabilitation programme will have to be drawn up.

The policy of fixing targets quite below the capacity of handlooms in the country is quite unjustifiable. Even to realise the targets set, arrangements were not made through the supply of raw materials and credit. The weavers are put to hardships due to Inadequate and irregular supplies of raw materials and fluctuating prices of yarn.zari, dyes and chemicals.

The removal of capacity restrictions, with the implementation of Textile Policy of 1985, worked against the interest of the handlooms. Steps should be taken to impose restrictions on the strict implementations of reservation policy to protect the handloom industry.

From the foregoing analysis, we can conclude that the Government should prepare a long term perspective plan for the development of the handloom industry. The technological developments in the handloom industry should be passed on to the weavers, and they should be convinced of the utility of the technology. The Government should take care of the private sector, while formulating the Handloom Development Plan. The fiscal concessions so far extended to powerlooms on par with handlooms should come to an end., and the powerlooms should be treated on par with mills. Free and adequate supply of raw material should continue to help the Handloom Industry., and the production targets of the Handloom Sector should take into consideration the optimal productive capacity of the industry. Steps must be taken to restructure the Textile Policy of 1985, and the compartmentalisation system should be reintroduced in view of protection required by the handloom industry.

A review of the Governmental policy towards Handloom industry should naturally be followed by an examination of socio-economic conditions of the handloom weavers. As such an attempt is made to present the socio-economic conditions of handloom weavers of Cuddapah district on the basis of the survey conducted by the researcher. As has been already stated there are remarkable differences between eastern and western parts of Cuddapah district in regard to the handloom industry.

It may be inferred that the socio-economic atatus of the weavers in eastern Cuddapah ia better than his counterpart in western Cuddapah. As such, an attempt has been made to specify the reasons for the regional disparities. It is also noticed that the sound economic position of the organisations concerned and the dynamism shown by the entrepreneurs of the eastern zone of Cuddapah district is responsible for the relatively better socio-economic position. The evolution of the handloom industry over a period of 20 years, shows that the handlooms in western zone were much better than in the eastern zone 20 years ago. But in western zone of Cuddapah district the industry has not made efforts for steady progress, where as the industry in eastern zone has improved a lot over period of time, by way of producing superior varieties of handloom fabrics such as pure zari sarees. It implies that the industry in western zone has the required potentials on par with the industry in the other zone, but lacking dynamic entreprenuership. Government strategy in this respect must change from providing temporary relief in the form of subsidy etc., to that of making the industry itself a self reliant one by encouraging the entrepreneurs to produce superior varieties. Efforts must be concentrated on shifting the productive skills of the eastern Cuddapah to that of western Cuddapah. Once the existing disparities are removed, it would be very easy to make the industry in western zone also a prosperous one and this would help to avoid the existing starvation deaths also.

Presently the productive operation of the mills and powerlooms are restricted to a large extent to protect the handloom industry from powerlooms and mills by reserving certain products to the handloom sector alone..Encroachment on the products reserved for handlooms by mills and powerlooms is often reported. All the efforts made in the direction of averting the cannibalisation appear to be ineffective.

The suggestions that have been made in this connection, are expected to help in the harmonious growth of all sectors simultaneously. Because the items produced in eastern Cuddapah cannot be produced on powerlooms and mills, the transfer of productive techniques practised in eastern Cuddapah to that of western Cuddapah would help the industry to improve on its own. It also implies that the industry need not depend on the Government assistance for marketing the products if the items produced in eastern Cuddapah are produced in western-Cuddapah also.

The impact of co-operative societies is being felt in western Cuddapah than in eastern Cuddapah. It is stated that most of the weavers couldn't market their products all by themselves independently. As such, many weavers became members of the co-operative societies so that they can free themselves from the responsibility of marketing their products. But in the process they not only lost their independent status, but are made to accept wages lower than those recommended by the State Government, since most of the co-operative societies, are in effect 'one man' (powerful man) societies.

It is rather disheartening to note that most of the raw materials supplied to the weavers under different organisations, are of poor quality. As such the durability of the product is reduced. This has led to a reduction in the demand for handloom products. Unless immediate steps are taken to arrest this trend and superior quality raw materials are supplied, the future of the industry would be in jeopardy.

The demand for handloom fabrics is not uniformly the same throughout the year. It is more during the festival seasons like (Sankranti, Ugadi, Dasara, Diwali) and during post harvesting seasons, than the other days of the year.

It is also reported that the consumption of cotton cloth is declining and the consumption of synthetic cloth is increasing. Statistics relating to per capita availability of cloth indicate that the importance of man made fibres increased stupendously between 1960-61 and 1990-91. Three decades earlier man-made fibers constituted only 8 per cent of the total cloth available, where as by 90-91 its proportion has increased to nearly 34 per cent. This does not, however, mean that the importance of handlooms has diminished. Looms are capable of making use of not only cotton yarn even even synthetic yarn. So to sustain the demand for handloom fabrics, it is necessary that the input mix should be changed with the introduction of artificial fibre such as Terlin, Terrycot and Polyester. The fabrics thus produced with the new input mix will meet the requirements of the people all through the year.

The survey has also revealed that most of the weavers are not in favour of subsidy extended by the Government for the development of Handloom industry. On the other hand they want that the Government should ensure supply of required raw materials—yarn and dye stuffs at —stable prices. They also want the Government to improve the marketing facilities for the handloom fabrics.

The most important and powerful rivals of handloom sector are the powerloom and mill sectors. It is too well known to require repetition that the mill and powerloom sectors have an edge over the handlooms.

The threat to handloom sector therefore is not imaginary, but a distinct possibility in a non-distant future. The handloom workers should be provided with alternative sources of employment near the place of their present day employment.

The Government should prepare a long term perspective plan for the development of the handloom industry. The technological developments occuring in the handloom industry should be publicised to the weavers and they should be encouraged to use the technology. The Government should also take care of the private sector while formulating the handloom development plan. The fiscal concessions so far extended to the powerlooms on par with handlooms should be discontinued and powerlooms should be treated on par with mills. Adequate and recular supply of raw material should also continue to develop the handloom industry and the production targets of the handloom sector should take into consideration the optimal productive capacity of the industry. Steps must be taken to revise the Textile policy of 1985, and the compartmentalisation system should be reinstated in view of protection required by the handloom industry.

It is anybody's guess whether the handloom industry can regain its past glory and survive in the face of stiff competition from the mill sector capable of turning out durable synthetic fabrics, whose demand has been increasing.

Can the handloom industry with products of artistic excellence, but slow processes of production stand against the wind and face the competition from the mill sector producing durable synthetic fabrics which are cheaper in the long run? It may be noted while reports of starvation deaths of weavers come from the neighbouring districts of Cuddapah, luckly the incidence of such cases appears to be nil in Cuddapah district. This indicates the resilience of the weaver in Cuddapah district and his ability to survive against odds. However, there is every need to train him to improve his skills and to produce the varieties that are in demand and not wait indefinitely for consumers to buy what has been producing for a long time without much of a change.

Bibliography

Reports

All India Handloom Board, *Fourth Report (1956-59)*, Govt. of India 1959.

Andhra Pradesh Legislative Assembly: *Committee of the House to Enquire into the activities of handloom Co-operative Organisations relating to Misuse of Rebate*, Govt of Andhra Pradesh, 1976.

Director of Handlooms and Textiles (A.P.): *State Administrative Reports* Hyderabad, 80-81; 81-82; 82-83; 83-84; 84-85; 85-86; 86-87; 87-88, 88-89 and 89-90.

The Employers Federation of India: *A Study of Central Wage Boards Reports*, A Monograph, Bombay, 1968.

A.P. Khadi and Village Industries Board: *Annual Report (70-71)*, Hyderabad, 1971.

A.P. Khadi and Village Industries Board: *Annual Administrative Report* (75-76), A.P., 1975.

Encyclopaedia of Britannica: *Vol 23*, USA, 1968.

Govt. of India: *Report of the Fact Finding Committee*, India 1942.

Govt. of India: *Textile Enquiry Committee Report, Kanungo*, 1952.

Govt. of India: *Handlooms of India.*, Ministry of Commerce and Industry, All India Handloom Board, Bombay 1958.

Govt. of India: All India Handloom Board, *Fourth Report* (1956-59).

Govt. of India: *Powerloom Enquiry Committee Report*, 1963.

Govt. of India: *Sivaraman Committee Report*, 1975.

Govt. of India: *Study of Handloom Development Programme, Programme Evaluation*, Organisation, Planning Commission 1967.

Govt. of India: *Report of the Study Group to Review the Working of the Reserve Bank of Indka, Scheme for Handlooms*, Development Commissioner for Handlooms, New Delhi, June 1978.

Govt. of India: *Ashok Mehta Committee Report, Integrated Textile Policy,* Ministry of Information and Broadcasting April 1979.

Govt. of India: *Report of the Expert Committee on the Textile Industry,* Ministry of Textiles and Supplies, April 1985.

Govt. of India: *Report of the Expert Committee on the Textile Industry,* Ministry of Supply and Textiles–1985.

Govt. of India: *Annual Report (85-86),* Ministry of Textiles, 1986.

Govt. of India: *Annual Report (1987-88),* Ministry of Textiles, Govt of India.

Govt. of India: *Annual Report (86-87),* Ministry of Textiles, 1987.

Govt. of India: *Annual Report (88-89),* Ministry of Textiles, 1989.

Govt. of India: *Report of the High Power Committee on Review,* The Working of Central/State Handicrafts Development Corporations and the Apex Handicrafts Co-operative Societies, 1987, The Development Commissioner, Ministry of Textiles, New Delhi, 1987.

Govt. of India: *Report of the Sub-group on Handlooms, Development Commissioner for Handlooms*—Ministry of Textiles, New Delhi, February 1989.

Govt. of India: *First Five Year Plan,* 1951, *Second Five Year Plan,* 1956, *Third Five Year Plan,* 1961, *Fourth Five Year Plan,* 1961, *Fifth Five Year Plan,* 1974, *Sixth Five Year Plan,* 1978, *Seventh Five Year Plan,* 1981, *Eighth Plan Report of the Subgroup of Handlooms,* Development Commissioner for Handlooms—February 1989.

Govt. of A.P.: *Performance Budgets (85-86), Dept. of Handlooms and Textiles,* 1985.

Govt. of A.P.: *(1984-85)*–1984.

Govt. of A.P.: *(1983-84)*–1983.

Govt. of A.P.: *Direct Gazetteer of Cuddapah,* 1967, p.362.

The Indian Cotton Mills Federation: *Report for the year 1986-87—1987.*

Khadi and Village Industries Commission: *Annual Report* (87-88), 1988.

Sastry, B.R.K: *Report of the Handloom Committee,* Industries and Commerce Department, Govt. of Andhra Pradesh, 1980.

All India Fabrics Marketting Co-op. Society: *Akhila Bharata Sammelanamu* Copy of Resolution, Bombay.

Books

A.P. Co-operative Societies Ltd.: *APCO, Year Book,* 1978-79, Hyderabad, 1978.

All India Handloom Organisation: *Memorandum submitted to Shri V.V. Giri,* President of India, Yemmiganur, Andhra Pradesh-1973.

Abdul Zahir: *Handloom Industry in Varanasi,* Unpublished Thesis, 1966.

Angadi: *Handloom Industry in Karnataka,* Unpublished Ph.D thesis.

Arasaratnam, S: *Weavers, Merchants and Company, The Handloom Industry in South Eastern India,* 1750-90.

Arterbunn J.Y.: *The Loom of Interdependence, Silk Weaving Co-operatives in Kanchipuram,* Hindustan Publishing Corporation (India), Delhi, 1982.

Commissioner for Handlooms and Textiles: *Bharatha Vastrala Nuthana Drukpatham,* New Delhi–1978.

Chowdhury Mukhtar Singh: *Cottage and Small Scale Industries,* Kitabistan, Allahabad, 1947.

The Cotton Textiles Export Promotion Council: *New Textile Policy of UK-India's Case,* Bombay, 1969.

Dept. of Information and Publication: *Twenty Years of Andhra Pradesh Handloom Industry Govt. of Andhra Pradesh,* Hyderabad, 1976.

Director of Handlooms and Textiles: *Handloom Textiles,* Andhra Pradesh Govt. of Andhra Pradesh, 1979.

Director of Economics and Statistics: *Socio-economic Survey of Bhilai Region,* Madhya Pradesh, Bhopal.

Gadgil, D.R.: The Industrial Evolution of India in Recent Times, 1860-1939, Oxford University Press, 1985.

Gandhi, M.P.: *The Indian Cotton Textile Industry, Its Past, Present and Future,* G.N.Mitra Esqn of the Book Companay, Calcutta, 1930.

Gandhi, M.K.: *Why and How,* Navajeevan Publishing House, Ahmedabad, 1955.

Goody, N: *From Craft to Industry,* Cambridge University Press, 1982.

Handloom Weavers Congress: *Crisis in Handloom Industry,* Nidubrolu, Andhra Pradesh, 1967.

Handloom Weavers Congress: *Handlooms and their Future,* Nidubrolu, 1964.

Handloom Weavers Congress: *Woes of Weavers,* Mimeo, Nidurbrolu, 1977.

Handloom Weavers Congress: *Souvenir on 70th Birthday of Sri Pragada Kotaiah,* M.P. Chirala.

Handloom Weavers Congress: *The First Andhra Pradesh Handloom Weavers Co-operative Societies Conference,* Nidubrolu, 1973.

Hariharan, S: *Handloom Industry in Trichy District,* National College, Tamilnadu, 1989.

Indian Cotton Mills *Federation*: *Handbook of Statistics on Cotton Textile Industry,* Bombay, 1988.

The Indian Cotton Mills Federation: *Report for the Year 1979-80, 1980.*

Kotaiah, Pragada: *Self Employment Solved Unemployment,* All India Handloom Weavers Congress, Nidubrolu, Andhra Pradesh, 1971.

Kotaiah, Pragada: *Whither Handloom*—All India Handlooms and Handicrafts Board, Nidubrolu, 1982.

Kotaiah, Pragada: *Handlooms and Some Problems*—1983.

Kakade: *Socio-economic Survey of Weaving Communities, Sholpur,* Gokhale Institute of Public Finance and Economics, Pune, 1947.

Mahapatro, P.C.: *Economics of Cotton Handloom Industry,* Ashish Publishing House, New Delhi, 1986.

Nagen C.Das: *Development of Handloom Industry, Organisation Production, Marketing,* Deep and Deep Publications, New Delhi, 1986.

National Council for Applied Economic Research: *Survey of Handloom Industry in Karnataka and Sholapur*–1959.

Public Relations Department: *Chenethaku Cheyutha*—Pragati, Govt. of A.P, Hyderabad (Years of publication not mentioned).

Public Relations Department: *Survey of Silk and Art Silk Industries,* New Delhi-October 1961.

Ramana Rao, A.V: *Economic Development of Andhra Pradesh (1766-1957),* Popular Book Depot, Bombay, 1958.

Ramaswamy Vijay: *Textiles and Weavers in Mediaeval South India*—Oxford University Press–1985.

Satyanarayana, H.N: *Handloom Exports*—Revew and Prospects, All India Handloom Convention, 24th July, 1974-pp. 20-22.

Sarangapani, B: *Organisational Pattern and Levels of Living of Handloom Weavers, A Study in Coastal Andhra Pradesh,* Unpublished Thesis, 1987.

Sastry, D.U.: *The Cotton Mill Industry in India,* Oxford University Press, Delhi, 1984.

Somappa, M: *All India Handloom Fabrics Marketing Co-operative Society Ltd,* Bombay, 1969.

Somappa, M: *Whither Handlooms,* All India Handloom Fabrics Marketing Co-op Society, Bombay, 1954.

Somappa, M: *Fair Deal to Handlooms,* Weavers Co-op Society, Yemmiganur, 8th Oct 1956.

Somappa, M: *Voice of Handlooms,* Weavers Co-op Society Ltd., Yemmiganur–1958.

Somappa, M: *Handlooms in Third Plan*—Weavers Co-op Society Ltd., Yemmiganur, 1958.

Somappa, M: *All India Handloom Fabrics,* Marketing Co-op Society Ltd. Bombay–1968.

Somappa, M: *Utilise Capacity of Handlooms in Full,* All India Handloom Convention, 24th July 1974, pp. 1-2.

Sudhakar, B: *Employment Factor in Handlooms,* National Institute of Rural Development, Hyderabad, 1986.

Surendra, S.T: *Co-operatives in Andhra Pradesh,* Hyderabad, Unpublished Thesis, 1984.

Thimmaiah, G: *Socio-economic Impact of Drinking State Lottery and Horse Racing in Karnataka,* Sterling Publishers Pvt. Ltd., New Delhi. 1967.

Vesanta Desai: *Problems and Prospects of Small Scale Industries in India* Himalayan Publishing House, Bombay, 1983.

Venkateswara Rao, Akurati: *APCO*—A Brochure—Year of publication not mentioned.

Newspapers

Boost for Handlooms, *Indian Express*, Feb 21, 1976, p.4 (NS)

Central Move to Give Impetus to Handlooms, *Times of India*, Aug 1, 1975, p.4

Dustulunessvariki Pasthulena Prathiphalam, *Eenadu*, (Telugu)1 7.1.89

Govt. Policy on Textile Mills Defended, *The Hindu*, 15.7.84.

Helping the Handloom Weavers, *The Hindu*, 19 Sep 1975, p.6.

Avineethi Salegutlo Chenetha Karmikula Gijagija, *Eenadu*, 10.11.88.(Telugu)

Artistic, Wide Rrange to Meet Consumer Needs, *The Hindu*, 12.10.84.

Assembly Told of Weavers' Plight, *The Hindu*, 10.3.89.

Aid to Handlooms, Editorial, *Financial Express*, 22 Jun 76.

A.P. Handloom Units in Dire Straits, *Financial Express*, 14 May 1983, p.3.

Boost to Handlooms, Editiorial, *The Economic Times*, 17, Jan 1977.

Call to Rejuvenate Cooperative Movement, *Indian Express*, 20 Nov 1978, p.4.

Controller Cloth, *The Hindusthan Times*, 21 Dec 1976, p.9.

Chandran Nair, Story of Kanchipuram Saree, *Financial Express*, 8 May 1982, p.4.

Chandra Sekhar C.P, Textile Industry, *Economic Times*, 10 Aug 1982, p.5.

Chenethaku Cheyutha, *Eenadu*, 16.5.84. (Telugu)

Chenetha Karmikula Bathukupogu Thegindhi, *Eenadu* 18.7.84.(Telugu)

Controlled Cloth for Handlooms, *Financial Express*, 7, June 1985.

Controductory Directives on Wages Hurt Handloom Weavers, *The Hindu*, 4.7.85.

Central Supply of Yarn Too Late, Too Little, *The Hindu*, 9.12.87.

Chenethapaniverala Dustiti tolaginchutetlu, *Adhra Patrika*, 15 Jan 1942, p.3.(Telugu)

Control Cloth Prices, 10 May 1943, *Andhra Pathrika*, p.2.(Tel)

Control on Handloom Cloth, 27 Oct 1947, *Andhra Pathrika*, p.6. (Telugu)

Economic Times Research Bureau, Handloom Industry, Poor Implementation of Plans at State Level, *The Economic Times*, 20 May 1978.

Fresh Look into Textile Policy Urged, *The Hindu*, 6, April, 1988.

Govt, Failed to Help Handloom Weavers, *The Hindu*, 24.3.88, p.3.

Handloom Sector, Editorial, *Financial Express*, 27, April 1977.

Handlooms and Powerlooms, *Financial Express*, 6, April 1978.

Handlooms in Distress, *Financial Express*, July 31 1981, p.5.

Handloom Exports, *Economic Times*, 10.1.82., p.6.

Handlooms, Problems and Prospects, *Indian Express*, 25th August 1978.

Handloom Weavers Plea to Prime Minister, *Indian Express*, 24.9.81

Handloom Development Corporation Soon. *Indian Express*, 4.12.80.

Handlooms Development, *Andhra Prabha*, 5 Apr 1980 (Telugu)

Handlooms, Staff Report, Plight of Industy in Southern States, *The Hindu*, 29.9.1981, p.17.

Handlooms from All Over India on Display, *The Hindu*, 3.4.84.

Handloom Reservation Act to be enforced strictly, *The Hindu*, 7.85.

Handloom Reservation Act to be enforced strictly, *The Hindu* 2.7.85.

Handlooms Capacity Should Be Frozen, *The Hindu*, 8.5.89.

Help to Handlooms, *Pathrika*, 6, April 1942, p.3. (Telugu)

Handloom Weavers of Yemmiganur, *Andhra Pathrika*, 13 May 1942, p.5.(Telugu)

Kotaiah Pragada, Plight of Handlooms, *The Hindu*, p.6.

Kendhra Vidhanam, Nethakarmikula Bathuku Baram, *Vudayam*, 10.3.89. (Telugu)

Manubhai Shah, The New Textile Policy, *Indian Express*, 2.7.85.

Moggalalone Magguthunna Bathukulu, *Eenadu*, 17th Feb 1984, p.2. (Telugu)

Noteworthy Contribution to Society, *The Hindu*, 28, June 1985.

Protection to Handlooms, *Financial Express*, 29.12.80, p.7.

Pande, K.R, Handloom Industy Strategies, for Marketing, *The Economic Times*, 20.5.81, p.5 & 6.

Panel to Study Weavers' Problems, *The Hindu*, 6 Jan 1981, p.12.

Plight of Handlooms, Editorial, *The Hindu*, 2, October 1981.

Paniki Chenetha Karmikula Valasa, *Eenadu* 17.1.89 (Telugu).

Ramakant Gupta, Handlooms in Maharashtra, *Economic Times*, p.5 Dt. 15.3.80.

Rebate on Handlooms, Andhra Prabha, 18 February 1987, p.2 (Telugu)

Reserving the Ancient Exquisite Art of Weaving, *The Hindu*, 17.10.86.

RBI Permits More Credit Flow to Weavers, Artisans, *The Hindu*, 1.12.87.

Rationing on Cloth, 27 Nov 1946, *Pathrika*, p.1. (Telugu).

Seventh Plan Should Provide More for Handloom Sector, *The Hindu* 7 Sept. 1984.

Saree and Dhoti to each Greencardholder At, *The Hindu*, 16.10.84.

Standard Cloth Scheme, 20th April 1943, *Andhra Pathrika*, P., 13th May 1943, p.4, 25th May 1943, p.3 (Telugu).

Small Industries and Employment, *The Hindu*, 9 July 1984.

Seshadri, N.P. Handlooms Provides Jobs to Millons, *The Indian Express*, 16 Dec. 1976, p.8.

Strategy for Handlooms, Editorial, *Financial Express*, 10.1.80.

Seshadri, Handloom for All Seasons, *Financial Express*, 15 Augugst 1982, p.6

Textile Policy Aim: More Cheap Cloth, *Financial Express*, 28 th February 81, p.7.

Text of Textile Policy, *Financial Express Bureau, Financial Express*, 7th June 1985, p. 8.

Textile Policy, Editorial, *Financial Express*, 8.6.1985.

What Ails Handlooms, Editorial, *The Hindu*, 6.2.84.

What Ails Handlooms in Coastal Andhra, *The Hindu*, 24.3.87.

Weavers, A Neglected Lot, *Indian Express*, 13.7.88.

War, Handloom Industry, Kotaiah Pragada, *Pathrika*, 13 June 1943, p.5 (Telugu).

Wage control, *Andhra Pathrika*, 29 Oct. 1947, p. 5. (Telugu).

Yarn for Handlooms, *Financial Express*, 25.11.80, Editorial.

Yarn Prices, Editorial, 24 Jan 1942, *Andhra Pathrika*, p.4 (Telugu).

Hiking Prices of Yarn, *Pathrika*, 29 May, 1943, p. 3 (Telugu)

Problems of Handloom Weavers, *Andhra Pathrika*, 3 Feb. 1945, Chenetha p.2 (Telugu)

Ramachandran, V.K.—*The Hindu–Supplement*–The Facts Speak Out–p.VIII, 26th Apr 1992.

Sreenivasan, R, Development of Handlooms, *Commerce*, 13th Oct. 1979, pp. 34-39.

Srinivasan, B.R., Development of Handlooms, *Commerce*, 13 Oct. 1979.

Sankara Subbaiayan, Organisation of Handlooms in Tamil Nadu, *Commerce*, 13 Oct. 1979.

Thomas, P.J. *'Modern Review' Journal*–Jan. 1924, p. 4.

Rajaram, A., Handloom Weavers Economic and Social Welfare Measures, *Chenetha*, March 81, p.21.

Rajaiah, K, Salem Type of Handlooms, *Chenetha*, Dec. 1982, p. 7, 9.

Ramakrishna Rao, B & Subramanyam, G, Handloom Industry, In Coastal Andhra, *Kurukshetra*, March 1987, pp. 14-34.

Rao, C.S., Employment in Handloom Industry, *Kurukshetra*, 1 Oct, 1973, pp. 20-22.

Ummat, R.C., Sivaraman Committee on Handlooms, *Eastern Economist*, 2 August 1974, pp. 194 & 195.

Venkateswara Rao, Akurathi, Indias Glorious Tradition of Hand, Weaving, *Chenetha*, Jan. 1982, p. 15 and Feb. 1982 pp. 11, 14.

Veeranjanyulu Goli, Ways and Means for Handloom Development, *Chenetha*, June 1982, p. 3.

Venkateswarlu, B., Inspection and Quality Control, *Chenetha*, Jan. 1984, pp. 11-12.

Vijaya Raghavan,. T.T, Textile Policy Revision, *Eastern Economist*, 2 May, 1980, pp. 889 and 890.

Venkatappa, K.N., Progress and Problems of Handloom Weavers, Co-operatives in Karnataka State, *Indian Co-operative Review*, Jan 1977, pp. 129-140.

Working of the Scheme for Handloom Finance, Editorial, *Eastern Economist*, 14, July 1978, pp. 99-104.

Yagaiah, Handloom Industry in India, *Yojana*, Dec. 1979, pp. 9-12.

Economic and Scientific Research Foundation, New Delhi, Survey of Indias Export Potential of Textiles, 1988, pp. 130-32.

Journals

Anand, Mulkaraj, Chenethaku Jejelu, *Chenetha*, April 79. p. 12. Telutu.

Anjayya, Punna, Protect Handloom Industry, *Chenetha*, June 1980.

Ansari, I.A. Pattern of Govt. Assistance to Handloom Industy, Jan 1970, *India Co-operative Review*, Jan. 1970, pp. 259-64.

Arsarathnam, S–*The Indian Economic and Social History Review*, July-Sep 1980, pp. 257-81, Vol. XVII, No. 3

Athre, A.V. Handloom Industy, *Mysore Economic Review*, Dec. 1975.

Batra, Jasbir, A Heritage As Old As Yesterday and As Young As Tomorrow, *Yojana*, 15, May, 1977, pp. 21-26.

Batra, J.D. Petrofils to the Aid of Handloom Co-operatives, *Kurukshetra*, 16 June, 1979.

Batra, J.D, Programme for Weavers Prosperity, Khadi Gramodyog, March 1977.

Bathaiah, D & Satyanarayana, K, Analysis of Optimum Product Mix in Cotton Textile Industry, *Decision*, Oct., Dec. 1986, pp. 265-267.

Correspondent—*Textile Industry and New Legislation for Handloom Protection*-pp 583-584.

Commerce Research Bureau, Handlooms Our Largest and Languishing Industry, Commerce, 23, Aug, 1975, pp. 315-321.

Clandius Murchison, Japan and the World Cotton Goods Trade, Americal Cotton Manufacturers Institute, New York, 1951.

Chowdary Ram Sevak, Role of All India Handloom Board in the Development of Handloom Co-operatives, July 1969, *Indian Co-operative Review*, pp. 499-512.

Eapen, M 'New Textile Policy' *Economic and Political Weekly*, Nos. 25 & 26–p. 1072.

George, A.L. Co. op. Spinning Mills Should Support Handloom Industry, *Commerce*, June 15, 1976, pp. 5-6.

Goswamy, Omkar—Indian Textile Industry (1970-84)—An Analysis of Demand and Supply, *Economic and Political Weekly*-Vol XX

Handlooms in Indian Economy, Special Correspondent, *Commerce* 19, 1979.

Indian Cotton Merchants Federation (ICMF) Journal Feb 1976.

Jaganmohan Rao, Ramunatham, Handloom Industry, Yarn Policy, Chenetha, p. 7. (Telugu journal)

Jain, L.C., End of Handloom Industry, *Mainstream*, 20 July, 1985.

Jain, L.C., Handlooms Face Liquidation, Powerlooms Mock at Yojana Bhavan, *Economic and Political Weekly*, 27, Aug 1983, pp. 1517-26.

Kundu Abanti, Pattern of Organisation of Handloom Industry in West Bengal, August 80, pp. 19-32 & Sep-oct. 1980, pp. 41-51. Social Scientist.

Kamat, G.S, The Yarn Requirements of Handlooms and the Role of Co-op Spinning Mills, July 1976, *Indian Co-operative Review*, pp. 337-343.

Kamble, Ram-Powerlooms In the Fifth Plan—*Commerce* 29, Dec. 1973, pp. 35-41.

Kakade, Socio-economic Survey of Weaving Communities, Sholapur, Gokhale Institute of Politics and Economics, 1947.

KrishnaMurthy, M.S., Handlooms *vis-a-vis* Powerlooms. *Khadi Gramodyoga*, pp. 1419-424.

Kulkarni, R.S, Improved Handlooms, *Khadi Gramodyog*, July 78, pp. 507-11.

Kotaiah Pragada, The Weavers Cry to Heaven, *Swarjya*, 26 March 1966.

Kotaiah Pragada, A Motherless Child, 11 July 1964, p. 9, *Swarajya*.

Khukraja C., Co-operativisation Programme in Handloom Sector, *Co-operator*, Feb. 1984.

Muchrikar, N.V, Weavers Creative Hhuman Beings, Chenetha, March 1982, p. 11.

Narayana Swamy, Mani, Handloom Development Programme, *Kurukshetra*, 1 Oct 1976, pp. 17-20.

Notes and Comments, How to Improve Performance of Handlooms, *Indian Cotton Mills Federation Journal*, Jan 1979, pp. 593-96.

Notes and Comments, Development of Handlooms, *Indian Cotton Mills Federation Journal* 13(1) 1976, pp. 1,33.

Naresh Kumar, Export Promotion of Handloom Goods, Indian Journal of Marketing, July, Aug, 1983, pp. 9-10.

Papa Rao, P., Pochampalle Tie and Dye Sarees, Chenetha, p. 9-10.

Podar R. Kantikumar, Organisation of Handlooms, *Commerce*, 23 Dec. 1978, pp. 21-29.

Padmanabhan, S., Handloom Industry in India, Its Past, Present and Future, All India Handloom Convention, Madras, 24th July 1974, pp. 18 and 19.

Radhakrishna, K.P., Poverty and Unemployment, The Case of Handloom Sector, *Khadi Gramodyog*, Nov. 1978, pp. 125-27.

Rajula Devi, A.K., Plight of Handlooms, A Study, *Kurukshetra*, 1 Jan 1983, pp. 17-22.

Ramakrishna Rao, B-Handloom Industry in Coastal Andhra—*Kurukhetra*-March 1987, p. 14.

Sadasiva Rao Damarla, Chenetha Rangamulo Harivillu, *Chenetha*, 29.7.78, p. 19, 15.6.79, p. 6. (Telugu journal)

Seshadri N.V., Joing Development Commissioner, Chenetha Rangamulo Sadhinchina Vijayalu, *Chenetha*, August 1979, p. 11.

Sivanna, M.S., Increase Productivity of Handlooms, *Chenetha*, p. 3.

Surendra Rao, S.T., Some Economic Aspects of the Gadwal Handloom Industries, *Chenetha*, 1983, pp. 7, 10 & Nov. 1983, pp. 3,5.

Shahin Sultan, Textile Mills *Vs* Handlooms, *Yojana*, Dec. 77, pp. 25-26.

Saaz, J.L., Hereditary Weavers of Pochampalli, *Kurukshetra*, August 68, pp. 25-26.

Shrivastav, K.G., Handloom Industry in Madhya Pradesh, *Yojana*, 1 Sep. 1980, pp. 28-29.

Sreenivasan, T.S, Handloom Industry, Looking for a New Deal, *Kurukshetra*, 16 May 1977, pp. 12-13.

Special Report, Elimination Middlemen in Handlooms, *Commerce*, 19 June 1982, pp. 1058-59.

Special Report, Handlooms in Indian Economy, *Commerce*, 19 May, 1979, pp. 847-51.

Index

C

D

E

F

G

T

U

V

W

Z